EQUALITY, THE THIRD WORLD
AND
ECONOMIC DELUSION

The Rubber Industry
West African Trade
The Economics of Underdeveloped Countries (with B. S. Yamey)
Economic Analysis and Policy in Underdeveloped Countries
Indian Economic Policy and Development
Markets, Market Control and Marketing Reform (with B. S. Yamey)
Dissent on Development

Equality, the Third World and Economic Delusion

P. T. Bauer

Methuen

First published in Great Britain in 1981 by
George Weidenfeld & Nicolson Ltd
91 Clapham High Street, London SW4

First published as a University Paperback in 1982 by
Methuen & Co. Ltd
11 New Fetter Lane, London EC4P 4EE

Printed in Great Britain by
J. W. Arrowsmith Ltd, Bristol

British Library Cataloguing in Publication Data
Bauer, P. T.
Equality, the Third World and economic delusion.
—(*University paperbacks 791*).
1. *Economics – History – 20th century*
I. Title
330'.09'04   HB87

ISBN 0–416–34230–2

Contents

ACKNOWLEDGEMENTS   vii

INTRODUCTION   1

Part One: Equality

1 The Grail of Equality   8
2 Class on the Brain   26

Part Two: The West and the Third World

3 The Population Explosion: Myths and Realities   42
4 Western Guilt and Third World Poverty   66
5 Foreign Aid and its Hydra-Headed Rationalization   86
6 Background to Aid   138
7 The Link Scheme of Aid   151
8 Costs and Risks of Commodity Stabilization   156
9 British Colonial Africa: Economic Retrospect and Aftermath   163
10 The Lesson of Hong Kong   185
11 Broadcasting the Liberal Death Wish   191

Part Three: The State of Economics

12 Economists and the Two Dollar Problems   214
13 Economic History as Theory   221
14 The Investment Fetish   239
15 Reflections on the State of Economics   255

NOTES   267

INDEX   283

Acknowledgements

As in the preparation of some of my earlier books, I again benefited greatly from discussions with many friends and colleagues in Britain and elsewhere. As such discussions are a perquisite of academic life, I hope that those who have thus helped me will accept this general expression of thanks without individual acknowledgement.

I wish to thank Mr Adolf Wood and Mr John Wood for the removal of many infelicities at various stages in the revision of this book.

During the final revision, I had the good fortune to work with Léonie Glen. Her incisive intelligence, particularly evident in her prompt grasp of the subject matter, and her intellectual stamina and consistent good humour made her editorial assistance altogether exceptional.

I must also thank Professor H. Myint for permission to use chapter 8, of which he was co-author, and Professor A. A. Walters who was my co-author in two articles, parts of which are incorporated in chapters 13 and 15.

My greatest debt is to Professor B. S. Yamey, who has been my collaborator for many years. In the preparation and revision of these studies, I have benefited greatly from the acuteness and precision of his mind, and from his wide-ranging and exacting scholarship. Indeed, we have collaborated so closely that the standard disclaimer that he is not responsible for the remaining errors does not apply as unequivocally as it does usually, since he has read and discussed each study in detail with me. I am also indebted to him for permission to use chapter 3 of which he is co-author.

It is a pleasure also to thank Mrs Anne de Sayrah for secretarial work both remarkable in quality and amount.

Finally I wish to thank the Trustees of the Leverhulme Fund for financial help towards editorial and secretarial assistance during my tenure of a Leverhulme Fund Fellowship in 1975–7.

These studies were written over the last ten years. Chapter 3 is a revised version of an address to the Annual Meeting of the Indian Economic Association in December 1979. It has not previously been published. Much of the material in the rest of the book has also not been published before. The status of the other chapters in this respect is as follows.

Chapter 1 has not been published before, but its nucleus appeared in *The Times Literary Supplement*, No. 3880, 23 July 1976.

Chapter 2 is a revised and enlarged version of a paper published by the Centre for Policy Studies in 1977.

ACKNOWLEDGEMENTS

Chapter 4 is a much revised and enlarged version of an article which appeared in *Commentary*, New York, Vol. 61, No. 1, January 1976.

Chapters 5 and 6 have not been published before. They incorporate in a much revised form scattered material from various articles published in different magazines between 1974–79. especially *Encounter*, London, Vol. XLII, No. 3, March 1974, and *Commentary*. Vol. 6, No. 6, December 1978.

Chapter 7 is a compressed version of two articles which appeared in *Lloyds Bank Review*, No. 109. July 1973, and No. 111, January 1974, respectively.

Chapter 8 is reprinted from *The Banker*, December 1976.

Chapter 9 is a much revised and enlarged version of a chapter which appeared in Peter Duignan and L. H. Gann (eds.) *Colonialism in Africa, 1870–1960*, Vol. 4, Cambridge, Cambridge University Press, 1975.

Chapter 10 is an extended version of an article which appeared in *Spectator*, Vol. 224, 19 April 1980.

Chapter 11 is a revised and extended version of an article which appeared in *Encounter*, Vol. LIV, No. 4, June 1980.

Chapter 12 is an amended version of an article which appeared in *Economica*, New Series, Vol. 38, No. 150, May 1971.

Chapter 13 is a revised version of an article which appeared in *Lloyds Bank Review*, No. 116, April 1975.

Chapter 14 has not been published before. It incorporates a few paragraphs from an article which appeared in *Fortune*, New York, Vol. 44, No. 3, September 1976.

Chapter 15 is a much revised version of an article which appeared in the *Journal of Law and Economics*, Vol. 18, No. 1, April 1975.

P. T. Bauer

London
July 1980

Introduction

The central theme of this book is the conspicuous and disconcerting hiatus between accepted opinion and evident reality in major areas of academic and public economic discourse since the Second World War. Review of intellectually and practically significant instances of this discrepancy provides the connecting thread between the studies presented in this volume. The book is ambitious in that it attempts to demonstrate the presence of this hiatus over a wide range of economics and politics and their academic study. This hiatus is evident in all three major areas covered by this book.

I argue that the widely accepted ideas examined here, many of which are staples of the economic literature and of the publications of leading economists, are demonstrably invalid, often evidently so. The received conclusions have served as a basis for major policies in the West, and in the less developed world. Policies based on these conclusions are at best inappropriate in terms of their proclaimed objectives, but more often counter productive or worse. It is often said that in politics myth is all. This now seems to apply to much of economics as well. Large parts of the subject have come to be perverted in the established sense of the term, that is, misapplied and turned away from their proper use.

Thoroughgoing criticism by an academic of ideas and methods of reasoning widely accepted or taken for granted in both academic and wider public discussion must baffle readers long exposed to the accepted opinions. Such criticism is at times regarded as a form of intellectual blasphemy, or even moral blasphemy, when the ideas rejected are thought to embody moral precepts.

Such criticism is therefore apt to evoke certain evident questions and predictable responses and reservations. It is likely to elicit the question whether the criticism is not an attempt to strain for effect, to startle the reader; and also whether the opinions examined have been presented fairly and are not misrepresentations, travesties or Aunt Sallies. I have indeed often encountered such reactions.

I do not intend to advance anomalous or paradoxical views to attract

1

attention, to startle the reader by the intellectual equivalent of Gerard de Nerval's practice of walking a lobster in the boulevards of Paris *pour épater le bourgeois*. Much of my argument rests on simple reflection, analysis or observation, the validity of which the non-technical reader can verify readily. Most readers interested in economic matters and public affairs will have been exposed to the ideas reviewed here. They will therefore recognize that the arguments and opinions I examine are not concocted by me, nor taken out of context. The abundant and at times extended quotations from academics, and the even more numerous references to reputable publications, are intended to reassure readers on this matter.

Many readers are, however, likely to ask a further question. How does it come about that leaders of opinion, including academic economists of world standing, accept and even propagate patently invalid or bizarre notions? I have often been asked this question, especially when lecturing on development economics. It is a question which cannot be answered conclusively. The validity of an argument can in principle be accepted or rejected decisively on evidence and logic. The success of a policy can be examined appropriately by comparing its outcome with the proclaimed objectives. But reflections on why people canvass or accept particular ideas or favour certain policies must involve an element of conjecture.

Nevertheless, the question is not futile. Nor are attempts to answer it necessarily uninformative. Although the answer cannot be conclusive, this is not to say that one answer or explanation is as good as another, since reasoning based on logic or evidence can be adduced for supporting one explanation rather than another. It is both understandable and legitimate to ask how it comes about that leading academics or other influential people canvass plainly insubstantial notions which much affect both the intellectual scene and the course of events. Indeed, even if these ideas are successfully refuted, some doubts are likely to remain in the minds of readers, unless the critic can suggest some acceptable reasons why these ideas have come to be advanced. Further, if policies are criticized and their reform is proposed, it is necessary to consider the forces behind the policies, including those behind their advocacy. I shall therefore now discuss some reasons for the wide acceptance of the notions examined in this book, and discuss at somewhat greater length what I consider the overriding reasons.

On two grounds I do so here rather than in the individual studies. Separate discussion of this matter in each context would involve avoidable duplication. Moreover, because this discussion is necessarily conjectural to some degree, it moves on a plane different from the examination of arguments and policies which is a principal theme of the particular studies. With one or two

2

exceptions it seemed preferable to omit this speculative element from the discussion in the individual studies. The main exceptions are the concluding sections of chapter 5 and much of chapter 6. For reasons set out in chapter 5 section 15, it seemed advisable to round off the discussion of foreign aid with proposals for reform, and this necessitated a discussion of the forces sustaining the policy of foreign aid.

The rapidity and pervasive character of social and technical change in recent decades; the vast expansion in the volume and diversity of information and messages reaching people or overwhelming them; the growth of specialization; the reduction in the extent and depth of shared experience – all these have often been noted as impediments to the exercise of critical faculty outside people's specialized concerns. Again, the inability of people in their individual capacity to influence public affairs even when these impinge on their lives disinclines them to look at arguments behind policies since there is little or nothing they can do about the policies. Such forces often make it difficult successfully to criticize even egregious errors, successfully that is in the sense of undermining their influence or survival. Economists and academics in cognate disciplines related to politics and public affairs are apt to be much affected by such wider influences. This consideration applies also to economic theorists. In chapter 15, I discuss some of these influences on academic economic discourse. But these forces do not by themselves adequately explain either the multiplicity of the extremely crude notions examined in most of these studies or their power of survival. Nor do they explain the acceptance of these notions by prominent academics, nor the readily observable non-random character of most of these lapses, notably the clear political thrust behind them.

I believe that these characteristics are in large measure explained by the effectiveness of some of the more articulate groups of the contemporary political nation. Since the Second World War, politicians, public servants, writers, mediamen, academics, teachers, and at times some churchmen and entertainers, have largely constituted the political nation in the West. They serve the same function also in the Westernized Third World, where, in addition to these groups, the politicized military also often plays a significant role.

These articulate groups play a major role in the discussion of public affairs, national and international. They dominate public discourse on the Third World. Their interests and preoccupations also colour academic discussion in disciplines close to public affairs, even when the treatment appears to be purely abstract. This consideration explains the emergence and survival of most of the transgressions reviewed in this book. Almost all of these promote

3

or underpin policies which enhance the role and power of groups which comprise a major part of the contemporary political nation. The acceptance of these transgressions therefore serves their emotional, political and material interests. These groups understandably promote and support ideas congenial to them. They also act as a phalanx protecting the most elementary transgressions, and also provide a jargon and technical facade which help to shield them.

These groups play a crucial role both in formulating and also in disseminating opinions. The great number and diversity of sources of messages available to people greatly enhance the influence of those who determine what issues are highlighted, what opinions are given prominence and what are pushed aside or drowned. All this goes a long way to explain the ineffectiveness of the criticism even of simple, important transgressions encountered in academic writings, and notably in mainstream development economics. In particular the dominance of these groups explains the continued widespread acceptance of evidently unsubstantial notions many years after their hollowness has been exposed. Notable examples of this situation will be presented in this book. One striking illustration is the continued use made of comparisons of national income estimates for widely different societies two decades after Professor Dan Usher had shown that such comparisons are worthless.

Readers will readily recognize the general direction and distinctive political thrust of many of the notions which I shall examine. But I may perhaps draw attention specifically to chapter 9 on the experience of British colonial Africa. According to the received stereotype, the history of British colonialism in Africa until about the Second World War was one of official neglect and private exploitation, while from about the 1930s and '40s more enlightened policies were adopted, designed to promote the interests of the colonial population. However, this stereotype of colonial history is the opposite of reality. It equates the interests of the political nation, especially of the politicians and intellectuals in the West and in the Third World, with the interests of ordinary people in the colonies. The colonial policies of the late nineteenth century and early twentieth century in British Africa benefited the population at large, but did not offer much scope for the Westernized groups. On the other hand, the policies of the terminal years placed the population at large at the mercy of the representatives of the new political nation in Africa.

Some of the ideas and issues discussed in these studies are encountered in several contexts, and this explains some overlap between a few of these studies. These instances of overlap were unavoidable if the coherence and independence of the individual studies were to be preserved. The alternative would have been a multiplicity of cross references irksome to the reader.

Although these are primarily essays in applied economics and closely related subjects, they should be readily accessible to the non-technical reader. There are a few exceptions, primarily in Part Three. But in every instance the substance of the arguments should be clear to the general reader.

The reader is also owed an explanation for the length of chapter 5. I have tried there to deal with foreign aid as comprehensively as possible, to examine every argument in support of official foreign aid, and also to analyse all major repercussions or implications of this ultimately far-reaching policy of global redistribution. This attempt inevitably makes for extended treatment. To facilitate the task of the reader I have outlined the principal topics and the order of their discussion at the beginning of that chapter.

There are various synonyms for Third World, including less developed, underdeveloped and developing world. In this book these terms are used interchangeably, as also is the term the South, the latest in the series.

PART ONE

Equality

1 The Grail of Equality
2 Class on the Brain

CHAPTER 1

The Grail of Equality

1

Why, in free and open societies such as those of Western countries, are some people better off than others – not necessarily wiser, nicer, happier or more virtuous, but better off? The precise causes of differences in income and wealth[1] are complex and various, and people will always disagree on how they apply to particular societies, groups or individuals. But in substance such differences result from people's widely differing aptitudes and motivations, and also to some extent from chance circumstances. Some people are gifted, hard-working, ambitious and enterprising, or had far-sighted parents, and they are therefore more likely to become well-off.

In an open and free society, political action which deliberately aimed to minimize, or even remove, economic differences (i.e. differences in income and wealth) would entail such extensive coercion that the society would cease to be open and free. The successful pursuit of the unholy grail of economic equality would exchange the promised reduction or removal of differences in income and wealth for much greater actual inequality of power between rulers and subjects. There is an underlying contradiction in egalitarianism in open societies.

2

When social scientists talk of social problems, they usually mean discrepancies between social reality and what they assume to be norms. Because they are largely preoccupied with discerning, announcing and emphasizing discrepancies between their assumed norms and reality, social scientists tend to generate social problems rather than solve them. This way of looking at social situations and reading problems into them is evident in the persistent and extensive concern of egalitarians with economic differences.

In recent years there has been a vast upsurge of interest in the subject of these differences: witness, in Britain, the Standing Royal Commission on the Distribution of Income and Wealth (Diamond Commission, 1975–1979) and throughout the West, the research activities and publications of academics,

8

the contents of university curricula, and the preoccupations of journalists, broadcasters, and other popularizers.

The appeal of egalitarianism is likely to persist. As Tocqueville observed, when social differences diminish – as they have diminished in the West – those which remain appear especially irksome and objectionable; and as he also pointed out, material advance is apt to engender discontent over failure to have achieved some other objective. The contemporary predilection for numbers and quantification, and also the emphasis on material conditions, further help to focus attention on economic differences.

Once the moral and political case for egalitarian policies is taken for granted, the movement for egalitarianism feeds on itself. If the results of egalitarian policies are deemed favourable, it is evidence that still more could be achieved by further and sterner measures; if on the other hand the policies are deemed to have failed, it is evidence that they were not drastic enough. Such reactions are fostered when it is widely assumed that the economic positions of people are properly the concern of official policy.

Political power enables rulers forcibly to restrict the choices open to their subjects. But possession of wealth does not by itself confer such coercive power in this crucial sense. Wealth can sometimes secure a degree of political influence, although the likelihood and significance of this possibility are apt to be much exaggerated. In any case, wealth as such does not imply coercive power. Indeed, those who are rich are vulnerable to envy and to criticisms founded on an unreasoning presumption in favour of economic equality. These attitudes have at times led to the persecution and even destruction of productive or prosperous groups, often ethnic minorities. Possession of wealth offers no sure protection against such dangers. Moreover, the effort usually required for economic success is apt to divert the attention of the rich from political affairs; and the ability to accumulate wealth is often accompanied by an indifference to political opportunities, or a failure to recognize political dangers.

In an open society income differences normally reflect the operation of voluntary arrangements. The absence of coercive power in most forms of successful economic activity is recognized in Dr Johnson's familiar observation that 'there are few ways in which a man can be more innocently employed than in getting money'. Keynes put the same idea more elaborately (*General Theory*, 1936, p. 374):

Dangerous human proclivities can be canalized into comparatively harmless channels by the existence of opportunities for money-making and private wealth, which, if they cannot be satisfied in this way, may find their outlet in cruelty, the

9

reckless pursuit of personal power and authority, and other forms of self-aggrandisement. It is better that a man should tyrannize over his bank balance than over his fellow-citizens. . . .

This conclusion is particularly evident in a modern open society. In such a society the accumulation of wealth, especially great wealth, normally results from activities which extend the choices of others, as is clear from the fortunes acquired in, say, mass retailing or the development of the motor car.

3

People differ in economic aptitudes as they do in artistic, intellectual, musical and athletic abilities. In particular they differ in their ability to perceive and utilize economic opportunities. Readiness to take advantage of economic opportunities is of great significance in explaining economic differences in open societies. This should be evident on a little reflection. The opportunities seized by such men as Thomas Edison, Henry Ford, Lord Northcliffe or Sir Isaac Wolfson were open to most people in their countries. The same applies elsewhere; witness the many Chinese and Japanese *nouveaux riches* in the East. Income differences resulting from readiness to benefit from economic opportunities will be especially wide if there is rapid social, economic and technical change, including the development of new products and the opening up of new markets.

Chance often plays a part in economic life, and thus in the emergence and perhaps persistence of income differences. But this is no different from other fields of human endeavour. And Pasteur's celebrated observation that chance visits the prepared mind applies as much to economic life as it does to scientific activity.

An unfounded belief in the basic equality of people's economic faculties has coloured the language of the discussion. If people are assumed to be equally endowed and motivated, then wide economic differences suggest that some undefined but malevolent force has perverted the course of events. Of course people are not equally motivated or endowed in their economic attitudes and attributes, and this explains substantial economic differences between them in open societies. This discrepancy between the unfounded belief (or assumption) and reality may partly account for the almost universal practice of describing differences as inequalities. Difference is plainly the more appropriate expression since it is neutral. It does not prejudge the issue – unlike the term inequality, which clearly suggests a situation that is unjust or otherwise objectionable. In recent years inequality has come to be used interchangeably with inequity, and equality with equity. That differences is a more appropriate term than inequality is also suggested by the accepted practice of referring to people's physical characteristics, such as height, weight and strength, as differences rather than inequalities, and never as inequities.

On the other hand, the term inequality is appropriate in discussing political power because that power implies a relationship of command between rulers and subjects. As I suggested above, those who have political power can coerce others by restricting their choices, while wealth does not by itself confer such power on the rich.

In contemporary parlance social justice has come to mean substantially equal incomes. Why should this be so? It is not obvious why it should be just to penalize those who are more productive and contribute more to output, and to favour those who produce less. This conclusion is reinforced when it is remembered that relatively well-off people have often given up leisure, enjoyment and consumption, and that these past sacrifices have significantly contributed to their higher incomes. This is but one instance of a wider issue. Income differences or changes in income and the nature of poverty cannot be discussed seriously without examining how they have come about. Although this matter is central to an analysis of egalitarian ideas and proposals, further discussion of it is left until section 9 below, after other matters which are more prominent in the espousal and presentation of egalitarianism have been considered.

Advocates of redistribution propose that results of economic processes should be separated from the processes themselves, that people should share the fruits of economic activities in which they have not participated. The idea of equality over the past two centuries has progressed, or declined, from equality before the law, through equality of opportunity, to equality of result (or even equality of one quantifiable aspect of the result).

The demands to divorce the results of economic activity from the processes leading up to them are one facet of the contemporary preoccupation with situations and the neglect of the antecedent sequences. Such practices reflect the unhistorical approach of much contemporary discussion of social issues, the amputation of the time dimension from our culture, to borrow from Sir Ernst Gombrich.

A given degree of concentration of income and wealth at a particular time has a very different meaning if the societies are fluid, such as, say, those of Malaysia or Western Europe, or more nearly stable or static as, for example, that of rural India. This rather basic consideration rarely enters into egalitarian rhetoric. Moreover, for a rounded view of income differences, incomes have to be considered beyond one generation. Economic differences may be extended or reduced, or rankings of individuals or families maintained or reversed over a span of a generation or two.[2] Again, this consideration is rarely reflected in discussions of income differences.

Egalitarians often suggest that the incomes of the rich, or property incomes, have been received at the expense of other people rather than earned by supplying valuable resources. A familiar instance is the use of the term unearned income, when in fact such income is no less earned than any other income.

Incomes, including those of the relatively prosperous or the owners of property, are not taken from other people. Normally they are produced by their recipients and the resources they own; they are not misappropriated from others; they do not deprive other people of what they have had or might have had.[3]

The misconception that the incomes of the well-off are somehow obtained by exploitation rather than earned has often had disastrous consequences: for instance, it has led to spurious justification of the expropriation, and even destruction, of economically productive groups to which I have already referred. The same misconception is behind the familiar references to shares (usually unequal shares) of different groups in the national cake, and behind assertions that certain groups have not shared in national or international prosperity – assertions which do not ask how much these groups may have contributed to it.

The terminology of the economic theory of distribution has a long history and a reputable ancestry. It has come to be accepted so generally that it is almost impossible not to use it. Nevertheless, the terminology is misleading. Distribution of income suggests a total income which somehow is there and is then parcelled out. But, as I have just noted, recipients of income normally produce their incomes: the distribution of income is connected with its production. Distribution also has a technical meaning in statistics (as, for instance, a normal distribution), which is quite different from the meaning of the term both in the theory of income distribution and in egalitarian discourse. These different uses of the term should not be confused.

In a market economy the production and distribution of income are two sides of the same process. The term redistribution is especially misleading because what happens in fact is that part of the income is removed from those who have produced it, and is transferred to others (after the costs of effecting the transfers have been deducted).

The general proposition that incomes, including those of the well-to-do, are generated, produced and not taken from others, is subject to partial qualification. The incomes of some people are augmented by the exercise of

12

monopoly power, which in serious and persistent instances reflects barriers to entry or other forms of restriction created or supported by the state. It has even been argued that state-supported restrictions have contributed materially to the extent of income differences in some Western societies, a contribution which would be eliminated if market forces were allowed freer play.

It is difficult to tell just how important this factor is. In any event, it does not mean that the incomes of these favoured groups (other than the recipients of straight state subsidies) are not generated by their members; what it means is that restrictions enable these groups to charge more for their services than they could otherwise. But it certainly does not follow that high incomes are usually achieved at the expense of the rest of the community. The levels of income of particular groups do not themselves indicate the presence or absence of restriction on entry. Successful businessmen, entertainers and athletes, for instance, can earn very high incomes even when they do not curtail their output, and when there are no contrived barriers to entry into their activities. Similarly, an expansion of demand can greatly increase the incomes of certain groups even when, again, there are no such barriers. On the other hand, even modest incomes of professional people, trade unionists or farmers may be inflated by barriers to entry.

4

The policy termed redistribution benefits some people by confiscating part of the incomes of others. The beneficiaries may be poor, but this is by no means always so. Major beneficiaries of redistribution include its advocates, organizers and administrators, notably politicians and civil servants, who are not among the poor. This outcome promotes the self-perpetuation of the process. And once the notion is accepted that economic differences are somehow reprehensible, the door is opened to forcible intervention on any number of different and shifting grounds and criteria. These include differences in income or wealth, and differences in their rate of change.

On the national level, the operation of the welfare state comprises two quite different forms of redistribution: wealth transfers between groups, and redistribution of responsibility between the agents of the state and private citizens. Welfare state policies do not always redistribute income between the rich and the poor. They do not necessarily redistribute income even among individuals. The same people may be taxed at some times and subsidized at others.

The substantial taxes, including direct taxes, paid by the poor in the welfare states of the West make clear that, contrary to what is widely believed, the welfare state is not simply an agency of redistribution from rich to poor. In Britain in 1978, a single man earning £25 a week (less than one-half of the average unskilled wage) paid direct taxes. Those who earn the average wage of manual workers and have two children pay substantial direct taxes. Both categories also pay heavy indirect taxes.

The substantial taxation of the poor in countries which have extensive provision of social services is one facet of the confusion of redistribution of income with redistribution of responsibility just noted. By now, egalitarians and other supporters of social services often recognize explicitly that state-financed old-age pensions, health care, education, susbsidized housing and food, welfare and unemployment payments and other social services do not represent solely or even primarily transfers from rich to poor. Heavy taxation of the poor, together with extensive provision of welfare services, reflects the self-perpetuating character of redistributive policies. The case for these continues to be taken for granted, even after it has become plain that to a considerable extent they benefit people other than the supposed beneficiaries.

Old age, ill-health, the bringing-up of children and interruption of earnings, these are contingencies of life to be paid for out of one's income, and for which adults can be expected to provide by saving or insurance. In many Western countries provision for these contingencies has come to be taken over largely by the state. Because the provision cannot be adjusted to the widely differing circumstances of individuals and families, it is apt to be both expensive and unsatisfactory. Such provision is necessarily financed by taxation. As a result many people's post-tax income becomes like pocket-money which is not required for major necessities and hazards of life because these are paid for by taxes largely levied on themselves. This policy treats adults as if they were children. Adults manage incomes; children receive pocket-money. The redistribution of responsibilities implied in the operation of the welfare state means the reduction of the status of adults to that of children.

There is a further result of large-scale redistribution of responsibility between the agents of the state and private individuals, a result which acts as an anomalous and even ominous force for perpetuating and extending the policy. Prudent people, even if poor, can normally provide for the contingencies of life by saving and insurance, but only if the value of money is reasonably stable. They are unable to do so when this condition does not hold. Heavy state spending on welfare in various ways promotes the erosion of the value of money, a risk against which many people cannot protect themselves, certainly not by saving and insurance. The difficulty, or impossibility, of protecting themselves effectively leads them to accept or to demand that tax-financed provision for these contingencies should be maintained or extended, even if this is recognized to be unsatisfactory. The result greatly reinforces political, administrative and other sectional interests in perpetuating and extending the welfare system.

Many people receive in subsidies or government services broadly the same amount as they pay in taxes. But the two transfers do not simply cancel out, leaving things unchanged. People subject to them are still unable to escape certain adverse consequences of redistributive policies. First, taxation usually has some disincentive effects, and so may eligibility for subsidies. Second, people's ability to dispose of their incomes has been shifted from themselves to the politicians and officials who design and carry out such policies, and this reduces their range of choice in the disposal of their income.

Proposals for redistribution, supposedly in order to reduce differences in incomes, are also often pretexts for measures for the political or economic benefit of some persons or groups at the expense of others, with no certainty, or even presumption, of a reduction in conventionally measured differences in income. That they do not ensure even approximate economic equality is suggested by the experience of Communist countries. International comparisons of the distribution of incomes are fraught with conceptual and statistical problems, some of them intractable. But there are evident wide differences in income in Communist countries after decades of Communist rule. And in the Soviet Union (a country often thought to be dedicated to the removal of economic differences), the differences in income and living standards are quite as pronounced as in some market-orientated societies – and this after more than half a century of mass coercion.

5

Equality of opportunity was until recently the principal theme of egalitarian ideology. For example, many Fabians, notably Tawney, thought that equality of opportunity would result in substantial equality of income; that any remaining differences would reflect merit, and would therefore be widely respected and readily accepted. These ideas bypass the fundamental and intractable problem behind the central dilemma of egalitarianism: granted that equals should be treated equally, how shall we treat those who are unequally endowed, motivated or placed? For instance, loving parents and a cultivated background benefit those fortunate to possess them. Good looks and other such advantages result in unequal opportunities.

An open society, one with *la carrière ouverte aux talents*, is the most familiar interpretation of the ambiguous concept of equality of opportunity. The concept is then certainly and obviously incompatible with substantial equality of income and wealth. This is so because individuals and groups differ in economic aptitudes and motivations. These differences are evident in the rise from poverty to prosperity of countless individuals and groups the world over. They are evident also in the wide and persistent differences in prosperity between religious and ethnic groups in different areas and societies. Instructive examples include the economic success of certain communities in the face of adverse official discrimination, such as Nonconformists, Huguenots and Jews in the West, and the Chinese communities in South-East Asia. An open society may well bring about greater economic and social equality than a closed or caste society, but wide economic differences are bound to emerge and persist in it.

Only the belief that everybody's aptitudes and motivations are the same – a belief which can have sinister consequences – supports the notion that an open society is practically synonymous with economic equality, or at any rate promotes or ensures it. It is extraordinary that this notion should have been entertained for so long, and is often still entertained, when the evidence to the contrary is both overwhelming and obvious.

The idea that the economic aptitudes and motivations of all people are the same derives from the doctrine of the natural equality of man. According to this idea, we are all the same except for differences in money and education; the poor are like the rich except for having less money; and the peoples of the Third World, themselves all much the same, differ from those of the West only in being poorer.

This scheme of things envisages economic differences between people as being the only difference of any significance. At the same time, it is assumed that the differences can be removed without changing people's behaviour and without affecting their economic performance significantly. The continued belief that the persistence of economic differences in open societies is abnormal or accidental then leads to proposals and measures which go counter to equality before the law or to the maintenance of equality of opportunity – witness educational quotas on a racial basis in the United States or elsewhere.

The champions of equality in the sense of *la carrière ouverte aux talents* used to argue that income differences would be readily accepted once it became clear that they reflected achievement. This assumption, too, is facile. Lack of economic success is apt to be keenly felt and resented when economic achievement is thought to be important, and when failure is thought to result from inadequacy rather than from, say, purely random forces. When faced with differences of economic achievement in an open society, many people react by denying that success reflects a contribution to society let alone that it reflects merit. Such reactions have contributed to the denigration of market economies in open societies, because economic differences have persisted in them.

6

The adverse effects of redistributive policies on economic performance are implied in such expressions as the trade-off between equity and efficiency, or between social justice and efficiency. These formulations recognize to some extent that economic activity is not a zero-sum game. But they still disguise the extent to which the outcome of economic processes depends on the performance of people – performance which can be promoted or obstructed by official policy.

I have already noted that it is by no means obvious why it should be unjust that those who produce more should enjoy higher incomes. And attempts to prevent them from doing so will affect adversely the average level of incomes. It will do so cumulatively because if everybody can expect to receive only something like an average of all income, this average itself will fall. A neat example of this process emerged from an experiment designed a few years ago by a teacher in an American university. The students demanded much greater equality in all walks of life, including the grading of their papers. In response to these demands the teacher announced that from a given date the students would be given equal grades for their weekly papers, and that the grades would be based on the average performance of the class. The experiment brought about a rapid decline in average performance and thus in the average grade, because the incentive to work declined greatly.

Because wide income differences have not disappeared in open societies, pressures for their further reduction or elimination have also continued. Hence the demands for increasing the scope and level of what is misleadingly termed redistributive taxation. However, redistributive taxation is coming to be seen as insufficient by some egalitarians who recognize the cultural and personal factors which underlie economic differences.

Many people envisage that special disabilities (additional to progressive taxation) should be imposed on groups and individuals with cultural and personal characteristics favourable to economic success. Special taxation of talented persons has been proposed on the argument that their talents should be regarded as communal property. Such proposals mean conscription of abilities, already to some extent implicit in progressive taxation. Again,

17

government measures have been implemented to prevent some people from earning incomes as high as they are capable of doing. Quotas handicapping the gifted and the ambitious have already been widely adopted in higher education and in certain areas of economic activity in the United States. And the removal of children from their parents, and even the attempted manipulation of the genetic code, have also been suggested as instruments for the promotion of equality, though dismissed at any rate for the time being.

There may be a further reason for measures attempting to prevent the earning of higher incomes as distinct from attempts to equalize net incomes. Gross income (i.e. income before the deduction of tax) is an indicator of achievement, a mark of status and recognition. If differences in status and recognition are considered objectionable, there will be pressure for measures to equalize incomes before tax. Here redistributive taxation is irrelevant.

7

Attempts to minimize economic differences in an open and free society necessarily involve the use of coercive power. They politicize economic life. And economic activity comes to depend to a great degree on political decisions. People's incomes and their economic *modus vivendi* come largely under the control of politicians and civil servants. The extent of these consequences will depend on the degree of economic equality the rulers wish to achieve; and also on differences in the capacities, ambitions and circumstances of the groups and individuals among whom economic differences are to be curtailed or abolished.

Extensive politicization of life enhances the prizes of political power and thus the stakes in the fight for it. This outcome in turn intensifies political tension, at least until opposition is effectively demoralized or forcibly suppressed. And because people's economic fortunes come to depend so much on political and administrative decisions, their talents and energies are diverted from economic activity to political life, sometimes from choice and often from necessity. These consequences are manifest in many societies, especially in multiracial societies.

In many countries politicization of life, often pursued in the name of equality, now means that the question of who are the rulers has become of the greatest importance. The effect of politicization on people's feelings and conduct is observable in many countries where there is some ethnic diversity, including the United Kingdom. It stands out starkly in the heterogeneous societies of the Third World, where the conduct of the rulers is often a matter of life and death for millions of people. The ferocity of the political struggle in many Third World countries cannot be understood without an awareness of the politicization of life there. This process has been helped along by the slogans of equality, and reinforced by the idea that high incomes, especially of minorities, have not been earned but have been taken from other people.

When the inequality in political power between rulers and subjects is pronounced, conventional measurements of incomes and living standards cannot even remotely convey the substance of the situation. Such measurements greatly understate the realities of inequality in a society where the rulers can command the available resources practically at will. They may use their power to secure for themselves large incomes; or they may choose austere forms of life. They still have vast power over the lives of their subjects, which they can use to secure higher living standards for themselves whenever they wish. Dzerzhinski, Nasser and Nyerere have been among rulers whose relatively simple mode of life has elicited sycophantic adulation from their admirers. But their simple mode of life has not prevented them from combining it with the ruthless exercise of their virtually unlimited power over their subjects.

It is now widely urged that differences in income and living standards should be reduced or eliminated not only within countries but between them, and indeed even globally. Hence the proposals for a New International Economic Order approved by the General Assembly of the United Nations. Because of the enormous and stubborn differences between peoples, policies designed to equalize their living standards would require world government with totalitarian powers. Such a government, to be equal to its ambitions, would be even more coercive and brutal than the totalitarian governments of individual countries.

The various adverse and often sinister consequences of the politicization of life promoted by egalitarianism are widely ignored or swept under the carpet, even when they are both pronounced and evident. A major reason for this neglect is that egalitarians, including many academics, are more interested in advocating the removal of economic differences than in enquiring either how they have come about or what is involved in their removal. It is the current situation which is considered offensive or objectionable – and the reasons for the situation and the consequences of the proposed treatment are neglected.

8

Economic differences are largely the result of people's capacities and motivations. This is evident in open societies, and also where societies are not open, nor yet completely closed or caste-bound. A disproportionate number of the poor lack the capabilities and inclination for economic achievement, and often for cultural achievement as well. Weak members of a society need to be helped. But large-scale penalization of productive groups for the benefit of the materially and culturally less productive, and for the benefit of those who administer wealth transfers, impairs the prospects of a society. This outcome is especially likely when the less productive receive support without stigma and, indeed, as of right; and even more so when those who are more productive are made to feel guilty on that account. These are precisely the stances and attitudes prominent in the advocacy and practice of redistribution.

The terminology of the negative income tax reflects the acceptance of the principle of support without stigma. The payment of income tax is a statutory obligation. A negative income tax is the inverse: the right to an income regardless of performance, simply by virtue of being alive and poor.

Personal and group differences in economic aptitudes and motivations will disappoint the expectation that the guarantee of a cash income would make it possible to abolish specific welfare services. These services will still have to be supplied to the many recipients of cash payments who will nevertheless fail to provide for the contingencies of life. Such people are likely to be disproportionately represented among the recipients of negative income tax. In Britain this is suggested, for instance, by the prevalence of avoidable ill-health and dental decay among children of unskilled workers who own television sets or motor cars.

Many recipients of either domestic or international wealth transfers are paupers, in the traditional sense of persons dependent on official charity. But because the support is given as of right and even envisaged as restitution for past wrongs, the paupers can not only insist on these transfers but can attempt also to prescribe the political conduct of the donors. This is evident in the advocacy of international wealth transfers from the West to the Third World.

9

Some modern egalitarians seem readier than their predecessors to recognize personal and group differences in economic endowment and in motivation. This acknowledgement brings into the open previously ignored dilemmas. The recognition of such differences has also induced these egalitarians to advocate the elimination not only of economic differences but also of differences in aptitudes and motivations; that is, the causes of economic differences. Hence some of the policies and drastic proposals noted above.

Although acknowledgement of the determinants of economic differences has helped to clarify some central issues and dilemmas of egalitarian policies, in other ways the level of discourse has remained unsatisfactory. Indeed, in recent decades the standard may even have deteriorated.

The uncritical reliance on statistics in egalitarian discourse and policies provides a major illustration. There is, for instance, the familiar practice of expressing the income or wealth of a small proportion of the population of a country as a percentage of the income or wealth of the whole population. The misleading, even meaningless, nature of this practice should be evident. Thus children have no incomes, or very low incomes; people normally cannot make appreciable savings until well into middle age; many married women have no cash incomes or only low cash incomes. Income differences need to be expressed on a basis which separates different age groups, and also men from women. In technical language, the differences have to be expressed on an age- and sex-standardized basis.

Further complexities and ambiguities ensue if we compare family incomes. A childless couple is likely to have a higher per capita income than a family with children. But it does not follow that the former is better off. The conventional method of calculating the national income implies that children are simply an unavoidable cost or burden, and assumes that people do not enjoy the generation and possession of children sufficiently to outweigh any differences in income per capita. It also results in paradoxes, such as the registering in conventional national income calculations of the birth of a calf or the survival of a cow as an increase in per capita income, while the birth or survival of a child is registered as a diminution. Further problems arise over the definition of 'capita'. For example, should a child be treated as equivalent to half an adult? Moreover, conventional income comparisons do not distinguish adequately between income and the cost of securing income, for instance in such contexts as the cost of training, or of enjoyment forgone in training, or in long hours of work, or in the cost of travel to and from work. And professional people who have invested heavily in a training which has enabled them to earn high incomes are disadvantaged in terms of real income compared with those who have used their time to learn to do things such as household repairs themselves – a consideration of some significance when direct taxation and the cost of labour-intensive services are high.

State-provided or guaranteed pensions represent another example of the intractable conceptual difficulties behind assessment of economic differences. Such pensions can be very valuable to particular individuals, and can represent the equivalent of large capital sums, notably when they are index-linked. But pension rights are unmarketable and cannot be turned into capital; and their value depends on the ability and willingness of future governments to honour them.

Finally, we now come to a wide issue, mentioned briefly earlier in this chapter, which is crucial to an examination of income differences and changes. Even when income statistics are free of problems of concept and measurement, which is unusual, by themselves they tell us nothing about the background of the situation they reflect. It is indispensable for sensible assessment and policy to know why people are poor and how income differences have arisen. For instance, those who are poor through crippling disease, or unavoidable or uninsurable accident, or erosion of savings through inflation, need to be treated differently from those people whose poverty has resulted from persistent overspending of large incomes. Again, incomes can become more equal as a result of more people dying or being forcibly sterilized. Yet conventional terminology describes this result as an 'improvement in income distribution'. Conversely, if more very poor people live longer, this registers as a so-called worsening of income distribution.

Some policies, popular beliefs and mores affect income differences between societies so greatly that they are central to any sensible discussion of such differences. The many obvious examples include the persecution of productive groups in Asia and Africa; the subordination of economic advance to egalitarian objectives as in Britain; the refusal to take animal life as in South Asia; or to let women work outside the home as in many Muslim countries. These pertinent matters are freely ignored by advocates of global redistribution who focus entirely on conventionally measured income differences. Altogether, we have become so preoccupied with quantifiable matters that even such an obvious distinction (and one formerly well-recognized) as that between sturdy beggars and needy poor has come to be neglected or even derided by egalitarians.

Disregard of such basic matters reflects the naive belief that statistics denote facts more effectively and exactly than does qualitative description, or that it is only statistics which objectively depict social facts. These habits of mind are of a piece with Mr Gradgrind's attitude in Dickens' *Hard Times*.[4]

As I have already mentioned, the time dimension of historical processes is widely neglected in contemporary discourse. This is especially notable and misleading in the context of international income differences. Income and living standards in the West are the outcome of many centuries of cultural and economic progress; they have not come about in one or two generations. It is therefore not surprising, abnormal or reprehensible that many Third World

22

countries (notably in Africa) which do not have centuries of progress behind them should have much lower incomes than the twentieth-century West. The pertinence of this long period of antecedent development is ignored in the advocacy of global redistribution. It is ignored also in the insistence that Third World countries should promptly reach Western levels of income by a process of virtually instant development. This insistence is apt to issue in coercive policies which not only inhibit a rise in living standards in these countries, but also provoke social tension, upheaval and political conflict.

10

Redistribution of income and reduction of poverty are often thought to be interchangeable concepts. Indeed, it is often taken for granted that egalitarian policies necessarily improve the condition of the poor. This is not so. The promotion of economic equality and the alleviation of poverty are distinct and often conflicting. To make the rich poorer does not make the poor richer.

The advocates of egalitarian policies focus on relative income differences, or the relative positions of different groups. They thereby divert attention from the causes of poverty, especially the causes which underlie real hardship, and from the possibilities of effective remedial measures. Relief of poverty, especially the improvement in the position of the very poor, has nothing to do with the pursuit of equality. The policies of egalitarianism often ignore the poor, especially those who are self-reliant and enterprising.

Except perhaps over very short periods, redistributive policies are much more likely to depress the living standards of the poor than to raise them. The extensive politicization brought about by large-scale redistribution diverts people's energies and ambitions from productive economic activity to politics and public administration. It also encourages attempts to benefit from politically-organised redistribution, or to escape its consequences. An even more evident result is that these policies systematically transfer resources from people who are economically productive to others who are less so. Thus such policies inhibit a rise in incomes and living standards, including those of the poor.

Besides such results of broadly egalitarian policies, many specific measures thought to be egalitarian often benefit middle income groups at the expense of both rich and poor. This is the likely outcome of such policies as, for instance, the granting of privileges to trade unions, official prescription of minimum wages, the imposition of rent controls, restrictive licensing of enterprises, legislation for the promotion of so-called equal opportunities, and heavy direct taxation of persons and of enterprises.

In sum, the pursuit of economic equality is more likely to harm than to benefit the living standards of the very poor by politicizing life, by restricting the accumulation and effective deployment of capital, by obstructing social and economic mobility at all levels, and by inhibiting enterprise in many different ways. Continued poverty, whether resulting from soi-disant egalitarian measures or from other causes, then serves as plausible argument or rationalization for further and more stringent egalitarianism. These repercussions are necessarily ignored when the promotion of equality and the alleviation of poverty are regarded as identical.

11

Disregard of the restriction of the opportunities of the poor effected by egalitarianism is promoted by a curious asymmetrical application of that environmental determinism which underlies so much contemporary discourse on social affairs. The poor are seen as helpless victims of their environment, people at the mercy of external forces and without wills of their own. The implication is that they are without the primary human characteristic of responsibility. This determinism, however, does not extend to the rich. They are seen as having wills of their own which are somehow deployed for selfish and even villainous ends. Poverty is thus a condition caused by external forces and not by personal conduct. Wealth, on the other hand, is the result of conduct which is purposeful but reprehensible. The poor are seen as passive but virtuous, the rich as active but wicked.

This picture is painted by certain groups who regard themselves as standing apart from rich and poor, and perhaps as above both. They are, in the main, politicians, social reformers, welfare administrators, social scientists, writers, artists, media people, churchmen and even entertainers. As noted in the Introduction, they now form much of what was once called the political nation. In their advocacy of redistribution and its misleading identification with the relief of poverty, a significant number of these people behave in a manner which has led Dr R. M. Hartwell of Oxford University to refer to them as the redistribution industry.

Many members of these groups, especially politicians, academics and media men, have in recent decades done much to articulate, institutionalize and organize envy and resentment against economically effective people. Envy and resentment may be as old as mankind,[5] but especially in the West and in the Westernized Third World countries these sentiments seem nowadays more insistent, persistent and extensive than they were formerly. Politicians and intellectuals have supplied articulation and a veneer of intellectual respectability to envy and resentment. They have argued that economic differences are abnormal and reprehensible, and also that they result from exploitation. They have effectively helped to provoke feelings of guilt among the more successful and affluent, and this in turn has helped to confer a spurious legitimacy on envy and resentment.

CHAPTER 2

Class on the Brain

1

It has become part of contemporary political folklore that the curse of British society is its restrictive class system. This belief, amounting to an obsession, has it that class is the major barrier to economic progress in Britain and a significant source of legitimate social discontent.

I shall first summarize the generally accepted opinion about class in Britain; then show that it is misconceived; and finally suggest that its widespread acceptance has led to harsh restrictions on mobility and freedom and that it threatens further and even more drastic restrictions.

My main contention is that the established view on class in Britain mistakes a differentiated but open society for a closed society – or even a caste society, i.e. one in which people's occupations are fixed by the class into which they are born. It confuses distinctions with barriers. In Britain, class distinctions do indeed exist, but they are not, and rarely have been, significant barriers to social or economic mobility.

2

Herr Schmidt, the West German Chancellor, once came out with a terse summary of received opinion on the subject of class in Britain. On an official visit in London in December 1975, when the pound was weak and the balance of payments poor, he was reported in the *Financial Times* (11 December) as saying: 'As long as you maintain that damned class-ridden society of yours you will never get out of your mess.' And indeed this is what foreigners are told all the time by the British intelligentsia. The *Financial Times* staff writer, who quoted Herr Schmidt approvingly, went on to say:

The single most important fault in Britain's social structure remains its propensity to accentuate class differences. . . . Most foreigners can see this, but many people in Britain are curiously blind to the grim reality behind the Chancellor's words.

This is part of a stereotype. For many years now, politicians, journalists and academics have blamed the class system for just about every form of economic adversity or social malaise in Britain. Some of the allegations are plainly far-fetched: for example, the idea that a rigid or antiquated class system is responsible for balance of payments difficulties, when the balance of payments can turn from deficit to surplus in a matter of weeks. And while the commentators often say that a weak pound reflects the class system, they do not often say the converse when the pound is strong. Thus, speaking again in London in October 1977, Herr Schmidt said that the British economy had improved greatly: but on that occasion he said nothing about class.

Neither the German Chancellor nor the writer in the *Financial Times* bothered to define the so-called mess, or to spell out what he meant by the class system, or how class accounts for the mess. Such basic and substantial omissions are typical in allegations about class. The underlying thrust is nevertheless clear, namely that the British class system is rigid and iniquitous because it leaves large reservoirs of talent unused, to the detriment of both social peace and economic efficiency. It is also alleged to be an instrument of exploitation. The allegations misconceive the character of British society and the nature of economic activity. They also ignore simple and undisputed facts of British history and of British social, economic and political life.

As I shall argue subsequently in this chapter, restrictive barriers have indeed emerged in Britain in recent years. But these have nothing to do with class as usually understood. The critics of the allegedly restrictive character of the British class system do not normally identify devices or mechanisms by which class distinctions restrict economic opportunity. On the other hand, as we shall see shortly, it is easy to identify the new restrictive devices and their methods of operation, which are unrelated to class.

The general case that Britain is an open society is established by the fact that for centuries there have been no identifiable class barriers to economic achievement in Britain. I introduce specific examples only to throw into relief the general position. These are not isolated cases. I have chosen them because they are readily verifiable and I believe them to be instructive. They can be multiplied.

It is sometimes objected that examples such as those given here refer only to exceptional persons. But this objection is irrelevant. Prominent, successful, rich, unusually industrious or enterprising people are exceptional by definition. What is pertinent is the absence of identifiable restrictive barriers related to class. I shall deal primarily with economic life since this is the principal concern of the most influential and articulate critics of class in Britain. And I shall then turn to other spheres of activity, including politics.

27

3

The stereotype of the role of class in British economic life is demonstrably unfounded. Those exposed to the stereotype could not guess that British industry is managed, and has been managed for decades or even centuries, by new men, people who have made their way often from humble beginnings. This is evident in the motor-car, food processing, electrical, chemical, retailing, entertainment, building, property and plantation industries. But it applies in large measure also to steel, transport, shipbuilding and the mass circulation newspapers. The British motor-car industry has always been in the hands of new men or of American companies; its troubles therefore cannot be attributed to class.

In the inter-war period the leading figure of the British motor industry was Lord Nuffield, who began as a bicycle repairer and had had little formal education. With part of his huge fortune he founded Nuffield College.

Unilever, one of the largest manufacturing companies in the world, grew out of a business started in the closing years of the nineteenth century by a Lancashire grocer who made his own soap. For many years the founder's successors as chairman and chief executive have been new men. Thus, from 1960 to 1970 the position was held by Lord Cole, son of a clerk. Cole had a very modest education and started work for the company at the age of seventeen. On retiring from Unilever, he became government-appointed chairman of Rolls Royce. (His son went to Eton and Oxford.) In mass retailing or catering the prominence of new men such as Sir Isaac Wolfson, Sir Charles Clore or Sir Charles Forte is familiar; that of Thomas Boot, the Sieffs, Salmons and Glucksteins (Marks and Spencer and Lyons) dates from a few decades back.

Less familiar are the names of Sir John Hay (1882–1964), undisputed leader of the British rubber industry of the inter-war and early post-war years; Sir John Ellerman (1862–1933), founder of the Ellerman shipping line, who at the time of his death was possibly the richest man in England; the first Lord Catto (1879–1959), chairman of Yule Catto, director of Morgan Grenfell, and finally Governor of the Bank of England. All three came from poor families and started their business careers in very modest jobs in City offices. Mr David Robinson, who recently gave £17 million to found a Cambridge college, is another self-made man.

It is quite usual to see items in the press complaining about the supposedly restrictive class system in Britain which is said to obstruct the economic advance of poor people, side by side with reports of the careers of people who started with nothing and became very rich. The obvious inconsistency reflects both the tenacity of the stereotype of class and the widespread inability to perceive even simple connections between readily observable phenomena.

To turn from commerce to politics. According to the stereotype Britain is governed by members of a traditional ruling caste. Yet Disraeli, whose origins are evident from his name, was Prime Minister more than a century ago; Lloyd George, an orphan brought up by an uncle who was a shoemaker, was Chancellor of the Exchequer by 1908 and Prime Minister from 1916 to 1922; and Ramsay MacDonald, illegitimate son of a fisherwoman, was Prime Minister 1923–24 and 1929–35. None of them went to university; Lloyd George and MacDonald had elementary education only, and Disraeli attended an obscure secondary school. And although Mr Heath and Mrs Thatcher did go to university, their backgrounds are certainly not upper class. Nor, of course, are those of Mr Callaghan and Mr Healey.

The higher Civil Service and Oxford and Cambridge have often been regarded as the exclusive preserves of the upper and upper-middle classes, at any rate before the Second World War. But the first Lord Stamp of Shortlands (1880–1941) began as a clerk in the Inland Revenue in 1896. He reached a high position in the Civil Service before he retired young, moved into industry, became a director of the Bank of England and chairman of the largest British railway company. The late Sir John Anderson, first Viscount Waverley (1882–1958), Governor of Bengal, Lord President of the Council and Home Secretary, was also a career civil servant with a middle-class background.

At Oxford and Cambridge it has long been the case that high and coveted positions have been held by new men of very modest background, including people who were not undergraduates there. For instance, Sir James Chadwick, the famous physicist, was a Fellow of Gonville and Caius College, Cambridge for most of the inter-war period, and became its Master in 1948. He was the son of an unskilled worker, and went to Manchester University on a scholarship.

Class domination of the British army before the Second World War is often regarded as so self-evident as to be not worth discussing. But for most of the First World War, the Chief of the Imperial General Staff was Sir William Robertson (1860–1933). Robertson was a man of lowly birth who enlisted as a private in the 1880s. He published his memoirs under the title *From Private to Field Marshal*. For most of his life he dropped his aitches.

Not even the diplomatic service was closed to people of humble origin. Sir Reader Bullard (1885–1976) was the son of a casual labourer. He entered the consular service before the First World War, having largely educated himself, and rose to become ambassador to Iran.

Such refutations of the accepted stereotype should not come as a surprise.

Prominent writers and scholars have recognized for well over a century the extensive social mobility in Britain, and especially in British economic life. Tocqueville commented on the ease of entry into the British aristocracy in the nineteenth century, and the rise of new men in society and in business has often been noted at length by academics and others.

A few years ago Seymour Martin Lipset and Reinhard Bendix, two American sociologists, published an authoritative book, *Social Mobility in Industrial Society*[1], in which they argued that the degree of social mobility, including that affecting business leadership, was much the same in Britain as in the United States. In that book they quote a study published in 1912 in the *Journal of the Royal Statistical Society* under the revealing title 'The Recruiting of the Employing Classes from the Ranks of the Wage Earners in the Cotton Industry'.[2] According to that study, over two-thirds of owners, directors and managers in the cotton industry had begun their careers either as manual workers or in modest clerical positions. Lipset and Bendix wrote:

The researchers, surprised by their own findings, attempted to check them by interviewing company executives, union leaders, and economic historians of the industry. They found general agreement with their findings. Sidney Webb, the Fabian leader, commented 'In Lancashire I think that practically all mill managers are taken from the ranks of the Spinners Union'.

The results of the cotton industry study by researchers who knew that industry well plainly exposed the inadequacies of the stereotype of the restrictive class system. These findings were endorsed explicitly by the leader of the Fabians. Two further considerations reinforce the interest of these findings. First, the British cotton industry at the time was a relatively old industry so that the large proportion of new men may be surprising. Second, the industry has contracted considerably since the First World War, which suggests that Britain's industrial decline has nothing to do with the class system.

There are many other academic studies which show the high degree of social mobility in Britain. They include books by left-wing authors critical of British politics and society who are nevertheless prepared to recognize evidence on this subject. Examples are works by D. V. Glass and John Westergaard.[3]

Recent academic study has again provided notable confirmation of social mobility in Britain. It has done so with evidence which is both detailed and wide ranging; and the results of the work have surprised the researchers themselves, in much the same way as did those of the Lancashire survey of about seventy years ago. The findings of a major survey carried out by a group of research workers under the direction of Dr John Goldthorpe, Fellow of

Nuffield College, Oxford, have recently become available. The results were noted in *New Society* of 10 November 1977 in an article which also emphasized the remarkable silence with which these highly interesting results were received. The article deserves to be quoted at some length:

> Over the past few months John Goldthorpe and his colleagues at Nuffield College, Oxford, have begun to publish the results of their analysis of social mobility in Britain in a variety of sociological journals. And these, for once, challenge rather than reinforce stereotypes.
>
> For they show that Britain is a much more mobile society than the received wisdom suggests: that we are a surprisingly open society, with people moving up and down the occupational escalators in a bewilderingly complex pattern. For example, only a quarter of those in social class I – managers and professionals – had fathers in the same category: rather less than the proportion drawn from a manual working class background (at least partly, of course, because the managerial class has been expanding so fast that it simply couldn't recruit from among its own members).
>
> Nor is the loud silence which has accompanied the publication of these findings an isolated example of the reaction to research which doesn't fit easily into conventional pigeon-holes.

The silence with which these findings were greeted is by no means unusual. The media rarely take cognizance of findings which discredit a stereotype accepted by themselves. However, the standard opinion on class has come to be disputed by scholars and by others in non-academic publications. Thus Professor Donald Macrae has written in a newspaper article:

> We have never, since Elizabethan times, had serious legal barriers to moving up or down social ladders, never had a closed nobility of the European kind. Our statistics, which on this matter take us back with some doubts to the early twentieth century, suggest a high and constant rate of mobility equal to that of the United States and greater than in Western Europe.[4]

Professor Macrae's observations were not disputed. Indeed, a subsequent article in the same newspaper referred to 'the turbulent chaos of British social life, in which about two people in every five end up in a social class different from that occupied by their parents'. On this point, a letter in *The Observer* is informative and entertaining:

> I was interested in your questionnaire on TV and had intended to complete it, until I noticed the usual horrid little box at the end, asking me to state my 'class'. According to the sociologists, I have two middle-class sisters and one working-class. I have one middle-class and one working-class daughter. My son-in-law was middle-class until the age of 23, then became working-class for three years. He is now middle-class again. From now on I refuse to fill in any questionnaire which perpetuates such absurdity.[5]

In British economic life such mobility goes back many centuries. The expression 'new rich' seems to have been used in England as early as the fifteenth century. And by the early eighteenth century Addison wrote:

A superior capacity for business, and a more extensive knowledge, are steps by which a new man often mounts to favour, and outshines the rest of his contemporaries.

Addison might almost have been anticipating the question asked by Lady Bracknell more than a century later in *The Importance of Being Earnest*: 'Was he born in what the radical papers call the purple of commerce, or did he rise from the ranks of the aristocracy?'

Mobility of course may be downward as well as upward. Relative decline in the position of some groups and individuals is the necessary mirror image of the relative rise of others. And the frequency of instances of absolute decline is recognized in the familiar saying about three generations from clogs to clogs. Altogether, the term 'class' applied to the British social scene is misleading because it suggests effective barriers to social mobility based on birth or some other clearly defined and firm criterion.

4

Since no significant branch of British industry or trade has ever been restricted to a particular class, class barriers have not obstructed economic progress in Britain. It is true that until well into the nineteenth century Catholics, Jews and Nonconformists could not enter politics, nor for that matter Oxford or Cambridge. But these restrictions probably promoted economic progress, in that the barriers induced ambitious people within these groups to go into industry and commerce. The restrictions may have contributed to the conspicuous role of the Nonconformists in the development of British industry and commerce in such activities as banking, brewing, engineering and textiles.

In the nineteenth and twentieth centuries the Nonconformists were joined by the Jews. Their economic success shows how misleading it is to think that the exclusion from political activity necessarily inhibits the economic prospects of a person or group. Jews had no political rights in Europe until well into the nineteenth century, by which time, however, many of them had become extremely rich and prominent in many forms of economic activity.

There are still no class barriers to wealth or access to positions of responsibility in Britain. Nevertheless, in other ways British economic society is now less open and less flexible than in the past. The reasons for this are very different from those suggested by the standard complaints about the British class system.

In Britain, the establishment and development of businesses from small beginnings has become much more difficult in recent decades. This is a result of the nationalization of many activities, the restrictive licensing of some activities, far-reaching bureaucratization and heavy taxation both of persons and of small businesses. Again, housing policy (primarily rent controls), trade union restrictions, minimum wages, so-called employment protection and closed shops all reduce mobility – both directly and by making it more difficult to start new businesses. These policies and measures have made it difficult for people to rise from poverty to prosperity by means of legitimate business activity. For people of modest background such progress is now largely restricted to those who can advance through the Civil Service or big-business bureaucracy, or to the small number who can do so in the free professions. Many gifted working-class children (as well as many other people) have the capacity to establish and run small businesses, but not the aptitudes or qualifications of a successful bureaucrat, or the skills required to succeed in a bureaucratic society.

Even journalism is becoming less open to talented and enterprising members of the working class. From the early nineteenth century until recently journalism presented one of the best opportunities for advance for talented people of working-class background and with little formal education. Some of the great figures of nineteenth-century and early twentieth-century British journalism, including outstanding and influential editors of *The Times* and *The Observer*, came from modest backgrounds and had scant formal education. Compulsory unionization and the widespread insistence on formal qualifications have made such careers less likely.

This closure of opportunities has recently come to be well recognized. An item in *The Times* of 8 December 1977 referred to the careers of Mr Louis Heren, deputy editor of *The Times*, and Admiral Sir Raymond Lygo, the Vice-Chief of Naval Staff. They were messenger boys together on *The Times* and rose to their exalted positions from this beginning. The report concluded that in journalism such careers are not possible today. Again, Mr Frank Johnson, who achieved a national reputation as editorial and Parliamentary sketch writer on *The Daily Telegraph*, was born of working-class parents, and his formal education terminated with one O level (in commerce). He started as a messenger boy on the *Sunday Express*. He has stated emphatically that such a career is no longer possible because of the widespread insistence by unions and management on formal qualifications and career structure.

As a result of these numerous restrictions, Britain is now much less of an open society or economy – in the sense of a society or economy with *la carrière ouverte aux talents* – than it was formerly. Indeed, contrary to what is generally believed, the British economy is at present beset by many more restrictions than it was in the past, especially in the eighteenth and nineteenth centuries.

It is not certain whether many working-class children would be affected by the further extension of what has come to be called, rather misleadingly, higher education, or would benefit from it financially or otherwise. But the closure of many avenues of advance, other than those for which formal qualifications are required, will ensure continued intense concern with the extent of higher education and with the background of students.

The prospects of many talented working-class children have been prejudiced also by the abolition of many schools catering to their needs, and the replacement of these schools by institutions intended to serve as social engineering laboratories rather than as educational institutions. But these are not what critics of the British class system complain about. The stereotype of the class system has in fact helped to bring about such recent obstacles to social and economic mobility. The belief that British society is class-ridden and therefore restrictive has paved the way for the politicization and bureaucratization of life. Measures introduced ostensibly to assist the poor and to promote greater equality of opportunity have, in fact, restricted social, economic and occupational mobility and made it more difficult for enterprising, ambitious and self-reliant working-class people to get on. In the prevailing climate of opinion these obstacles to movement come to be attributed to a restrictive class system, an attribution which is then used spuriously to justify further extension of restrictive measures and the erection of further obstacles.

5

People in Britain have for centuries displayed acute awareness of fine distinctions. The difference between a CB and a CBE is recognized to this day throughout the Civil Service, and often beyond it. Civil Servants and public figures are unhappy to receive a CBE when they expect a CB or an OBE when they hope for a CBE. Perception of differences extends far down the social scale – witness saloon bars, lounge bars and public bars in pubs.

Over a wide area, including education, speech and dress, there are many differences in Britain which are related to social standing and class. These were, at any rate until recently, freely accepted. Their presence is an important political and social fact. In this sense Britain has always been a class society. But for about eight centuries Britain has not been a closed society, much less a caste society. Britain has not had a closed aristocracy or nobility since the early Middle Ages. Marriage, money, services or official favour enabled many aspiring members of the working class and middle classes to enter the aristocracy, including the highest ranks. Wolsey was the son of a butcher. Queen Elizabeth I was descended from a serf.

Differences in conduct related to social class, including modes of speech, habits of eating and dress, and even taste, may in Britain extend over a wider area of behaviour than in other countries. The relationship between social class and different types of secondary schooling is a familiar, indeed well-worn example. Again, in Continental countries or in America, unlike in Britain, the midday meal is not called by a different name by the working class and by the rest of society, nor is a preference for weak or strong tea, or for dry or sweet sherry, related to social class. Most British people are exceptionally perceptive of small differences and nuances in these matters. These conditions encourage the idea of Britain as a class-ridden society. But it is nevertheless an open society. A middle-class person may talk about lunch (or even luncheon) when the working-class person talks about dinner; or he may drink China tea, or even espresso, rather than strong, sweet Indian tea. But the same middle-class person may be a former working man or woman, or at any rate the child of one.

The presence and the unenforced acceptance of social distinctions and differences, including small differences and fine distinctions, were the outcome of centuries of relatively peaceful history. And, in an open and mobile society, such differences and distinctions do not restrict talent or inhibit economic progress. In fact, they promote ambition and achievement because they offer inducement, something to go for.

But to complain about the acceptance of such distinctions or differences in conduct is to object to people's preferences, even if these preferences do not restrict the opportunities of others. Indeed, the sentiment behind many of the allegations about the class system is no more than an objection to differences in conduct and to arrangements which permit these differences. Egalitarians regard a varied scene as objectionable. They consider reprehensible all differences in behaviour unless based on criteria devised or sanctioned by themselves. When it comes to differences between their own behaviour and that of others who may be less prominent or successful, they ignore these differences, or even commend them.

It would much reduce the effectiveness of the critics of the class system if it were acknowledged that at bottom they were merely expressing their disapproval of the conduct of others, conduct which does not reflect or erect

35

restrictive social barriers or economic barriers. In fact, as we have seen, differences in social standing or behaviour are not effective barriers to mobility or enterprise; nor do they by themselves bring about economic malaise, or engender social discontent. But these differences lend plausibility to the sentiments and activities of people who for various emotional or financial reasons are disgruntled, or who hope to derive personal or political benefit from criticisms of the social and economic arrangements. This background to the criticism in no way validates the idea of a restrictive class system, but rather underlines its hollowness.

The British upper classes usually absorb new men very easily, reflecting the adapatability and flexibility of British society. Indeed, the new recruits soon become indistinguishable from the class into which they have been recruited. The ease with which the upper classes absorb new men is apt to mislead casual observers and to lend plausibility to criticism: superficially it suggests a static society or even a rigid system. No one could have guessed the background of the late Sir James Chadwick, whom I have already mentioned, from his conduct as Master of Gonville and Caius College, Cambridge, which was founded in 1348, and of which he became Master exactly 600 years later. Much the same could be said about Sir John Hay and Lord Cole and others whom I have already mentioned.

After only a single generation persons of working-class origin can merge completely into the aristocracy. Thus the career, connections and even the physical appearance of the late Lord Robertson of Oakridge (1896–1974) would have suggested that he was an aristocrat. He was a general, British High Commissioner, Commander-in-Chief in the Middle East, ADC to two monarchs, company director and chairman of the British Transport Commission. He was the son of Field Marshal Sir William Robertson, who was a plebeian in appearance and in some of his manners.

The conjunction of assumed rigidity and actual flexibility of the social system sets up pitfalls which can trap the unwary. When Sir Sydney Caine became Director of the London School of Economics one newspaper said that he had been educated at Harrow; in fact he had attended Harrow County School, a very different establishment.

6

Some variants of the principal line of criticism of the British class system deserve notice. One of these is the suggestion, sometimes explicit, sometimes implied, that the prosperity of the well-to-do has been extracted from the rest of the population. As already noted in chapter 1, even in relatively open societies and market economies groups and individuals often derive economic benefit from monopoly, restrictionism, state subsidies and political manipulation. This has also applied to Britain. But even in the aggregate such instances have not been of overall significance in the making of industrial and commercial fortunes over the past two hundred years. Nor have these influences been related to class. In recent decades, political muscle has become significant in raising the incomes of politically effective groups, notably recipients of state subsidies or members of strong trade unions, and also certain groups of bureaucrats. It is evident that this has nothing to do with the traditional class system, especially since trade union members are major beneficiaries.

The allegedly exclusive character and class bias of English education are often blamed for various economic and social difficulties. However, the educational system did not preclude rapid British economic progress in the eighteenth and nineteenth centuries, promoted and propelled largely by people with little formal education, a phenomenon which academics and educationalists seem reluctant to recognize. Moreover, neither the presence nor the privileges of Oxford and Cambridge, nor the prestige of the public schools, prevented or hindered other groups from setting up academies and schools. There was no general state education in England until well into the nineteenth century, but there was no official barrier to the setting up of educational institutions. Again, the educational system in Scotland was quite different from that in England. There were old universities in Scotland, and these were not restricted to members of the Church of England nor controlled by it, and the school system there was also more extensive than in England. Yet Scotland has not outdistanced England either in economic performance or in industrial relations. Nor is it sensible to describe the restrictions of the educational system as class-bound, when those against whom it discriminated included aristocrats such as the Catholic Dukes of Norfolk.

Much has been made of the large proportion of Prime Ministers and cabinet ministers in the twentieth century who were at Oxford or Cambridge. This is not evidence of the allegedly closed character of British politics. It reflects the prestige which ability and education commanded in British politics until recently; the inclination of those with political ambition to go to university, coupled with the emphasis at Oxford and Cambridge on studies helpful in political life; and the access of gifted persons from all ranks of society to these universities. The careers of Sir Harold Wilson, Mr Heath, Mrs Thatcher and Mr Healey reflect the open nature of Oxford and Cambridge rather than the closed character of British political life.

7

The relatively peaceful history of Britain, the absence of foreign invasion or occupation and of violent revolutions (at any rate since the mid-seventeenth century) and the ready acceptance of differences, including social differences, imparted poise and self-assurance to the upper and upper-middle classes and to the representatives of traditional institutions. This poise made it possible to resist outside pressures. A Cambridge college, an institution widely regarded as class-ridden and insular, has unhesitatingly elected foreigners to highly coveted fellowships at times of substantial unemployment, or at times when the country was swept by xenophobia. Similarly, it was able to elect to a Fellowship a scholar from Communist China a few days after a Chinese force defeated a British regiment in Korea with heavy casualties. Such action is far less likely, perhaps even unthinkable, in American and Continental universities, which are generally thought to be much less class-ridden and restrictive than Oxford and Cambridge.

But the prolonged and largely unquestioned acceptance of differences and distinctions also made for vulnerability, in that the upper and upper-middle classes were not forced to examine or rationalize their position. They were thus ill-placed to face the upsurge of egalitarianism in the Western world. Having taken their situation for granted, they could not analyse or explain it. Their spokesmen or representatives knew and could probably articulate the distinction in rank between a baron, a baronet and a knight, or even between a CB and a CBE, but not that between a differentiated yet open and mobile society on the one hand and a restrictive, closed or caste society on the other hand. Nor were they able to scrutinize effectively such arguments as, for instance, that which says that the incomes of the well-to-do are secured at the expense of the poor. They were thus unable to counter the arguments for egalitarian policies or for the far-reaching privileges granted to trade unions. More generally, they were unable to resist effectively the arguments and sentiments which resulted in the politicization of social and economic life, a politicization often deemed necessary to offset the alleged restrictive class bias in British politics.

The upper and middle classes were intellectually unarmed to meet the egalitarian thrust, perhaps even more than are businessmen to meet the more specifically economic arguments of the egalitarians. The resulting loss of poise and nerve was aggravated by the emergence of a guilt feeling over the presence of differences in the face of the growing belief that all such differences are abnormal and reprehensible.

8

The long and relatively peaceful continuity of British history and society may have promoted the acceptance of the stereotype of the British class system. The absence of violent change has suggested a static social system headed by an impregnable and static ruling class.

The unobtrusive ease with which new men are assimilated, and become indistinguishable from their erstwhile social superiors soon after having risen from modest backgrounds, has also served to lend plausibility to the notion of an upper class of unchanging composition, part of a caste-like system. The liberal, tolerant nature of British society in these matters has eased the path of its detractors.

Moreover, the open and mobile character of British society compared with Continental society has made the aristocracy and prosperous groups more conspicuous and certainly more accessible than on the Continent, and therefore more readily envied and resented. The British upper and upper-middle classes have for centuries been more accessible to members of other groups, including writers, than the corresponding classes elsewhere. They therefore are more obvious targets than their counterparts abroad. This mattered little when envy and resentment were less virulent than now.

PART TWO

The West and the Third World

3 The Population Explosion: Myths and Realities
4 Western Guilt and Third World Poverty
5 Foreign Aid and its Hydra-Headed Rationalization
6 Background to Aid
7 The Link Scheme of Aid
8 Costs and Risks of Commodity Stabilization
9 British Colonial Africa: Economic Retrospect
10 The Lesson of Hong Kong
11 Broadcasting the Liberal Death Wish

CHAPTER 3

The Population Explosion:
Myths and Realities

The simple and sensational answers obtained may well be wrong and could cause serious damage to civilization and mankind. We must have the courage to accept that population economics is a complex subject, where one man's problem is another man's solution and where most people's long-run interests are likely to be best served by intellectual humility and undogmatic policies.

Julian L. Simon

1

Rapid population growth in less developed countries (ldcs) is widely regarded as a major obstacle to their material progress and a major global economic and political problem. According to the Pearson Report: 'No other phenomenon casts a darker shadow over the prospects of international development [the latter a synonym in the Report for the development of ldcs] than the staggering growth of population.'[1] Mr Robert McNamara, President of the World Bank, is even more emphatic:

To put it simply: the greatest single obstacle to the economic and social advancement of the majority of peoples in the underdeveloped world is rampant population growth.... The threat of unmanageable population pressures is very much like the threat of nuclear war.... Both threats can and will have catastrophic consequences unless they are dealt with rapidly and rationally.[2]

Such opinions are surprising. The recent rapid increase in population in ldcs reflects a steep fall in mortality. This development represents substantial improvement in conditions, since people value a longer life. Yet the fears epitomized in these passages have been advanced in support of drastic measures for reducing population growth, including even forcible sterilization.

42

These fears are unfounded. Their implausibility is suggested by observation of the contemporary world and by reflection on recent and earlier history of both the less developed world and the West.

Rapid population growth has not been an obstacle to sustained economic advance either in the Third World or in the West. Between the 1890s and 1930s the sparsely populated area of Malaysia, with hamlets and fishing villages, was transformed into a country with large cities, extensive agricultural and mining operations and extensive commerce. The population rose from about one and a half to about six million; the number of Malays increased from about one to about two and a half million. The much larger population had much higher material standards and lived longer than the small population of the 1890s. Since the 1950s rapid population increase in densely-populated Hong Kong and Singapore has been accompanied by large increases in real income and wages. The population of the Western world has more than quadrupled since the middle of the eighteenth century. Real income per head is estimated to have increased by a factor of five or more. Most of the increase in incomes took place when population increased as fast as, or faster than, in the contemporary less developed world.

Received opinion, widely accepted across the political spectrum, has it that the effects of population growth on economic achievement and progress depend largely on physical resources and capital per head, primarily the former. Yet this conventional reasoning is plainly inadequate, as our examples show. Either the reasoning fails to identify the principal determinants of economic progress, or the factors underlying the reasoning do not interact in the manner assumed. We shall argue that the accepted reasoning suffers from both these shortcomings. We argue further that much of the discussion of the welfare effects of population growth, and also those of population density, rests on a misleading index of economic welfare. We also show that demographic forecasts have been seriously unreliable, and that this is pertinent to their use as basis for policy.

2

In societies (other than simple subsistence economies) there are, and always have been, substantial differences in economic performance, and therefore in incomes, among individuals and groups with access to the same physical resources, including land. This is so, and has always been so, both in the less developed world and in the West. Such differences could not be explained if it were true that physical resources were a decisive or a major determinant of economic achievement.

43

There are pronounced differences in economic performance between ethnic and cultural groups in the same country. Examples include differences between Chinese, Indians and Malays in Malaysia;[3] between Chinese and others elsewhere in South-East Asia; between Parsees, Jains, Marwaris and the rest of the population in India; between Greeks and Turks in Cyprus; between Armenians, Jews, Greeks and the rest of the population in the Levant; between Asians and Africans in East Africa and Central Africa; between Ibos and others in Nigeria; and between Chinese, Lebanese and West Indians in the Caribbean.

In some of these cases the more prosperous groups have been relatively recent immigrants, who mostly came in empty-handed but were ambitious, energetic, industrious and resourceful. The fact that emigrants are usually not a random selection of the population in the country of their origin does not affect the present argument, which is concerned with the role in economic performance of natural resources per head. Similarly, whether or not differences in performance persist is also irrelevant here.

In many of these instances the now more prosperous groups were discriminated against in access to land, and often barred from owning land. This was true of the Chinese in South-East Asia and the Asians in Africa. And in South-East Asia the Chinese, with higher incomes on average, live in more densely populated areas than the Thais, Burmese, Malays and Indonesians in the various countries. There are similar examples in the West. The economic achievement and prosperity of the Huguenots, Jews and Nonconformists were attained without owning land. Indeed in much of Western Europe Jews could not own land until quite recently, by which time they nevertheless had become relatively prosperous.

In both the less developed world and in the West some of the most prosperous countries and regions are extremely densely populated. Hong Kong and Singapore are probably the most densely populated countries in the world, with originally very poor land. Hong Kong consists largely of eroded hill sites, and much of Singapore was empty marshland in the nineteenth century. In the advanced world Japan, West Germany, Belgium and Holland are examples of densely populated countries. Conversely, many millions of extremely backward people live in sparsely populated regions amidst cultivable land. Examples include the backward peoples in Sumatra, Borneo, Central Africa and the interior of South America. They have ready access to vast areas of land – for them land is a free good. In South Asia, generally regarded as a region suffering from over-population, there is much uncultivated land, land which could be cultivated at the level of technology prevailing in the region. In its first Five Year Plan the Government of India classified one quarter of the land surface of the country as uncultivated but cultivable. In West Malaysia, a small and relatively densely populated country, well over half the land is still uncultivated. Much of this uncultivated land is of the same quality as that currently cultivated, and is virtually as readily accessible.[4]

Such contrasts are not new. The Indians in North America before Columbus had unlimited land and were wretchedly poor. The land was not infertile, as European immigrants soon made clear. They came from Western Europe which had far less land per head and was already advanced and rich. Venice was built on a few mud flats and became a wealthy world power. Much of Holland was drained from the sea and it became a prosperous commercial country and a centre of culture and learning.

Within the last hundred years or so, very large areas of the less developed world which had been sparsely populated by poor people were effectively transformed. Examples include the establishment and development of the estates and smallholdings in South-East Asia, primarily in Malaysia and Indonesia, but also in Thailand and the former Indo-China, and estates and farms in much of Africa and Latin America. These instances of transformation were effected very largely by people with meagre capital and with only simple technology at their command, and who worked under difficult conditions. Their progress reflected sustained effort, the adoption of improved methods and the reinvestment of income.

Altogether, it is clear that natural resources do not explain differences in development and living standards. There is also no substantial ground for the belief that population growth in the Third World will be a major obstacle to material progress, much less that it will create critical shortages of natural resources. (We shall revert to this in somewhat greater detail in section 4 below in the context of food production and of the availability of land and mineral resources.) Indeed, over large parts of the Third World the extreme sparseness of the population presents obstacles to the economic advance of enterprising people, obstacles which are more effective than those supposedly presented by population pressure. A sparse population precludes the construction of transport facilities and communications, and thus retards the spread of new ideas and methods. In this way it circumscribes the scope for enterprise.

Of course, by extrapolating any increase in population sufficiently far ahead it is always possible to conclude that eventually there will be standing room only left on earth. Given enough time, this would be true even if population increased by only one person every century. But such extrapolations are not informative or sensible. No one can predict social and technological change beyond a decade or two. Nevertheless, one particular prediction can be made confidently. If rapid population growth should substantially threaten living standards, this would induce people to modify their reproductive behaviour.

The predictions of doom through population growth rest on the idea that economic achievement, progress and welfare all depend primarily on natural resources, supplemented by physical capital. There is a vaguely commonsensical appeal about the neo-Malthusian notion that prosperity depends on ample land and rich mineral resources. This neo-Malthusian notion is then supplemented by the very non-Malthusian idea that people in ldcs have no will of their own and are simply passive victims of external forces: in the absence of Western-directed pressures, people in the less developed world would procreate heedless of consequences. This reasoning is invalid. People in the less developed world do adapt their conduct to circumstances, and do not procreate without thought for the morrow.

It may be convenient to forestall three lines of objection to the proposition, emphasized in the preceding discussion, that natural resources and physical capital are relatively insignificant as pre-requisites of economic achievement.

The gold and silver flowing into Spain after the Spanish conquest of Latin America, and the riches of contemporary oil producing countries, are often instanced as evidence of the value of natural resources in conferring prosperity on their owners. But the precious metals of the Americas did not promote economic progress in pre-Columbian America, and their capture did not serve to ensure substantial development in Spain. The oil resources of the Middle East and elsewhere were valueless until found and developed by the West; it must be conjectural how far they will lead to sustained economic advance. It is true, however, that the interplay of political and ideological forces determine largely who benefits primarily from such geographical 'windfalls', windfalls activated by Western enterprise and technology.

Second, rapid population growth is often said to inhibit development in that it absorbs investible funds which could otherwise have been available to support economic development. A typical formulation is by Mr McNamara:

> The irrefutable reason is that these governments must divert an inordinately high proportion of their limited national savings away from productive effort simply in order to maintain the current low level of existence for the expanding population. . . . Capital that ought to have been invested was not available. It had been dissipated by the ever-rising tide of children.[5]

This contention is seriously defective. To begin with, it assumes that the increasing numbers of children are looked upon by their parents as a burden, not as a boon. Further, it ignores the direct economic contribution made by the very young in many ldcs. It also exaggerates the expenditures in ldcs called forth by high fertility rates. For instance, primary education even on a large scale need not be costly, because for both climatic and social reasons school buildings can be simple inexpensive structures. The volume of investible funds in any case is a minor factor in economic development. Much capital formation takes forms more closely analogous to consumer durables than to instruments for increasing production and promoting further economic growth.[6] It is unwarranted, further, to assume that the governments of the ldcs in question would use the investible funds more productively if they did not have to use them to provide for expanding population. The investment record of many Third World governments has been deplorable.

Third, it is argued that population growth must be detrimental to overall productivity by reducing land and capital per head. As we have seen, land is in abundant supply in large areas of the less developed world. And the fertility of the land is largely the result of human activity, notably effort, science and technology. Moreover, the factor price of land as such is a small part of the national income in most countries. Where rents are high relative to the income of farm tenants and agricultural labourers, this clearly reflects the low value of unskilled labour, itself the reflection of lack of skill, enterprise or ambition rather than of population pressure. Of course, population increase can substantially reduce the marginal productivity of labour in the short period; but this phenomenon has little to do with long term development. It can also reduce productivity per head by increasing the proportion of the young and the old in a population. But to regard this as a reduction in welfare is to accept the unstated and, as we shall see, unwarranted assumption that children and old people are unwanted burdens whose life is of no value.

3

National income per head is used extensively as an index of economic welfare, as a measure of goods and services yielding economic satisfaction or benefit. The psychic income derived from health, prolongation of life and possession of children is a major component of satisfaction. That this is so is evident in the readiness of people to pay for services to have their health improved and their own lives and those of their children and parents prolonged. These forms of psychic income are disregarded in national income statistics.

Disregard of these forms of benefit brings about anomalies. The birth of a child immediately reduces income per head within the family, and also that in the country as a whole. But do the parents feel worse off? Would they feel better off if they could have no children or if some of them died?

The familiar references in the development literature to the so-called burden of dependency, represented by a relatively large proportion of children and old people in the population, imply that children are only a cost or a burden, not a blessing; and that the survival of people into old age is of no benefit to anybody, not even to the survivors themselves. These references also ignore both the current and prospective economic contribution of children to the incomes of their parents.

It is sometimes suggested that high birth rates in ldcs, especially among the poorest, result in life so wretched as not to be worth living: over a person's life suffering or disutility exceeds utility. If this were so, fewer such lives would increase the sum total of human happiness. This type of reasoning, which implies that external observers are the appropriate judges of the moral and emotional status of others, was often heard in the late nineteenth century and early twentieth century in discussions of the conditions of the poor in Britain. It is inconsistent both with simple observation and with widely accepted ethical notions. Even when people are poor they prefer to live rather than not to live, as is indeed shown by their decision to strive to remain among the living.[7] This is not to say that their lives may not be unhappy, but merely that it is not legitimate to suppose that their lives are not worth living.

The rapid population growth in the less developed world in recent years has served to widen differences in recorded per capita income between advanced countries and ldcs compared to what these would have been otherwise. Somewhat similar changes have taken place within individual countries between richer and poorer groups. The results of such developments are all too often deplored as representing a greater inequality of income – a so-called worsening of income distribution. Yet since the poor also like to have children and to live longer, this so-called worsening of income distribution reflects an improvement in their condition.

The concept of optimum population (whether the population size which maximizes real income per head or that which maximizes real income per head multiplied by the size of the population) occasionally surfaces in discussions of population growth in ldcs. This concept is of little intellectual or practical significance. It again ignores any psychic income from children and from longer life. Its proponents usually also fail to specify such critical magnitudes as the period over which average or total income is to be maximized and the rate at which expected future income is to be discounted.

4

If population pressure and population growth do not jeopardize economic performance and progress significantly, they should not bring about persistent specific adverse results either. However, certain specific untoward results are often attributed to population growth. These results are thought to bring about quite special problems and also by themselves to obstruct material progress. The most significant of these are thought to be a threat to food supplies through lack of land, and to other components of living standards through the exhaustion of mineral resources. The emergence of large-scale unemployment is said to be another major threat.

Food supplies and exhaustible resources. Population growth is often said to undermine living standards in the less developed world, or even world wide, through increasing the demands made on land and exhaustible minerals. In this particular context population growth in advanced countries is supposed to be especially harmful because people there use more of these resources per head.

People in the West do indeed consume much more food and minerals per head than do people in ldcs. But the difference in production between the two categories is even greater. Not only does the production of developed countries pay for all the consumption there, but in addition it finances the export both of commercial capital and of subsidized capital to the less developed world.[8]

There is no danger of worldwide malnutrition or starvation through shortage of land resulting from population growth. Contemporary famines and food shortages occur mostly in sparsely populated subsistence economies with abundant land. There is no shortage of land in areas such as Ethiopia, the Sahel, Tanzania, Uganda and Zaire. The recurrent famines in these countries and elsewhere in the less developed world usually reflect conditions typical of subsistence or near-subsistence economies. They reflect in particular the absence of reserve stocks and lack of access to external supplies, largely the result of poor communications and ineffective storage facilities. The effects of these conditions are exacerbated by widespread official restrictions on the activities of traders, by a lack of public security and sometimes by official restrictions on the movement of food. In some instances the shortages are brought about by the maintenance of unproductive systems of rights to land, such as tribal systems of land rights which inhibit improved productive activity. These various influences have nothing to do with population pressure on land. It is notable that no famines are reported from such densely populated regions of the less developed world as Taiwan, Hong Kong, Singapore, Malaysia and cash crop producing areas of West Africa.

The small size of farms and the low level of agricultural productivity over most of the less developed world reflect lack of skills, ambition and energy, or

49

social beliefs and customs adverse to economic achievement – and not a shortage of land. In many of these regions additional land is freely available, and yet agricultural holdings are very small. And in much of the less developed world, only a single annual crop is taken from the land where double or treble cropping is feasible with little or no increase in input other than more work by the family in different seasons.

In the developed world the cost of land is a small proportion of the resource cost of food. For instance, land rent as a proportion of the factor cost of food was estimated for the United States as representing no more than 5% in 1972.[9] Most of this modest proportion represents not the original qualities of the land, but the enhancement of its value through human activity and the application of knowledge – processes which will continue *pari passu* with population growth. The productivity of land in both the developed and less developed world depends very largely on human activity.

It should be clear that there is no unequivocal or even sensible answer to the frequently asked question how many people a country, a region or the world can support. Those who ask such questions often fail to specify even the standard of living they envisage. But even if this were specified, such questions would not be sensible. The number of people who can live in any area at the specified standard of living is not determined by the extent of land or of other physical resources available there. It depends very largely on the personal qualities, social institutions and mores and political arrangements of the population, on the state of technology and on external market conditions for imports and exports.

Except for fossil fuel, mineral deposits do not represent exhaustible resources. They are concentrations of minerals. The extraction of these deposits and also of minerals in a more dispersed form depends on price, cost, technology and government policy. When minerals are used they do not disappear. In large measure they can be recovered by processes governed by the same factors as those governing their discovery and extraction. Fossil fuel is an exception because when used as energy it disappears in the atmosphere. But there is no danger of population growth posing a threat to long term energy supplies. A substantial and lasting increase in the real cost of fossil fuels would encourage the use of other sources of energy and also various methods for saving energy. Moreover, fossil fuel is not used extensively as a source of energy in Asia and Africa, the home of the great majority of the peoples of the less developed world. Thus population increase in these areas would not be a major factor in raising the cost of fossil fuel.

Any substantial long term rise in the real cost of food and minerals would induce technical change designed to mitigate their relative scarcity. It would also affect people's reproductive behaviour. To ignore this amounts to assuming that in one of the most important aspects of people's lives their conduct remains unaffected by changes in their circumstances.

Thus population growth in the less developed world would not endanger long term supplies of food and minerals. On the other hand, governments of many ldcs pursue policies which affect these supplies adversely. Over much of the less developed world both current agricultural output and the extension of capacity, and thus long term supply, are impaired by heavy taxation of farmers, forcible collectivization of agriculture and restrictions on the activities of traders. In many ldcs there are also severe restrictions on the access of energetic and enterprising local groups to land, whether already cultivated or unused. (Examples include the Ibo in Nigeria, Asians in Africa, and Chinese in South-East Asia.) Further, farm production is inhibited by ubiquitous restrictions on the import or use of tractors, harvesters, intertillage machines and other mechanically-powered farm implements.[10]

Supplies both of food and of minerals, including fossil fuels, are impaired also by policies and measures such as expropriation of assets and enterprises, unilateral alteration of terms of agreements and insistence of local participation in mining and plantation enterprises. Besides reducing current supplies, these widespread policies raise risks and costs and inhibit the flow of capital into plantation agriculture, the exploration and production of minerals and related activities, and thus reduce the long term supply of foodstuffs and minerals.[11]

Population growth and unemployment. It is widely believed that population growth in the less developed world is responsible for heavy current and prospective unemployment. This opinion is the acknowledged basis for the large scale World Employment Project sponsored by the World Bank and the International Labour Office.

This opinion is superficially plausible but nevertheless unfounded. It clearly does not envisage unemployment as a consequence of lack of effective demand, that is unemployment of a Keynesian or cyclical character. The larger population means more consumers as well as more producers. There is no reason why an increase in numbers as such should cause unemployment. The large increase in population in the West over the last two centuries has not brought about persistent mass unemployment. Substantial unemployment emerged in the twentieth century when population growth was already much slower than it had been in the nineteenth century. And when in the 1930s and 1940s an early decline in population was widely envisaged, this development was thought to make for more unemployment. It is evident also from recent and current experience in the less developed world that even rapid increase in population does not result in persistent unemployment, and also that this issue cannot be discussed sensibly on the basis of numbers and physical resources. Rapid population growth in Hong Kong did not bring about unemployment there.[12] Again, Singapore is extremely densely populated and only very recently experienced a rapid population growth. There is far less land per head of population in Singapore than there is in neighbouring Malaysia. Yet many people move from Malaysia to Singapore as short term or long term migrants or as permanent settlers in search of employment and higher wages. Their numbers represent an appreciable proportion of the labour force of Singapore and are significant in relation also to the labour force of Malaysia.

The suggestion that increased population results in unemployment implies that labour cannot be substituted for land or capital in particular activities, and also that the pattern of production cannot be altered in the direction of more labour intensive activities. In technical language the suggestion implies that the elasticity of substitution between labour and other resources is zero in both production and consumption. These conditions are not present in the less developed world. This is shown by the development of more intensive forms of agriculture in many ldcs and the frequent changes in the composition of their national output. Obvious examples include the development of double and treble cropping or the shift from pastoral activity to arable farming. The suggestion that population growth causes large scale and persistent unemployment in the less developed world involves other unrealistic and inadmissable assumptions such as absence of foreign trade, unchanging technology and reproductive behaviour uninfluenced by economic conditions and prospects.

There are, however, certain characteristics of labour markets in some ldcs which do lead to unemployment, but they have nothing to do with population pressure. An important instance is the operation of formal or informal minimum wage controls above the equilibrium level for the type of labour involved. This need not in itself cause unemployment but merely a reduction in the numbers employed in these activities. However, the attraction of being employed at these wages, together with the need to be available for employment when required, results in the formation of pools of unemployed or intermittently employed labour. This situation, which is unrelated to population pressure or growth, is observable in the urban labour markets of many ldcs.

5

The foregoing discussion of the implications of population growth and density can now be linked to recent demographic experience and prospects in the less developed world.

Treatment in largely broad brush terms is appropriate for the present purpose on several grounds. The first is the ethnic and cultural diversity of the less developed world and even of individual ldcs. Specific treatment of demographic experience would require separate discussion of the conduct and experience of the main ethnic and cultural groups in particular regions and countries. This is not feasible here. Moreover, demographic statistics of most ldcs, notably in Africa and South Asia, are often no more than rough estimates with wide margins of error. Registration of births is seriously incomplete in most ldcs. Statistics are sometimes manipulated for political purposes. On the other hand, incomplete censuses may result in underestimated numbers. The appropriate procedure for the present purpose is therefore to rely on broad information or reasonable estimates. In certain contexts this information can, however, be supplemented by detailed specific studies carried out by observers with no specific axe to grind.

The population explosion is simply a shorthand expression for a rapid sharp decline in mortality over a period during which birth rates have remained high. Although statistics are patchy, the overall picture is clear.[13]

Between the 1920s and the 1960s mortality in the less developed world approximately halved. It declined from about thirty-one per thousand in the 1920s to about seventeen per thousand in the 1960s.[14] Life expectation at birth in the less developed world as a whole is estimated to have increased from about thirty-five years in 1950 to about fifty-three years by 1972, that is by one half in the life span of one generation. The decline in mortality and the increase in life expectation have occurred far more rapidly than they did in more developed countries with initially similar levels of mortality. In Western countries for which comparable information is available such an increase in life expectancy took place over several generations. The decline in infant and child mortality in the less developed world has been particularly rapid, but mortality seems to have declined substantially in all age groups.[15] The general and sharp decline in mortality and the consequent rise in life expectation in ldcs have not been accompanied or as yet been followed by a correspondingly substantial or widespread decline in fertility.

The demographic picture of the contemporary world can be presented in the following general terms. In most of the less developed world fertility has remained high but mortality has fallen sharply. In the developed world, in contrast, both fertility and mortality have been at much lower levels for several decades, even allowing for somewhat higher fertility rates in the first two decades or so after the Second World War. Thus there is one large group of societies with crude birth rates of about thirty-five to forty per thousand or more, a population increase in the region of about 2% per annum or more, and a gross reproduction rate of over 2.5%; and there is another large group with crude birth rates of about eighteen to twenty per thousand, a population increase of under 1% per annum, and a gross reproduction rate of about 1.2%. There are some societies with intermediate levels of fertility at around thirty per thousand, with population increasing at around 1% per annum. These are mainly in certain Far Eastern countries with appreciable Chinese populations, a few island countries elsewhere (for example, Sri Lanka, Mauritius and the Caribbean) and some South American countries in the temperate zone with substantial populations of European origin. But this intermediate group is relatively small.

Thus there is a distinct dichotomy in recent demographic experience and current demographic patterns between the West (including Eastern Europe), Japan and Australasia on the one hand, and most of Asia, Africa and Latin America on the other hand. The distinction between these two groups is much clearer and much more pronounced in terms of demographic statistics than it is in terms of statistics of national income per head, for which there is no clear discontinuity in the international range of incomes. There are many relatively prosperous countries, especially in the Middle East and Latin America, where fertility has remained at levels much higher than those in some European countries with comparable or even lower per capita incomes.

The high gross reproduction rates and the large proportion of young people will ensure significant population increases in the principal regions of the less developed world over the next few decades. These increases would occur even if age-specific fertility were to decline appreciably. As we shall see in the next section, ambitious population projects have often been wide of the mark. But the unambitious prediction can be made with some confidence that over the next decade or two the rate of population growth of the less developed world as a whole is unlikely to fall significantly below 2%, and may for some years continue in the region of $2\frac{1}{2}$%. The only circumstances likely to upset rough estimates would be a huge increase in mortality as a result of a series of catastrophes, or a dramatic reduction of fertility as a result of a sudden, rapid and pervasive Westernization of much of the less developed world. The occurrence of either development is exceedingly improbable, and the first would in any case be accompanied by other cataclysmic changes.

6

Current levels of fertility in the less developed world have greatly exceeded expectations. It used to be widely believed that the precipitate fall in mortality in ldcs would be followed by an early and substantial fall in fertility. This was thought especially likely if the decline in mortality were accompanied by a significant rise in incomes and in the extent of urbanization. It was also thought likely that a decline in infant and child mortality would bring about a reduction in the birth rate, because a wish to replace children who had died young was regarded as a major reason for large families.

In the West the rising incomes and general living standards in the nineteenth century were accompanied first by a widespread decline in mortality which was then followed relatively soon by a decline in the birth rate. This sequence resulted in a slow rate of population growth in the late nineteenth century and in the twentieth century, with much reduced mortality and fertility rates compared with the early stages of this period of transition in the eighteenth century and early nineteenth century. This Western experience came to be regarded as a norm. It served as the basis for the theory of demographic transition, from which its exponents predicted in the early post war years that similar sequences were about to take place in the less developed world.[16]

Throughout the 1960s and 1970s fertility in most of the less developed world remained much higher than had been expected. In particular, fertility in some of the poorer countries of Europe in the inter-war years was much lower than it has been in recent years in many ldcs, including countries with higher incomes than these European countries had before the Second World War.[17]

For at least two reasons the confident predictions based on the theory of demographic transition derived from Western experience should have been suspect at the time.

The first reason was the notable failure of predictions of an early decline in population widely canvassed in the 1930s and 1940s. Substantial early decline in population, primarily in the West but to some extent worldwide, was then generally predicted. Confidence was buoyed up by belief in improvements in demographic forecasting techniques, notably the development and use of the concepts of gross and net reproduction rates. Economists, sociologists and demographers also predicted that the decline in population would entail unfortunate or even disastrous results. These were thought to include widespread unhappiness in a world populated largely by old people; an increased burden of dependency on income earners because the greater proportion of old people in the population would more than offset the smaller proportion of children; a lack of adaptability of the economy; difficulties of maintaining full employment because the incentive to invest would be reduced; and widespread social pessimism and dejection accompanying these changes. Even the extinction of the species was seriously envisaged in some writings of prominent academics under such headings as 'The End of the Human Experiment' or 'The Suicide of the Race'.

In less than the span of one human generation the population problem has come to mean the exact opposite of what it had been held to be. The earlier scare of a decline in numbers has come to be replaced by the scare of an increase in numbers, in both the developed and less developed worlds. The scare has remained but the sign has been reversed. In view of this startling change one wonders what would have happened if proposals for increasing fertility had been adopted in the 1930s and 1940s and had successfully increased the number of people in the reproductive age groups. But before the more drastic proposals could be introduced, the predictions on which they were based were already discomfited by population growth.

Population forecasts have often proved wildly inaccurate. It is, nevertheless, hard to think of a precedent for an error in direction such as that of the forecasts of the 1930s and 1940s. The belief of the practitioners in their predictions and their readiness to base far-reaching policies on them were also new. Much the same confidence is evident in current population discussions, and they again serve as bases for policy.

Faith in the extension of the conventional theory of demographic transition to the less developed world was misplaced also. The initial conditions from which the demographic transition in the West occurred were in critical respects radically different from those in the contemporary less developed world. The level of material culture in many Western countries was then higher than that in most of the Third World. Moreover, marriage patterns in Europe in the eighteenth century also may have been exceptional, possibly unique. This is the theme of a justly celebrated and often quoted article by Professor John Hajnal.[18] According to Hajnal:

> The marriage pattern of most of Europe as it existed for at least two centuries up to 1940 was, so far as we can tell, unique or almost unique in the world. There is no known example of a population of non-European civilisation which had had a similar pattern. The distinctive marks of the 'European' pattern are (1) a high age at marriage and (2) a high proportion of people who never marry at all. The 'European' pattern pervaded the whole of Europe except for the eastern and south-eastern portion.

This pattern contributed to a fertility appreciably lower than the norm in other societies, including most present day ldcs. Hajnal's findings have been acclaimed widely. Hajnal suggests that the distinctive marriage pattern emerged around the middle of the seventeenth century (although there are more recent suggestions of an earlier origin). That its emergence was soon followed by a substantial acceleration of material progress bears out the significance of attitudes and mores on economic performance.

7

In the contemporary less developed world economic improvement has at times been accompanied by an increase in birth rate and an even greater rate of increase in population because of increased survival rates (including those of women of childbearing age and of their young children). Statistical association between economic improvement and increases in the birth rate has been observed in the inter-war period and in the 1950s in a number of countries including Taiwan, Singapore, Malaysia and Mauritius. (This was found in conditions in which the rise in the birth rate could not be attributed to the correction of previous under-reporting.)[19] In particular, in many parts of Africa fertility has increased in the course of progress from a nomadic life to sedentary agriculture, and from the first to the second generation of sedentary agriculture. In these early stages of economic advance the improvement leads to increased fertility and survival at a time when parents do not wish to restrict the number of their children. Dr James Kocher found that in rural Tanzania parents generally would have liked to have more children than the number of their children surviving over their reproductive life. He argues that his findings apply widely in sub-Saharan Africa and that they are confirmed by other studies.[20]

Various demographic inquiries in West Africa, notably those of Professor Caldwell and of his associates, found that fertility may have increased in recent times, and that there was no significant difference between fertility in the towns and in the countryside, notably in the Yoruba society of Western Nigeria.[21] Professor Petersen shows that a number of inquiries into urban and rural fertility reveal wide differences in experience in the less developed world. In many ldcs, for example Malaysia, India, Pakistan and Algeria, urban fertility is not lower than in the countryside; urban fertility relative to rural fertility appears to be highest in Nigeria and lowest in some Latin American and Caribbean countries. In the West, on the other hand, low urban fertility has been routine for a long time.

The relationship between fertility, social class and occupational statistics is also much more varied in the less developed world than in the West. Some studies of fertility in Egypt have suggested that fertility on the one hand, and education and occupation on the other, are positively correlated in rural areas but negatively in urban areas. Practically throughout the less developed world, however, the Westernized strata in business, politics, administration and the professions tend to have smaller families. These groups are a small fraction of the total population in South Asia, Africa and much of Latin America.[22]

Altogether, fertility in the less developed world does not depend simply either on the level of income or on the degree of urbanization. Adoption of Western attitudes will induce people to restrict the number of their children; but neither higher incomes nor increased urbanization by themselves will bring this about.

8

The number of children people desire depends on personal attitudes and preferences. These in turn are much affected by social beliefs, values and institutions. The economic costs and benefits also affect the number of children people wish to have.

Social values, beliefs and institutions differ widely among and often within societies. The more narrowly economic costs and benefits of children again differ greatly with the economic opportunities open to parents and children both as producers and as consumers. These opportunities in turn are influenced by social and religious values, institutions and arrangements.[23] Thus one would expect substantial differences in fertility and family size both among societies and among groups within societies. Various influences interact with one another, and their impact may change. Fertility and family size in a given society may therefore be expected to change over time. Both the nature and speed of demographic response to a particular economic change, such as an increase in income, may differ greatly in different societies and groups and may vary through time.

Diversity and complexity of social and economic phenomena themselves do not preclude valid generalization. Indeed, they present a challenge to theorists. We now note two bold attempts at a theory of the determination of family size. One is in terms of modern microeconomic theory; the other is based on inter-generational flows of wealth.

The microeconomic theory of fertility applies modern economic analysis to the determination of fertility and family size. It proposes to explain family size in terms of various factors susceptible to economic analysis; these include the pleasure (i.e. utility) derived from children, the costs of raising them, the current and expected income accruing from children to parents, and the prices of goods and services.

58

The theory is valuable for imposing a pattern on disjointed phenomena, and for reconciling the results of cross-section studies of fertility with the results of the analysis of time series.[24] It may well provide successful predictions of fertility over relatively short periods or in stable conditions, especially in industrial societies. But its usefulness for predicting longer-term demographic change in ldcs is likely to be limited. This is so chiefly for two reasons. First, the theory addresses itself only to some of the determinants of the decisions on fertility (unless the utility derived from children and the costs of raising them are defined so widely as to be tautological); and these are not always the most important. Second, the parameters and their modes of interaction with the variables used in the analysis are apt to differ considerably among the diverse societies of the less developed world, and are apt to change in the changing conditions of that world. This applies, for example, to the cost of children and to their likely contribution to family income and to the support of parents in their old age.

Thus even if the demographic experience of the West could be explained largely in terms of the modern economic theory of fertility, it is unlikely to provide a sound basis for predicting prospective fertility in ldcs over the next few decades.

The theory that the direction of the inter-generational flow of wealth determines fertility was developed by Professor Caldwell. His investigations and inferences are among the most informative on this subject. His enquiries were conducted mostly in West Africa, and his findings are summarized in the major article already mentioned. Their significance and novelty warrant extended discussion.

For the purpose of demographic analysis Caldwell classifies the societies of the less developed world into primitive, traditional and transitional societies. The first two types of society reward a high fertility, which is advantageous to the society and may even be necessary to maintain it. The primitive society has barely emerged from subsistence production. Mortality is very high and there is scant protection from internal and external enemies. Traditional society is much more orderly as well as significantly less poor. Settled agriculture, cash crops, trade and crafts emerge. In both primitive and traditional societies the extended family prevails. Caldwell recognizes and lists the familiar advantages of the extended family in the early stages of development. But he also observes and emphasizes certain other characteristics rarely noticed in discussion of the nuclear family and the extended family which bear on demographic prospects.

The most important of these characteristics is that in primitive and traditional societies the inter-generational flow of wealth is overwhelmingly from the children to the parents, and more generally from the younger to the older generation. The contribution of children who work in the field or in the household exceeds the cost of maintaining them. The young continue to be net contributors to their elders until they set up on their own. Indeed, they often contribute even after leaving the household or compound, especially by supporting their relations. The young do not resent the system, because they know that they in turn will be supported when they grow old. The participants adopt and accept a long-term horizon; for instance, young women frequently refer to the need to have many children and even grandchildren to support them when they grow old.[25]

When the inter-generational flow of wealth is from the young to the old, it is an economic advantage to have many descendants and young collateral relatives. Thus the system conduces to high fertility. Higher incomes and more urbanization will not by themselves reverse the inter-generational flow of wealth and bring about demographic transition. Thus in Nigeria many of the social, political and economic advantages of having many children continue in urban conditions. Indeed, it is more likely in the towns than in the country that the political and material benefits of having one really successful relative should outweigh the cost of bringing up a number of unsuccessful ones.

It is in the transitional society which follows a traditional society that the inter-generational flow of wealth is reversed. The transitional society is significantly more modernized than the traditional society. Many people in it have adopted Western attitudes to a considerable extent. Caldwell rightly insists that modernization is only a euphemism for Westernization. Adoption of Western attitudes conduces to a reversal of the direction of the inter-generational flow of wealth. People come to subsidize their children and young relatives generally, instead of being subsidized by them. This change then promotes family limitation.

Caldwell supports his contentions with the results of close study of the availability and use of contraception in Nigeria, notably Ibadan and Lagos. He confirms other evidence that both traditional and modern contraceptive methods are widely known and readily accessible in Southern Nigeria. However, only a minority practise contraception to restrict family size. Even when contraception is practised, this is not primarily in order to limit family size, but rather for various other reasons such as avoidance of detection of pre-marital or other extra-marital sexual activity. The demographic innovators, those women who regularly practise contraception in order to restrict family size, are a small minority – a small minority even of educated women, and also of those who use contraceptives. They are women who deliberately accept Western attitudes towards child-bearing and child-rearing, almost certainly as a result of exposure to Western education, contacts and media. They are as yet only a very small fraction of women of child-bearing age.

Caldwell's conclusions are original, imaginative and suggestive. His findings may explain the sustained high fertility in most ldcs, in circumstances when a substantial decline could have been expected on the basis of the theory of demographic transition. Nevertheless, even if Caldwell's conclusions were valid and capable of generalization to other parts of the less developed world, they still could not serve as a secure basis for forecasting long-term fertility trends. It is impossible to predict how far and how fast the different societies will accept Westernization and Western patterns of inter-generational flow of wealth. Westernization has made headway in the less developed world. It may be expected to make further headway, and if so, it would bring about smaller families. But there has also been resistance to Westernization, even substantial movement in the opposite direction. Examples include the resistance in rural India both to birth control and to the slaughter of cattle, and the revival of Muslim orthodoxy in parts of the Middle East.

The microeconomic theory of fertility and the Caldwell theory based on the direction of the inter-generational flow of wealth are complementary. The latter relies more explicitly and extensively on the effects of cultural change. Together the two theories help considerably with an understanding of the determinants of family size. But for the reasons indicated, notably the impossibility of forecasting the extent and speed of Westernization, prediction of long term fertility trends in the less developed world as a whole must involve much conjecture. It is unwarranted to go beyond saying that it is virtually certain that for the rest of the century the population of the less developed world will increase appreciably, even though it is likely that age-specific fertility and the rate of population growth will diminish.

9

The preceding discussion has assumed that parents plan the size of their families and tend to have the number of children they wish to have. The typical family size, in turn, depends on various cultural, social and economic factors.

The comparatively high fertility and large families in many ldcs should not be regarded as irrational, abnormal, incomprehensible or unexpected. They accord with the tradition of most cultures and with the precepts of religious and political leaders. These precepts have been expressed by leaders of non-proselytizing cultures, such as Hinduism, which suggests that they do not reflect merely a desire for the power or prestige conferred by large numbers of followers or subjects. It is highly plausible that the desire for self-fulfilment and for the perpetuation of one's family or one's society or culture has been important in traditional insistence on the value of large families. The larger the number of children, the more likely are these objectives to be attained, especially for people looking beyond their immediate descendants. A sense of continuity in the society is likely to encourage people to have large families.[26]

Notwithstanding certain clearly definable exceptions, the wish of the great majority of mankind to have at least some children has extended across the ages, across cultures and across social classes. This is evident from the multiplication of the human race as well as from widely-held ideas and widely-practised behaviour.[27] The Biblical injunction to be fruitful and to multiply is familiar. Less well known in the West is the traditional greeting adressed to brides in India: 'May you be the mother of eight sons'. By contrast, the discontent or unhappiness of people, especially of women, with no children, and the happiness of the fertile are common themes of both the sacred and the profane literature of diverse cultures; it is reflected also in the uniformly unfavourable connotation of the term barren.[28] The widespread practice of adoption and the growing demand for artificial insemination in some countries also reflect the desire for children and a family.

Altogether, in the less developed world as elsewhere the great majority of people want the children they have. Children give satisfaction; they are outlets for affection; and they enable people to project themselves into the future. They also yield economic benefits: they often contribute significantly to the family income; they serve as a source of security or form of insurance for old age; and they sometimes bring prestige and influence. In all these contexts the benefits from one highly successful child exceed the cost of the others.

It is often thought that people in ldcs have many children because they do not know about birth control or have no access to cheap contraceptives. But this is wrong. Fertility is well below fecundity in most societies. Traditional methods of fertility control such as coitus interruptus were widely known and practised in societies technically and culturally much poorer and more primitive than populations with high fertility in the contemporary less developed world. Moreover, people in high fertility areas do have access to cheap Western-type goods and simple equipment of all sorts. Mass demand for such cheap Western-type consumer goods as soft drinks, hardware, watches and cameras has been conspicuous for many decades in South Asia, the Middle East, Southern Ghana, Southern Nigeria, Latin America and elsewhere. The transistor radio was ubiquitous in South Asia, the Middle East and Latin America a few years after it became available in the West. Contrast this with the relatively slow spread of condoms, inter-uterine devices and the pill, long after their extensive use in the West, and also long after the decline of mortality in the less developed world. The ready availability of cheap consumer goods and the relatively limited use of cheap contraceptives, which moreover are often subsidized, suggest strongly that there is only limited demand for them.

Much of the discussion of population in the development literature assumes or implies that in the high-fertility ldcs children are somehow uncontrollably visited on their parents, and that they are to a large extent unwanted burdens both on the parents and on society at large. On the contrary, however, the children who are born are generally desired. Children at any rate are avoidable. To deny this is to suggest that parents in ldcs procreate without an understanding of the consequences or without the will or sense of responsibility to prevent them. This view treats people of the less developed world with altogether unwarranted condescension or contempt.[29]

10

Western observers often chide parents in ldcs for alleged exploitation of their children and of the young generally. Such complaints are inconsistent with the frequent assertions that the large proportion of children in their populations represents a heavy burden of dependency. Neither of these inconsistent notions is valid.

In ldcs quite young children often participate in economic activity. They contribute to the family income through agricultural activity and by undertaking household chores, thereby freeing parents for other activities. In rural Uganda even five and six year old children regularly participate in simple agricultural and pastoral work.[30] A detailed survey of a large area of Bangladesh found that children contributed substantially to family income by working in the field and in the home.[31] Even in towns young children are often active in various forms of trade. This is a well known feature of economic life in West Africa.[32]

The contribution of children to family income, and thus to the national income, is considerable in the aggregate.[33]. The contribution of young children may well exceed the cost of maintaining them. But this does not mean that parents exploit their children. As already noted, the children can expect similar support when they grow up.

In ldcs as elsewhere people take note of surrounding social and economic conditions in their procreative habits. And if they find that they have as many children as they can support, they will either stop having more or adjust their economic circumstances. People in ldcs as elsewhere who are materially ambitious for themselves or for their children will adopt one or other or both of these courses. The adoption of more intensive forms of agriculture, the development of cash crops and the readiness of people to move between activities and places are familiar examples of such responses.

It is argued at times that even if parents largely have the families they desire, they may have larger families than is socially desirable because they do not bear the full costs of having and raising children. According to this argument there is an externality in that some of these costs are met by public expenditure, as on hospitals, schools and family allowances. Taxpayers subsidize parents. Consequently the total number of children is greater than if parents themselves had to bear all or a larger part of the costs.

These effects are likely to be more material in developed than in less developed countries because the public expenditures involved are less significant in the latter. However, the remedy lies in the reduction of these expenditures, or a modification of their incidence so that the parents of larger families are not so heavily subsidized. Further, the presence of some of these externalities does not depend on family size. For instance, while a small family may be subsidized by the taxpayers if the children receive publicly financed university education, a much larger family may not be so subsidized if the parents bear the cost of their school education.

Western observers often press governments of ldcs to restrict family size because of the adverse consequences of larger families, including the consequences of externalities. At the same time these observers often also urge more government help for the poor, including those with large families. Advocacy of fertility control will not be effective if parenthood is subsidized at the same time. Even if the incomes of the poor were increased by subsidies not geared to family size, this is still more likely to lead to larger families than to smaller ones because these higher incomes would not result from a change in attitudes.

11

Allegations or apprehensions of adverse or even disastrous results of population growth are unfounded. They rest on seriously defective analysis of the determinants of economic performance; they misconceive the conduct of the peoples of ldcs; and they employ criteria of welfare so inappropriate that they register as deterioration changes which are in fact improvements in the conditions of people.

Misconceptions and defective reasoning have promoted policies designed to reduce fertility and family size. Where these policies involve no more than dissemination of information about birth control techniques, or even the subsidized distribution of contraceptives, they may do little harm, and may at some cost improve the range of alternatives open to people. Even then, however, the policy may set up tensions and provoke feelings of insecurity and vulnerability if its announcement and implementation are accompanied by official propaganda insistently deprecating prevailing attitudes and behaviour. Moreover, people in many ldcs, especially in rural areas, are often dependent on officials for favours, for example in the allocation of subsidized credit or subsidized goods. Education and persuasion in favour of reduced fertility may in practice shade into coercion.[34]

Pressures for population control in the less developed world largely emanate from the West. The pressures and their sources were evident in India, where a sustained and mounting pressure for birth control reached its peak in the compulsory mass sterilization campaign 1975–77 in which the number of people sterilized against their will, often brutally and in insanitary conditions, is reported to have run into several hundred thousand.[35] Substantial sums have later been spent in trying to rehabilitate some of the victims of this coercive population policy.

Even drastic policies of population control will not be able to achieve the favourable effects claimed for them within the foreseeable future, certainly not within the time horizon of interest to national and international politicians and administrators. On the other hand, population policies which involve open or disguised coercion, or which in other ways are repugnant to the people concerned, will rapidly produce anguish, anxiety, tension and conflict, with a damaging effect on personal and social well-being and on economic performance. Such coercion is objectionable on moral grounds as well as for its economic results. Those who seek urgent and dramatic solutions to a problem they claim to have discovered are apt to propose or prescribe policies which generate difficulties and problems for the people directly affected far more acute than those they would otherwise experience.

CHAPTER 4

Western Guilt and
Third World Poverty

Come, fix upon me that accusing eye.
I thirst for accusation.

W. B. Yeats

1

Yeats' words might indeed have been written to describe the wide, even welcome, acceptance by the West of the accusation that it is responsible for the poverty of the Third World (i.e. most of Asia, Africa and Latin America).[1] Western responsibility for Third World backwardness is a persistent theme of the United Nations and its many affiliates.[2] It has been welcomed by spokesmen of the Third World and of the Communist bloc, notably so at international gatherings where it is often endorsed by official representatives of the West, especially the United States. It is also widely canvassed in the universities, the churches and the media the world over.

Acceptance of emphatic routine allegations that the West is responsible for Third World poverty reflects and reinforces Western feelings of guilt. It has enfeebled Western diplomacy, both towards the ideologically much more aggressive Soviet bloc and also towards the Third World. And the West has come to abase itself before countries with negligible resources and no real power. Yet the allegations can be shown to be without foundation. They are readily accepted because the Western public has little first-hand knowledge of the Third World, and because of widespread feelings of guilt. The West has never had it so good, and has never felt so bad about it.

2

A few characteristic examples will illustrate the general theme of Western responsibility. To begin with academics. The late Paul A. Baran, Professor of Economics at Stanford, was a highly regarded development economist. He was a prominent and influential exponent of Western guilt in the early days of contemporary development economics. He contributed the chapter on economic development to the *Survey of Contemporary Economics* published by the American Economic Association, and his book *The Political Economy of Growth* is a widely prescribed university textbook. In it Baran wrote:

> To the dead weight of stagnation characteristic of pre-industrial society was added the entire restrictive impact of monopoly capitalism. The economic surplus appropriated in lavish amounts by monopolistic concerns in backward countries is not employed for productive purposes. It is neither plowed back into their own enterprises nor does it serve to develop others.[3]

This categorical statement is wholly and obviously untrue because throughout the underdeveloped world large agricultural, mineral, commercial and industrial complexes have been built up through profits re-invested locally.

Professor Peter Townsend of Essex University is perhaps the most prominent British academic writer on poverty. In his book, *The Concept of Poverty*, he wrote:

> I argued that the poverty of deprived nations is comprehensible only if we attribute it substantially to the existence of a system of international social stratification, a hierarchy of societies with vastly different resources in which the wealth of some is linked historically and contemporaneously to the poverty of others. This system operated crudely in the era of colonial domination, and continues to operate today, though more subtly, through systems of trade, education, political relations, military alliances, and industrial corporations.[4]

This again cannot be so. The poorest and most backward countries have until recently had no external economic contacts and often have never been Western colonies. It is therefore obvious that their backwardness cannot be explained by colonial domination or international social stratification. And there are no industrial corporations in the least developed countries of the Third World (the so-called Fourth World) such as Afghanistan, Chad, Bhutan, Burundi, Nepal and Sikkim.

In this realm of discourse university students echo what they have learnt from their mentors. About ten years ago a student group at Cambridge published a pamphlet on the subject of the moral obligations of the West to the Third World. The following was its key passage:

> We took the rubber from Malaya, the tea from India, raw materials from all over the world and gave almost nothing in return.

This is as nearly the opposite of the truth as one can find. The British took the rubber *to* Malaya and the tea *to* India. There were no rubber trees in Malaya or anywhere in Asia (as suggested by their botanical name, *Hevea braziliensis*) until about 100 years ago, when the British took the first rubber seeds there out of the Amazon jungle. From these sprang the huge rubber industry – now very largely Asian-owned. Tea-plants were brought to India by the British somewhat earlier; their origin is shown in the botanical name *Camilla sinensis*, as well as in the phrase 'all the tea in China'.

Mr Charles Clarke, a former President of the National Union of Students, said in his presidential address delivered in December 1976: 'For over a hundred years British industry has been draining wealth away from those countries.' Far from draining wealth from the less developed countries, British industry helped to create it there, as external commerce promoted economic advance in large areas of the Third World where there was no wealth to be drained.

Western churches and charities are on the same bandwagon. Professor Ronald J. Sider is a prominent American churchman. In an article entitled 'How We Oppress the Poor' in *Christianity Today* (16 July 1976), an influential Evangelical magazine, he wrote about the 'stranglehold which the developed West has kept on the economic throats of the Third World' and then went on to say, 'It would be wrong to suggest that 210 million Americans bear sole responsibility for all the hunger and injustice in today's world. All the rich developed countries are directly involved . . . we are participants in a system that dooms even more people to agony and death than the slave system did'. These are evident fantasies. Famines occur in Third World countries largely isolated from the West. So far from condemning Third World people to death, Western contacts have been behind the large increase in life expectation in the Third World, so often deplored as the population explosion by the same critics.

Many charities have come to think it advantageous to play on the theme of Western responsibility. According to a widely publicized Oxfam advertisement of 1972:

Coffee is grown in poor developing countries like Brazil, Colombia and Uganda. But that does not stop rich countries like Britain exploiting their economic weakness by paying as little for their raw coffee as we can get away with. On top of this, we keep charging more and more for the manufactured goods they need to buy from us. So? We get richer at their expense. Business is Business.

A similar advertisement was run about cocoa. Both advertisements were subsequently dropped in the face of protests by actual and potential subscribers. The allegations in these advertisements are largely meaningless, and they are also unrelated to reality. The world prices of coffee and cocoa, which were as it happens very high in the 1970s, are determined by market forces and not prescribed by the West. On the other hand, the farmers in many of the exporting countries receive far less than the market prices, because they are subject to very high export taxes and similar government levies. The insistence on the allegedly low prices paid by the West to the producers and the lack of any reference to the penal taxation of the producers locally are examples that this guilt literature is concerned more with the flagellation of the West than with improving the conditions of the local population.

The intellectuals outside the academies and churches are also well to the fore. Cyril Connolly wrote in an article entitled 'Black Man's Burden' (*Sunday Times*, London, 23 February 1969):

> It is a wonder that the white man is not more thoroughly detested than he is. . . . In our dealings with every single country, greed, masked by hypocrisy, led to unscrupulous coercion of the native inhabitants. . . . Cruelty, greed and arrogance. . . characterized what can be summed up in one word, exploitation. . . .

If this were true, Third World countries would now be poorer than they were before Western contacts. In fact, they are generally much better off.

Insistence that the West has caused Third World poverty is collective self-accusation. The notion itself originated in the West. For instance, Marxism is a Western ideology, as is the belief that economic differences are anomalous and unjust, and that they reflect exploitation. But people in the Third World, especially articulate people with contacts with the West, readily believed what they were told by prominent academics and other intellectuals, the more so because the idea accorded with their interests and inclinations.

Inspired by the West, Third World politicians have come habitually to insist that the West has exploited and still exploits their countries. Dr Nkrumah, a major Third World figure of the 1950s and 1960s, was a well-known exponent of this view. He described Western capitalism as 'a world system of financial enslavement and colonial oppression and exploitation of a vast majority of the population of the earth by a handful of the so-called civilized nations'.[5] In fact, until the advent of Dr Nkrumah, Ghana (the former Gold Coast) was a prosperous country as a result of cocoa exports to the West, with the cocoa farmers the most prosperous and the subsistence producers the poorest groups there.

Julius Nyerere, President of Tanzania, is a highly regarded, almost venerated, world figure.[6] He said in the course of a State visit to London in 1975: 'If the rich nations go on getting richer and richer at the expense of the poor, the poor of the world must demand a change. . . .' When the West established substantial contact with Tanganyika (effectively the present

Tanzania) in the nineteenth century, this was an empty region, thinly populated with tribal people exposed to Arab slavers. Its relatively modest progress since then has been the work primarily of Asians and Europeans.

The notion of Western exploitation of the Third World is standard in publications and statements emanating from the Soviet Union and other Communist countries. Here is one example. The late Soviet Academician Potekhin was a prominent Soviet authority on Africa. He is worth quoting because Soviet economic writings are taken seriously in Western universities:

> Why is there little capital in Africa? The reply is evident. A considerable part of the national income which is supposed to make up the accumulation fund and to serve as the material basis of progress is exported outside Africa without any equivalent.[7]

No funds are exported from the poorest parts of Africa. Such remittances as there are from the more prosperous parts of the continent (generally very modest in the case of Black Africa, to which Potekhin refers) are partial returns on the resources supplied. In the most backward areas there are no foreigners and no foreign capital. It is the opposite of the truth to say that the reason there is little capital in Africa is that much of the national income is 'exported . . . without any equivalent'. In Africa as elsewhere in the Third World, the most prosperous areas are those with most commercial contacts with the West.

I could cite many more such allegations, but the foregoing should suffice to illustrate the general theme. In subsequent sections I shall note more specific allegations, some of them even more virulent than those already quoted.

3

Far from the West having caused the poverty in the Third World, contact with the West has been the principal agent of material progress there. The materially more advanced societies and regions of the Third World are those with which the West established the most numerous, diversified and extensive contacts: the cash-crop producing areas and entrepôt ports of South-East Asia, West Africa and Latin America; the mineral-producing areas of Africa and the Middle East; and cities and ports throughout Asia, Africa, the Caribbean and Latin America. The level of material achievement usually diminishes as one moves away from the foci of Western impact. The poorest and most backward people have few or no external contacts; witness the aborigines, pygmies and desert peoples.

All this is neither new nor surprising, since the spread of material progress from more to less advanced regions is a commonplace of history. In medieval

Europe, for instance, the more advanced regions of Central and Eastern Europe and Scandinavia were the areas with most contacts with France, the Low Countries and Italy, the most advanced parts of Europe at the time. The West was materially far ahead of the present Third World countries when it established extensive and diverse economic contacts with them in the nineteenth and twentieth centuries. It was through these contacts that human and material resources, skills, capital and new ideas, including the idea of material progress itself (and, incidentally, that of Western guilt too) flowed from the West to the Third World.

In recent times the role of external contacts in promoting economic advance in the Third World has been much more significant than that of similar contacts in the earlier history of Europe. To begin with, and as just noted, the very idea of material progress in the sense of sustained, steady and increasing control over man's environment is a Western concept. People in the Third World did not think of these terms before the advent of Western man. Scholars of such widely differing philosophical and political persuasion as, for instance, J. B. Bury and Christopher Dawson, have for long recognized the Western origin of the idea of material progress. The Western impulse behind economic advance in the Third World has also been acknowledged by writers who recognized this progress but warned against the disturbing, even corrosive, results of the sudden impact of contact with materially much more advanced societies.[8]

The West developed multifarious contacts with the Third World in the nineteenth and twentieth centuries, when the difference in economic attainment between the West and these regions was very wide, much wider than such differences had been in the past. Thus these contacts offered correspondingly greater opportunities, especially in view of the great improvements in transport and communications over the last two hundred years or so.

Since the middle of the nineteenth century commercial contacts established by the West have improved material conditions out of all recognition over much of the Third World, notably in South-East Asia; parts of the Middle East; much of Africa, especially West Africa and parts of East and Southern Africa; and very large parts of Latin America, including Mexico, Guatemala, Venezuela, Colombia, Peru, Chile, Brazil, Uruguay and Argentina. The transformation of Malaya (the present Malaysia) is instructive. In the 1890s it was a sparsely populated area of Malay hamlets and fishing villages. By the 1930s it had become the hub of the world's rubber and tin industries. By then there were large cities and excellent communications in a country where millions of Malays, Chinese and Indians now lived much longer and better

71

than they had formerly, either in their countries of origin or in Malaya.

Large parts of West Africa were also transformed over roughly the same period as a result of Western contacts. Before 1890 there was no cocoa production in the Gold Coast or Nigeria, only very small production of cotton and groundnuts, and small exports of palm oil and palm kernels. By the 1950s all these had become staples of world trade. They were produced by Africans on African-owned properties. But this was originally made possible by Westerners who established public security and introduced modern methods of transport and communications. Over this period imports both of capital goods and of mass consumer goods for African use also rose from insignificant amounts to huge volumes. The changes were reflected in government revenues, literacy rates, school attendance, public health, life expectation, infant mortality and many other indicators.

Statistics by themselves can hardly convey the far-reaching transformation which took place over this period in West Africa and elsewhere in the Third World. In West Africa, for instance, slave trading and slavery were still widespread at the end of the nineteenth century. They had practically disappeared by the end of the First World War. Many of the worst endemic and epidemic diseases for which West Africa was notorious throughout the nineteenth century had disappeared by the Second World War. External contacts also brought about similar far-reaching changes over much of Latin America.

The role of Western contacts in the material progress of Black Africa deserves further notice. As late as the second half of the nineteenth century Black Africa was without even the simplest, most basic ingredients of modern social and economic life. These were brought there by Westerners over the last hundred years or so. This is true of such fundamentals as public security and law and order; wheeled traffic (Black Africa never invented the wheel) and mechanical transport (before the arrival of Westerners, transport in Black Africa was almost entirely by human muscle); roads, railways and man-made ports; the application of science and technology to economic activity; towns with substantial buildings, clean water and sewerage facilities; public health care, hospitals and the control of endemic and epidemic diseases; formal education. These advances resulted from peaceful commercial contacts. These contacts also made easier the elimination of the Atlantic slave trade, the virtual elimination of the slave trade from Africa to the Middle East, and even the elimination of slavery within Africa.

Although peaceful commercial contacts had nothing to do with the Atlantic slave trade, in the contemporary climate it is impossible not to refer to that trade in a discussion of Western responsibility for Third World poverty.

Horrible and destructive as was the Atlantic slave trade, it cannot be claimed legitimately as a cause of African backwardness, still less of Third World poverty. Asia was altogether untouched by it. The most backward parts of Africa, such as the interior of Central and Southern Africa and most of East Africa, were largely unaffected by it.[9]

The slave trade between Africa and the Middle East ante-dated the Atlantic slave trade by centuries, and far outlasted it. Slavery was endemic over much of Africa long before the emergence of the Atlantic slave trade, and it was eventually stamped out by the West. Arabs and Africans do not seem to feel guilty about slavery and the slave trade; but Western Europeans and Americans often do and are made to do so. And yet it was due to their efforts that these practices were largely eliminated. Guilt is a prerogative of the West.

Western activities – supplemented at times by those of non-Western immigrants, notably Chinese, Indians and Levantines whose large-scale migration was made possible by Western initiative – have thus transformed material conditions in many parts of the Third World. All this is not to say that over the past hundred years there has been substantial material advance uniformly throughout the Third World. Large areas, especially in the interior of the Third World, have had few contacts with the West. Moreover, in much of the Third World the political, social and personal determinants of economic performance are often uncongenial to economic achievement. And the policies of many governments plainly obstruct economic achievement and progress. Again, people often refuse to abandon attitudes and mores which obstruct economic performance. They are not prepared to give up their established ways for the sake of greater prosperity. This is a preference which is neither unjustified not reprehensible.

Such considerations in no way warrant the allegations that Western contacts have obstructed or retarded Third World progress. Wherever local conditions have permitted it, commercial contacts with the West, and generally established by the West, have eliminated the worst diseases, reduced or even eliminated famine, extended life expectation and improved living standards.

4

Many of the assertions of Western responsibility for Third World poverty imply that the prosperity of relatively well-to-do persons, groups and societies is achieved at the expense of the less well-off. These assertions express the misconception emphasized in chapter 1 that the incomes of the well-to-do have been taken from others. In fact, with a few clearly definable exceptions, which do not apply to the relations between the West and the Third World, incomes whether of the rich or of the poor are earned by their recipients. In the Third World it is an article of faith of the most influential and articulate groups that their societies have been exploited by the West, both by Western individuals and Western companies, and also by locally resident ethnic minorities such as the Chinese in South-East Asia, Asians in East Africa, and Levantines in West Africa. The appeal of these misconceptions is all too familiar. They are especially useful to politicians who have promised a prosperity which they cannot deliver. But they are also useful to other influential local groups who expect to benefit from policies inspired by these ideas, especially from the expropriation of foreign enterprises or discrimination against minorities.

In recent decades certain readily recognizable influences have reinforced the notion that the prosperity of some group means that others have been exploited. The impact of Marxist-Leninist ideology has been one such influence. In this ideology any return on private capital implies exploitation, and service industries are regarded as unproductive. Thus, earnings of foreign capital and the incomes of foreigners or ethnic minorities in the service industries are evidence of forms of exploitation. Further, neo-Marxist literature has extended the concept of the proletariat to the peoples of the Third World, most of whom are in fact small-scale cultivators. In this literature, moreover, a proletariat is exploited by definition, and is poor because it is exploited.[10]

The idea of Western responsibility for Third World poverty has also been promoted by the belief in a universal basic equality of people's economic capacities and motivations. This belief is closely related to egalitarian ideology and policy which have experienced a great upsurge in recent decades. If people's attributes and motivations are the same everywhere and yet some societies are richer than others, this suggests that the former have exploited the rest.[11] Because the public in the West has little direct contact with the Third World, it is often easy to put across the idea that Western conduct and policies have caused poverty in the Third World.

The recent practice of referring to the poor as deprived or under-privileged again helps the notion that the rich owe their prosperity to the exploitation of the poor. Yet how could the incomes of, for example, people in Switzerland or North America have been taken from, say, the aborigines of Papua, or the desert peoples or pygmies of Africa? Indeed, who deprived these groups and of what?[12]

5

The principal assumption behind the idea of Western responsibility for Third World poverty is that the prosperity of individuals and societies generally reflects the exploitation of others. Some variants or derivatives of this theme are often heard, usually geared to particular audiences. One of these variants is that colonialism has caused the poverty of Asia and Africa. It has particular appeal in the United States where hostility to colonialism is traditional. For a different and indeed opposite reason, it is at times effective in stirring up guilt in Britain, the foremost ex-colonial power.

Whatever one thinks of colonialism, it cannot be held responsible for Third World poverty. Some of the most backward countries never were colonies, as for instance Afghanistan, Tibet, Nepal, Liberia. Ethiopia is perhaps an even more telling example (it was an Italian colony for only six years in its long history). Again, many of the Asian and African colonies progressed very rapidly during colonial rule, much more so than the independent countries in the same area. At present one of the few remaining European colonies is Hong Kong – whose prosperity and progress should be familiar.[13] It is plain that colonial rule has not been the cause of Third World poverty.

Nor is the prosperity of the West the result of colonialism. The most advanced and the richest countries never had colonies, including Switzerland and the Scandinavian countries; and some were colonies of others and were already very prosperous as colonies, as for instance North America and Australasia. The prosperity of the West was generated by its own peoples and was not taken from others. The European countries were already materially far ahead of the areas where they established colonies.

In recent years the charges that colonialism causes Third World poverty have been expanded to cover 'colonialism in all its forms'. The terms 'economic colonialism' and 'neo-colonialism' have sprung up to cover external private investment, the activities of multinational companies, and indeed almost any form of economic relationship between relatively rich and relatively poor regions or groups. Reference to 'colonialism in all its forms' as a cause of Third World poverty is a major theme at UNCTAD meetings. This terminology has become common currency in both academic literature and in the media. It regularly confuses poverty with colonial status, a concept which has normally meant lack of political sovereignty.

One unusually direct formulation of these ideas (which are normally expressed in much more convoluted form in the academic and official literature) was provided in an editorial in the June 1978 issue of *Poverty and Power* published by War on Want, a British charity:

We see poverty in the Third World as a result of colonial looting in the past and neo-colonial exploitation in the present.

The demise of political colonialism has probably been another important factor behind the shift in terminology. Disappearance of colonial rule has forced the accusers of the West to find new ground for their charges. Hence the terminology of neo-colonialism and economic colonialism. The usage represents a shift in the basis of accusation and at the same time it retains the benefits of the older, familiar terminology. The influence of Marxist-Leninist doctrine has also promoted the new terminology. According to Marxist-Leninist ideology, colonial status and foreign investment are by definition evidence of exploitation. In fact, foreign private investment and the activities of the multinational companies have expanded opportunities and raised incomes and government revenues in the Third World. Reference to economic colonialism and neo-colonialism both debase the language and distort the truth.[14]

6

The West is now widely accused of manipulating international trade to the detriment of the Third World. This accusation is a major theme of the demands for a New International Economic Order. In particular, the West is supposed to inflict unfavourable and persistently deteriorating terms of trade on the Third World. Among other untoward results, this influence is said to have resulted in a decline in the share of the Third World in total world trade, and also in a large volume of Third World foreign debt. These allegations are again irrelevant, unfounded and often the opposite of the truth.[15]

The poorest areas of the Third World have no external trade. Their condition shows that the causes of backwardness are domestic and that external commerical contacts are beneficial. Even if the terms of trade were unfavourable on some criterion or other, this would only mean that people do not benefit from foreign trade as much as they would if the terms of trade were more favourable. People benefit from the widening of opportunities which external trade represents. Besides this last and basic conclusion, there are many other objections to the notion that the terms of trade are somehow inherently unfavourable to the Third World, and external commercial contacts damaging to it.

As the Third World comprises most of the world, the aggregation of the terms of trade of all its countries has a very limited meaning. The terms of trade of some Third World countries and groups of countries move differently and often in opposite directions from those of others; the effect of the OPEC price increases on many Third World countries is only one recent and familiar example.

Again, except over very short periods, changes in the terms of trade as conventionally measured are of little welfare significance without reference to changes in the cost of production of exports, the range and quality of imports, and the volume of trade. In so far as changes in the terms of trade do affect development and welfare, what matters is the amount of imports which can be purchased with a unit of domestic resources. This figure cannot be inferred simply from the ratio of import and export prices because these do not take into account the cost of production of exports. (In technical language, the comparisons relevant to economic welfare and development are the factoral terms of trade, which allow for changes in the cost of production, and not the simple ratio between import and export prices, i.e. crude commodity terms.) Further, expressions such as unfavourable terms of trade are meaningless except by reference to a base period. In recent decades, however, even the crude commodity terms of trade of Third World countries have been exceptionally favourable. When changes in the cost of production, the great improvement in the range and quality of imports, and the huge increase in the volume of trade are taken into account, the external purchasing power of Third World exports is now relatively high, probably more so than ever before. This situation has made it easier for governments to retain a larger proportion of export earnings through major increases in mining royalty rates, export taxes and corporation taxes. The imposition of substantial export taxes, often very high in the Third World, makes clear that the terms of trade of a country do not determine people's ability to buy imports, much less their living standards.

The exponents of the idea that the terms of trade of the Third World deteriorate persistently rarely specify the period they envisage for this process. Yet it must come to an end at some stage before the terms of trade decline to zero.[16] Nor is it usually made clear why there should be such a deterioration. It is often implied that the West can somehow manipulate international prices to the disadvantage of the Third World. But the West cannot prescribe international prices. These prices are the outcome of innumerable individual decisions of market participants. They are not prescribed by a single individual decision-maker, or even by a handful of people acting in collusion.[17]

The share of a country or group of countries in total world trade is by itself no index of prosperity or welfare. Similarly, reduction in this share has by itself no adverse economic implications. It often reflects the expansion of economic activity and trade elsewhere, which does not normally damage but usually benefits those whose relative share has declined. For instance, since the 1950s the large increase in the foreign trade of Japan, the reconstruction of Europe, and the liberalization of intra-European trade have brought about a decline in the share of other groups in world trade, including that of the United States and the United Kingdom. Furthermore, the share of a country or group of countries in world trade is often reduced by domestic developments, and in particular by policies unrelated to external circumstances such as increased domestic use of previously exported products, or domestic inflation, or special taxation of exporters, or the intensification of protectionist policies. Merely as an aside, it is worth noting that since the Second World War the Third World's share of total world trade has in fact much increased compared with earlier times. It is evident that this share has increased hugely under Western influence in the modern period. Before then, the areas forming the present Third World had little external trade. Of course, if international trade harmed the peoples of the Third World as the critics of the West so often allege, then a decline in the share of the Third World in this trade would be beneficial. Ultimate economic bliss would be attained when the Third World no longer had external economic relations, at any rate with the West.

The external debts of the Third World are not the result or reflection of exploitation. They represent resources supplied. Indeed, much of the current indebtedness of Third World governments consists of soft loans under various aid agreements, frequently supplemented by outright grants. With the worldwide rise in prices, including those of Third World exports, the cost even of these soft loans has diminished greatly. Difficulties of servicing these debts do not reflect external exploitation or unfavourable terms of trade. They are the result of wasteful use of the capital supplied, or inappropriate monetary and fiscal policies. Again, the persistent balance of payments deficits of some Third World countries do not mean that they are being exploited or impoverished by the West. Such deficits are inevitable if the government of a country, whether rich or poor, advancing or stagnating, lives beyond its resources and pursues inflationary policies while attempting to maintain overvalued exchange rates. Persistent balance of payments difficulties mean that external resources are being lent to the country over these periods.

The decline of particular economic activities, as for instance the Indian textile industry in the eighteenth century as a result of competition from cheap imports, is habitually instanced as an example of the damage caused to the Third World by trade with the West. This argument identifies the decline of one activity with the decline of the economy as a whole, and the economic interests of one sectional group with those of all members of a society. Cheap imports extend the choice and economic opportunities of people in poor countries. These imports are usually accompanied by the expansion of other activities. If this were not so, the population would be unable to pay for the imports.

The so-called brain drain, the migration of qualified personnel from the Third World to the West, is another allegation of Western responsibility for Third World poverty or stagnation. This is a somewhat more complex issue than those noted so far, but it certainly does not substantiate the familiar accusation. The training of many of the emigrants was financed by the West. Again, formal education is not an indispensable instrument nor even a major instrument of emergence from personal poverty or economic backwardness – witness the rapid progress to prosperity of untrained or even illiterate people in many Third World countries. The enforced exodus or outright expulsion of many enterprising and skilled people from many Third World countries, the maltreatment of ethnic minorities or tribal groups, and the refusal of many Third World governments to allow foreigners to work inhibit development much more than do voluntary departures. And many of these emigrants leave because their own governments cannot or will not use their services. It is not the West nor the emigrants who deprive the society of productive resources: it is these Third World governments.[18]

The West is also said to have damaged the Third World by ethnic discrimination. But the countries in which such discrimination occurred were those where material progress was initiated or promoted by contact with the West. The most backward groups in the Third World (aborigines, desert peoples, nomads and other tribesfolk) were quite unaffected by ethnic discrimination on the part of Europeans. Many communities against which discrimination was often practised – the Chinese in South-East Asia, Indians in parts of South-East Asia, Asians in Africa, and others – have progressed greatly. In any case, discrimination on the basis of colour or race is not a European invention. In much of Africa and Asia and notably in India it has been endemic for many centuries. Finally, any ethnic discrimination by Europeans was negligible compared with the massive and sometimes brutal persecution of ethnic and tribal groups systematically practised by the governments of many independent Asian and African states.

Altogether, it is anomalous or even perverse to suggest that external commercial relations are damaging to development or to the living standards of the people of the Third World. They act as channels for the flow of human and financial resources and for new ideas, methods and crops. They benefit people by providing a large and diverse source of imports and by opening up markets for exports. Because of the vast expansion of world trade in recent decades, and the development of technology in the West, the material advantages from external contacts are now greater than ever before. The suggestion that these relations are detrimental is not only unfounded but also damaging. For instance, it has often served as a specious but plausible justification for official restrictions on the volume or diversity of these relations.

The basic realities of the results of external contacts have been obfuscated by the practice, rife both in public discussion and in the contemporary development literature, of confusing governments or elites with the population at large.[19] Many Third World governments and their local allies do indeed often benefit from state economic controls, and in particular from the restrictions on external commerce. Such restrictions enable governments to control their subjects more closely, a situation from which the rulers benefit politically and materially. Other articulate and influential local groups also benefit politically and financially from organizing or administering economic controls. These realities are concealed in allegations that the West had forced imports on Third World countries. It is, of course, the rulers who object to the imports desired by their subjects.

The allegations that external trade, and especially imports from the West, are damaging to the populations of the Third World reveal a barely disguised condescension towards the ordinary people there, and even contempt for them. The people, of course, want the imports. If they did not the imported goods could not be sold. Similarly, the people are prepared to produce for export to pay for these imported goods. To say that these processes are damaging is to argue that people's preferences are of no account in organizing their own lives.

The disparagement of external contacts is relatively recent. Before the Second World War the role of these contacts as instruments of economic advance was widely recognized in academic and public discussion. Their role in providing both external markets and incentive goods, as well as transforming people's attitudes, was a conspicuous theme of the classical economists, including writers as different in their outlook as Adam Smith, John Stuart Mill and Marx.

7

Apart from the damage allegedly caused to the Third World by external trade, it is frequently said nowadays that the mere existence and day-to-day activities of the peoples of the West also harm the Third World.

Cheap consumer goods developed and used in the West and available also in the Third World are said to obstruct development there because these goods supposedly encourage spending at the expense of saving. The mainstream development literature calls this the international demonstration effect. This contention disregards the level of consumption and the extension of choice as criteria of development. Yet these matters are what economic development is about. The notion of a damaging international demonstration effect also ignores the role of external contacts as an instrument of development. It overlooks the fact that the new consumer goods have to be paid for, which usually requires improved economic performance including such things as more work, additional saving and investment, and readiness to produce for sale instead of for subsistence. Thus this accusation neglects the obvious consideration that a higher and more varied level of consumption is both the principal justification for material progress and an inducement to further economic advance.[20]

An updated version of the international demonstration effect proposes that the eager acceptance of Western consumer goods in the Third World is a form of cultural dependence engendered by Western business. The implication here is that the peoples of the Third World lack the ability to decide for themselves how best to spend their incomes. They are looked on as children, or even as mere puppets manipulated by foreigners at will. In fact, however, Western goods have been accepted selectively and not indiscriminately in the Third World where they have been of massive benefit to millions of people. This charge of cultural dependence is often accompanied by the accusation that the West also damages the Third World through its patent laws. Thus, both the provision of Western goods and also the alleged withholding of them are said to be damaging.

As is not surprising, allegedly lavish consumption habits and the pollution and plunder of the environment in the West have also been pressed into ideological service. A standard formulation is that per capita consumption of food and energy in the United States is many times that in India, so that the American consumer despoils his Indian opposite number on a large scale. Professor Tibor Mende is an influential and widely-quoted writer on development. A few years ago he wrote: 'According to one estimate, each American has twenty-five times the impact on the environment – as a consumer and polluter – as an Indian' (*Newsweek*, 23 October 1972). Note the reference to each American as consumer and polluter, but not as a producer.

Even babies are drafted into the campaign to promote Western guilt, notably in the familiar pictures of babies with distended bellies. An article entitled 'The Greed of the Super Rich' in the London *Sunday Times*, 20 August 1978, opens as follows:

81

One American baby consumes fifty times more of the world's resources than an Indian baby. . . . The wheat need of the people in Africa's Sahel region could have been met by a twentieth of the wheat European countries use each year to feed cattle.

The West has even come to be accused of mass cannibalism. According to Professor René Dumont, the widely-known French agronomist and consultant to international organizations: ' . . . in over-consuming meat, which wasted the cereals which could have saved them, we ate the little children of Sahel, of Ethiopia, and of Bangladesh.'[21] This grotesque allegation has come to be widely echoed in the West. According to Miss Jill Tweedie of *The Guardian* (London): 'A quarter of the world's population lives, quite literally, by killing the other three-quarters' (*The Guardian*, 3 January 1977). And another article prominently featured in *The Guardian* of 11 June 1979 referred to the

social cannibalism which has reduced over three-quarters of mankind to beggary, poverty and death, not because they don't work, but because their wealth goes to feed, clothe, and shelter a few idle classes in America, Europe, and Japan . . . money-mongers in London and New York and in other Western seats of barons living on profit snatched from the peasants and workers of the world.[22]

Such ridiculous statements could be multiplied many times over. Their expression by prominent academics and by journalists in the so-called quality press tells much about the contemporary intellectual scene.

The West has not caused the famines in the Third World. These have occurred in backward regions with practically no external commerce. The absence of external trading links is often one aspect of the backwardness of these regions. At times it reflects the policies of the rulers who are hostile to traders, especially to non-indigenous traders, and often even to private property. As a matter of interest, it has proved difficult to get emergency supplies to some of the Sahelian areas because of poor communications and official apathy or hostility. Attempts permanently to support the populations of such backward areas with Western official donations would inhibit the development of viable agriculture there.

Contrary to the various allegations and accusations noted in this section, the higher level of consumption in the West is not achieved by depriving others of what they have produced. Western consumption is more than paid for by Western production. This production not only finances domestic consumption but also provides the capital for domestic and foreign investment as well as foreign aid. Thus the gap between production in the West and in the Third World is even greater than the gap in consumption.

8

The West has indeed contributed to Third World poverty, in two senses. These, however, differ radically from the familiar assertions.

First, Western activities since the Second World War have done much to politicize economic life in the Third World. In the terminal years of British colonial rule the traditional policy of relatively limited government was abandoned in favour of close official economic controls. As a result of this change in policy in most British colonies outside the Far East and South-East Asia, a ready-made framework for state-controlled economies or even for totalitarian states was presented to the incoming independent governments. The operation of official Western aid to Third World governments, reinforced by certain strands in its advocacy and by the criteria of its allocation, has also served to politicize life in the Third World.[23] These controls have wasted resources, restricted social and economic mobility and also external contacts. They have also provoked fierce political and social strife. These consequences in turn have brought about poverty and even large-scale suffering.

Many independent Third World governments would presumably have attempted in any case to politicize their economies extensively, because this greatly enhances the power of the rulers. But they are unlikely to have gone so far as they have in recent years, or to have succeeded in their attempts, without Western influence and assistance. But all this does not validate the position of the exponents of Western guilt. The most vocal and influential critics both of colonial rule and of Western contacts with the Third World have emphatically urged large-scale economic controls and other forms of politicization of life in the Third World. Indeed, they have blamed colonial governments and Western influence for not promoting such policies sooner and more vigorously.

Second, Western contacts with the Third World have helped bring about the sharp decline in mortality in the Third World which is behind the recent rapid population growth there. These Western contacts have therefore enabled many more poor people to survive and have thus increased apparent poverty. But, as I have argued in chapter 3, this outcome represents an improvement in the condition of people, and is not the result of deprivation.

9

The allegations that external contacts damage the Third World are plainly condescending. They clearly imply that Third World people do not know what is good for them, nor even what they want. The image of the Third World as a uniform stagnant mass devoid of distinctive character is another aspect of this condescension. It reflects a stereotype which denies identity, character, personality and responsibility to the individuals and societies of the Third World. Because the Third World is defined as the whole world with the exception of the West and a handful of Westernized societies (such as Japan and South Africa) it is regarded as if it were all much of a muchness. Time and again the guilt merchants envisage the Third World as an undifferentiated, passive entity, helplessly at the mercy of its environment and of the powerful West.

The exponents of Western guilt further patronize the Third World by suggesting that its economic fortunes past, present and prospective, are determined by the West; that past exploitation by the West explains Third World backwardness; that manipulation of international trade by the West and other forms of Western misconduct account for persistent poverty; that the economic future of the Third World depends largely on Western donations. According to this set of ideas, whatever happens to the Third World is largely our doing. Such ideas make us feel superior even while we beat our breasts.

A curious mixture of guilt and condescension is also discernible behind the toleration or even support of inhuman policies of many Third World governments. The brutalities of the rulers are often excused on the ostensible ground that they are only following examples set by the West. For instance, when Asian or African governments massively persecute ethnic minorities, they are excused by their Western sympathizers as doing no more than adopting a local variant of ethnic discrimination by Europeans. Similarly, the most offensive and baseless utterances of Third World spokesmen need not be taken seriously because they are only Third World statements, a licence which has been extended to their supporters in the West. In this general scheme of things, neither Third World rulers nor their peoples have minds or wills of their own: they are envisaged as creatures moulded by the West or, at best, as being at the mercy of their own environment. Moreover, like children, they are not altogether responsible for what they do. In any case, we must support them to atone for alleged wrongs which our supposed ancestors may have perpetrated on their supposed ancestors.[24] And economic aid is also necessary to help these children grow up.

Insistence on Western foreign aid is a major theme of the recent literature of Western guilt. But whether or not linked to patronization (and it usually is so linked), the idea of Western guilt is not only unfounded but is also a singularly inappropriate basis for aid. It leads to a disregard of the effects of aid in the recipient countries and of the conduct of the recipient governments. It discourages even cursory examination of the likely political, social and economic results of Western alms. The prime concern is with divesting the West of resources, not with the effects of its donations.

A feeling of guilt has nothing to do with a sense of responsibility or a sense of compassion. Exponents of guilt are concerned with their own emotional state and that of their fellow citizens, and not with the results of the policies inspired by such sentiments. These policies damage the West. They damage the ordinary people in the Third World even more.

CHAPTER 5

Foreign Aid and Its Hydra-Headed Rationalization

Do not attempt to do us any more good. Your good has done us too much harm already.

Sheik Muhammed Abduh,
an Egyptian in London, 1884

1

Who can possibly object to aid for the less fortunate? Foreign aid (or its synonym overseas aid) is the transfer annually of billions of dollars of Western taxpayers' money to distant governments directly or through international organizations.[1] To call these transfers aid simultaneously disarms criticism, prejudges the effects of the policy and also obscures its realities and results. On both practical and intellectual grounds this policy calls for critical examination. Its many little-understood repercussions, and the multiplicity of the rationalizations put forward, necessitate extended discussion.

Such an extended discussion needs, however, to be prefaced by an unequivocal statement of the principal outcomes of this policy. The primary result of official Western aid has been the creation of the Third World as a collectivity confronting the West, and one which, as a collectivity, is hostile to it. The second major consequence has been the contribution of aid to the politicization of life in the Third World. These momentous and far-reaching results will continue as long as foreign aid continues. Discussion of such matters as the more specific economic results of aid, its statistics, the arguments in its support, or the background to it, may be useful or even necessary in specific contexts. For instance, an extensive consideration of these matters is appropriate in this chapter and the one following which attempt a detailed examination of this policy. But such a discussion should not be allowed to obscure the paramount results of aid, namely the creation of the Third World as such and the promotion of the politicization of life there or to divert attention from these results. This reminder is especially necessary at the beginning of a long discussion which aims to cover the arguments behind foreign aid as well as its diverse results.

Since this chapter is unavoidably long, the reader may find it useful to have an outline of its contents.

Section 2 explores the concept of the Third World. Section 3 elaborates the point that the case for aid is generally taken as self-evident, an uncritical attitude which gives rise to numerous anomalies such as those illustrated in section 4. Detailed examination of a series of different arguments for aid is introduced in section 5. Sections 6 to 9 examine the central argument that aid is necessary for satisfactory economic development in the Third World, and indeed promotes it. Aid and the relief of poverty in the Third World are the subjects of sections 10 and 11. Sections 12 and 13 deal respectively with aid and international income redistribution, and with aid as restitution for past and present wrongs. Section 14 examines the contention that aid serves the political and economic interests of the donor countries and their people. Aid and population pressure in the Third World is briefly discussed in section 15, and some further rationalizations will be found in section 16. Section 17 considers how various measures, including the reform of aid, can achieve several of the proposed objectives of aid which present policies and practices do not and cannot achieve.

2

Foreign aid is central to the economic relations between the West and the Third World. It will remain so long as there is a Third World. The Third World and its antecedents and synonyms, such as the underdeveloped world, the less developed world and the developing world (all still used) and now also the South, are for all practical purposes the collection of countries whose governments, with the odd exception, demand and receive official aid from the West. The concept of the Third World or the South and the policy of official aid are inseparable. They are two sides of the same coin. The Third World is the creation of foreign aid: without foreign aid there is no Third World.

The concept of an underdeveloped world eventually to become the Third World was invented after the Second World War. It did not exist before then. From its inception, the unifying characteristic has been that the Third World is in practice the aggregate of countries whose governments demand and receive Western aid. In all other ways the unity or uniformity is pure fiction.

The fictitious unity has made it worthwhile, possible and apparently sensible for the United Nations and its affiliates to organize concerted action by these countries for this purpose. It has made opposition to the West a source of political or financial benefit to Third World leaders and to influential groups in the West. To represent the world as if it included two sharply divided categories, namely a rich and developed West and a wretchedly poor Third World, makes it easier to advocate international wealth transfers.

The Third World comprises about two thirds of mankind. Its societies range in evolution, culture and income from aborigines to materially very advanced groups and societies, notably in South-East Asia, the Middle East and Latin America. It includes many prosperous individuals, groups and regions in these areas. Several oil-producing countries were also included in the Third World, and received aid even when they were already rich; Saudi Arabia and Kuwait received Western aid at least as recently as 1979. Thus poverty is not the unifying characteristic of the Third World. Nor is stagnation. Since the Second World War, many Third World countries have progressed very rapidly, much more so than many Western countries, including the United States and Britain.

Nor is the Third World a collection of politically non-aligned countries. Many Third World rulers, perhaps most, have been critical of the West, and some virulently hostile to it.[2] As a collectivity the Third World is always hostile to the West. This is perhaps not surprising. The *raison d'être* of the Third World as a collectivity is to extract resources from the West. With loss of self-confidence, feelings of guilt and internal dissension in the West, a hostile stance is appropriate for the Third World to adopt.

It is sometimes thought that skin colour provides a unifying feature of the Third World because its peoples are predominantly non-white. But they are also predominantly non-black, the majority being brown and yellow. In fact, in the Third World as a whole the whites outnumber the blacks. Negative definition, that is defining a category in terms of what it is not, rarely tells us much about a social or economic category. But it is a familiar, and sometimes effective, device of political rhetoric.[3]

What is there in common between, say, Papua-New Guinea and Mexico, Indonesia and Peru, Malaysia and Lesotho, India and Chad, Afghanistan and Chile? In most Third World countries, people often do not even know of the existence of other Third World countries. Much less do they think of their populations as brothers. Many of them are engaged in international hostilities or open warfare. These include India and Pakistan, Algeria and Morocco, Angola and Zaire, Tanzania and Uganda, Ethiopia and Somalia, Guatemala and Belize and Kampuchea and Vietnam. Many are also rent by acute, undisguised and persistent conflict within, including civil war. Familiar recent examples include Indonesia, Malaysia, Iran, Lebanon, Uganda, Chad and Nigeria, among others.

The frequency and intensity of the internal conflict in these countries is often the result of the politicization of life in the Third World. This politicization has greatly raised the stakes in the battle for power. It has also often helped to bring to the fore governments more sympathetic to the Soviet bloc than to the market societies of the West. These governments incline more toward the Soviet bloc because they too favour state-controlled economies. This politicization has been much assisted by official aid.

It is often urged that protracted debate of foreign aid is unwarranted because the amounts involved are too small to justify it. The far-reaching political results of this policy make it clear that this reasoning is invalid. Further, as we shall see, current levels of aid have substantial economic results, even in the West. The repercussions in the Third World are even more pervasive and, for reasons to be shown later, they are brought about by amounts of aid which represent modest percentages of the national income of donors and recipients. And many influential supporters of aid envisage its substantial expansion and indeed regard its present flow as only a small beginning of global redistribution.

3

Foreign aid is perhaps the least questioned form of state spending in the West. It is never questioned in principle. It is often criticized on the ground that it is insufficient. Past aid programmes have been criticized at times as inappropriate, as for instance aid which has financed spending which was obviously wasteful, or which has gone to governments or for projects which subsequently became politically unpopular in the West. But such criticism is not allowed to question aid as such. It leads to proposals that aid should be increased, or redirected to targets deemed more appropriate.

Indeed, foreign aid has been elevated above political discussion. In Britain, spokesmen of the major political parties have for many years insisted explicitly and repeatedly that aid to the Third World was above political debate. This approach was confirmed when in November 1978 the Prince of Wales joined the Commonwealth Development Corporation which is an official agency under the Ministry of Overseas Development.[4]

In continental Europe also, aid is above political criticism. That this is so in Scandinavia and the Netherlands is familiar. But it is true, too, in the Federal Republic of Germany, a country widely regarded as a hardliner in economic affairs. Yet its government spends heavily on foreign aid at a time when the high level of taxation and the large inflationary budget deficits have been in the foreground of German politics. At a conference in January 1979, the President of the Federal Republic, the official leaders of the three political parties, the Presidents of the Confederation of German Industry and of the Federation of Trade Unions, and the leaders of the main churches agreed unanimously that in the years ahead official German Third World aid should be increased by more than other forms of public spending. In the United States there is some sporadic and rather ineffective criticism of aid which does not affect mainstream discussion at all, and official policy apparently not much either. The fact that official aid has effectively been removed from political discourse does not make it any less political. It is taxpayers' money which goes to foreign governments, and these are political matters.

Altogether, the mainstream advocacy of aid rarely addresses itself to its actual operation, and notably not to its efficacy in terms of its proclaimed objectives. The advocates do not examine whether aid actually promotes development or improves the lot of the poor. Nor do they examine its adverse repercussions. Many advocates seem more interested in removing resources from the West than with the effects of these transfers in the recipient countries, or with the promotion of the welfare of the people there. We shall return to this later.

This uncritical approach is reflected in the language of the discourse. Giving more aid is equated with doing better; increased aid is used interchangeably with improved aid performance; and countries giving a higher percentage of their national income in official aid are described as better performers than others giving a small percentage. The implications of this axiomatic status of aid were neatly summarized a few years ago in an editorial in *Nature* (26 May 1972): 'If 1 per cent, in total, is the present target, what is wrong with 2 per cent?' Why stop there? Indeed, to take for granted that giving more aid is the same as doing better is to equate cost with benefit – which no one in his right mind would normally apply to his own affairs.

The nomenclature of the aid agencies again reveals this approach. They are invariably termed development agencies or organizations, which prejudges the effects of the donations they disburse. Again, in aid discussions it is only advocates and administrators of aid who are termed experts; the few people who from time to time question aid are never so designated, whatever their experience or qualifications.

The axiomatic approach means that whatever happens in recipient countries can be adduced to support the maintenance or extension of aid. Progress is evidence of its efficacy and so an argument for its expansion; lack of progress is evidence that the dosage has been insufficient and must be increased. Some advocates argue that it would be inexpedient to deny aid to the speedy (those who advance); others, that it would be cruel to deny it to the needy (those who stagnate). Aid is thus like champagne: in success you deserve it, in failure you need it.

Aid seldom responds to economic adversity in the donor countries. In Britain, large-scale aid continued throughout the various sterling crises of the 1960s and 1970s even when spending both at home and abroad was severely restricted, including foreign investment and private travel. When *in extremis*, such as the acute sterling crisis of 1976, aid was reduced slightly, the reductions were generally the first of the state spending cuts to be restored. And in 1979, for example, overseas aid was running at around one-quarter to one-third of the current account deficit.

In the financial year 1978–9 United Kingdom overseas aid was about £800 million. This sum was equal to about ten per cent of all state old age pension payments. It was also about ten per cent of the Public Sector Borrowing Requirement, and of the central government total borrowings at the time when the amount of this borrowing was a matter of widespread anxiety and the scope for its reduction a major issue of policy. The Labour government proposed large increases in aid from 1979 onwards. The Conservative budget of June 1979 also proposed an increase in aid in both money and real terms, while suggesting substantial actual cuts in some other forms of spending. [5] However, the official White Paper published in November of that year pegged overseas aid in real terms for 1979–80 and 1980–1 at its 1978–9 level. At the same time the government announced substantial reductions in spending on schools, transport and housing compared with previous years, and also a large rise in prescription charges under the National Health Service.

The bulk of aid is in the form of grants, the rest in loans at zero or nominal rates of interest. This has been happening when both in Britain and the United States the government, large industrial companies and also millions of house owners have had to borrow at double-figure interest rates.

In the 1970s, both the US and British governments continued offiical aid, often on a large scale, when their own currencies were weak. For instance, in 1978 US foreign economic aid was equal to over one-half of the current account deficit (and about one-sixth of the federal budget deficit). At this time Western governments and international organizations chided the American government for the large current account deficit and the weakness of the dollar. Yet they simultaneously urged the United States to expand aid to the Third World. In March 1979, Secretary of State Vance urged further expansion of American aid, as being both a moral duty and matter of self-interest. He said this at a time when the dollar had greatly declined on the world's foreign exchange markets, and when American economic aid was expected to be about equal to the current account deficit for 1979.

Large-scale American and British aid, given when their currencies are weak, entails worldwide financial repercussions. The dollar and the pound are major reserve currencies. Governments and individuals throughout the world hold much of their reserves in them. A fall in their exchange rates inflicts large losses on those, including many in the Third World, who were prudent enough to build up reserves, and foolish enough to hold them in these currencies. Inflation in reserve currency countries, moreover, is powerfully stimulated by government spending of which aid is now a significant part. And inflation in these countries has contributed substantially to the international inflation which has created so much havoc in the Third World and elsewhere. Again, the continuing auctions of part of the gold reserve of the IMF – the proceeds of which are to be handed to Third World governments – are also inflationary in a minor but unambiguous way, because they convert accumulated reserves into current spending. All these consequences are ignored because aid is regarded as virtuous by definition.

Firm forward commitments for several years ahead represent another corollary of the axiom that aid must be desirable. Such commitments for Britain in 1979 exceeded £750 million, excluding multilateral aid commitments. No one knows what governments will be in power in the recipient countries by the mid-1980s, let alone what their policies will be. The anomaly was shown up in 1977 when the British Foreign Secretary expressed regret that EEC aid to Amin could not be terminated because much of it was firmly committed.

Western donors also face contingent liabilities in the form of the uncalled share capital of the World Bank, whose operations are steadily increasing and can confidently be expected to continue to do so. Moreover, some widely canvassed objectives of aid, to which Western governments have committed themselves with varying degrees of firmness, imply completely open-ended commitments. These include the Pearson Commission's proposal for sufficient aid to raise the growth rate of developing countries by one-fifth. Other much publicized aims are the elimination of absolute poverty, in which a billion people are said to live, and the establishment of a guaranteed minimum income everywhere. Their vagueness aside, such objectives mean open-ended commitments, as they cannot be secured from outside but depend on policies, attitudes and conduct in the Third World. The reduction or elimination of international income differences is another widely canvassed objective which implies an open-ended commitment, because while transfers reduce the incomes of the donors, they cannot by themselves raise those of people in the Third World.

Meanwhile, the aid lobbies persistently press Western governments and public for more aid. As already noted, official Western organizations including the OECD urged more American aid to the Third World at the same time as they complained about the size of the American current account deficit. Even if a country gives more aid, the aid lobby is apt to complain that aid has not increased by as much as some other economic magnitude, or is still not as large in absolute terms, or as a percentage of the national income, as it happens to be in some other country. Virtually any change in financial flows has come to be invoked in the advocacy of aid. If private flows to the Third World increase, this is used to advocate more official aid to prevent or arrest a reduction in its share in the total flow. If private flows decline, more aid is urged to offset this decline.

<h1 style="text-align:center">4</h1>

Disregard of the conduct of governments and of political and economic conditions in their countries results in many anomalies. In 1977, the government of Vietnam received over $200 million of Western aid. Substantial aid (including British aid) continued in 1978 and till at least as late as July 1979, long after the Vietnamese government had suppressed practically all private economic activity outside subsistence production, and when it also brutally persecuted millions of its most productive subjects. As a result of these policies, hundreds of thousands of these people had to leave the country. Very large numbers perished in the course of their escape. Most of those who survived descended on other aid-recipient countries, notably Thailand, Malaysia and Indonesia, where they caused much social tension and political embarrassment. In August 1978, when the suppression of private economic activity and large-scale persecution were already in full swing in Vietnam and people were fleeing the country in large numbers, the World Bank announced a $60 million interest-free loan to the government. The disbursement of this loan was subsequently halted, presumably as a result of a public outcry in America.[6]

Notable recent anomalies have included large-scale Western aid to Mrs Gandhi at a time of forcible sterilization of many thousands of people in India; substantial aid to Amin in Uganda; to Mengistu in Ethiopia when the slaughter of large numbers of Ethiopians, both political opponents and ordinary people, was widely reported in reputable Western newspapers; to Mobutu in Zaire during the expulsion of traders indispensable for an exchange economy; and very large-scale aid to Nyerere in Tanzania amidst instances of political executions, and the enforced herding of millions of unwilling people into distant, so-called Socialist villages, themselves often mere sites.[7] More remarkable still is that Western aid continued to be sent to the Pol Pot government of Kampuchea at least as late as 1977, at a time when its atrocities were already known in the West.

In 1978 and 1979 much Western aid went to the repressive dictatorship of Afghanistan, where resistance to the government manifested itself in large-scale civil war. And that government, long after asking America to reduce the size of its embassy, continued to receive substantial aid from the International Development Association, to which the US is much the largest contributor. A paradoxical result of taking for granted the case for aid is that most aid recipients routinely spend heavily on arms to be directed against their own subjects or against other aid recipients. For example, in 1979, substantial additional aid to Tanzania was canvassed to meet the cost of military action against Amin, another aid recipient. Other examples include India and Pakistan, Algeria and Morocco, Ethiopia and Somalia, Kampuchea and Vietnam.

Altogether, the conduct of aid recipients produces an extensive and varied list of obvious anomalies. As we have occasion to note in several different contexts, many aid recipients openly persecute the most productive groups in their countries, maltreatment which frequently extends to expulsion. They almost routinely circumscribe the economic activities of productive groups, especially those of economically effective minorities. Familiar examples include the treatment of the Chinese in South-East Asia and Asians in East Africa. Again, aid-recipient governments generally restrict the inflow of private capital, and also the way it may be deployed. Since a low level of capital is the ostensible rationale of aid, such policies are evidently anomalous. Less familiar but equally anomalous is the practice of aid recipients to give aid to other governments. India, Libya, Turkey, Nigeria and Yugoslavia have been among those who, for political reasons, have passed on some of the aid they received, which they were said to need for their own development or relief of poverty.

British aid to the Seychelles in the late 1970s combined anomaly with a touch of comedy. In 1977 and 1978 aid was of the order of £5 million a year. The Seychelles are a holiday paradise with a total population of about 65,000 people. The official car of the High Commissioner in London was at that time a new Rolls Royce. Such anomalies do not disturb either the flow of aid or its advocacy. When particular policies which might upset aid supporters can no longer be ignored, their mention in the press is apt to be coupled with an insistence that these policies must not stand in the way of aid.[8]

Aid to governments which pursue such policies reflects the view which emerged in the 1960s, that to examine the conduct of the recipients would improperly infringe their sovereignty. This idea has come to be widely accepted by both donors and recipients. In the words of the United Nations Declaration on the Establishment of a New International Economic Order passed at the Sixth Special Session of the General Assembly in 1974:

> Every country has the right to adopt the economic and social system that it deems to be most appropriate for its own development and not to be subjected to discrimination of any kind as a result.

Discrimination here means not to be given Western taxpayers' money. Such an interpretation is not just anomalous. It is perverse, because the policies of recipient governments directly affect the level of incomes and the rate of development in these countries. So it is bizarre to insist that the donors should not question these policies. Yet the Western representatives, including those of Britain and the United States, did not dissent from the Declaration. Thus American and British governments, which habitually examine the conduct of their own state and local authorities to whom they give taxpayers' money, are not permitted to do this with foreign governments to whom they also give their taxpayers' money. For instance, it is a rule of the World Bank that no political strings whatever should be attached to funds which are provided to it and its affiliates, such as the International Development Association (part of the World Bank group and administered by the Bank) which provides grants or extremely soft loans to Third World governments.

It is plainly anomalous to give taxpayers' money to foreign governments without examining, or even questioning, their policies. It also goes counter to what was until not so long ago firmly established constitutional practice in Britain. Until well after the Second World War, it was a recognized principle in the allocation even of modest grants from Britain to colonial governments that the grants had to be confined to governments for whose conduct the Secretary of State for the Colonies was answerable in Parliament to the elected representatives of the taxpayers.

Other anomalies arise from the disregard of economic conditions in the recipient countries. Thus Western aid, including aid from Britain, went to major OPEC countries in the 1960s and 1970s, including among others Bahrain, Iran, Iraq, Kuwait, Libya and even Saudi Arabia. Some of these countries with vast oil reserves and revenues had average incomes much higher than those of several donor countries, and were then often unable to spend their foreign exchange revenues. At the same time some of these governments, including those of Iraq and Libya, expropriated Western assets. Western aid also goes regularly to Third World countries where the local customs and institutions plainly retard or even ensure poverty, a matter to which I shall return later in this chapter. Some specific forms of aid which are currently widely canvassed and extensively practised plainly exacerbate poverty rather than alleviate it and retard development rather than promote it. Their espousal reflects the uncritical approach which pervades the discussion of official resource transfers to the Third World. Commodity agreements and debt cancellation are examples. Commodity agreements are discussed at length in chapter 8. Debt cancellation is conveniently examined here.

The burden of indebtedness of Third World countries is a major plank in the advocacy of official aid. In particular, the proportion of export earnings required to service the debts is a major theme in these discussions. Debt cancellation is widely advocated. It is also freely practised. In 1978, the British government wrote off £1 billion of debts owed to the United Kingdom by Third World governments. In 1974, the American government cancelled $2.2 billion equivalent of rupee debt owed by the Indian government, a debt which was payable in local currency.

In the advocacy of debt cancellation it is rarely made clear that the debts represent real resources which had been supplied to the debtors. Most of the official debts of Third World countries since World War II have resulted from soft loans, often very soft loans, under various aid agreements. Even after large-scale cancellations such as those just noted, much of the remaining debt still represents such soft loans. The burden of servicing these debts has been much reduced by the worldwide inflation of the last decade, and often reduced further as a result of defaults and deferments. The familiar references to the large proportion of export earnings absorbed by the servicing of debts also omit to note that the volume of these earnings depends crucially on domestic policies, especially financial policies. Any difficulty in servicing the debts is clear evidence that the capital was supplied to governments who have wasted resources they received, or who refuse to honour their obligations. Debt cancellation thus favours the incompetent, the improvident and the dishonest. Moreover, the poorest countries and groups (such as nomads and aborigines) do not benefit from debt cancellation, as these countries and groups are largely outside the exchange economy and have no external debts. Many governments whose debts have been cancelled are those of relatively well-off

Third World countries such as, for instance, Turkey, Ghana and several Latin American countries.

While debt cancellation favours governments who have wasted capital or who refuse to honour their commitments, it simultaneously damages the credit standing of those Third World governments who are willing and able to honour their obligations – and thus it also damages the prospects of those best able to use capital productively.

The advocacy of debt cancellation is in any case paradoxical. A standard argument for aid is that the West is unwilling to lend enough money to the Third World. Pressure for debt cancellation implies that the West has lent too much – too much, that is, in relation to the results achieved by the recipients' use of loans.

Some of the current ideas in the advocacy of aid are also rather surprising. It is often suggested that to impose conditions on the recipients would amount to blackmail; as if those who give money are the blackmailers, not those who receive it. It is also commonly advocated that recipient governments should have a large say in the volume and distribution of official aid. This is akin to suggesting that banks should be run by borrowers, or charities by the recipients of alms.

There is one minor exception to the idea that the conduct of aid recipients must not be questioned. It arises when this axiom clashes with other precepts of aid supporters, notably the advocacy of comprehensive planning, or the expropriation of prosperous groups (e.g. of land owners in the name of land reform). Governments pursuing such policies are favoured by aid agencies, while those respecting voluntary arrangements and property rights or freely accepted traditional hierarchies are apt to be castigated. But such discrimination does not offset the anomalies of the aid fetish, and indeed, as we shall see shortly, often even compounds them.

5

The case for aid has come to be taken for granted: nevertheless, arguments in its support are often put forward, primarily for the benefit of audiences not yet regarded as firm supporters. The most familiar arguments are that aid is indispensable for development; that it relieves poverty; that it is an instrument for international redistribution of income; that it is restitution for misconduct; that it serves the interests of the donors; and that it is made necessary by the unprecedented population growth in the Third World, which it will help to control: to put it more succinctly, development, poverty, redistribution, restitution, self interest and population growth. These arguments are mere rationalizations which shift with the vagaries of intellectual and political fashion. Thus restitution did not figure much in the 1950s, when the white man's guilt had not yet become accepted dogma in the West. Again, when addressing conservative audiences, aid advocates say that aid is an instrument of political and military strategy; when addressing egalitarians, they emphasize poverty and redistribution; and when addressing businessmen and trade unionists they say that aid maintains exports and employment. The practice of major shifts in these rationalizations has come to be known as changing emphasis.

It is these frequent shifts which make it so difficult to examine the case for aid systematically and in manageable form. Yet the arguments must nevertheless be examined at length. While assessment of a policy is inevitably affected by value judgments, arguments adduced in its support can be examined conclusively on the basis of logic and evidence. The arguments are also of interest because they are influentially canvassed, often by prominent academics: they can, therefore, inform us about the intellectual climate. Finally, even though the case for aid is taken for granted, the rationalizations often affect the conduct both of donors and of recipients, and the volume and direction of aid. They are therefore pertinent to policy.

6

In the early stage of foreign aid, preoccupation with growth, and the belief that it depended on investment, were the order of the day. Then the prime argument for aid was that it was indispensable because the incomes of underdeveloped countries were too low for the investment required to achieve higher incomes. This argument was popularized as the vicious circle of poverty. But it is plainly untrue that poverty is self-perpetuating, that poor persons and societies cannot emerge from it without external alms.[9] If it were true, countless individuals, groups and societies both in the West and elsewhere could never have emerged from poverty as they did. Indeed, since the world is a closed system, development could never have sprung up from the once-universal ur-poverty. The means by which people and societies do escape from poverty differ in time and place. Even poor individuals and societies can generate capital, and indeed have often done so. They have, for instance, sacrificed leisure for work, including the clearing and improvement of land. In many once-poor areas, people have transferred labour and land to more productive uses, often replacing subsistence production with cash crops. Again, initially penniless traders have often accumulated capital in the process

98

of opening up local markets, and have thereby also made new opportunities available to the people there.

Nor does material progress depend on large investible funds. The establishment and improvement of agricultural properties, the building up of small traders' inventories, or the establishment of workshops and small factories requires little finance. Conversely, some of the most expensive types of capital formation, especially buildings, are more akin to durable consumer goods than to instruments or production. Capital formation is indeed a very small factor in long term development. Professor Kuznets has estimated that increase in physical capital and in labour together accounted for less than one-tenth of long term growth in the West over the last two centuries. Moreover, investible funds are by no means always embodied in productive capital.

The West began poor and progressed without external aid. And large areas of the present Third World progressed rapidly long before foreign aid, as for instance much of South-East Asia, West Africa and Latin America. Moreover, Western societies progressed in conditions far more difficult than those facing the Third World, which can draw on huge external markets, on external capital markets, on a vast range of technology and on diverse skills unavailable before. Plainly, official aid is not indispensable for progress. Even if a society were caught in a vicious circle of poverty, this could not be broken by aid, for reasons examined later in this section and also in section 16 below.[10] All this underlines the point that having money is the result of economic achievement, not its precondition. The notion of the vicious circle of poverty confuses poverty with its causes: a low income is poverty, not its cause.

According to a variant of the argument, aid is required because external payments difficulties are inherent in the early stages of development. Indeed it has even been argued that absence of payments deficits reflects governmental neglect of development.[11] Yet payments difficulties cannot possibly be necessary concomitants of development. All Western countries, and many Third World countries, progressed rapidly without experiencing them. On the other hand, both rich and poor countries encounter such difficulties when governments promote monetary demand in excess of available resources or, in the popular phrase, live beyond their means.

It is sometimes urged that while the West could advance without alms, the Third World cannot do so because the pre-conditions for development are now much less favourable than they were in the past. But as we have already seen, external conditions are now much more favourable to the material progress of poor areas than they were formerly, which helps to explain the rapid advance of many poor countries over the last hundred years or so.

In so far as development prospects of many Third World countries are unfavourable, this has nothing to do with external factors. Economic achievement depends on people's attributes, attitudes, motivations, mores and political arrangements. In many countries the prevailing personal, social and political determinants are uncongenial to material progress: witness the preference for a contemplative life, opposition to paid work by women and widespread torpor and fatalism in certain countries. Moreover, policies of many Third World governments are plainly damaging to economic achievement.

The argument that aid is indispensable for development runs into an inescapable dilemma. If the conditions for development other than capital are present, the capital required will either be generated locally or be available commercially from abroad to governments or to businesses. If the required conditions are not present, then aid will be ineffective and wasted. Foreign alms do not enrich the personal, social and political factors which are decisive for economic development. There is not a single instance in history when external donations were required for the economic development of a country. The Marshall Plan for Western Europe after 1945 was no exception, as we shall see in section 15 of this chapter.[12]

The argument that external subsidies are not necessary for economic achievement, and that they generally do not secure it, is not invalidated by such bonanzas as the discovery of precious metals, or their acquisition by conquest, or the success of the OPEC cartel. These are windfalls which accident or the play of political forces has conferred on the owners or controllers of potentially valuable resources. By themselves, such occurrences have not hitherto led to sustained development.

It might be argued that while aid is not indispensable for progress, it is required to accelerate what would otherwise be very slow progress. This contention differs substantially from the widely canvassed vicious circle, but it is still invalid. Official aid played no part in the progress of the West, nor in the very rapid progress of many Third World countries since the closing decades of the nineteenth century. It is patronizing to suggest that the peoples of the Third World crave for material progress, but unlike people in the West, they cannot progress at a reasonable rate without external donations. This condescension is misplaced.

7

Even though foreign aid can alleviate immediate shortages, it cannot appreciably promote the growth of the national income. It is more likely to retard this growth. Countries where government or business can use funds productively can borrow abroad. The maximum contribution of foreign aid to development in the sense of the growth of the national income cannot therefore exceed the avoided cost of borrowing. As a percentage of the national income of large Third World countries this maximum contribution is at best minute, a fraction of 1%, far too small to register in the statistics.

An example may help here. According to the official statistics external aid to India in the late 1970s was around 3% of GNP. If the cost of capital is put as high as 20% per annum, then the avoided cost of borrowing in this case is 0.6% of the officially estimated GNP, provided that aid is a free and untied grant. It is less because some aid is tied and some of it is repayable. The maximum contribution to development turns out to be even smaller when it is remembered that the actual GNP of a country like India much exceeds (probably by a factor of about three) the official estimate when expressed on a basis comparable to that of the United States.[13]

Even if aid is used productively, the maximum benefit to development cannot exceed the avoided cost of obtaining capital by borrowing. And aid is most unlikely to be productive. That it is likely to be unproductive is evident when its declared objective is redistribution, relief of poverty or some other purpose unrelated to development. But the productivity of aid is likely to be low even when development is the declared objective. Aid is not expected to yield a commercial return, and its use, unlike commercially supplied capital, is therefore not adjusted to market circumstances or to general local conditions. Official gifts and loans can be written off at no cost to aid administrators whose fortunes do not depend on the productive use of the funds supplied but primarily on the amount of spending they advocate and administer. Aid therefore need not be deployed productively, and often is not so deployed.

Moreover, as has been noted, when investible funds are highly productive they will be generated locally or will be available from abroad on commercial terms to governments or business enterprises. Further, development does not depend on large investment spending. Much spending conventionally classified as investment is in any case not intended to promote development, including categories of investment which absorb substantial monetary savings, such as housing or some forms of public investment. Again, much spending undertaken or directed by government and termed investment does not represent capital formation on any sensible interpretation, but is merely spending on various activities and projects deemed useful to the government and its agents. And aid brings about a host of repercussions which adversely affect the basic determinants of development and are likely far to outweigh any benefit from aid. This major matter is the subject of the next section.

These considerations would apply even if aid flows were much larger than at present. Indeed, the adverse repercussions in particular would be intensified. And the temptation would be stronger to allocate aid receipts to expenditures contributing little or nothing to economic development.

However productive the use of aid may be in a particular instance, its contribution to development can never exceed the avoided cost of borrowing the investible funds. Of course, the cost of borrowing would be lower where the probable or intended uses of the investible funds were seen to be productive and the borrowing government had a good record in economic policy and debt servicing. Again, the need to service loans would discourage wasteful or less productive use of funds, so that a given volume of funds can be expected to be more productive when borrowed commercially than when received as aid. It is often argued that Third World governments cannot borrow abroad for risky projects, or for projects whose return is distant or whose benefits diffuse. But in these conditions governments can still borrow from abroad because they are able to service the capital from their tax revenues.

The conclusion that even in the most favourable circumstances the contribution of aid to Third World development cannot be significant follows from evidence, from inference about the availability of capital where it can be used productively, and from the pertinent magnitudes, that is, the avoided cost of capital and the amount of aid as percentage of the national income. In view of the adverse repercussions of aid (section 8), the presumption must be that official aid is more likely to retard development than to promote it.

This adverse presumption is supported by evidence of various kinds. Thus the difficulties of many Third World governments to service even very soft loans suggests that the capital has not been used productively because it has not raised incomes and taxable capacity. If, on the other hand, the governments could service these loans but refuse to do so, this response would reveal attitudes clearly harmful to development on the part of the recipients.

The adverse presumption is strengthened by the conditions in many recipient countries after decades of aid, including very low living standards, recurrent famine, and breakdown of the exchange economy and of public security and health (sometimes aptly termed disdevelopment). It is supported also by the distinct shift in the advocacy of aid from development to other objectives.

It is often thought that the effects of aid could be established from statistical evidence with the help of statistical analysis. This is not so. As it happens, the statistical evidence is conflicting. Some studies have found significant correlation between aid received and the growth of the national income.[14]

Others, including those of the Pearson Commission, have found no such correlation.[15]

But even if there were a consistently high correlation between aid and development (which there is not), this would show at most that capital could be used productively in the recipient countries. (At most, because it is impossible to isolate the effects of the inflow of investible funds from the many other factors which affect development, all of which operate with different time lags; and also because of the very wide margins of error in the statistics of Third World incomes, which are neither uniform for all countries nor stable over time.) Even if it were established (which is in practice impossible) that aid funds over a period proved highly productive in their overall effects, the maximum contribution of aid would still be restricted to the avoided cost of borrowing as the funds could have been obtained commercially from abroad. Thus the statistical exercises at times undertaken to establish the contribution of aid to development are beside the point.

8

As we have seen, the contribution of aid to Third World development cannot be more than extremely small. And aid is not manna from heaven: its receipt sets up major adverse effects which can be expected to exceed by far the necessarily very small beneficial effects.

It may seem paradoxical that a flow of aid resources which cannot do much good is nevertheless likely to do much harm. But the paradox can be readily resolved. On two grounds the possible benefits of aid and its adverse effects are asymmetrical. First, the maximum possible benefits are modest and result from a reduction in the cost of investible funds, the volume of which is not a major factor in economic development. The basic determinants are personal, social and political. Second, the adverse effects are brought about by amounts of aid which, while small in relation to the national income, are nevertheless large compared with government revenues or foreign exchange earnings in the recipient countries. These are the relevant magnitudes, because aid goes to governments and increases the resources and foreign exchange at their disposal. And it is largely government policies, backed by these resources, which are responsible for the unfavourable repercussions by operating adversely on the basic personal, social and political determinants of economic achievement. Indeed, the adverse repercussions not only retard development but often bring about acute and massive hardship.

Since official wealth transfers go to governments and not to the people at large, they promote the disastrous politicization of life in the Third World.

The tendency towards politicization operates even in the absence of these transfers, but is much buttressed and intensified by them. Aid increases the power, resources and patronage of governments compared with the rest of society and therefore their power over it.

Foreign aid has thus done much to politicize life in the Third World. And when social and economic life is extensively politicized, who has the power becomes supremely important, sometimes a matter of life and death – witness Burundi, Kampuchea, Ethiopia, Indonesia, Iraq, Nigeria, Pakistan, Tanzania, Uganda, Vietnam and Zaire among countries whose governments have received substantial Western aid. In such conditions, people at large, especially those who are alert or ambitious, become much concerned with what happens in politics and in public administration, as decisions taken there come crucially to affect their livelihood and even threaten their physical destruction. People divert their resources and attention from productive economic activity into other areas, such as trying to forecast political developments, placating or bribing politicians and civil servants, operating or evading controls. They are induced or even forced into these activities in order either to protect themselves from the all-important decisions of the rulers or, where possible, to benefit from them. This direction of people's activities and resources must damage the economic performance and development of a society, since these depend crucially on the deployment of people's human, financial and physical resources.

These conditions provoke political tension and centrifugal forces, particularly in the multiracial or multitribal societies of the Third World. The tensions, the centrifugal forces and the attempts to suppress them lead to conflict, and even to large-scale civil war. Such sequences have occurred in recent years in a number of Third World countries, including some where such conflicts had been unimportant before. The tensions and conflicts of politicization of life create a climate which encourages inhuman policies, sometimes including large-scale expulsion or even massacre, tolerated, encouraged or perpetrated by the rulers. By helping to politicize life, aid has contributed to such policies and results. It has also facilitated these policies by enabling governments for a time to conceal from their own people some of the worst economic results, and also by conferring respectability on these governments by suggesting external endorsement of their activities.

As we have insisted, official aid is the common characteristic and unifying bond of the Third World. But for the reasons just noted, these official transfers so far from promoting amity provoke and exacerbate domestic political conflict. The same applies also and often between countries because of conflict over the sharing of these transfers. This latter result is likely to be especially

104

pronounced where the transfers are regarded as instruments of egalitarianism.

The tendency of aid to politicize life, and the results of this politicization, have both been reinforced by the inclination of official aid agencies to favour governments trying to establish state-controlled or state-dominated economies.

Since the early 1950s, the mainstream official and academic literature on development and aid has insisted that extensive state planning of Third World economies is helpful or even indispensable for development. This notion has become dogma in influential groups within international organizations and aid agencies. Since the 1960s, the need to promote economic equality in the Third World has also come to be widely adduced in support of closely controlled economies. Development and equality are the principal arguments for replacing the market system in the Third World by comprehensive state controls and by largely socialized economies (at any rate, in sectors outside subsistence production). This bias against the market is rife in the mainstream development literature, in the international organizations and in the aid agencies.

The establishment of state-controlled economies is clearly not necessary for economic development. It is indeed much more likely to obstruct development, especially a rise in living standards. The conclusion is evident, both on a little reflection and from the historical experience of the West, the Communist bloc and the Third World.

The adverse results are particularly pronounced in the Third World. State economic controls usually reduce domestic mobility and also the volume, variety and local dispersion of external commercial contacts. Domestic mobility and external contacts, especially the latter, are potent instruments of economic advance in emerging economies. For instance, by suggesting new wants, crops and methods of production to the local population, they bring about uncoerced erosion of attitudes, mores and modes of conduct uncongenial to material advance. In these and other ways external contacts in particular promote the modernization of the mind necessary for sustained economic advance. Reduction of mobility and restriction of external contacts are correspondingly damaging to economic development.

The policies of the governments of state-controlled economies in the Third World are not designed to promote development, or to reduce income differences or improve the lot of the poor. This is evident from such widely pursued policies as the penal taxation of small farmers by state export monopolies, extensive official support of uneconomic activities, large-scale spending on show projects, suppression of private economic activity especially trade, forcible collectivization of farming, restriction on the inflow of capital, and persecution of both rich and poor members of unpopular groups such as Tamils in Sri Lanka, Asians in East Africa and Ibo in Nigeria. Such policies impair actual and prospective living standards of ordinary people and bear especially harshly on the poor. They are extensively supported or even made possible by official aid.

Third World rulers use economic controls primarily to promote their own political and financial purposes, including the undermining or destroying of opponents and rewarding of supporters. Such use of state economic controls is taken for granted practically throughout the Third World. Development and equality are mere rationalizations for state controls, introduced for purposes other than the declared objectives. The rationalizations have enhanced the plausibility of granting large-scale aid to governments attempting to run state-controlled economies, or even fully socialized economies. For instance, President Nyerere received very large amounts of Western aid, especially from the World Bank, amidst extensive socialization, forced mass migration and large-scale confiscation. Not surprisingly, these policies have much impaired economic development there, notably food production.[16]

Indeed, Tanzania under President Nyerere has been described in the Western press, probably correctly, as Mr McNamara's favourite African country; and the aid to Tanzania under Nyerere has also been termed by sympathetic observers, and again rightly so, as indispensable for the survival of his government. Many Third World governments could not operate their numerous and far-reaching economic controls without foreign help, including personnel financed by aid.

Official aid retards development in many other ways, some of which will be considered briefly and one at greater length. As already mentioned many, perhaps most, aid recipients much curtail the inflow and deployment of private capital. Foreign capital is usually banned from a wide range of activities. It is further restricted in others by limiting the percentage of capital in an enterprise which can be owned by foreigners, or even by certain locally resident and distinct ethnic groups; for example, Chinese, Indians or Europeans in South-East Asia, and Asians or Europeans in Africa. Such restrictions are anomalous, even perverse, in terms of such commonly declared objectives of aid as economic development and the relief of poverty or unemployment. They are perverse because shortage of development capital is often the basic argument advanced for aid.

These restrictions must obstruct economic development. They immediately reduce the available amount of productive capital. Moreover, the inflow of productive capital extends external economic contacts generally and introduces new ideas, methods and attitudes which promote material progress. The adverse effects of restricting the inflow of capital extend far beyond the immediate result of diminishing its supply. The main purpose of these policies is to strengthen the control of governments over their subjects. Aid makes such restrictions politically easier by suggesting that it is more advantageous to rely on subsidized funds from abroad.

Official aid encourages unsuitable external prototypes such as Western forms of industry, even where these are quite inappropriate (e.g. national airlines and steel works in Africa). Such models are wasteful. They also often lead to political and social tension. And even hopelessly wasteful projects, which have to be subsidized from local resources, are often continued for political reasons long after it has become clear that they represent a drain on the local economy.[17] Developments of this kind are particularly likely where aid takes the form of supplies of specific equipment or plant rather than generalized purchasing power. On the other hand, another form of specific aid distorts relative prices in the recipient economy and so discourages particular activities. Aid in the form of free supplies of food has had this effect in India and elsewhere, and has discouraged local food production.

Insistence on the need for external donations obscures the necessity for the people of the Third World themselves to develop the faculties and to adopt the attitudes and conduct required for sustained material progress – that is, if they want higher incomes sufficiently to give up their established ways. The proviso is both important and necessary. Many people may reasonably prefer to retain their traditional attitudes, modes of conduct and institutions, and to remain poor. They may welcome the good things of life but may consider the cost too heavy.

In a subtle way, aid tends to perpetuate ideas and modes of conduct adverse to material progress. For instance, advocacy and inflow of aid lends support to the idea that improvement in one's fortunes depends on other people, the government, the rich, one's superiors, or foreigners. Here again aid pauperizes the recipients. They are encouraged to expect success without achievement, to believe that material reward depends on windfalls, and to want the results of economic success without the antecedent process. Aid promotes the delusion that a society can progress from indigence to prosperity without the intermediate stage of economic effort and achievement. Moreover, the particular argument much canvassed in the Third World, that aid is restitution for exploitation, spills over into domestic discussion where it affects attitudes as well as policies.

It has often been observed that rapid discontinuous change has unsettling effects on people in the Third World. Hostile reactions to rapid change vary from sullen apathy to violent rejection of further change.[18]

Official aid is much more likely to set up acute strains than do commercial contacts. The latter are usually more closely geared to local conditions, conduct and resources. This is so because in commercial activity economic return depends on correct assessment of local conditions, including local customs, susceptibilities and hierarchies. Those who direct taxpayers' funds from far away are under no such constraint. Moreover, the disturbing effect of Western commerce is partial, gradual, tentative and almost casual. For example, in the late nineteenth and early twentieth centuries, commercial contacts pervasively transformed South-East Asia and West Africa. For West Africa, the extent of the transformation was epitomized by McPhee[19] as a super-imposition of the twentieth century AD on the twentieth century BC. Yet the far-reaching changes engendered by commercial contacts did not bring about such violent responses as those evoked by the attempted forced modernization in Iran.

When rulers attempt forcibly to transform a society, many people will be lost between two cultures. In such circumstances, they are directed neither by traditional rules nor by Western incentives, and may well decline into an apathetic, inert mass. They may be capable of violent political action, but are less able to benefit from economic opportunities than they had been before the attempted transformation. Such an outcome is probable, especially when people come to believe that their prosperity depends on political development rather than their own economic exertions. In many Third World countries, notably Ghana, ordinary people now seem less interested in or able to utilize non-political economic opportunities than a generation ago. It has incidentally been suggested that such a response to coercive modernization is also observable outside the Third World, notably in the rural areas of the Soviet Union.

Such sequences and effects are especially likely because aid places resources in the hands of new rulers who see established customs and traditional hierarchies as an obstacle to their authority. They therefore wish to undermine or even destroy modes of life and traditional hierarchies hitherto freely accepted by the population.[20] Thus former President Obote of Uganda overthrew the popular Kabaka with a large force of tanks amidst much bloodshed. Aid resources are at the disposal of the local representatives of the new, centralizing, Westernized bureaucracy. They serve to undermine social structures and accelerate the disintegration of traditional society, with results of the kind just noted (except when the interests of the new and traditional rulers are politically linked, usually in a fortuitous and unstable alliance).

Finally, some more strictly financial repercussions of official transfers are also damaging. The inflow of aid tends to raise the exchange rate, to support overvalued exchange rates or to increase domestic money supply. These effects depend on the financial policies of the recipients, but aid tends to bring them about.[21] To the extent that it does so, it damages the international competitive position of the recipients. If aid increases the real productivity of resources, as the inflow of commercial capital does normally, this damage can be offset. But such an offsetting effect is most unlikely since aid is not linked to increases in productivity. When aid increases money supply in recipient countries, it reinforces inflationary tendencies there.

Balance of payments deficits are a useful argument both for requesting external assistance and for imposing domestic controls. Governments favour such controls for various reasons, notably because they extend the power of politicians and civil servants and also because in many Third World countries they provide excellent opportunities for making money. Balance of payments deficits are especially effective as arguments for aid when they accompany policies such as extensive state economic control, which are regarded by aid agencies as evidence of laudable efforts to speed up progress. Official aid thus does not constrain governments from pursuing inflationary policies and from running down their reserves. Inflation, payments difficulties and exchange and price controls engender insecurity, or even a crisis atmosphere. Such a sequence inhibits domestic saving and productive investment and induces a flight of capital. All this then serves as argument both for further controls and for more aid.

The inflationary effects noted here are on top of any such effects in donor countries which may be brought about by official aid, especially multilateral aid (which is more likely to be inflationary).[22] Inflation in the Third World, however it originates, exacerbates social and political tension and promotes politicization of life.

9

The discussion in sections 6–8 suggests strongly that aid cannot significantly promote development and is more likely to retard or obstruct it. The presumption is that aid is more likely to be prejudicial than beneficial to economic improvement. There are three familiar objections to this strong presumption.

First, aid advocates often refer to the results of some statistical enquiries which suggest a significant correlation between aid and the development of the recipient countries. In fact, the statistical evidence is conflicting. More important, it is altogether irrelevant for the reasons set out in section 6 above.

Second, aid advocates often cite the success of particular projects financed by aid. Assessment of the economic productivity of such projects requires systematic examination of their costs and benefits, notably including the cost of capital over the life of the project. There have been few such methodical assessments. And if a project is genuinely viable it could be financed commercially, so that the contribution of aid is again limited to the avoided cost of borrowing. Moreover, the outcome of one project says nothing about the overall effects of aid on the economy, including the repercussions of aid discussed above.

Third, the success of the Marshall Plan is a recurrent theme in the advocacy of aid. But the Marshall Plan is irrelevant to the case for Third World aid. The peoples of Western Europe had the faculties, motivations and institutions favourable to development for centuries before the Second World War: rebuilding, not development, was the task after the war. Hence the rapid return to prosperity in Western Europe and the termination of Marshall aid after four years, in contrast to the economic plight of many aid recipients after decades of aid, and their failure to repay loans obtained on favourable terms; and in contrast also to the proposals for indefinite continuation of official aid.

It is also of interest that over the few years of the Marshall Plan, West Germany had to absorb millions of refugees, among whom there were disproportionate numbers of old people and children, as well as to pay substantial reparations to the Soviet Union. Yet soon after the end of the Marshall Plan, West Germany was already a prosperous country, a substantial exporter of capital and a major donor of aid. Western Europe would have recovered without the Marshall Plan, though somewhat less rapidly.

10

Relief of poverty has always been a major theme in the advocacy of official aid, though the emphasis on it has varied considerably. For instance, in recent years aid advocates have come to emphasize poverty rather than development – witness the title of the report of the British Ministry of Overseas Development published in 1975: *Overseas Development: The Changing Emphasis in British Aid Policies: More Help for the Poorest* (Cmnd. 6270).

Many supporters of aid are apt to think of official aid as akin to voluntary charity. This analogy is altogether unwarranted. And while relief of poverty appears as an irreproachable, unambiguous and perhaps even simple objective of aid, it becomes evident on a little examination that the pursuit of this aim is shot through with anomalies and contradictions.

Official aid does not go to poor people, to the skeletal figures of aid propaganda. It goes instead to their rulers whose spending policies are determined by their own personal and political interests, among which the position of the poorest has very low priority. Indeed, to support rulers on the basis of the poverty of their subjects is more likely to encourage policies of impoverishment than to deter them. The familiar references of 'aid to the poorest', to describe transfers to governments of countries with very low incomes, confuses rulers with their subjects. This practice is but one instance of the familiar tendency to equate the government with the population, itself an example of treating an aggregate as if it were a single decision-making unit, or one the components of which have identical interests.

Even if aid should reach the declared beneficiaries – that is, the poor of the Third World as distinct from the governments – it would do so through a long chain of intermediaries with heavy service charges deducted.

The pattern of spending by aid-recipient governments is unrelated to help for the poor. This spending often aggravates the position of the poor, since recipient governments often spend heavily on politically inspired prestige projects made possible by external aid: airlines, inefficient industries, Western-type universities whose graduates cannot find jobs, and the creation of new capitals at vast cost (Brasilia, Islamabad, Dodoma in Tanzania and Lilongwe in Malawi). These often have to be subsidized by local taxes, including those on the poor. When demanding aid from the West, Third World governments emphasize the poverty of their people, whose condition is a major plank in aid advocacy. But the policies of most Third World governments are not designed to relieve poverty. The poor, particularly the rural poor who are the great majority, are politically ineffective and thus of little interest to the rulers. In fact in many, perhaps most, Third World countries, organized state relief of poverty does not accord with local mores, and no machinery exists for this purpose. Again, the most indigent groups in the Third World are largely outside the orbit of aid, as, for instance, the many millions of aborigines, pygmies and desert people. These latter groups are largely ignored in the literature of aid and development, perhaps because they do not include articulate, Westernized people who have contacts with the international organizations, or with Western academics and the media.

Much aid-supported state spending in the Third World benefits the more articulate, educated, skilled, enterprising and, above all, the politically influential groups, who are usually urbanized and at least partly Westernized people. Politicians, civil servants, academics, urban businessmen, and at times the military, are prominent direct or indirect beneficiaries. Moreover, as we shall see in chapter 8, some categories of official aid such as commodity agreements benefit the relatively well-off, and often directly harm the poor. There are many prosperous people in aid-recipient countries, especially in the government sector and in other activities related to it. Their presence in countries where there is much abject poverty shows that the rulers while demanding external donations are not much interested either in domestic redistribution or in the lot of the poorest. These realities are obscured by the use of statistics of per capita incomes, that is of average incomes. The adoption of low per capita income as a criterion for aid also leads to major anomalies. Many aid-recipient rulers have pursued policies which promptly reduce per capita incomes in their countries and simultaneously aggravate the lot of the poorest. Thus many have persecuted or expelled large numbers of people for political or racial reasons, or suppressed or constrained their activities. Such policies have been pursued through the length and breadth of Asia and Africa, in countries ranging alphabetically from Afghanistan to Zambia and geographically from North Africa to the Far East. In many of these countries, relatively enterprising and prosperous groups have been disproportionately represented among the immediate victims: for example, the Chinese in South-East Asia; Indians in Burma; Armenians, Greeks and Jews in the Middle East; Asians in East and Central Africa; Levantines in Central Africa and West Africa; Ibo in Nigeria, and Europeans in many countries. Because these groups are relatively prosperous and are also prime agents of economic advance, such policies reduce per capita income and also its growth in these countries, most obviously when people are expelled or killed. The suppression of private trade has closely similar results. Many people are forced to remain in subsistence production, or to revert to it, instead of producing for sale. This outcome deprives the population of skills, consumer goods and markets for cash crops, and causes shortages and even famine. Although the most immediate victims tend to be relatively prosperous, the policies bear harshly on the poor, especially in the countryside. Again, practically all aid-recipient governments restrict the inflow and deployment of private capital, a policy which both keeps down per capita incomes and aggravates the lot of the poor.

On the criterion of the poverty of their subjects, governments pursuing damaging policies such as those just listed nevertheless qualify for more aid. This criterion for giving aid in no way penalizes governments which pursue policies leading to the impoverishment of the mass of their subjects. As already noted, official aid has also often contributed to political tension and conflict and thereby aggravated the condition of the poorest groups.

Per capita income as a criterion of aid involves further anomalies. If more of the poor died, say, as a result of disease, this would bring about higher per capita incomes and provide an evidently perverse reason for reducing aid. Again, the meaning of riches and poverty depends crucially on people's requirements and thus on physical and social living conditions. This is obvious for physical conditions, notably climate. But it applies also to social conditions, including customs and values. If as a result of a change in mores women come to be discouraged from taking paid work, this would register as a fall in income, even though this would not indicate impoverishment as commonly understood, nor should it serve as an appropriate ground for more aid. All this is apart from the very wide margins of error in estimates of per capita incomes in the Third World. The arguments and examples in this section again show clearly that poverty and changes and differences in income cannot be sensibly discussed without taking cognizance of their antecedents and their backgrounds.

11

Attempts to avoid some of the major anomalies noted in the preceding section by trying to give official aid directly to the poorest, or by prescribing the policies of the recipient governments, would be resisted and sabotaged by Third World governments. If this resistance could be overcome, other intractable problems would arise.

The poorest, whether entire societies or the poorest groups within one society, are unlikely to possess the aptitudes and motivations for economic achievement to the same extent as those who are more prosperous, which is why relief of poverty and promotion of development differ radically as objectives, or indeed are largely at variance. They differ in much the same way as alms to a beggar differ from scholarships to promising students, or as assistance to an invalid differs from loans to young people to establish themselves in business.

The poorest groups in Third World countries tend to be materially unambitious. Official handouts to improve their economic conditions will have to be continued indefinitely if the beneficiaries are not to relapse into their original poverty. Poor people can therefore be turned into paupers. Whole societies can be pauperized in this way. The Navajo Indians, heavily subsidized by the United States government for many decades, are a familiar example. A less familiar but informative and pertinent recent example is that of the large-scale pauperization in the United States trust territory of Micronesia in the Pacific, described in a lively and first-hand report in the

Washington Post, 27 July 1978. This report is so vivid and convincing that it is worth quoting at some length. After referring to the familiar saying about the difference between the results of giving a man a fish (which feeds him for a day) or teaching him how to fish (which feeds him for life), a local politician is quoted as saying that United States policy was to give people a fish a day. The report goes on:

> US trusteeship in Micronesia has created a society dependent on government jobs and benefits, an island welfare state whose people are so inundated with handouts that they are abandoning even those elemental enterprises – fishing and farming – that they had developed before the Americans came.
>
> 'We've smothered them', said a veteran US administrator with the trust territory government, 'and it will take them a long time to come out from under this blanket. . . .'
>
> 'Any kind of work here is very hard work', said Elizabeth Uduim, an economist with the trust government. 'And now you can live here without working. . . .'
>
> The US administration is universally blamed for the islanders' dependency, even by current administrators. The only argument is over whether the United States deliberately conspired to promote it or merely bungled in its humanitarian zeal. . . .
>
> The Kennedy administration poured in funds for education, health, and welfare. Since then, annual appropriations for Micronesia have risen from about $5 million to about $100 million, and $30 million more is given yearly to the inhabitants on categorical programs such as food, special education and direct welfare.

The report also suggests that United Nations pressure had contributed to this policy of pauperization.

Intervention by the donors to avert pauperization by instilling in the recipients the requirements for economic achievement is not feasible. In many societies of the Third World such attempts would require wholesale reform of local beliefs and values, including some of those most deeply felt. Such attempts would involve far-reaching coercion of the supposed beneficiaries. These realities are obscured in such ambiguous phrases as the need to modernize agriculture or to reform institutions. But what the proponents of such objectives envisage is not so much the reform and modernization of a sector or of an activity, but of the people engaged in them; not so much of beliefs and values, but of those who hold them; and not so much of institutions, but of those who participate in them. What is to be transformed is people, meaning persons and groups of persons, not abstract entities such as activities, sectors or institutions.[23]

Many aid-recipient governments, as well as their populations at large, would refuse aid if receiving it involved coercive transformation of people and their *transport then into free world Indians, Nigerians, etc.*

values and attitudes. And such policies are much more likely to aggravate poverty than to relieve it, because they would set up determined resistance which could be overcome, if at all, only at the cost of turning the population into an apathetic mass incapable of effort and enterprise. It is therefore just as well that, in practice, official aid stops short of such drastic attempts purporting to relieve poverty.

These considerations also show how inappropriate it is to judge material conditions the world over by present-day Western middle-class criteria. The attitudes, values and beliefs which keep many people poor are often an integral part of their lives. They often also give meaning to their lives, so that attempts forcibly to eradicate them could lead to spiritual collapse. People's desire for children, often for large families, is an example.[24] The sanctity of the cow in rural India is another. The results of an enforced change cannot be gauged sensibly in terms of the values of a totally different culture.

It is now commonly asserted that conditions in much of the Third World are so desperate that life is barely tolerable, and that a worthwhile culture cannot be developed or sustained. People, it is said, have a basic need for such facilities as safe water and universal primary education, and a basic right to have this need satisfied. It is said further that the Third World has a moral right to have these facilities provided by the West. Yet on this reasoning, the world's population until recently was everywhere deprived of the satisfaction of these basic needs (and of its supposed basic human right in this sense), because the West itself did not have these facilities until they were created in the nineteenth century.

In most Third World countries economic conditions, including the lot of the poorest, have much improved in the twentieth century, especially since the Second World War. They may be expected to improve further, but such improvement would not by itself remove wretchedness. Ever since President Truman's Point Four programme, the advocates of aid have equated poverty with wretchedness. This equation is misleading, since wretchedness and contentment are not simply matters of income or income differences, even within a single society. This is much more evident globally. If there is a sensible and objective measure of wretchedness of life felt by the people who experience it rather than as envisaged by outside observers, it is the suicide rate. This is much higher in the West than it is in the Third World. Thus, if wretchedness were the appropriate basis of wealth transfers, as many people believe it to be, the transfers should be from the Third World to the West, as this would at least enable the wretched to become even more comfortable. This exposure of the confusion between poverty and wretchedness may appear merely flippant. But as we shall see when we come to consider official aid in support of sterilization programmes, the confusion can have serious consequences.

Even if official aid helped the poorest, which it clearly does not, its operation would still differ radically from the discharge of a moral duty, a claim so often invoked on its behalf. Foreign aid is Western taxpayers' money. Its advocates do not give away their money, but demand taxes on others. The donors are the taxpayers, who are forced to pay whether they like it nor not, and often do not even know that they pay for aid let alone how much.

12

World income redistribution, implicit in aid advocacy from its inception, has become much more prominent since the upsurge of articulate egalitarianism in the 1960s. Major implications of redistribution, and the far-reaching consequences of political egalitarianism, stand out in especially clear relief in global redistribution. World income redistribution and relief of poverty are quite different as objectives of aid. Indeed, they are largely inconsistent because redistribution reduces global productivity of resources, and is therefore likely to inhibit development and alleviation of poverty. But the same assumptions and arguments are often behind them, so that to examine the advocacy of these two objectives means inevitably going over the same ground twice. There is therefore some unavoidable overlap between this section and the one immediately preceding.

What is called world income is a statistical aggregate of the estimates of countless incomes produced in widely different physical and social environments in the numerous societies of the world. International redistribution means that part of the income of taxpayers in the developed countries is confiscated, and transferred to those who administer and dispense these funds in the West, in the international organizations and in the Third World.

International wealth transfers are now widely regarded as an appropriate extension of progressive taxation.[25] But unlike progressive taxation, aid, a transaction between governments, is in no way adjusted to the personal and family circumstances of donors and recipients. Even in progressive taxation within a country this adjustment is often imperfect, for reasons such as the neglect of the manifold and widely differing costs and sacrifices in preparing for a career, or the largely arbitrary element in distinguishing between income and the cost of earning it. In official aid there is no adjustment at all for the widely differing conditions of the payers (being the taxpayers in the donor countries) or of the various recipients and beneficiaries of the transfers. Many taxpayers in donor countries are far poorer than many people in Third World countries where, moreover, aid often benefits the prosperous rather than the needy, and where the governments who demand international redistribution do not practise it at home.

To assume that to give money to the government of a poor country leads to a more equal international distribution of income is to treat the government as if it were the same as the country, or the society. In the context of redistribution it is particularly misleading to treat a collectivity as if it were a single person or decision-making unit, or as if the interests, circumstances and inclinations of its constituents were the same.

The advocacy of redistribution clearly implies a basic similarity of requirements between those affected by it. But on a global level there is not even the semblance of such a similarity. People in the Caribbean area require fewer clothes and less fuel than people in Canada. Hence international comparisons of conventionally measured incomes are abstract to the point of being meaningless.

Nor is this so only because of differences in physical conditions. In what order would we rank the headman of a New Guinea tribe of head hunters, a British labourer and a Buddhist priest in Thailand who depends for his survival on voluntary charity? According to conventional income statistics the labourer is the richest. But within his local society he is much poorer and has less prestige than either of the two others. Redistributive taxation on the basis of conventional income comparisons transfers resources from British or American recipients of welfare payments, who are regarded as poor by themselves and by others, to Indian landowners and African chiefs, who locally are men of substance.

Differences in social institutions and political arrangements also undermine the usefulness of international comparisons. The familiar reluctance or refusal to kill animals in South Asia reduces the supply of food and severely circumscribes agricultural operations. In India, cattle compete with people for food rather than contribute to it. Is it appropriate to tax people in the West to equalize their incomes with those of people who voluntarily maintain practices which reduce their incomes? Or should American and British men and women be taxed to equalize incomes with people whose poverty is caused partly by forbidding women to take paid work?

Nor is it sensible to use differences in incomes and living standards between societies at widely different stages of evolution as grounds for redistribution. Some parts of the Third World are extremely primitive, and large parts have been so until very recently. Some areas are still in the Stone Age. It is not surprising that many Third World societies have no Western-type medical

117

services. If they were made available externally, the facilities would have to be manned and maintained from abroad, sometimes indefinitely.

As we have seen, the policies of many aid-recipient governments reduce current and prospective incomes in their countries. Redistribution from rich to poor countries as an objective of policy brings it about that lower incomes resulting from the policies of Third World governments serve as grounds for taxing Western citizens for the direct benefit of those who brought about these lower incomes.

Global egalitarianism is based on the idea that people's requirements are fundamentally the same everywhere. As we have seen, this idea is obviously unfounded. In addition, advocacy of egalitarianism usually assumes that people's capacities, attitudes, values and beliefs are uniform, so that differences in income and wealth among both societies and individuals result from accident or exploitation. If that were so, redistribution (i.e. confiscation) would be both just and relatively painless. Moreover, if income differences reflected only accident or exploitation, redistribution would not reduce the total aggregate income of the groups between whom income had been redistributed, except for the disincentive effects of the process. In fact however attitudes, motivations and policies differ greatly among societies. These differences provide the underlying causes of visible differences in income and living standards. Once the reasons for income differences are recognized, certain corollaries about global egalitarianism follow.

First, the process of politically organized global redistribution will need to be continued endlessly. This is so because otherwise the determinants of economic performance would assert themselves and produce renewed differences in incomes.

Second, once it is realized that visible income differences reflect differences in the operation of the underlying determinants of economic performance, egalitarians would be forced to attempt to extend the levelling process to these underlying determinants. Such attempts must involve far-reaching coercion if a significant reduction in income differences were envisaged. The process of coercion would certainly have to include not only much higher taxation in Western countries, but would also have to involve, as we have noted, a massive attempt to re-mould people and societies. Such far-reaching policies could not be attempted by national governments with any hope of success. They could only be implemented by an international or even a global authority with totalitarian powers. The policies of many Third World governments would have to be determined from outside. If global egalitarianism were pursued seriously, it would involve coercion well beyond that expected from totalitarian governments of single countries. These are the

118

corollaries of the idea that everybody everywhere, simply by being alive, is entitled to a substantially higher income than at present (and one based on Western norms).

Third, because the personal attributes, social institutions and economic policies which promote economic advance are much more prevalent in most donor countries than in most recipient countries, international wealth transfers reallocate resources from those who can use them more productively to those who use them less so. This outcome reinforces any disincentive effect or any other adverse repercussion of the transfers from the West to the Third World. These transfers reduce total world income.

International redistribution thus cannot realize its stated aims, even though it can reduce both total world income, and incomes in different societies both rich and poor. Uncritical acceptance of such an ambiguous and defective idea as world income redistribution, as in the New International Economic Order, inspires policies which are both destructive and unsuitable for achieving their declared purposes. But even if, for whatever reason, economic differences came to be reduced, both between and within countries, this would not abate the pressures for further redistribution. When social differences have narrowed, those that remain, however small, appear particularly offensive.[26]

The radical objections to global egalitarianism are reinforced by the inadequacies of the statistics on which policy claims to be based. We have already emphasized that straightforward international income comparisons on a world-wide basis are most misleading guides to social reality, and thus to policy. This conclusion holds even if the statistics were reliable and informative. In fact they are vitiated by problems of concept and measurement. For instance, the proportion of the children is much higher in the Third World than in the West. The incomes and requirements of children are lower than those of adults. Statistics not adjusted for differences in age composition inextricably confuse differences in age and differences in income, and thereby exaggerate Third World poverty. And income comparisons between widely differing societies always involve arbitrary elements, especially when they involve people who have little or no exchange outside their own restricted group.[27] Thus it is not surprising that national income estimates and comparisons of Third World countries are subject to very wide margins of error and bias. They also entail wide differences of interpretation, even though there is now much agreement that the conventional statistics much exaggerate international differences in living standards.

It was in 1963 that Professor Usher first showed that these biases (which, moreover, do not remain constant over time) amount to several hundred percent, and it was in 1968 that he explained this in great detail. His findings have been authoritatively endorsed.[28] It has also become evident that the population statistics of some large Third World countries are quite unreliable.[29] Yet advocacy of aid for redistribution still relies on conventional national income statistics which claim to estimate Third World incomes to a few percentage points.

The need to reduce a wide and widening gap in incomes between rich and poor countries is now much invoked in support of international wealth transfers, although there are aid advocates who rightly maintain that this idea is irrelevant to the case.[30] This particular argument suffers from all the defects of international income comparisons, and several others as well. If international income comparisons which involve the Third World are themselves largely meaningless, this applies even more to estimates of a gap between arbitrarily chosen bundles of such incomes. And if Third World governments pursue policies which directly reduce income in their countries, this immediately widens actual and prospective international income differences. This is yet another example which shows that income differences and changes cannot be discussed sensibly without an examination of their background. Moreover, while aid certainly removes resources from the donors, it does not necessarily, or even generally, raise incomes in the recipient countries. It may, therefore, not reduce the gap between them. And even if it does, this comes about much more by reducing incomes in the West than by increasing them in the Third World.[31]

Changes in incomes and in the degree of equality can result from any number of different causes which evoke altogether different responses. Most people would regret greater equality if this came about because more poor people died or better-off people were killed. On the other hand, most people would normally favour greater equality brought about by an increase in the amount of productive capital, or by a widening of employment opportunities or external contacts, or by technological advance of a kind which benefits mainly the relatively poor. So yet again we see that changes and differences in income cannot be examined sensibly without considering how they come about.

13

Redistribution and restitution are closely linked in egalitarian discourse, primarily because of the notion that income differences are the result largely of exploitation. The link is clearly present in the context of what is called social justice, interpreted as substantial equality of incomes, and often laced with suggestions of redress for some form of past or present misconduct. Proposals for redistribution to eliminate international income differences, and as restitution for exploitation of the Third World, are often combined in the case for international wealth transfers, although they are logically quite distinct.

In spite of the wide currency of restitution as ground for aid, I shall deal with it here briefly since I have examined it at length in chapter 4. The West has not caused the relative poverty of the Third World. The opposite is the case. The contacts established by the West have resulted in improved living conditions, longer life expectation and much wider choice for hundreds of millions of people in the Third World.

I need not labour this argument further. But it may be useful to supplement it by a few observations directly pertinent to restitution. While the idea that Western colonialism has caused Third World poverty is demonstrably unfounded, there have been many victims of colonialism in history, such as people killed or maimed in colonial wars and tribal farmers dispossessed by colonialists. These people are by now dead and cannot be helped – even by the World Bank.[32] Their descendants have gained from being born into the colonial or post-colonial world, rather than into the circumstances of pre-colonial Africa and Asia, where epidemic and endemic disease, tribal warfare, and lack of public security were widespread or universal. Indeed, millions of people who would otherwise have died survived because of Western techniques and ideas, notably medicine and public security which came with colonial rule.

Even if it could be established that colonialism was on balance harmful to the colonized, this would still not provide an argument for Western aid generally. Some major aid donors never had any colonies or dependencies of significance. But even in the case of colonial powers whose predecessors may have inflicted damage on certain groups, any theories of restitution would still fail. This is so because, except over very short periods, historical wrongs cannot be put right. For example, what date would we fix after which the crimes would be considered as justifying compensation? How far back in history should we go – a hundred years, a thousand years or longer? How would we identify the descendants of the criminals and of the victims? And would all historical crimes be invoked or only those perpetrated by the West, or more precisely by the supposed forebears of people living in the West against the supposed forebears of some Third World people?

Should Outer Mongolia (or its actual masters) pay compensation to Poland, Hungary, Turkey and several OPEC countries for the depredations of the Mongols many centuries ago, because the Mongols came from Central Asia? Should the Soviet Union compensate the descendants of the people displaced or killed in the Russian colonization of Siberia in past centuries?

Should the United States pay compensation to some African countries for the activities of some nineteenth-century American slavers, even if this involved taxing American negroes for the benefit of present African governments? Should present-day Americans be taxed to make amends to American Indians when most of the taxpayers are descended from immigrants who entered the country long after the time of any wrongs perpetrated against the ancestors of the Indians? A statute of limitation on historical wrongs is more than just: it is unavoidable.

Acceptance of the idea of restitution may serve to reinforce the feelings of guilt in the West, but, as is all too familiar, attempts to assuage such feelings have nothing to do with improving the condition of people in the Third World. Feelings of guilt unaccompanied by a sense of responsibility for the consequences of the policies inspired by them have brought about results which are extremely harmful to many of those affected by these policies.

14

Official aid is often advocated as serving the economic and political interests of the donors.

It is frequently argued that aid promotes exports and employment. According to the crudest form of this argument, aid sustains employment because it is used to buy exports. But as aid is financed by people in the donor countries, aid reduces the domestic demand for other goods which would have been bought had taxes and inflation been lower. To argue that aid helps the domestic economy is like saying that a shop-keeper benefits from having his cash register burgled so long as the burglar spends part of the proceeds in his shop. Subsidies given directly to domestic industry would be more effective than aid in promoting exports and employment. This method would also generate more employment, because less money would leak abroad – in the sense of not being spent on the exports of the donors – to the detriment both of employment and the balance of payments. Besides being more effective, such subsidies would make clear the purpose of the policy and also its costs to the taxpayer.

According to another version of this argument, aid benefits the donor economies and sustains employment by promoting the long-term development of the recipients. By assuming without question that aid is necessarily effective, this argument prejudges the issue. It also ignores the alternative and more productive uses of the resources given away as aid.

The play of political forces helps the specious argument that aid maintains employment. Aid is financed by millions of taxpayers; its cost is widely dispersed. The benefits of exports bought with tied aid, on the other hand, accrue to limited sectional interests. The obstacles to moving to new jobs in modern economies add plausibility to the idea that tied aid is desirable because it supports domestic employment by keeping workers in their present jobs. Sectional interests further benefit if aid makes it easier to impose restrictions against Third World exports by diminishing political resistance to these measures.

Aid is often advocated, particularly in America, as an instrument of Western political strategy, especially by helping to keep the Third World outside the Soviet orbit. But this too is unfounded. To serve Western political interests, aid would need to be geared to the strategic importance and to the conduct and location of the recipients. It would then be a form of political or military subsidy with clear conditions attached. In fact, aid operates without such criteria. Indeed, no political conditions are imposed on the recipients, as is evident from aid to Angola, Mozambique, Tanzania, Vietnam and others. Much of it goes to countries of no military, political or economic significance. The human and economic resources of many aid recipients are extremely meagre; their political effectiveness derives only from Western guilt and consequent weakness, or from conflict and dissension among and within Western donor countries.

About one-third of all Western aid is multilateral, i.e. it is channelled through the official international organizations.[33] In the allocation of aid, these organizations are not permitted to take account of the political interests of the donors. Indeed, multilateral aid has been widely supported on the specific ground that the interests of the donors do not influence its allocation. It has even been supported on the argument that in multilateral aid the donors cannot impose conditions on the recipients, and thus cannot blackmail them. As noted earlier in this chapter, this is a curious use of language where those who give money are the blackmailers. Finally, the Soviet bloc is represented in the United Nations and can thus influence the allocation of multilateral UN aid such as the substantial United Nations Development Programme even though its own contribution to such aid is extremely small.

In practice Western interests are also largely ignored in bilateral aid, as this is given regardless of the conduct of the recipients, and also of their political significance. Wholesale expropriation of Western enterprises has not stopped aid to Algeria, Ethiopia, Ghana, Mozambique, Sri Lanka, Tanzania, Vietnam, Zaire, and Zambia, among others. Official aid also often arouses the resentment of the recipients who do not receive as much as they want or feel entitled to. Many recipients insult and thwart the Western donors as best they can. And when the governments of India and Pakistan sought external mediation in the Kashmir dispute in 1965, they turned not to the United States or Britain but to the Soviet Union, despite the fact that they had for over ten years been receiving much American and British aid.[34] Thus the idea is altogether unwarranted that official aid serves the political interests of the West. It had never seriously been envisaged as an instrument for this purpose. If it had been, it would be administered by the political sections of foreign ministries or by the defence departments of the donors. The staffs of the domestic and multilateral aid agencies are not qualified or trained to serve the political interests of the Western donors and are rarely inclined to do so.

According to a variant of the argument that aid serves Western political interests, it is said to prevent the spread of Communism in the Third World by promoting economic improvement there. This contention again assumes that aid ensures prosperity. It assumes also that acceptance of Communism depends on low levels of income. Both these assumptions are invalid.

Indeed, the baffling disregard of the political and strategic interests of Western donors arouses suspicions in the recipient countries. It suggests that aid is an insidious attempt to buy influence, or an instrument for dumping unsaleable goods. Such allegations are frequently advanced even by relatively friendly aid recipients, who are nevertheless not prepared to believe that aid is motivated either by feelings of guilt or by a supposedly disinterested desire to do good.

15

The suggestion that aid will reduce population growth to the benefit of both donors and recipients straddles several arguments for aid, including development, poverty, redistribution (on the ground that reduced population growth in the Third World will reduce international income differences) and self-interest (on the ground that smaller numbers in the Third World will benefit the West in various ways).

Western aid to reduce population growth often takes the form of support for specific birth control programmes. More often, however, aid advocates argue that it reduces population growth by promoting a general improvement in economic conditions. They envisage a cumulative and beneficial three-stage spiral between aid, incomes and population growth: aid raises incomes; higher incomes lead to smaller families; smaller population growth leads to higher incomes. Each stage in this reasoning is inconclusive or invalid.[35]

Higher incomes as such do not necessarily reduce population growth (even if aid served to raise incomes). Higher incomes and reduced fertility often go together, though by no means invariably. When they are found together, they reflect changes in prevailing attitudes and motivations, notably greater

124

interest in improved material conditions, which leads both to improved economic performance and to smaller families. Thus, both the higher incomes and the smaller families reflect the operation of the determinants of economic performance. But a rise in incomes without these other changes raises fertility and population growth even more, because of higher survival rates. Also, if people are better off they can afford more children, and they will have more, unless the higher incomes are accompanied either by a change in motivation or by a relative rise in the cost of children. Higher incomes as such, therefore, will not reduce fertility or population growth.

Reduction in the rate of population growth cannot normally increase income appreciably, because the level and the rate of growth of income depend largely on personal, social and political factors, not on physical resources. As discussed fully in chapter 3, this relationship is evident throughout the Third World.

Besides the notion that development depends largely on physical resources per head, insistent advocacy of fertility controls for the Third World reflects two other ideas. The first is that children are merely a burden and not a source of satisfaction, nor are they contributors to current and prospective parental incomes. The second idea is that Third World people are unable to control their fertility.[36] Both ideas are misconceived. People in the Third World, as in the West, are generally fond of children. And in addition to the emotional satisfaction of having children, the latter often contribute to family income. Nor do people in the Third World procreate like animals heedless of consequences. That they do not do so is clear, for instance, from the gap between fecundity and fertility. They know about a wide range of both traditional and modern methods of contraception.

The ideas criticized in this section are the ideas behind Third World birth control programmes which have enjoyed much Western aid, especially from the World Bank. The Indian government in the late 1960s and in the 1970s was among the beneficiaries of such support. Its policy included far-reaching official coercion to force people to limit the number of their children, and eventually compulsory sterilization on a large scale.

Compulsory sterilization in India was an outstanding instance of the invention of a problem by external observers where no problem existed before. It was not a problem for the North Indian peasant that he was very poor by Western standards. Western observers, especially economists and sociologists, declared that his poverty presented a problem sufficiently acute to justify drastic policies. They therefore encouraged and supported forcible sterilization, thereby depriving him of children he wanted and creating desperate problems for the supposed beneficiaries.

125

In fact, policies of compulsory limitation of births cannot raise even conventionally measured incomes. They are expensive to enforce, and popular resistance imposes further economic costs. In India people fled from areas where they were most threatened with forcible sterilization, and also abandoned farming there. If the policies had been pressed home successfully, they would have left behind an abject and dejected population.

16

The immediately preceding sections have examined the most prominent and relatively durable rationalizations in the advocacy of global wealth transfers from the late 1940s to 1980. I will now take note of two further rationalizations which surfaced in the late 1970s and which may prove relatively durable. But whether they prove durable or not, they again are quite insubstantial.

The first of these rationalizations is based on the failure of the development policies of many aid recipients. The argument is that because these policies have been supported by Western aid or even made possible by it, the West is now under obligation to continue or to extend aid. This particular argument bears a distinct family resemblance to another idea in support of aid, rarely expressed in public but often heard privately. According to this unpublicized idea, the West must support the Third World because Western contacts have disturbed the pristine simplicity and innocence of the peoples of the Third World, and thrust them into the modern world for which they are not really fitted without further tutelage from the West, and without much Western support. Such ideas reflect the patronizing notion that the West is primarily responsible for whatever happens in the Third World, and especially so if that is deemed objectionable on some criterion or other.

An article in the *Financial Times*, 2 July 1980 presented an unusually explicit formulation of Western responsibility for the policy of a major aid recipient. This policy, which involved the enforced uprooting of many families, failed completely in terms of its declared economic objective. The article entitled 'Why Tanzania's Socialist Experiment is Failing to Work' reported on the agricultural policy of the government. It referred to the ' . . . socialist "Uja'maa" programme under which some thirteen million people are being regrouped into 8,000 villages . . . Professor Dumont points to the adverse impact on soil conservation and agricultural production of the "villagization" programme. . . . Two thirds of the development budget is externally funded, thus if things are going wrong donor countries might feel some degree of responsibility.'

Such explicit formulation of Western responsibility in this context is relatively recent. But as adverse economic policies supported by aid can confidently be expected to continue all over the Third World, this particular rationalization may well persist or recur as yet another argument for further aid.

The other recent and much canvassed argument is based on the rise in oil prices in the 1970s. According to this argument, the increase in oil prices has blighted the development prospects of non oil-producing Third World countries and has posed balance of payments problems in these countries which are practically insoluble without external assistance. The significance of this issue for Third World development and poverty is much exaggerated. There are six Third World countries the import bills of which have increased particularly heavily as a result of the OPEC price increases of 1979. These are Brazil, South Korea, India, Taiwan, the Philippines and Thailand. Among these, India is the only really poor country. Between 1973 and 1977 the increase of the cost of imported oil was about 1% of India's official estimated GDP. The poorest countries import little oil, and even in the few instances where they import appreciable quantities, as do a few smaller countries in Africa, Latin America and the Caribbean, the higher prices should cause no severe or insuperable problems.[37]

Material progress does not depend on the price of oil. This conclusion is obvious on very little reflection. It is confirmed by the recent experience of many Third World countries which have no oil of their own. South Korea, Taiwan, Hong Kong, the Ivory Coast, Kenya and Colombia progressed rapidly throughout the 1970s after the OPEC price rises. Relative price movements are a familiar contingency of economic life to be met by setting aside the reserves and by economizing on commodities the prices of which have risen. Should the price of oil come to fall, this is likely to be adduced in support of Western aid to oil exporting countries, but not in support of cuts in aid to the oil importing countries.

17

Highly critical assessment of a major and widely acclaimed policy is apt to be dismissed unless it is rounded off with proposals for policy. In popular discussion, criticism unaccompanied by such proposals is apt to be branded as unconstructive or merely negative. According to a more sophisticated reaction, criticism is deemed inconclusive or otherwise inadequate unless a preferred alternative is specified. Such contentions are unwarranted. When arguments behind a policy claim to be based on evidence and logic, they can be examined legitimately on the same basis. The policy itself can be examined appropriately by considering whether it has achieved, or can achieve, its stated objectives. All this need not be followed by proposals for policy. But because this is so widely expected from a highly critical discussion, I conclude with some proposals.

These suggestions will be relatively brief. Some follow from what has gone before. In any case, detailed discussion of specific proposals would not be appropriate here. The discussion is also necessarily on a different plane to that of the earlier sections of this chapter. Worthwhile policy proposals must take note of what is politically and administratively conceivable: that is, of considerations which are often much affected by local conditions. Policy proposals normally also involve value judgements. For these reasons, the acceptance or rejection of the proposals that follow has no bearing on the validity of the argument of the preceding sections of this chapter. The record of the advocacy of foreign aid is one of intellectual failure but political success. The implications and results of official wealth transfers make it clear that they ought to be terminated. But this is not feasible at present.

The momentum of existing commitments and the forces behind these transfers preclude this course. This is so even though other policies could contribute much more towards such declared objectives as the development of Third World countries or the relief of poverty in them. These are the objectives of aid which enjoy some genuine popular support, and the attainment of which is actually obstructed by official aid. The resulting dilemma is evident. The longer the period over which a policy has been pursued and the greater its costs, the more difficult it becomes effectively to call into question the principles behind the policy. The difficulty is aggravated when the prolonged pursuit of the policy has created formidable vested interests, as is conspicuous with foreign aid.[38] International wealth transfers cannot therefore be terminated soon.

The first task, performed in the preceding sections, is to call into question the axiomatic approach to aid, to convince policy makers and those who influence them that the case for aid should not be taken for granted. The next task is to examine how certain declared objectives of official transfers can best be attained, how the worst anomalies can be avoided or at least contained, and how this can be achieved by methods which erode rather than reinforce the interests behind official aid. I shall now look more closely at these objectives and at the methods for achieving them.

Relief of need

This aim of many generous-minded aid supporters should be left to voluntary agencies, with certain obvious exceptions such as assistance to disaster victims.[39] Ordinary citizens already voluntarily contribute large sums for these purposes. If governments were to make clear that this function was the province of voluntary charities, these contributions would probably increase greatly, especially if in some countries like Britain the tax treatment of charitable donations were liberalized.

There are other significant advantages in leaving the relief of need to charities, particularly those charities which are not largely politicized.[40] They know far more than Western governments about the local conditions in distant societies, where circumstances differ greatly from country to country, and differ also from those in the West. Genuine charities are also usually more interested in assisting the poorest and most distressed than are Third World rulers. Nor do the activities of charities directly promote the politicization of life, or increase the prizes of political power, or exacerbate political tension, or sustain the pursuit of harmful, oppressive or inhuman policies. Indeed, insofar as voluntary agencies provide an alternative source of help to Third World people, their activities may even reduce marginally the power of the rulers over their subjects. Further, voluntary aid is financed by people who give freely to help their fellow men. Official aid, in contrast, is tax money which has to be paid. Many Third World people sense this difference, and are suspicious of claims that aid is inspired by charitable and disinterested motives. Many in the West also seem aware of the difference. Voluntary donations serve also to refute the claims of Third World leaders that aid is a matter of right not of charity.

A specific example is pertinent. In June 1976, a referendum was held on a Swiss government proposal to provide substantial funds to the official International Development Association for handouts to Third World governments. The proposal was supported unanimously by the media, the churches, the universities and schools. For constitutional reasons it had to be tested in a referendum. In this referendum – the first popular vote ever taken in the West on foreign aid – the proposal was heavily defeated. At the same time the Swiss voluntarily contributed very large sums to a fund for the victims of an earthquake in Italy as well as to many Third World charities. Thus the public can distinguish official aid from voluntary charity.

However, voluntary charity for helping the poor in the Third World, though greatly preferable to official aid, also needs to be administered with considerable care if it is not to bring about untoward results. If it is envisaged as a long-term process of giving out alms rather than as disaster relief, it can easily lead to permanent pauperization. It is also likely to encourage feelings of superiority in the donors and of dependence in the recipients, as often happens under official aid as well.[41]

129

International political strategy

If the aim of official transfers is to promote the political interests of the donors, they should take the form of political and military subsidies. Such payments would have nothing to do with routine aid. As we have seen, handouts of the usual kind are at best ineffective for this purpose. They are indeed often counter-productive, by arousing suspicions of undisclosed motives or by encouraging recipients to thwart donors to show their independence.

Third World development

The West can contribute to Third World development best by reducing its barriers against Third World exports. The damaging results of these barriers in restricting markets and external contacts are compounded by frequent and unpredictable increases in their scope and severity. The threat of increases in trade barriers when some Third World industries expand their exports inhibits productive investment, exacerbates unemployment and retards the spread of skills. Substantial reduction of these restrictions together with assurances that they would not be increased could much accelerate material progress in those Third World countries, especially in the Far East, South Asia and Latin America, in which the domestic determinants of economic achievement are favourable.

There are familiar obstacles to more liberal Western trade policies. These are likely to become more severe in view of the increasing competitive strength of many Third World industries, the growing difficulties to internal adjustment in the West, and the apparently ever-increasing effectiveness of pressure groups. There is every prospect that Western consumers will continue to pay inflated prices and Western taxpayers be mulcted for the benefit of workers, managers and owners in protected industries.

In order to facilitate economic adjustment, it might be sensible to make a determined attempt to lift some of these restrictions, and simultaneously to redirect some aid expenditures to compensate groups damaged by cheaper Third World imports. Such a course would involve major drawbacks. For instance, why should the victims of certain sorts of economic change be compensated and others not? Still, if found practicable, such a policy might be the lesser of evils compared with the indefinite continuation of even more severe import restrictions and ever increasing aid.

Possible trade liberalization invites the question of liberalizing the immigration policies of some donors. It is not possible to develop this matter at length here, as it clearly raises the widest political, social and cultural issues. Extensive trade liberalization is clearly easier. Should this make substantial headway, one could then consider the conditions under which freer immigration policies might be practicable in certain countries. It would of course need to be considered how such policies could be implemented and financed, possibly by using aid funds, so as to benefit both the present donors and Third World countries with least upheaval.

Reform of aid

Official aid will still continue even if these various changes were to take place. The immediate political task, albeit a second-best solution, is therefore to try to improve aid while looking forward to its eventual termination and doing one's best to bring that about.

The first requirement is that aid should take forms which make it possible to identify its costs and its benefits. This rules out commodity agreements. These schemes damage the interests of the poorest both in the West and in the Third World, and benefit people who are relatively well-off in their societies. They thus set up demands for more redistribution. This form of aid bypasses even the semblance of parliamentary control. Its overall quantitative effects are also impossible to assess. Finally, commodity agreements, the effective operation of which involves official quotas for sharing out profitable activities, are apt to set up political tensions within and between the countries participating in these arrangements.

As a form of aid, subsidized loans are less appropriate than straightforward cash grants. Such loans confuse handouts with lending and thereby set up tensions; the donors see them as gifts and the recipients as burdens. The grant element in these is usually very large. Describing these transactions as loans conceals the cost to the donors. At the same time, these loans also lead to subsequent demands for debt cancellation, which, among various other perverse results, does nothing to help the poor. The aid element in subsidized loans is often difficult to compute. This is so on at least two grounds: first, because such calculations require some estimates of the commercial terms the borrowers would have had to pay, and second, because the servicing of these loans is open to all kinds of manipulation.

As long as official aid continues, it would be best if it were confined to untied cash grants. Tied aid confuses assistance to exporting interests with aid to the recipients. This form of aid arouses the suspicion that it is only a device for exporting unemployment or getting rid of unsaleable surpluses. These suspicions are not allayed by the fact that these objectives of tied aid could often be achieved more effectively by domestic subsidies.

If it is agreed that untied cash grants are the most appropriate form of official aid, the question is whether they should be bilateral, i.e. given direct

131

from the donor government to the recipient government, or whether they should be multilateral, channelled through the official international organizations. Supporters of the multilateral approach claim that it removes aid from the political arena, divorces it from the political interests of individual donors, and generally makes its allocation more disinterested, objective and conducive to development. This is not so. Transfer of taxpayers' money to foreign governments is inevitably political. All that the multilateral approach achieves is to reduce the modicum of parliamentary control over these expenditures in favour of control by those running the international organizations. Indeed, neither the donors (the taxpayers) nor their elected representatives can control the disbursement of multilateral aid. They are often formally barred from controlling the disbursement of these transfers. This is so because, in allocating multilateral aid, international aid organizations are not allowed to take into account the political interests of the donors. The World Bank does not accept contributions to which conditions are attached.

Staff members of international aid organizations have distinct personal, political and professional interests. Most of their constituents are Third World governments and they increasingly regard themselves as spokesmen for the Third World. Professor Martin Bronfenbrenner has observed trenchantly:

> What seems to have developed is a collection of self-serving ldc theories of international economic relations. . . . Of this collection . . . UNCTAD (in concert with other ldc-dominated UN agencies) has become the leading world spokesman.

Many of the most influential staff members of these organizations favour the expansion of aid and the preferential treatment of governments trying to impose extensive state controls. These priorities please their constituents and also create more influence and power for themselves. Moreover, many staff members and consultants of such organizations, especially those most influential and active, tend to be hostile to the internal arrangements of Western society, especially to the market system.

Multilateral aid also severs the last vestige of contact between the recipient governments and donor taxpayers and their representatives. This reduces further whatever limited effectiveness aid has in promoting development, because contact between the suppliers and users of capital increases its productivity. As explained in chapter 7, multilateral aid is also likely to be more inflationary than is bilateral aid. Further, under multilateral aid the donor governments cannot restrain patently wasteful or even barbarous policies of the recipients, because it becomes virtually impossible to withold aid; and the conscience of the individual donor government is laundered by the passage of its (taxpayers') money through the multipartite organizations.

Multilateral aid is also widely regarded as a more effective instrument for the worldwide equalization of incomes than bilateral aid. It is also often seen as an early phase of this policy, the purpose and operation of which are open to the most serious objections.

There is yet another reason for preferring bilateral cash grants to other forms of aid, and it is one which many people might regard as particularly significant. The elected representatives of the taxpayers can assess the cost, destination and results of bilateral cash grants more effectively (or at least less ineffectively) than is possible under any other form of aid.

Bilateral grants should be given for only limited periods. Donors should firmly refuse long forward commitments, as it is totally impossible to foretell who the eventual recipients will be, or what they will do. The donors should also make it clear that these transfers do not represent restitution for alleged misconduct, nor an instrument for global redistribution, nor for securing specified rates of growth or levels of income. Otherwise the donors will be subject to sustained blackmail, or made to accept completely open-ended commitments.

The next question is that of the selection of the recipients. To begin with, aid should not go to governments whose external policies conflict with the interests of the donors. The allocation should also favour governments which pursue liberal foreign trade policies and which offer security for private investment both foreign and domestic. Such conditions would benefit the peoples of the recipient countries, because their acceptance would promote foreign trade and investment, which conduce to economic progress, extend people's opportunities and reduce the power of the rulers to restrict the choices of their subjects.

The donors can, and should, however, go even further. In allocating aid they should favour governments which within their human and financial resources try to perform the indispensable tasks of government, but who refrain from close detailed control of the economy – briefly, governments who govern rather than plan. This would promote liberal economic systems, minimize coercion, reduce political tensions and favour material progress.

The choice between budgetary aid and project aid, that is between a general supplement to the budget and assistance for specific projects, needs also to be considered. Project aid seems preferable, even when the grants go to governments who pursue liberal economic policies. It places greater restraint on the politicization of life and government patronage than do unrestricted cash grants. It is also likely to contribute more directly to economic productivity.

Such criteria might well reduce some of the major anomalies of aid, such as continued support for governments pursuing brutal policies which clearly damage the economic position or prospects of their subjects. Their adoption would also simplify the administration of aid and dispel some of the mystique surrounding it. The simplification would reduce the cost of administering aid, and thus the service charge attached to it. It would reduce also the influence of the staffs of the international and domestic aid organizations. It would thus help to cut down the official aid organizations in size and to size. This result in turn would make it somewhat easier eventually to phase out official wealth transfers.

These various constraints in the allocation of aid are neither demeaning nor unreasonable. The direction of domestic policy, notably including public spending, is normally determined by the representative of the taxpayers. It is perverse that the policies of foreign governments receiving money from the taxpayers should not be scrutinized by their own elected representatives, when the policies of their local authorities are scrutinized by them as a matter of course. That this evident anomaly has largely escaped public attention is another corollary of the prevailing axiomatic approach to aid.

Moreover, as aid goes to governments it necessarily affects the political scene in the recipient countries; the only question is the character of the influence. The criteria proposed here would, quite simply, reverse the bias towards governments which attempt to establish state-controlled economies, often by coercion. These criteria would replace this bias by a more liberal influence which would counter the inherent bias of government-to-government aid towards state control and politicization. The adoption of such criteria is likely to affect considerably the policies of Third World governments, both those of current aid recipients and also those of prospective recipients of official aid. The policies of an aid recipient are the appropriate concern both of donors and other recipients. Both of these groups have an interest in the productive use of aid by particular governments. This is so because aid represents gifts of scarce capital, and the demand for aid always and necessarily exceeds the amount available. Aid to one recipient both diminishes the resources of the donors and reduces the amount of aid available to others.

The methods and criteria of Western aid could evidently be much improved. But even the most enlightened aid programme can contribute to development only marginally. Reduction in trade barriers could promote development much more than even the most enlightened aid policies.

These suggestions for reforming aid accord with its principal declared objective; namely, to improve the living conditions of the peoples of the Third World. They will not appeal if other objectives, such as world-wide egalitarianism or greater power for international organizations, are considered more important.

The Wide and Widening Gap

1

I have argued in section 12 that the idea of a wide and widening gap offers no justification for aid. The concept is nevertheless persistently canvassed as an argument for international wealth transfers. The radical shortcomings of the concept as basis for policy are habitually ignored. A brief discussion of these shortcomings is in order, on a slightly more technical level than the reference in the text.[43] In considering the matters discussed in this appendix, the reader should remember firmly that the statistics of income differences and gaps are of no interest unless the reasons for the differences are examined and understood. This is a matter which has been noted explicitly and repeatedly in this chapter, and also in chapter 1.

It may be convenient to list seriatim some of the basic limitations or misconceptions in the notion of the gap in international income differences.

(i) The international range of incomes is largely a continuous spectrum. There is no substantial gap in income between the poorest developed country and the richest less developed country. Any such discontinuity would be swamped by the errors and biases in international income comparisons. Moreover, in most countries there are substantial regional and group differences in income. Large regions and groups in many countries classified as poor have incomes higher than the average incomes of many countries classified as rich, and much higher of course than are those of particular groups and regions in the latter category.

As there is no clear discontinuity in the international range of incomes, it is arbitrary to place the line of division on the basis of income between the two global aggregates, i.e. the collectivities of rich and poor countries. But the difference in average incomes between the two aggregates (whether absolute differences, or ratio of incomes) depends on where the line is placed. The size of the gap is therefore arbitrary. Moreover, it is often left rather nebulous which countries are included in one or other of these aggregates. For instance, the treatment of the Soviet bloc, the OPEC countries and of certain Southern European regions is often ambivalent, and has sometimes changed. The People's Republic of China is often left out of account.

(ii) Even if the coverage of such huge collectivities were clearly specified, which it practically never is, it would still not be sensible to aggregate and average the incomes of vast and diverse societies, ranging from Stone Age people and aborigines to highly sophisticated communities, differing widely in physical and social living conditions and mores. The purported calculation of the average income of the entire less developed world and its comparison with the average income of the West (that is, aggregates which between them cover most of mankind) is a meaningless exercise though it may be politically effective.

(iii) National income estimates and comparisons which involve the Third World are subject to errors so wide as to render comparisons largely meaningless. For various reasons, such as the replacement of subsistence production by production for the market, these errors and biases do not remain constant over time.

(iv) Because of differences in age composition and in rates of population growth between developed and less developed countries, notably the much larger proportion of children in the latter, any worthwhile discussion of the gap would need to be based on age-standardized statistics. Such age standardization of incomes on a global basis is not possible.

(v) The relative economic position of societies undergoes changes through time. These changes are evident throughout the course of history, and also in more recent experience: witness the relative position of say Japan, West Germany or France compared with that of Britain, not to speak of the rapid growth of many Third World countries. Thus the period over which income differences are supposed to widen needs to be specified.

(vi) Both because of changes in the relative economic position of different countries and for various other reasons (mainly political), countries are often promoted from the less developed to the more developed category. Thus the composition of the two collectivities changes through time, and this precludes valid comparisons of their relative incomes over long periods.

(vii) It is rarely specified whether the gap refers to absolute differences in average incomes, or to the ratio of average incomes between the global aggregates of developed and less developed countries. Yet these are quite different concepts. The two types of difference often move in opposite directions, and, as a mathematical necessity, change at different rates.

(viii) If, over a period, there is a more pronounced decline in mortality among poorer people, this tends to widen the absolute and proportionate differences in income between rich and poor. Thus, a relatively greater decline in mortality of the poor widens the income gap. Yet this change reflects a relative improvement in the position of the poorer group. This consideration is particularly pertinent in our context, in view of the large decline in mortality in the Third World in recent decades. This has already been examined in chapter 3, above. For the present purpose, we will revert to it briefly in the next section.

2

Thus, statistics of the celebrated gap cannot lead to worthwhile examination of international income differences or of policies of redistribution. This conclusion supports Sir Arthur Lewis's contention, already noted, that living standards in poor countries, and not international income differences, are pertinent to the welfare of people in the Third World.

There is, however, one gap between the Third World and the West which is clear, and which is more significant and more precise than the nebulous gap in incomes or living standards. This is the difference in life expectation. As we have seen in chapter 3 above, in recent decades this difference, or gap, has contracted sharply. Life expectation has increased much more in the less developed world because of the more pronounced decline in mortality there in recent decades. The difference in life expectation between the two aggregates diminished greatly over this period, both as a ratio and as an absolute difference.

Here is a conceptually unambiguous gap. In recent decades it has not widened, but has contracted greatly. The increase in life expectation reflects a major improvement because in the less developed world, as in the West, people like to live longer, that is they prefer life to death. Yet this evident improvement in well-being is not included as an element in national income statistics.

Longer life expectation normally goes with better nutrition, housing, clothing and medical care. Therefore the differential reduction in mortality between the West and the Third World over the last few decades itself casts doubt on the idea of a widening gap in average living standards between the two aggregates, if such a nebulous concept can ever be interpreted sensibly.

The increase in life expectation is, of course, behind the much lamented Third World population explosion, which in fact reflects improved material conditions. The steep fall in mortality in the Third World has simultaneously increased the absolute size of the population in the Third World, and its size relative to the West. This by itself would have widened conventionally measured differences in income (not standardized for age) between the two global aggregates, or at least held down the rate at which they otherwise would have narrowed.

Very recently some doubts about the reality of the widening gap, especially when it is expressed in the form of a ratio of incomes, have crept into the development literature. According to a study sponsored by the World Bank, the average per capita GNP of the aggregate of less developed countries (including the People's Republic of China) has grown in recent decades at a rate faster than the aggregate of developed countries.[44] Both the global aggregation and also the underlying statistics in that study are open to serious objection. Nevertheless, this expression of doubt about the widening gap is worth mentioning.

CHAPTER 6

Background to Aid

Ambition comes behind and unobservable
Sin grows with doing good . . . .

T. S. Eliot

1

We saw in the preceding chapter that the arguments proposed by advocates of aid are no more than insubstantial rationalizations. How then did it happen that on such a slender basis so far-reaching and momentous a policy came to be advanced; that it was widely supported by public men and prominent academics, many of whom put forward these rationalizations; and that despite patent anomalies it finally achieved the status of an undeniable axiom? All this is especially baffling because when aid started there were no significant pressure groups or constituency interests behind it. Within about twenty years, the advocates of official aid have become one of the world's most effective lobbies, perhaps the most effective.

To examine the sources behind the progress of the aid lobby may therefore be instructive. It is also of practical importance. Realistic policies for reforming aid must take into account the forces and passions behind it. What are they? Why people accept particular arguments or find particular policies attractive cannot be discerned with certainty. But the element of conjecture does not mean that one explanation is as good as another. To trace connections and sequences by means of evidence, inference and reflection can prove informative.

The Charter of the United Nations, drawn up in 1945, enjoined its members to promote the social progress of all the people of the world, but it did not spell out the implications of this modest proposal. Nevertheless, from the early days of the United Nations, a few people in the academies and the media envisaged official aid from the West to the rest of the world. The policy was effectively launched by President Truman's Message to Congress of 20 January 1949. Point Four of that message urged a bold programme to use the fruits of Western economic progress to help the underdeveloped countries, where over one half of mankind was said to be living in sickness and wretchedness.[1]

The Point Four programme came about largely by accident. In November 1948 Mr Ben Hardy, then a virtually unknown newspaper reporter who had, however, a contact in the White House, embodied the central idea of Point Four in a memorandum which he circulated among friends in Washington. His contact in the White House passed the idea to the President, who insisted on including it in his message to Congress in the face of strong opposition by senior State Department officials, who pointed out that the proposal was extremely vague and therefore dangerous. Mr Hardy subsequently became the first Public Relations Officer of the Point Four programme in the State Department.[2]

Although the Point Four programme was a chance product of journalistic inspiration, it inaugurated a far-reaching policy and a supporting terminology. Point Four was an early instance of lumping together the non-Western world into one aggregate or collectivity. This collectivity was envisaged simultaneously as broadly uniform, and also designated as a candidate for Western donations. As was made plain in chapter 5, from 1949 to date Western aid has provided the only unifying characteristic and effective bond of the diverse, often antagonistic, even warring components of the underdeveloped world, the present Third World or South.

The policy launched by President Truman's Point Four made rapid headway. In 1952 Mr Charles Malik of the Lebanon, a moderate spokesman of the underdeveloped world, argued at the United Nations that to make any impact, the Point Four programme must be increased at least a hundredfold. In 1953 President Eisenhower spoke of large-scale aid to the underdeveloped world as necessary for world-wide social justice. In the 1960s spokesmen of the aid agencies expressed regret when the governments of Sri Lanka and Cambodia appeared to hesitate before accepting official aid, and they expressed the hope (mostly well-founded) that the aid agencies could prevail on those governments to accept aid. By the 1970s large-scale and practically unconditional wealth transfers came to be widely regarded as a matter of right of the recipients, and as no more than the satisfaction of legitimate expectations. The right of the Third World countries (that is, of their governments) to receive international wealth transfers was a major theme at international gatherings practically throughout the 1970s. And when, in August 1976, the British Ministry of Overseas Development granted £5 million of British aid to Mozambique, and it aroused some fleeting and ineffectual criticism, the spokesman of the Ministry said that this aid was only what a country in Mozambique's position could expect, thus implying that aid was a kind of drive-in handout, available on request.

There were certain distinctive landmarks in the progression of aid. These included the United Nations *Report on the Economic Development of Underdeveloped Countries* (1951); the first UNCTAD (United Nations Conference on Trade and Development) 1964; the *Report of the Commission on International Development* (Pearson Report) 1969; the United Nations *Declaration on the Establishment of a New International Economic Order* 1974; and *North-South, a Programme for Survival* (Brandt Report) 1980. The trend was unmistakable, from the suggestions for relatively modest amounts of aid to insistence on international taxation for global wealth transfers. To date, the Brandt Report is the high-water mark in the insistence on large-scale transfers to the Third World, and on far-reaching international fiscal policies to effect them. It should be evident from the repercussions of global transfers, as discussed in the preceding chapter, that the report is not a programme for survival. Rather, it is a signpost to political conflict, and a recipe for economic waste.

2

Many supporters of official aid are genuinely and humanely concerned about the conditions of people in the Third World. They are generous and well-intentioned but not well-informed. Many are unaware of the political and social realities in the recipient countries or of the adverse repercussions of official aid. They are apt to look on foreign aid as being the same thing as voluntary charity. They rarely appreciate the radical differences between the two, differences which must affect the operation and results of foreign aid. As we have seen, uncritical support for official aid leads to results which conflict with the objectives of these well-meaning and generous supporters. These objectives, in so far as they are attainable, can be promoted far more effectively by voluntary charity. But, as we shall see, many of the advocates of official aid are by no means so selfless or disinterested.

Chance, ideology, interests, organization and entertainment, the interplay of which is the very stuff of politics, have been closely linked and indeed inextricably interwoven in the rapid and remarkable progress of official aid from the apparently modest purpose of Point Four to the goal of global redistribution.

I have already mentioned the role of chance behind President Truman's Point Four programme. Chance events also shaped the subsequent history of aid. Mr McNamara's appointment as President of the World Bank arose out of the need to find him a suitable post after his resignation as Secretary of Defense, since when he has become the leading Western advocate and exponent of aid.

When the Point Four programme was launched there were no discernible pressure groups behind it. But here was an idea whose time had come. The climate of sentiment and opinion was highly favourable. In the West, the rapid erosion of traditional values, loyalties and ties, the failure of prosperity to

140

yield the happiness widely expected of it, and the disenchantment which came in the wake of the Second World War, all provided a restless, promiscuous search for new causes. The underdeveloped countries, vaguely known to many people either by brief war-time experience, or from their occasional and highly selective treatment by the media, provided one such brave new cause.[3] Again, the evangelical zeal of churches for foreign aid has increased simultaneously with the decline of traditional religious faith. Politics and philosophy, no less than nature, abhor a vacuum. With the decline in their spiritual role, churches came increasingly to look upon themselves as social welfare agencies, and especially so in the Third World because in the West the scope for such activities had come to be much circumscribed.

The widespread, though unfounded, feeling of guilt in the West has been a major factor behind the progress of official aid. I have already dealt with this feeling at some length. One of its consequences is especially pertinent here. Its prevalence may help to resolve a notable paradox in the advocacy of global wealth transfers. From the earliest days of aid to the present advocacy of worldwide redistribution or restitution for past wrongs, Western governments and institutions have financed the academic and other advocates of wealth transfers, both in the West and in the Third World. The West has also financed the Third World spokesmen who have assailed it most consistently and virulently, and it has also provided the platforms for these opinions. The feeling of guilt, as well as dissension in the West, may have something to do with this curious situation.

The terminology of aid itself has much assisted its uncritical acceptance. Above all, this applies to the term aid. The expression itself suggests help to one's fellow men, implying humane and compassionate conduct. The very word obscures the fact that it refers to official inter-governmental wealth transfers, to the transfer of taxpayers' money to foreign governments. Aid also suggests plainly that it must inevitably be of benefit to the peoples of the recipient countries, and in particular that it promotes development and relieves poverty and suffering. As we have seen, these assumptions are unwarranted, and indeed often the opposite of the truth. It is the rulers who usually benefit, and not the population at large.

Other obvious examples of aid terminology useful to its advocates include even the standard references to development in the titles of the agencies administering these wealth transfers. Nomenclature such as the Ministry of Overseas Development and Agency for International Development serves both to prejudge the effects of the policy and to reinforce the case for it.

In Britain, overseas aid also conjures up images of missionary activity, or of other past endeavours which are thought to have benefited both Britain and the peoples of the former colonies. Such ideas and images appeal especially to the older generation of conservatives who are themselves far from free of patronizing attitudes to 'lesser breeds (formerly) without the law', an example of the condescension which pervades the advocacy of official aid. Indeed, some of their number are much involved in the advocacy and operation of overseas aid.

The upsurge of egalitarianism, of the idea that economic equality is or ought to be a universal norm, has also much helped the aid lobby. Egalitarians condemn the West both because they regard its domestic policies as insufficiently levelling, and because it is more prosperous than most of the Third World. Egalitarians are therefore apt to support policies which remove resources from this corrupt metropolis, or which otherwise undermine its position. Moreover, egalitarians often object to market-oriented economies. Aid simultaneously becomes an instrument for promoting international equality, for reducing the power of the West and for encouraging state-controlled economies wherever possible.[4] There are also various disaffected groups in the West which have come greatly to dislike private property and the market system. Some of these groups envisage the Third World as a weapon in what is in effect an undeclared, one-sided civil war in the West. Some of these groups have consistently and effectively promoted the cause of wealth transfers from the West.

The progress of aid has also been helped by the widely prevalent and uncritical contemporary approach to quantifiability. The inclination to identify the quantifiable with the significant promotes the idea that economic performance and progress depend on physical and financial resources. These are factors which can be quantified and which, moreover, can be provided by the West. They are deemed more important in mainstream discussion on aid and development than personal, social and political factors. These cannot be readily quantified or provided by the West. This misplaced emphasis has been reinforced by the prevailing investment fetish, the idea that any spending termed investment is bound to be productive. And the spending of aid by the recipient governments is apt to be called investment, even if it has nothing to do with an increase in productive assets.

Preoccupation with the quantifiable has been reinforced by the practice of contrasting sharply the developed world and the less developed world. The aid lobbies habitually imply that the distinction in terms of income between the two is clear and durable, and that incomes, conditions and policies within each collectivity are broadly uniform. In fact, the distinction on the basis of income is arbitrary and shifting, and incomes, conditions and policies within the global aggregate differ greatly. The following three formulations by well-known authorities illustrate the widely prevalent and misleading practice:

It is on the ethical plane that the present situation is scandalous. One-third of the world lives in comfort and two-thirds in misery.[5]

One third of mankind today lives in an environment of relative abundance. But two-thirds of mankind – more than two billion individuals – remain entrapped in a cruel web of circumstances that severely limits their right to the necessities of life . . . . The gap between the rich and poor nations is no longer merely a gap. It is a chasm.[6]

The political tensions implicit in the inadequate progress of two-thirds of the world's population have become increasingly clear. The difficulties of peaceful co-existence between nations that are poles apart on the income-scale are appreciated even by those who reject the Marxist categories of social and historical analysis.[7]

Statements like this, stressing the gulf between the wretchedness of the two-thirds majority and affluence of the one-third minority, have helped the cause of aid from its earliest days.

In fact there is a continuous range of incomes between the societies of the world, and no clear gap, let alone chasm. Until recent times no one had the facilities or commodities the absence of which is said to deny the necessities of life to the peoples of the Third World. And as we have also seen, large parts of the Third World have progressed extremely rapidly in recent decades and very large numbers of people there are more prosperous than are many people in the West.

The large-scale and rapid expansion of social studies, especially economics, has also served the cause of aid. This expansion has much increased the number of people who claim to have discerned the existence of economic problems, and who claim also that they can both diagnose the nature of the problems and prescribe appropriate remedies.

We have seen in chapter 1 that a social problem is a discrepancy between a norm and social reality. We have also seen that because they are preoccupied with discerning and announcing such discrepancies, social scientists are apt to generate what are called social problems. There is no Third World development problem. Rather there are innumerable societies with widely differing conditions of life and expectations for the future. Like everybody else, people in the Third World would like to have more of the good things of life. But it is not informative to describe this as a development problem. The so-called Third World development problem was created by those who lumped together the innumerable societies of the Third World, and then declared that their low level of incomes compared with the West posed a problem to be solved or mitigated by wealth transfers.

143

3

Once aid got under way, it soon became clear that it served the political and financial interests of many people who accordingly joined in its support and administration. Staff members of the official national and international aid organizations have been an influential category, as have been, to a lesser extent, politicians close to them. The staff members and consultants of the United Nations and its affiliates have become a powerful force. They have often discarded even the appearance of neutrality to become, in effect, union organizers for the Third World.

The situation is epitomized by the position and opinions of Dr Mahbub ul Haq, Director of Policy Planning in the World Bank and one of Mr McNamara's speech writers:

A major part of the bargaining strength of the Third World lies in its political unity. This unity is going to be even more important in the struggle ahead. . . . One of the essential tactics of the Third World should be to proceed through the process of collective bargaining so that whatever bargaining strength its individual members possess is pooled together.[8]

This passage, which encapsulates the argument of Dr Mahbub's book, is typical of the dominant opinion in the international organizations on the subject of economic relations between the Third World and the West. It is but one example that, in the insistence on global wealth transfers, even the semblance of an argument has now been largely abandoned in favour of threats, albeit empty threats.

The official international organizations have done much to popularize the idea of a homogeneous less developed world with a common interest. They have organized representatives of the most diverse Third World countries to act in concert as a sort of trade union of the world's (alleged) poor – to borrow from President Nyerere – in extracting resources from the West. Thus, staff members of the various regional commissions of the United Nations provide briefs for Third World representatives at UNCTAD meetings and help these representatives coordinate their activities. Aid administrators derive both political and financial benefits from these activities. As we have seen, aid helps to promote state-controlled economies in the Third World, which many aid administrators favour. Official aid also secures them impressive and lucrative positions. Their financial benefits may appear to be fortuitous, as if Adam Smith's invisible hand were to work in reverse, so that those who sought the public good achieve what was no part of their intention, namely personal prosperity. As so often happens, people who set out to do good do well.

144

Professor Thomas Sowell's vivid and celebrated observation of the poor as a goldmine applies conspicuously to official international wealth transfers supposedly in the interests of the world's poor:

> To be blunt, the poor are a gold mine. By the time they are studied, advised, experimented with and administered to, the poor have helped many a middle-class liberal to attain affluence with Government money.[9]

Academics, especially academic economists, are also both major beneficiaries and effective supporters of aid. There is indeed an umbilical link between development economics and foreign aid. Before the Second World War, development economics did not exist as an academic subject. [10] It owes its existence very largely to the worldwide interest in foreign aid and the less developed countries. These concerns have led to a proliferation of posts in universities and foundations. There are now development centres, institutes and advisory groups the world over, often with close ties to major foundations and government departments. The burgeoning of development studies and related subjects has affected the substance and tenor of the academic study of much social science, the widespread effects of which may well be lasting. Development economists can also aspire to well-paid influential posts with international organizations, domestic aid agencies or organizations supported by them. This expansion of development studies serves to promote political systems favoured by mainstream development economists.

The media and the entertainment industry also became agents and beneficiaries of the aid campaign at an early stage. Since the 1950s the so-called quality press in the West has focused persistently on such matters as the poverty and wretchedness of the Third World. Familiar themes are hunger, malnutrition and famine, overpopulation, the exploitation of the Third World by the West (and of the Third World workers by multinational companies and by local employers) and the lack of medical, sanitary and educational facilities there. The illustration of such conditions by pictures of starving children, shacks and shanty-towns full of people, crowds of people everywhere, workers receiving pittances as a wage, has become a staple for documentary films, television programmes and press photography. These presentations are addressed to Western audiences unfamiliar with local realities, and unlikely to appreciate, for instance, that the inhabitants of shanty-towns are often stable communities, and that people migrate there because this improves their lot; or that the so-called starvation wages or pittances often represent substantial incomes locally. These presentations engender a mixture of horror, self-satisfaction, guilt, fear and titillation in different and varying proportions. But singly or in combination, these sentiments support the aid crusade.

Mr Hugh O'Shaugnessy, a prominent British aid advocate, put this well. Mr O'Shaugnessy is the principal correspondent for Latin America of the *Financial Times*. The rapid economic progress of Latin America is a frequent theme of articles in the *Financial Times*, often illustrated with photographs of the skyscrapers and skylines of its cities.

> Continually confronted by the media with images of how wretched life is for the majority of the world's population, people in this country, even in these comparatively lean times, accept that they have a duty to do what they can to palliate such wretchedness.[11]

The frequent and effective contacts between mainstream development economists and the media have enhanced the influence of both these groups.

4

Aid also benefits more specifically commercial interests. Exporters in the donor countries, including exporters of services (for instance economic and engineering consultants and other professional groups), often benefit greatly. This result is evident in tied aid, which is always in part an export subsidy from the taxpayers to the exporters. The subsidy element to exporters is often considerable as, for instance, in the provision of ships by the United Kingdom to India and Poland under the United Kingdom Aid Programme in the 1970s. Exporters, especially exporters of capital goods, in Britain and on the Continent, have for many years past been articulate and effective supporters of official aid and evident beneficiaries of tied aid. According to press reports (which were probably accurate) in Western newspapers in the autumn of 1978, lobbying by two large Western companies, one state-owned, the other private, with large contracts to supply tractors and trucks to Vietnam, was the prime influence behind continued EEC aid to the Vietnam government in 1978. This was at a time when hundreds of thousands of its most productive people were forced to leave the country.[12] Tied aid also often helps both governments and commercial interests to get rid of embarrassing commodity surpluses. While tied aid most obviously benefits exporters, they often derive benefit from untied aid too, when the expected orders financed by aid are more important to them than any orders possibly forgone in their own countries because of the reduction in purchasing power resulting from aid.[13]

Multinational companies with subsidiaries in the Third World also benefit if aid reduces the risk of expropriation, as it may have done in some instances.

But this outcome is by no means general. The governments of the donor countries are often unable or unwilling to assist these companies, while the operation of aid often promotes governments hostile to private enterprise. Multinational companies often support aid for reasons of public relations, especially to improve their standing with both Western and Third World governments. If companies support official aid, they can claim they are public-spirited organizations – good corporate citizens, in the modish phrase. Creditors of Third World governments may also benefit if aid improves their chances of getting their money back by putting aid money into the hands of debtor governments. The vocal support for aid in the 1970s by the large international banks seems to reflect this consideration.

From about the late 1960s, business and labour interests in the West have come to support aid from self-interest. Western donors severely restrict imports from the Third World to protect their own domestic industries. These restrictions have become progressively more severe and extensive. Two altogether different influences emanating from unrelated sources have promoted this result. The first of these has been the increased competitive power of many Third World industries. These competitive industries now include not only the familiar examples of textiles, footwear and shipbuilding, but also technologically sophisticated industries such as electronics, especially in the Far East. The second influence behind the proliferation of import restrictions in the West has been the increased effectiveness of pressure groups. In the present context, this latter influence reflects the strong resistance to industrial change in many Western economies, especially where the change leads to unemployment, even if this is only temporary. By what may be termed a self-protection racket, Western governments are ready to assist domestic sectional interests and buy votes at the expense both of Third World exporters and of their own taxpayers and consumers. In donor countries, protection against Third World imports resembles tied aid given to the Third World. Tied aid is in part a subsidy to exporters in donor countries, while import restrictions are a form of subsidy to domestic production; the same interests may benefit under both headings.

Official barriers against Third World imports lend some surface plausibility to the advocacy of aid. Because protection in the West restricts the opportunities open to Third World countries (compared to what they would be otherwise), feelings of Western guilt are reinforced. Aid takes on the character of conscience money. The Western beneficiaries of restrictions can look kindly on aid. It costs them little compared with their gains, and it reduces political resistance to the protection from which they benefit.

Western aid lobbies are apt to treat these restrictions lightly, and may even tacitly condone them. They may perhaps regard the barriers as useful arguments for more aid. Because of the restrictions, self-reliant development in the Third World is retarded: fruitful contacts with the West are reduced. The resulting difficulties for self-reliant enterprises add plausibility to the claim that aid is a continuing necessity although in fact, as we have seen, the material progress of many Third World countries, as manifested by their competitive strength, plainly refutes some of the more widely canvassed arguments for aid. Self-reliant progress threatens to put aid administrators and advocates out of a job, while the trade restrictions promise at least some job security. Professional humanitarians do not favour self-reliant groups who can dispense with their ministrations. Professor Thomas Sowell has clearly observed this phenomenon in a most illuminating article in which he also drew attention to some of its damaging and distasteful consequences:

the hostile reception accorded to any good news about black progress suggests a large vested interest in social pathology – as a source of accusations and demands on society, and as a reason for giving money, power, and patronage to the accusers and denouncers . . . .[14]

The powerful and articulate groups behind aid have created an effective claque which has managed to silence discussion of the subject, including worthwhile reform of aid.[15] This claque has also helped to divert attention from the evident anomalies of aid, and from its far-reaching consequences. Such activities and their effectiveness are helped by the fact that the public in the West necessarily knows less about conditions in the Third World than it does about domestic affairs.

An exception to the consensus is the critique of aid on the part of the far left, which regards aid as a neo-colonialist enterprise to secure Western political and economic domination over the Third World. But this exception is apparent rather than real. These critics generally object to aid because it does not go far enough in promoting international redistribution, or in bringing about confiscation of the relatively prosperous groups, or in the establishment of socialist economies in the Third World. Thus the activities of this group of critics reinforce the general direction of the operation of aid. Another possible exception is presented by a handful of individual critics of aid who, because of their small number, can be easily discredited as eccentrics or outright cranks. Thus the arguments of neither group of critics affect the overall magnitude, operation or direction of international wealth transfers.

5

As a result of the successful advocacy of aid, many people in the West have come to envisage the world as comprising two sharply distinct categories. One category is the people of the Third World, sunk in poverty, helpless and at the mercy of their environment, exploited by the West, caught in a vicious circle of poverty, unable to control their own fertility, devoid of will and with little capacity for individual action. In short, they are like paupers or children. On the other side of a vast gulf are the prosperous people of the West, partly conditioned by their environment but with a will of their own, active but malign, responsible for the plight of the world's poor and unwilling to improve it.

There is no doubt which is the superior group in this scenario. The West emerged from poverty; the Third World cannot without massive help. The poverty of the Third World is the result of exploitation by the West; its chance of a better future depends on Western aid. Past, present and future, whatever happens to the people of the Third World is decided by the West. The people of the West can thus feel superior, even while they accuse themselves. What poses as compassion involves a great deal of condescension. Condescension in turn readily leads to coercion. To assist the helpless people of the Third World, the West first taxes its own citizens and organizes international wealth transfers. It then presses for domestic redistribution within Third World countries. And it does not shrink from organizing the lives of the poor in their own best interests. Hence the close link between official aid on the one hand, and comprehensive planning and other schemes of coercion and social engineering on the other. The social engineers often insist that the declared objectives of their coercive policies must be pursued at whatever costs. The sacrifices are not borne by those who so warmly advocate their imposition, and who usually benefit from the policies on which they insist. They are borne instead by ordinary people in the West and especially in the Third World. The longer the policies continue, the greater the sacrifices and the more difficult it becomes to question the cause in the name of which they have been exacted.

A most formidable array of interest groups has grown up in support of aid, including politicians, staff members of the international organizations and of Western government departments, churchmen and a variety of business groups and trade unions. Indeed, there are people who argue that the influence of interest groups is the decisive factor behind foreign aid. For instance, a senior British academic said recently, in response to a lecture criticizing foreign aid, that its protracted examination is misleading. He argued that official aid is simply a racket which benefits Third World politicians, the staffs of aid agencies and Western exporters at the expense of Western taxpayers and of ordinary people in the Third World. To the extent that he is right, discussion of aid serves only to divert attention from this basic reality.

6

By now the power of vested interests involved in aid is daunting. Every Western country has a government department dispensing aid. These organizations, including the British and German aid ministries, spend heavily on what they call aid education, both in schools and in the media, so that the taxpayer must also be convinced and have his children convinced of the value of his compulsory donations.[16] This official propaganda is a revealing example of the powerful force of self-perpetuation of official aid organizations, a force which, for reasons already suggested, is even greater in this area than in the purely domestic sphere. Aid has become a major task and often even the sole task of extremely powerful official international organizations, which also spend lavishly on promoting it. Compared with the resources of their opponents and critics, the resources of the aid organizations are unlimited; they receive taxes, their critics pay them.

The World Bank group, the most powerful aid organization in the world, epitomizes the far-reaching activities, interests and ramifications of some of these organizations. The group includes the International Development Association which effectively gives money away. World Bank bonds are widely held by banks, insurance companies, pension funds, corporations, churches and individuals. The value of these bonds would decline, possibly heavily, if there were any threat that a major Western government would withdraw its support from the Bank, especially if there were any suggestion of withdrawal by the United States. Moreover, substantial curtailment of the activities of the World Bank group would endanger not only its own staff, but also the interests of many beneficiaries of its activities in the Third World and the West, in politics, business, the professions, the media, the academies, and in the other international organizations.

Over the imprint of the Bank, senior staff members have been able to publish reports and studies which are riddled with simple violations of common sense, fact and logic.[17] The paucity of critical comment, indeed often the commendation of altogether incompetent World Bank publications, reflects in part the prestige and strength of the Bank, and in part the approval of its ideology by the academies and the media. The Bank has given aid used to support inhuman and coercive policies in the Third World (e.g. Ethiopia, Tanzania) – all without endangering the position or prestige of the Bank, and mostly without eliciting critical comment.

With such powerful support, these official wealth transfers are clearly here to stay for the foreseeable future. Their operation ensures that they will be self-perpetuating.

CHAPTER 7

The Link Scheme of Aid

1

It is widely proposed, as part of a package of international monetary reform, that Special Drawing Rights (SDRs) should be issued by the International Monetary Fund (IMF) to less developed countries (ldcs) as a form of foreign aid. This proposal for the creation of additional international money has come to be known as the Link, or the Link scheme, because it links foreign aid to the creation of international liquidity. In this chapter, which is not concerned with the merits of foreign aid as such, I argue that acceptance of the Link scheme would reinforce world-wide inflation.

The purpose of the Link scheme is to effect a transfer of real resources from the richer donor countries to the ldcs, which purpose implies that the latter must soon spend the Link SDRs issued to them, and not simply add them to their reserves. This conclusion applies whether the newly-created international money is issued to individual ldcs, or issued in the first instance to an international organization, such as the International Development Association, for subsequent disbursement to individual ldcs. Thus will the Link promptly result in additional spending. Supporters of the scheme argue that any inflationary effect would be small, usually on the ground that the sums involved would be modest and, moreover, that any inflationary effect could be counteracted by appropriate monetary and fiscal policies by the donor countries. It should be evident, on the basis of this latter argument, that no policy need ever be inflationary as, in principle, any inflationary effect could be offset by counteracting measures.

I contend that such offsetting action is improbable; that even if it were undertaken it would be delayed; and also that, if the Link scheme is accepted, the volume of SDRs issued under it is likely to be larger than at first proposed. The crux of the argument is that from the point of view of donor countries there are radical differences between foreign aid given in the familiar form of routine aid, whether bilateral or multilateral (i.e. channelled through international organizations) on the one hand, and a transfer of an equivalent amount of resources under the Link scheme on the other.

In the 1970s the multilateral component of foreign aid increased steadily

151

and considerably. This form of aid is more likely to have a net inflationary effect than is bilateral aid. This result is probable because any expansionary effect of spending by the recipients is less likely to be monitored by the donors of multilateral aid. The donors are less likely to take account of the additional spending by the recipients of aid, and also less likely to try to influence these recipients to take heed of any expansionary effects of their spending policies. The inflationary effects of the Link scheme, which involves the creation of high-powered international liquidity, are likely to be more pronounced than those of even multilateral aid, and much more so than those of bilateral aid. The difference is likely to be particularly pronounced when routine aid is not financed by the creation of additional money.

It is common ground between supporters and opponents of the Link that exports from individual countries bought with Link SDRs would be paid for in internationally acceptable currency. Nevertheless, in the aggregate the exporting countries would experience a drain on their real resources because Link SDRs do not represent the creation of resources, but only the creation of claims on resources. Indeed, if these exports were requited *in toto*, in the sense of being paid for by their equivalent in real resources, there would be no aid element in the operation of the scheme. In the aggregate, that is, the exporting countries donate real resources to the recipients by financing the Link scheme.

2

Aid represents specific claims on the resources of individual donor countries. This effect is direct and obvious, and in inflationary conditions it is likely to lead to some offsetting fiscal and monetary measures, whether from choice or necessity. Under the Link scheme the claims on the resources of the donor countries are just as real as under ordinary aid. But the direct nexus between this form of aid and the claim on resources is broken, the effects diffused, and offsetting measures correspondingly less likely. The basic reason why they are much less likely is that although Link SDRs represent additional claims on real resources, their spending cannot be anticipated by individual governments.

Like any other category of government expenditure, routine aid represents a readily perceivable, indeed obvious, claim on a country's real resources. This claim is taken into account by a donor government in assessing the overall effects of its policies on the economy. It is, therefore, a factor which directly affects estimates of the general state of the economy, and thus of the monetary and fiscal policies appropriate to achieve desired internal and external economic results.

An increase in routine aid is an expansion of one category of government spending, and is clearly visible as competing with other forms of such spending. Whatever the general state of the economy, this additional spending requires either higher taxation or reduction in other forms of public spending, increased borrowing from non-bank sources or the creation of new money.

The domestic consequences of any of these measures are of a kind which cannot be ignored. Donor countries must therefore keep some control over the volume of routine aid, and the consequences for the domestic economy tend to act as a brake on its expansion.

The effects of the provision of routine aid on a donor country's external reserves tend to act as a further brake on the volume of aid. When aid is spent outside a donor country, the effect on a country's external resources is direct and obvious. When the money is spent within the donor country, it is part of total spending. The connection between aggregate spending and the external balance is now well understood.

Under the Link scheme these effective brakes are likely to be absent or weak. The issue of SDRS to less developed countries by an international organization has no direct, predictable or readily perceptible impact on the domestic economies of individual donor countries. This measure will not, therefore, seem to call for offsetting action. Nor will the issue of SDRS and their use by the recipient countries affect the external reserves of any individual donor country in any clearly foreseeable or evident fashion. Indeed, although in the aggregate the countries financing the Link SDRS must experience a loss of foreign exchange, some individual countries may well enjoy an increase as a result of the creation and spending of SDRS.

Under the Link scheme the transfer of real resources to the initial recipients of these SDRS is financed by the creation of additional international money. For the collectivity of donor countries such a measure will have inflationary effects similar to those of an equivalent increase in their ordinary aid (assuming no offsetting financial action is taken). But the causal chain leading to any inflationary effects will be masked, and the effects themselves diffused. Furthermore, some of the repercussions on the domestic economies of individual donor countries could be warded off if these countries drew from the IMF their own authorized quotas of ordinary SDRS. Thus the governments of individual donor countries will be much less inclined to address themselves to the potential inflationary effects of the process of the transfer of resources. They will also be less concerned with the total volume of SDRS issued under the Link scheme than they are with the financing of routine aid.

It may be objected that the issue of SDRS under the Link scheme would lead to a reduction in the volume of ordinary aid. However, since the prime purpose of the Link scheme is to expand the volume of aid, any reduction in ordinary aid is extremely unlikely. Moreover, the donor countries will be under no great inducement to reduce their own aid, for the reasons already indicated. The issues of Link SDRs will therefore form an independent source of potential inflation.

It may be said, by way of further objection, that the volume of Link SDRs currently envisaged is too small to have any appreciable inflationary effect. However, in the contemporary climate the volume of SDRs issued periodically under the Link scheme will probably be larger than currently suggested by its advocates. This is especially likely if the economic development of the ldcs is deemed unsatisfactory on one or other of the many different criteria canvassed in discussions about the less developed world. Moreover, as already noted, individual donor countries will not be much concerned with the volume of Link SDRs, and will therefore have little reason to resist pressures for their expansion.

It is especially pertinent here that the volume of SDRs under the Link scheme would be decided by an official international organization. Resistance to the expansion of this form of aid is then likely to be less than when the amount of aid is determined by individual countries, because each country bears only part of the cost of the total expansion determined by the collective decision.

3

Whatever one thinks of foreign aid, there is no sensible reason for linking it to international monetary reform. The Link proposals appeal because they make aid appear costless to individual donor countries. The real resources transferred in the aid process are represented in the first instance by SDRs, and thus appear to be created out of thin air. In this respect the Link scheme bears a family resemblance to public spending on the poor financed by the creation of money rather than by taxation. Both domestic and international creation of money is politically popular because the costs of the process are concealed. For this very reason the political, social and economic costs are likely to be greater.

The proposed introduction of a scheme which is likely to be inflationary is highly paradoxical at a time when the donor countries are attempting to grapple with inflation. The adverse social, political and economic effects of this inflation are recognized in the far-reaching measures being introduced in Britain and elsewhere in attempts to control inflation, or at least some of its politically more embarrassing manifestations.

Prolonged inflation is likely to be accompanied by appreciable international differences in rates of inflation. These differences have contributed to international currency crises and thus to the resurgence of protectionism. Protectionism damages the economic position and development prospects of ldcs. Trade restrictions in the West and their adverse effects on ldcs are apt to lead to demands for further assistance, which may well take the form of Link aid. As we have already noted, aid under the Link scheme is more inflationary than ordinary aid.

The Link proposal is one of many anomalies in the discussion of international monetary reform. The whole SDR concept was originally advanced to avert a threatened shortage of international liquidity which it was feared would impart a deflationary bias to the world monetary system. Creation of appreciable additional reserve assets is now proposed after years of alarming inflation, and at a time when the international movement of massive liquid funds presents major problems to monetary management. The ultimate paradox here is one which reflects on the state of the political climate and the level of public discussion. At present the credibility of governments and international bodies is at a distinctly low ebb. At the same time wide powers of decision about the creation and distribution of international money are proposed for organizations set up by governments who are themselves unable to manage successfully their own domestic monetary systems.

CHAPTER 8

Costs and Risks of Commodity Stabilization

1

International commodity policy is often envisaged as an instrument both for stabilizing prices and incomes of primary producers and also for transferring resources from rich countries to poor countries. These twin objectives are apt to be regarded as closely related or even as identical. In fact they differ radically.

Unless clearly defined stabilization is an altogether vague concept which can be interpreted in a number of different and conflicting ways. But on none of the accepted meanings of the term is it the same as a resource transfer. The stabilization of prices and of incomes received by people cannot be identified legitimately with the systematic transfer of resources to them or from them. We shall first discuss some issues of stabilization, and then turn to commodity agreements as instruments of resource transfer.

Stabilization as an objective of commodity policy is difficult to examine because the idea is so vague. It is often not even made clear whether stabilization is to be applied to world market prices or to prices and incomes within particular producing countries. Again, stabilization sometimes refers to maximum prices or incomes, that is, to the imposition of a ceiling; and at other times to minimum prices or incomes, that is, to the establishment of a floor. What it clearly cannot mean, though this is rarely made explicit, is the indefinite maintenance of prices and incomes at a constant level.

In practice, stabilization is usually interpreted as an attempt to maintain prices or incomes at a fixed level (or within a specified range), varying them subsequently by means of abrupt changes; or as the smoothing of random fluctuations around a trend. But even when stabilization is distinguished from a transfer of resources, and when maintenance of prices or incomes followed by abrupt changes is distinguished from the smoothing of random fluctuations, there still remain basic ambiguities in the concept. For instance, advocates of stabilization rarely make clear whether it refers to money values or to real terms in some sense or another; what mechanism is envisaged for retaining or regaining contact with the long-term trend of prices; over what period the smoothing process is to operate or prices are to be kept constant before an abrupt adjustment; what relationship is envisaged under locally operated schemes between world market prices and the domestic prices received by producers (a guaranteed price at a small fraction of the market price does not help producers); whether prices are to be adjusted to compensate for variations in output, such as harvest variations; who is to be covered by a proposed stabilization scheme, and how actual and potential producers not covered by it are to be treated; how to allow for the inevitable changes through time in the composition of the body of producers; or why wide abrupt adjustments should be preferable to frequent oscillations in prices.[1]

This is an incomplete list of issues which need to be faced in any sensible discussion of commodity stabilization. Otherwise stabilization becomes a completely vague omnibus expression which can be invested with any number of different meanings. These interpretations can then be invoked in support of widely differing, and indeed conflicting, policies. Thus stabilization has been invoked in support of commodity cartels designed to raise prices and incomes; and also in support of the confiscation of the bulk of the sales proceeds of cash crop producers by the state export monopolies in West Africa, East Africa and Burma. For a commodity stabilization scheme to deserve serious consideration, the objectives envisaged and the methods of implementation have to be set out clearly. These requirements are rarely satisfied.

A review of the principal interpretations of international or domestic commodity stabilization would require book-length treatment. It is neither appropriate nor feasible to attempt this here, especially because commodity policy is usually envisaged as an instrument for transferring resources to the Third World; stabilization is merely a misleading euphemism for this policy. We shall examine in subsequent sections the principal issues of commodity agreements as a form of resource transfer. We shall first, however, consider matters pertinent to stabilization in the sense of attempted reductions in the fluctuations in prices and incomes of primary producers.

2

Exponents of stabilization schemes are apt to suggest that their proposals would improve on the haphazard and irrational operations of commodity markets. In particular, it is still often claimed that the administrators of international buffer stocks or of domestic marketing boards can disregard short-period changes in market sentiment. It is claimed further that managers of such organizations can mitigate frequent and disturbing price fluctuations by focusing on underlying long-term trends in supply and demand.

These claims are unfounded. The future course of prices of particular commodities is unpredictable. There is no way of telling whether a particular price change will be followed by further movement in the same direction, let alone by how much or for how long, or whether it is a short period fluctuation to be reversed soon. Those who can assess market conditions and prices more rationally than can the commodity markets would accumulate vast wealth. Diligent search has failed to uncover many such examples among politicians, civil servants and academics who claim explicitly or implicitly to be able to perform better than participants in commodity markets. It is because prospective price movements are unpredictable and the penalties of mistakes extremely heavy that prices fluctuate widely. Private traders and speculators themselves bear the risks and costs. Administrators of buffer stocks and of state monopolies can throw the costs on to others; and the costs of their operations are often concealed.

If they have sufficient control over total supply and demand, administrators of international stabilization schemes can keep market prices within prescribed limits. Similarly, administrators of local marketing boards can support product prices indefinitely if they have access to sufficient funds; and they can keep down domestic prices indefinitely if they have the sole right to export. But such possibilities have nothing to do either with superior foresight or with stabilization in any meaningful sense. They are analogous to abolishing unemployment by conscripting the unemployed or putting them into prison.

The allegedly damaging consequences of price fluctuations on the position and prospects of Third World economies are often adduced in support of international stabilization measures such as buffer stocks, which are said to be able to reduce or eliminate unnecessary price fluctuations. As we have already noted, they are unlikely to do so. Moreover, international action is not necessary in order to cushion the impact of price fluctuations on a local economy and on its producers. This cushioning can be achieved by local fiscal and monetary policies, designed to accumulate reserves in times of prosperity and to draw on them in periods of adversity. The impact of world price fluctuations on producers can also be reduced by variable export taxes. This latter method also has the advantage that it can take into account fluctuations in local output if this is thought desirable. Sliding-scale export duties operate widely in Third World countries. They could be extended and refined to promote the smoothing of fluctuations in prices and incomes. This method, however, raises problems such as that of maintaining contact with the trend of market prices; the repercussions of variations in export duties on the world market price; and possible destabilizing effects on producer incomes if the rates do not allow for variations in output. What one needs to remember is that the impact of market price fluctuations on local producer prices and incomes (or on the domestic economy as a whole) can be cushioned by local action, but that this involves risks and costs, as do measures which sever contact with market prices. Incidentally, such smoothing measures do not require state export monopolies such as the familiar marketing boards in the former British dependencies. Such export monopolies are always liable to become instruments of taxation.

An alternative approach which does not involve the disadvantages of such stabilization schemes is to encourage the use of forward contracts by small producers and traders, and the development of organized commodity markets in local centres. This can be promoted by the spread of modern financial institutions and the banking habit in the rural areas, and by the extension of the activities of the traders who form the vital communication links between the smaller and larger market centres. In practice, so far from attempting to improve the operation of markets and to extend the activities of traders, many Third World governments severely limit the range and scope of their activities. This not only has the effect of discouraging output, but frequently serves to widen the local price fluctuations both of internationally traded goods and of domestic produce.

Government action could also encourage the accumulation of financial reserves by producers. Public discussion of stabilization schemes often treats the peoples of the Third World as if they were children incapable of taking thought for the morrow. As far as the peasant producers are concerned, this prejudice seems to be plainly unwarranted – witness the readiness of millions of West African and Malayan producers to plant tree crops such as cocoa and rubber which take many years to reach maturity. Third World governments, on the other hand, often spend heavily on investment projects (the returns of which are frequently doubtful and at best delayed) at the expense of keeping foreign exchange reserves, which are often deemed unproductive. Governments which fail to keep foreign exchange reserves are, of course, vulnerable even to relatively modest fluctuations in commodity prices.

Even sharp fluctuations in the prices of primary products are not necessarily damaging; and even effective smoothing of such fluctuations would not necessarily be advantageous. For instance, temporary high prices may help to attract resources into certain activities such as clearing the jungle and thereby extending capacity. This new capacity will not be abandoned even if prices subsequently decline. Nor do wide fluctuations in export prices normally set up political tensions in ldcs. In many cases farmers can readily divert their effort and resources from the temporarily unprofitable (or less profitable) product to other products and activities, including susbsistence production.[2] This flexibility cushions the effects of adverse price movements of particular export commodities. Moreover, in the absence of specific import controls the volume of imports responds readily to changes in domestic demand. Thus a rise in export prices does not bring about a sharp rise in the price of imports. Ample experience in less developed countries both before and since the Second World War confirms the operation of these processes of smooth adjustment.

3

The commodity schemes widely canvassed at meetings of the United Nations Conference on Trade and Development (UNCTAD) and elsewhere are clearly seen as instruments for resource transfer to the Third World and, by clear implication, as a transfer from rich to poor. They are singularly inappropriate for this purpose. Here are some reasons.

Exporters of primary products are not generally poor, let alone invariably so. Rich countries are often net exporters of major primary products. One need only look at the OPEC countries to show how inappropriate it is to identify primary producers with poor people, even within the Third World. The countries exporting primary products are usually among the more prosperous (even apart from petroleum exporters) as, for instance, countries exporting rubber, cocoa, coffee and copper. And within the exporting countries the main beneficiaries of commodity agreements are relatively prosperous producers, including at times shareholders and employees of mining and plantation companies, as well as politicians, businessmen and administrators. It is the opposite of the truth to suggest, as is often done, that commodity agreements are necessary to improve the lot of the desperately poor. The poorest countries and groups in the Third World rarely produce for export.

Commodity agreements are normally regressive. To raise prices these schemes have to restrict supply, which means restriction of output or export and normally also exclusion of potential producers. Those subject to these restrictions, especially the frustrated producers, are usually poorer, often very much poorer, than those who benefit from the operation of the schemes. This applies within countries, especially when the controlled commodity is the only source of cash income or one of the few sources of cash income available in certain areas. But it also applies internationally, as many countries which have to be barred from producing or exporting the controlled commodity, or have to be restrained from increasing their production or exports, are much worse off than are the established exporting countries.[3] The analysis applies closely to the current tin scheme, and with varying degrees of approximation to schemes operating intermittently, and to those proposed for cocoa, coffee, rubber, tea and some other primary products.[4]

The controlled commodities are often the principal source of cash income in many rural areas of the Third World, where their production is a major instrument for replacing subsistence production by production for the market. Forcible exclusion from production implies not only a loss of income for many of the rural poor, but also the restriction of mobility between activities and places, and thus a restriction on their economic, social and even cultural horizons. These considerations apply both within countries and also internationally.

While exclusion from production is a substantial penalty, the right to produce or to export under a commodity scheme may be a valuable asset, as is readily ascertainable from the high prices paid for the right to produce, export or to establish capacity. The right to allocate such valuable privileges as export quotas increases the prizes of administrative and political power. Such a situation leads to political tension both within particular countries and also between them. The quota aspect of commodity agreements reinforces the misconception that incomes are extracted from other people rather than earned by the recipients. Quota systems lend plausibility to this notion, because an increase in the quotas of some producers reduces those available to others.

Besides their effect on the position and prospects of frustrated producers, commodity agreements are regressive also because they raise the prices of commodities of mass consumption in both rich and poor countries. Many Third World countries import commodities covered by these agreements. The impact of the OPEC cartel on the import prices of many Third World countries is a familiar instance of a more general phenomenon. Many raw materials and foodstuffs are produced in relatively prosperous Third World countries and imported into others which are much poorer. Indeed, commodity agreements in a sense raise prices twice over: they raise prices by restricting output in order to increase the incomes of producers.[5] But they also inflate costs by protecting higher-cost producers, and at times by enforced under-capacity working. Prices have to rise sufficiently to secure higher incomes after compensating for the higher costs.

The users of the controlled products and the frustrated producers bear the primary economic costs of commodity schemes. Their incidence is not only repressive, it is also arbitrary, difficult to calculate and largely concealed. Thus it does differ from that of routine foreign aid channelled through the budget.

Some of these results of commodity agreements are both anomalous and evident. Their neglect in the advocacy of these measures shows yet again that as long as a policy removes resources from the West its advocates can ignore even its most evidently damaging impact on the welfare of the ostensible beneficiaries, the poor of the Third World.

The argument so far has assumed that commodity agreements are effective and lasting. Further problems and tensions arise from the frequent instability of commodity schemes. Their success in raising the prices, and thus the incomes of the favoured producers and producing countries, depends on effective control of output and supply both of the commodities covered and of their close substitutes, whether agricultural or manufactured. Higher prices by themselves stimulate the search for new sources and new substitutes. Except where a controlled commodity can occur in a few places only, output is likely to expand in areas not covered by the scheme, a development often accompanied by the accumulation of unsold stocks which are very expensive to finance. And the collapse of a commodity scheme results in abrupt and disrupting changes in incomes and prices, and is likely to exacerbate domestic and international tensions. Moreover, excluded producers and producing countries are likely to become restive, especially when the scheme has succeeded in maintaining or raising prices. And success of this kind is in any case likely to set up tensions in the periodic negotiations on the allocation of production and export quotas. Such developments are familiar from the history of many arrangements for raising prices of primary products, including coffee, cotton, copper, rubber and sugar.

CHAPTER 9

British Colonial Africa: Economic Retrospect and Aftermath

1

The stereotype of the economic experience of the British colonies in Africa can be readily summarized. It is in two parts. According to the first and principal part, during most of the colonial era these territories stagnated, even retrogressed, as a result of administrative neglect and commercial exploitation. According to the second part, toward the end of colonialism the rulers somewhat mended their ways and showed a more active concern for the welfare of their subjects. I shall start with some characteristic expressions of this stereotype and then show at length that neither part of it bears any relation to reality.

I do not wish to argue here the case either for or against colonialism. Rather, I want to try and set the record straight on some central issues. I shall try to make clear that both the course of events and the character of some perplexing problems of policy (many of which still persist) differ radically from those of the received picture of African experience during colonialism.

2

Kwame Nkrumah, first President of Ghana, was one of the most influential African politicians to emerge after the Second World War. He helped to shape opinions and events far beyond West Africa. About the processes and results of colonial rule he had this to say in his book *Africa Must Unite*:

They [the colonial powers] were all rapacious; they all subserved the needs of the subject lands to their own demands: they all circumscribed human rights and liberties; they all repressed and despoiled, degraded and oppressed. They took our lands, our lives, our resources and our dignity. Without exception, they left us nothing but our resentment. . . . It was when they had gone and we were faced with the stark realities, as in Ghana on the morrow of our independence, that the destitution of the land after long years of colonial rule was brought sharply home to us.[1]

Before colonial rule, conditions in the Gold Coast were extremely primitive and life was short and perilous . People's circumstances improved out of all recognition during the colonial period. The passage from Kwame Nkrumah's book is an example of effrontery playing on guilt and ignorance.

Statements of international bodies with substantial Western participation habitually incorporate unquestioned acceptance of the notions of colonial stagnation and of Western responsibility. Here are two examples.

The Pearson Commission was organized by the World Bank as a grand assize on development. Five of the seven members of the commission were unambiguously Western. Professor Sir Arthur Lewis and Professor Sabuto Okira are *de facto* Westerners in our context, although the former is of West Indian extraction and the latter is Japanese. According to the Annex of the Pearson Report, which was regarded by the commission as part of the report and published between the same covers:

Compared to the rest of the developing world, Africa has been a late starter in economic development. Only three countries, UAR, Ethiopia and Liberia, were independent before 1950, and most attained independence between 1955 and 1963. Despite the late start there have been impressive growth performances in such countries as the Ivory Coast, Kenya and the main oil exporting countries. The relatively recent start on development programmes and in many cases the past failings of colonial administration explain to a large measure Africa's great scarcity of skilled personnel.[2]

General Principle XIV of the 1964 United Nations Conference on Trade and Development (the first UNCTAD) provided another example of the notion that colonial rule necessarily means stagnation. Indeed it epitomized the idea: 'Complete decolonization ... is a necessary condition for economic development and the exercise of sovereign rights over natural resources.' As is evident from experience throughout the world, colonial status as such does not preclude economic progress. It has not precluded it in the contemporary East: witness Malaysia and Singapore, among many other examples. It did not preclude it in the past either, in Australia and New Zealand in the south, or in the United States and Canada in the west and north. Yet at this conference, largely organized and financed by the West, there were only two countries out of 114 which voted against this self-evident untruth. When the vote was taken in 1964 the rapid progress and competitive economic strength of Hong Kong already caused much apprehension in the West and led to restrictions against the exports from there. According to UNCTAD General Principle XIV, colonial status is incompatible with material progress. Hong Kong then was one of the few remaining Western colonies.

In Black Africa also, many colonies progressed rapidly during the colonial period, contrary to the passage just quoted from the Pearson Annex. Familiar examples include Nigeria, the Gold Coast, the Ivory Coast, Kenya, Uganda and Rhodesia. Indeed, and as noted in chapter 4 above, much of British colonial Africa was transformed during the colonial period. In the Gold Coast, there were about 3,000 children at school in the early 1900s, whereas in the mid-1950s there were over half a million. In the early 1890s there were in the Gold Coast no railways or roads, but only a few jungle paths. Transport of goods was by human porterage or canoe. By the 1930s there were railways and good roads; journeys by road required fewer hours than they had required days in 1890. In British West Africa public security and health improved out of all recognition over the period. Peaceful travel became possible; slavery, slave trading and famine were practically eliminated, and the incidence of the worst diseases greatly reduced. British West Africa was not even mentioned in the passage I have quoted from the Pearson Annex and according to which colonial Africa stagnated.

At the end of the nineteenth century Kano and other towns in Northern Nigeria were regular slave markets; and by the 1930s they had become centres of the groundnut trade. As a result of such changes mortality in British colonies fell greatly, with a consequent increase in population. A greatly increased population came to live longer and at a much higher standard of living than before British colonial rule. And the extensive progress brought about by improved communications and the enlargement of peaceful contacts within Africa and with the outside world extended far beyond the material aspects of life.

Professor Sir Arthur Lewis has explicitly recognized the substantial economic advance of colonial Africa. A few years ago he wrote:

The tropics were transformed during the period 1830 to 1913 . . . . In 1913 Sub-Saharan Africa's exports were only 6.2 per cent of tropical trade. By 1937 they were 13.3, by 1955 18.2 . . . per cent of tropical trade.[3]

The passage from the Pearson Annex also specifically blames the colonial adminstrations for the lack of trained personnel in ex-colonial Africa. This is a familiar accusation which does not mention either the much more conspicuous lack of such personnel in independent Ethiopia and Liberia, or its complete absence in pre-colonial Africa.

Economic change was not uniform within individual colonies, especially the larger ones, and even less so over the vast and diverse regions of British colonial Africa. The economic experience of the many and diverse societies of British colonial Africa ranged from comparatively little change to large-scale transformation. In Nigeria, for instance, economic progress during the colonial period was very different in Southern Nigeria from, say, that among the Tiv people in the north. Such diversity of experience is only to be expected.

165

There are regional and group differences in economic attainment throughout the world. These are inescapable in the early stages of economic development, since economic advance must necessarily begin in some places before it can spread to others. This outward spread depends on various factors, primarily the state of physical communications, and on the personal, social and political determinants of economic progress. Economic differences between groups and regions are likely to be pronounced in large countries which encompass diverse societies and areas where communications are poor. The differences are accentuated when change is initiated largely by foreigners and by contacts established with the area by materially more advanced societies. All these conditions were conspicuous in British colonial Africa.

The characteristic experience of the many and diverse societies of colonial Africa was not stagnation but uneven progress with some groups affected sooner and to a much greater extent than others. But everywhere in Black Africa modern economic life began with the colonial period.

3

Many perplexing problems facing colonial governments (and their successors) arose from the impact of sudden and uneven change which, in any one period, affected some groups and regions much more than others. For instance, personal and social difficulties resulted from the transformation of a subsistence economy into a money economy, and from the concomitant processes of detribalization and urbanization. Such problems for governments would not have arisen in stagnant societies.

Social and economic change was so rapid that the governments and their advisers had little time to examine some of its implications and consequences. This circumstance may partly explain the land policies of the British colonial governments, notably the decision to reserve large areas of land for particular sectors of the population, including the establishment of native reserves and the maintenance or promotion of communal tenure of land. These policies were widely regarded as necessary to protect the indigenous population. Humanitarians and missionaries advocated them strongly and also pressed for the prohibition of foreign-owned plantations in West Africa.

Since the 1950s prominent scholars have criticized these arrangements. Professor Frankel has argued that they have obstructed the material progress of both the indigenous and non-indigenous populations and also that they have often provoked political tension rather than alleviated it.[4] Professor Colson has suggested that the promotion of communal tenure misconceived the needs of the population and misinterpreted the pre-colonial systems of land usage in Africa.[5]

Had the colonial governments been less pressed by rapid change their land policies might have been based on a more thorough understanding of social realities. Opinion on such matters as the establishment of native reserves or the ban on foreign-owned plantations in Africa has changed greatly in recent decades. The opinions of Professors Frankel and Colson differ greatly from those of the most influential scholars of the 1940s and 1950s who usually emphasized the benefits of communal tenure of land.

The extreme material backwardness of pre-colonial Africa exacerbated the difficulties and complexities of sudden change. Except for simple bush tracks, there were practically no man-made communications in sub-Saharan Africa on the eve of colonialism. The huge area depended on muscle power for transport and communications, usually human muscle. As I have already noted, the basic ingredients of modern, social and economic life, including public security and health, wheeled transport, modern forms of money and scientific agriculture, were brought to sub-Saharan Africa by Westerners in the nineteenth and early twentieth centuries. They were introduced by the colonial administrations, or by foreign private organizations or persons, under the comparative security of colonial rule and usually in the face of formidable obstacles.

Much of the recent academic and official literature ignores the evident and radical changes which occurred during the colonial era. They were, however, recognized by many knowledgeable and authoritative writers before the Second World War. These writers also saw that these changes took place under the impact of external contacts and that their suddenness presented major social, political and administrative difficulties.

At the turn of the century Mary Kingsley, a well-informed and sympathetic traveller, wrote extensively about the problems of the impact of nineteenth-century Europe on West Africa. She considered that the material culture of the region was roughly at the stage of early medieval Europe. She urged the colonial administrators to be mindful of the difficulties created by this impact.[6]

A generation or so later, but long before African development became an international political issue, Allan McPhee, a distinguished historian of West Africa, wrote that the central problems of policy in British West Africa arose from difficulties of adjustment brought about by 'the superimposition of the twentieth century after Christ on the twentieth century before Christ' following the establishment and rapid spread of cash crops and a monetized economy. He aptly entitled his book *The Economic Revolution in British West Africa*.[7]

Some perceptive and telling observations by Sir Keith Hancock apply both to the colonial period and to the present:

In some periods of European history – in our own day, for example, or in the day of the first steam-engines and power mills – the European world has seemed to be transformed. Europe nevertheless has remained the same world, spinning very much faster.

But in Africa change means more than acceleration. Europe's commerce and its money-measurements really have brought the African into a new world. . . . He retains something of his old social and religious and mental life and habit – these things are very slow in dying – but they are distinct from his new economic life and habit.[8]

These remarks were written towards the end of the colonial period by a historian critical of white rule and of much of colonial policy. Thus the salient characteristics of the African scene in the nineteenth and early twentieth centuries were widely acknowledged until the Second World War. Since then they have been widely ignored or even denied. The idea of stagnation caused by Western oppression and neglect understandably appeals to African politicians. It also appeals to diverse and articulate influential groups in the West who derive emotional satisfaction or even political or financial benefit from the idea that the West has caused the backwardness of Africa.

Few people in the West know how extremely backward this area was until very recently, and mostly still is in spite of much rapid advance over the last hundred years or so. The drastic foreshortening of historical perspective, so familiar in contemporary discourse, contributes to this lack of understanding. The influence of left-liberal academics and media men in the West, the importance of the black vote in the United States, and various recent intellectual fashions have all served to obscure African realities, including the results of Western economic contacts and of colonial rule.

Exposure of the stereotype of colonial stagnation is required in the interests of historical truth. It should help also to show up recent categorical statements such as those quoted in section 2 above, which appear objective and authoritative but which are in fact evident distortions of reality. Furthermore, for an understanding of the post-colonial African scene it is necessary to remember that many of the problems there result not from stagnation but from rapid and uneven change.

4

It is easy to establish that British colonial Africa did not stagnate, but in the nature of things it cannot be shown so readily and conclusively whether colonial rule promoted or retarded economic advance there. Nevertheless, it can be confidently stated that colonial rule promoted rather than obstructed economic advance and, indeed, that it was necessary for it. The confidence of this assertion derives both from the conditions in pre-colonial Africa and the conditions in independent Black African countries, whether Ethiopia and Liberia, or the more recently independent Black African states.

The role of external commercial contacts in initiating and promoting material progress in the Third World is one of the major themes of this book. In Africa this role was conspicuous and far-reaching.

Even more than elsewhere, these contacts were here indispensable for material advance. They brought about the establishment of public security and the construction of transport facilities. These facilities made possible the establishment and enlargement of links between Africa and the outside world and within Africa itself. There, even more than elsewhere, external contacts brought new commodities as well as new ideas, methods and crops to the notice of the local population, and simultaneously provided large markets for their products. They were often the first to acquaint people with the possibilities of change in the immemorial order of things. Millions of Africans took advantage of the opportunities presented.

There were many external contacts in pre-colonial Africa, including peaceful commercial contacts. But Western colonialism greatly increased their volume, variety and effectiveness. A few examples will illustrate these considerations.

The typical communities of pre-colonial Black Africa were generally small and isolated. Without railways, roads and public security, communication was hazardous and difficult even over short distances. Colonial rule and metropolitan support secured both the capital and the skills for the construction of railways and practically all the roads in Africa. Without public security and basic transport facilities there could have been no substantial production of cash crops in the interior, let alone large-scale mining operations. And without railways, roads and wheeled and mechanical transport Black Africa would have continued to depend on exceedingly rudimentary forms of communication.[9] It is noteworthy, though this is very rarely mentioned, that for non-rudimentary transport Black Africa even in 1980 depends largely on facilities constructed and maintained by foreigners.[10]

All agricultural exports from British West African colonies were produced by Africans, mostly on their own farms. The same applies to major cash crops in Uganda and Tanganyika (part of present-day Tanzania). The production of these crops makes it clear that it is misleading to describe the advanced sectors and activities of African economies as mere enclaves owned and operated by foreigners, enclaves which do not materially benefit the local people and may even harm them. But even when the enterprises in the advanced sectors are owned and largely manned by expatriates, they still

169

benefit local people. They provide employment opportunities, generate government revenues, suggest new methods of production and offer opportunities for acquiring new skills.

5

Colonial conquest was usually attended by bloodshed. The extent of bloodshed and of other forms of coercion differed greatly in the various areas. In the British colonies it was generally slight, especially in East Africa; in West Africa, especially in Ashanti and Nigeria, there was more. But on the eve of colonial conquest civil wars, local wars, slavery and slave trading were endemic in most areas, notably in West Africa. Indeed, these conditions usually provided the occasion or the excuse for external intervention. It is highly probable that over most of British Africa colonial conquest saved lives rather than destroyed them: this is virtually certain for instance of Northern Nigeria.

After the establishment of colonial rule coercion was also often used in the recruitment of labour for public employment and at times for private employment. The use of forced labour was not peculiar to Africa. It was widely used in Europe before the nineteenth century. In Africa both indigenous and colonial governments employed forced labour in partly monetized economies. Forced labour is a form of taxation in kind. There were other forms of taxation in kind in Africa as well as elsewhere. Thus in the early days of British rule in East Africa people were allowed to pay taxes in cattle. This system was soon abandoned because taxes came to be paid in old and diseased beasts which died on the collectors' hands. Similarly, chiefs required to supply people for forced labour were apt to enlist the weakest and least efficient men for the work. Nevertheless, forced labour was often employed when the establishment of public security or other public works were difficult and expensive in incompletely monetized economies with sparse populations and poor communications. In British colonies forced labour was limited in extent and duration. The rate at which it diminished was determined by the spread of the cash economy and also by political and moral pressures. Nevertheless, it can be argued that even where it promoted the progress of the indigenous population, coercion was objectionable, especially when applied by alien rulers who often did not understand local sentiments, beliefs and institutions, and whose ways were often incomprehensible to the subjects.

All taxation implies compulsory levies. The burden of forced labour is difficult to gauge adequately because it is bound up with processes and conditions which are not susceptible of measurement. In the British colonies the periods to be served were usually short and conditions reasonably humane. We cannot assume that without colonial rule there would have been less coercion. Before colonial rule local wars, slavery and slave raiding were widespread and endemic. British rule did away with these forms of coercion. The great majority of people came to live longer, more securely and with more freedom than before. The conditions prevailing over much of Africa before colonial rule and since independence suggest that colonialism diminished rather than increased the extent and intensity of coercion.

The extent of disruption in social and family life caused by large-scale migration of labour is much disputed. Where migration was an aspect of forced labour, it no doubt involved hardship and disruption. But forced labour was a small proportion of total migration. Most of it was voluntary response to wider opportunities, especially opportunities for rural people to earn a cash income. As a result of greater public security, many people were encouraged to travel over long distances in search of higher incomes. This judgment is supported by evidence from many regions in Africa and else-where. Examples include the large-scale, long-distance voluntary migration to the cocoa-producing areas of the Gold Coast; the continuing inflow into the towns throughout Africa; the sustained attempts and efforts of many Africans from distant countries to find employment on the Copper Belt and in South Africa; the large-scale voluntary labour migration from China and India to different parts of South-East Asia, the Caribbean and elsewhere; the importance of the backward parts of Europe and Asia as sources of mercenary soldiers from the sixteenth century to the twentieth; and the contemporary large-scale migration, often short-term, of individuals and families from Southern Europe and Turkey to the more industrialized countries of Europe, and of people from Pakistan and India to the Persian Gulf.

Over the past two hundred years or so, most migrants in Africa (as in Asia) were bachelors, or men without their families, who had first considered them-selves as temporary migrants. But the reason for this lay in the supply side rather than the demand side. Employers often preferred family migrants to unaccompanied men, as the former constituted a more permanent labour force, and so were more likely to acquire skills. But tribal chiefs and authorities preferred temporary movement of unaccompanied men to more permanent migration of families, as the movement of families would have disrupted and diminished the tribe much more; and they exercised pressure accordingly. Moreover, the migrants often wished to retain their rights in the tribal lands, and these would have been endangered by permanent or family migration.

Neither extensive migration of labour nor the preponderance of unaccompanied men among migrants was a phenomenon peculiar to colonial Africa. The great expansion of labour migration in colonial Africa was a

171

major consequence of the widening of opportunities and the greater security of movement. It is arguable, of course, that the social disruption caused by economic change and the response to new opportunities by voluntary migrants brought much unhappiness. But criticism of this kind raises issues about the nature and implications of economic change and progress which have nothing to do with colonialism as such.

In summary, the balancing of the costs and benefits of economic changes as vast as those brought about by colonial rule in Africa is an exercise which involves large elements of judgment. But it is certain that the far-reaching changes which attended colonialism provided these territories with such elements of a modern society and economy as there are in Africa. These changes were achieved in the face of great obstacles. The coercion and the hardships, though far from negligible, seem slight when we think of both pre-colonial and post-colonial Africa, and of the character and extent of the changes brought about by colonial rule. The number of Africans who lived longer, more securely, in materially better conditions and in peaceful contact with their fellow men was much greater, probably by several orders of magnitude, than the numbers who were harmed. And before the Second World War most British colonial rulers in Africa addressed themselves to improving the lot of their subjects, which they did with some success.

It is sometimes argued that there would have been economic progress in Africa sooner or later even without colonial rule. This suggestion of eventual progress without colonial rule envisages a time-span which not only far exceeds the colonial era but is also open-ended. Without colonial rule there would have been far fewer external contacts and much less economic progress of the kind which extends people's horizons and widens their range of choice generally. In sections 10 and 11 I shall, however, note a very important and damaging legacy of colonial rule, unrelated to the usual criticisms of the system. But this legacy can only be considered after a review of the policies of the terminal years of colonial rule.

These various observations are not intended to support either colonial rule or the methods employed in its establishment and operation. Rather, they may serve as a reminder that in political action and judgment the choice is usually between courses that many people would regard as evils.

6

From the mid-nineteenth century to the early 1920s free trade was the accepted policy in Britain and the colonies. In the 1920s and early 1930s Britain itself moved away from free trade towards protection. But in Africa the change of policy was at first very small. In the construction of public works colonial government at times favoured British rather than foreign tenders, but this preference was very limited. Southern Rhodesia, Sierra Leone and Gambia gave modest preference to imports from Britain. From 1934 quotas were imposed in some of the colonies on Japanese exports. But these were minor exceptions to an open-door policy.

In the British African colonies the state played a major role in the development of what is often known as the infrastructure, especially the transport system. Colonial governments built most of the railways and ports. Publicly financed infrastructure absorbed much capital over the colonial period, and it was important in the economic life and subsequent development of these territories.[11] It is impossible to say what the cost of private financing of these projects would have been. The issues involved are much the same as those of state investment in such projects elsewhere.

State intervention in economic life in British colonial Africa came to be much extended in the late colonial period. In particular, from about the early 1930s a wide range of economic controls was introduced in British colonial Africa. The controls differed in the various colonies. Information about them is not always readily available. Some of the measures were embodied in enactments and ordinances, while others were announced in obscure local regulations and notices or emerged in administrative practice. In Nigeria, for instance, the important decision to bar expatriates from trading in local food stuffs was conveyed by the administration to the United Africa Company in 1932, without public announcement. But the general trend was unequivocal: the volume and scope of state economic control were increasing steadily. This movement accelerated during the Second World War, in the course of which State export monopolies, comprehensive exchange controls and import licensing were introduced. The scope of these measures went far beyond such familiar purposes as denying supplies to the enemy, securing them for Britain and its allies, and ensuring the foreign exchange proceeds for the sterling area currency pool.

By the end of British colonial rule in Africa state economic controls and related measures included state monopoly of export of all major crops; extensive restrictive licensing of commercial activities in the areas of industry and transport and also foreign trade; the establishment and operation of many state-owned and operated enterprises and also state-sponsored cooperatives; control of the number and kind of traders allowed to operate in certain areas, and also of the commodities and grades of produce that could be traded; large-scale subsidies to certain activities and enterprises; restrictions on the employment both of expatriates and of African internal migrants (strangers); prescription of minimum wages; and widespread price controls. Most of these remained in force to the end of colonial rule. They were generally maintained and often intensified by the independent governments. Most of the discussion of their effects therefore applies to the present also.[12]

The emergence and spread of the belief that state control of economic life was desirable on social, political and economic grounds was a major factor behind the burgeoning of controls. The most influential British civil servants in charge of African affairs in the 1930s and 1940s shared this belief. They also welcomed policies which enhanced their power and status. By restricting competition the measures often benefited influential private interests, both expatriate and African. Towards the end of the period controls were often operated specifically to secure for African businessmen a share in lucrative commercial activities. At times they were imposed or maintained specifically for this purpose, as in the import trade in Nigeria in the 1950s.

Economic controls first introduced in one region soon spread to others. For instance, in the early 1930s there were more official restrictions on commercial activity in British East Africa and Central Africa than in West Africa. Thereafter however, more such controls were introduced in West Africa. The civil servants in London and their local counterparts instanced the controls in East Africa as enlightened policies and a good example to be followed by West Africa also. On the other hand comprehensive import licensing and state monopoly of agricultural exports were introduced first in West Africa and spread subsequently to East Africa. In the late colonial period the centralization of policy-making in the Colonial Office in London and in the local secretariats encouraged both an extension of state control and greater standardization of policy both within the various colonies and also between them.

The principal effects of state economic control are familiar, and have been mentioned in earlier chapters. They politicize life and provoke tension. They restrict the movement of people, ideas, commodities and financial resources. They curtail the volume and diversity of external contacts, and inhibit productive capital formation and obstruct both economic change and the effective deployment of human, financial and physical resources. They divorce economic activity from consumer demand. They also fragment the economy and thereby narrow the markets for commodities and services. Their operation confers monopolistic or windfall profits and benefits on some people and inflicts losses on others. Most of these effects were, and still are, particularly significant in Africa. Much of the cost falls on farmers who are discouraged from producing for the market when their terms of trade deteriorate. Especially in outlying areas they may find it more advantageous or even necessary to revert to subsistence production. Restriction of external commercial contacts is also especially damaging in Africa. These contacts provide sources of imports and markets for exports. More important, they are potent instruments for bringing about voluntary changes in attitudes and mores unfavourable to economic advance. More generally, they encourage that modernization of the mind which for good or ill promotes material advance. The more varied these contacts and the more widely dispersed among the population, the more effective they are for these purposes.

The various adverse effects of state controls are compounded by physical, ethnic and tribal diversity, and by the relatively poor communications of most British territories in Africa. These measures accentuate the fragmentation of the African economies in the narrowing of markets and the restricting of mobility. Local shortages and surpluses and price differences and fluctuation become more pronounced. Differences in employment opportunities are more likely to persist, which increases unemployment. Ethnic and tribal diversity further compounds both the political and the narrowly economic results of state economic control. For instance, this diversity exacerbates the political tension brought about by the imposition of restrictions. Moreover, state-supported restrictions are also most likely to be invoked and enforced effectively against people who can be distinguished readily on ethnic and linguistic grounds from the rulers, and from the advocates and beneficiaries of the restrictions. In Africa since about the Second World War state controls have notably discriminated against Asians, Europeans and Levantines. This discrimination has had damaging economic effects because these groups have been prime agents of economic progress in Africa. On the other hand, restrictive controls have also often operated against Africans not related to the ruling group.

The various economic controls were introduced as a result of the play of political forces, the pressure of sectional interests and the vagaries of intellectual fashion. They were not designed specifically to benefit ordinary Africans, but have always been useful to the politicians and civil servants who impose and administer them. In the private sector such measures obviously benefit those whom they protect from competition. Until well into the 1950s this latter category of beneficiary often included expatriates. To take but one of the many examples, the restrictive licensing of cotton ginneries in Uganda benefited primarily expatriates, particularly Indian owners of ginneries, for whom they often secured large windfall profits. These profits were secured at the expense of the producers of cotton, and also at the expense of people who could not obtain a licence.

Subsequently, state-organized and state-controlled cooperative societies, especially their administrators, became major beneficiaries of the imposition of restrictive controls. African businessmen, especially those with political contacts, also benefited considerably. These controls harmed the economic position and prospects of the population at large, and the costs were borne largely by the unorganized and politically ineffective rural population.

As a result of the far-reaching and comprehensive economic controls, a framework of quasi-totalitarian regimes was handed over to the incoming independent governments. Their eager and understandable maintenance of these controls inevitably increased the stakes in the fight for political power. Some of the implications of this were exemplified in the operation of two particularly significant controls; namely, comprehensive licensing of imports and state monopoly of agricultural exports. I shall review their operation in the next two sections.

7

Extensive import licensing in British colonial Africa was introduced during the Second World War. With occasional relaxations it has continued ever since. Import licensing has generally been accompanied by formal or informal controls of the prices charged by importers and wholesalers.

In Black Africa as in other less developed areas, the results of such arrangements go beyond those familiar in the West. At the retail level neither rationing nor price control is effective and is often not even attempted. Most consumers pay market-clearing prices which equate demand with available supply. This supply is determined by the operation of import controls. The market-clearing prices often much exceed the landed costs of imports which, with the costs of their distribution, provide the basis for controlled prices where there are price controls. In such a situation there are windfall profits. These are often large and their size can be readily ascertained by comparing the final retail prices with the costs of imports or with controlled prices.[13] Tensions and conflict are inevitable here. Import merchants are accused of favouritism when they distribute supplies below market-clearing prices, and of profiteering when they sell at or near these prices. Matters are complicated by the ability of many politicians, civil servants and other favoured customers to buy supplies of licensed goods at controlled prices, which they may then resell at the much higher market-clearing prices. They therefore have a powerful interest in the maintenance of these controls.

The windfall profits which arise here do not represent a reward for genuine economic services. They are the direct result of import controls when there is no effective rationing. Such a situation reinforces the misconceived notion that commercial profits represent privilege and exploitation rather than a reward for skills and commercial risk-taking. In principle, the windfall profits can be eliminated by imposing or raising excise duties. Such measures do not affect the prices paid by most consumers who, in any case, buy at market-clearing prices. But they are difficult to apply, partly because supply and demand conditions often change rapidly, and partly because controls benefit influential interests, including the recipients of licences and their employees, and also their favoured customers who obtain supplies below market-clearing prices.[14]

The colonial governments generally failed to appreciate the fundamentally simple economics of these controls. They also underestimated the political tensions which resulted when the allocations of supplies conferred large windfall profits. Such tensions created a highly charged atmosphere in British Africa in the 1940s, and contributed significantly to the resulting disturbances such as the Accra riots of 1948 in which a number of lives were lost. The colonial administrators did not seriously investigate the possibilities of restricting imports by tariffs instead of by direct controls, or of equating supply and demand and eliminating windfall profits by excise duties, or by the auctioning of supplies or of licences.

8

By the end of colonial rule the great bulk of agricultural exports from British colonies in Africa, including practically all exports produced by Africans, was handled by state export monopolies known as marketing boards. These organizations, established in West Africa in the early years of the Second World War and subsequently introduced in East and Central Africa, became the most important single instrument of state economic control in British Africa. Their political results have been far-reaching. For instance, the funds of the Gold Coast Cocoa Marketing Board provided the financial power base for Kwame Nkrumah. The operation of the marketing boards has been extensively discussed in readily available publications.[15] I shall therefore present a succinct outline only, largely in terms of West African experience. The operation of similar organizations elsewhere in British Africa resembled those of their West African counterparts which were, however, much larger. The export monopolies in Uganda were the most important of these organizations outside West Africa.

Monopoly of the export of cocoa was introduced in British West Africa in 1939. In November 1939 the British government announced that it would buy all West African cocoa through an official monopoly at seasonally fixed prices in order to avoid a threatened collapse of the local price of cocoa.[16] Such a collapse was feared because of a shortage of shipping and the closure of important overseas markets. Monopoly of export was subsequently extended to all other major West African agricultural exports of which oils and oil seeds were the most important. This extension was said to be necessary to increase supplies of oils and oil seeds (palm oil, palm kernels and groundnuts).

As should have been obvious, the declared purposes of these measures did not require a monopoly of export. A guarantee by the government to act as a residual buyer at fixed prices would have sufficed to maintain the local price of cocoa. Monopoly of export was clearly unnecessary for the expansion of the supplies of oils and oil seeds. In fact, it obstructed an increase in supplies because the relevant marketing board paid farmers far less than the market price or the price paid by the Ministry of Food for bulk supplies from other sources.

The official cocoa export monopoly was set up at the suggestion of the West African merchants. Within a week or two of the outbreak of war the Cocoa Committee of the Association of West African Merchants submitted to the Colonial Office a detailed scheme for the war-time control of West African cocoa. The scheme had obviously been prepared long before. It proposed that exports of West African cocoa should be handled by an official organization with the sole right to export cocoa. It proposed that only established merchants should act as buying agents for this organization, and should do so in accordance with quotas based on pre-war market shares. The scheme provided further that merchants who had bought more than their quota had to pay penalties for the benefit of those who had bought less. The Colonial Office adopted the scheme a few days after the merchants submitted it. The same arrangements (official monopoly of export, government guarantee to buy at seasonally fixed prices all supplies offered for export, and buying quotas restricted to established merchants) were adopted subsequently for all other major West African agricultural exports.

Maintenance of the local price of cocoa and expansion of the exports of oils and oil seeds were the declared purposes of the war-time control of West African exports. Monopoly of export was irrelevant to one purpose and damaging to the other. Similarly, the quota system was also irrelevant to the first purpose and damaging to the second. Nor did an official monopoly of export require buying quotas. It is perhaps worth noting in passing that no such arrangements operated in the export trade of other British territories during the war.

In West Africa state monopoly of export was a fortuitous by-product of restrictionism. And the introduction of quotas was evidently anomalous. The official guarantee to buy all supplies at seasonally fixed prices meant that the market for these products locally was unlimited. The arrangements themselves revealed the anomaly because the quotas did not refer to fixed amounts. They were shares in unspecified and indeed unlimited totals. The quotas represented statutory extension and enforcement of the pre-war market-sharing arrangements (pools) of the West African merchants, and were designed to protect profit margins by restraining competition in buying for export. Such measures are easier to administer and enforce when there is only one ultimate buyer who is prepared to operate and enforce a quota system. This is why the merchants promoted the establishment of state monopolies of export. The arrangements for the calculation of the quotas and for the penalties and compensations for excess and shortfall of purchases were absolutely identical with those of the merchants' own cocoa-buying agreement of 1937. This agreement, which was not in fact abandoned until the introduction of the official wartime arrangements, had sparked off the Gold Coast cocoa producers' strike of 1937.

Between 1944 and 1948 the British government and the West African colonial governments announced in a series of official publications that the marketing boards would be made permanent. The main reason given was that monopoly of export was necessary to stabilize producer prices. One of the official documents said with rather unusual candour that it would be regrettable to abandon an established organization.

As the marketing boards had the sole right to export and to buy for export the crops they controlled, they were in a position to pay producers far less than the world market prices. In the documents which announced that these export monopolies would be made permanent the British government gave the most emphatic and unequivocal assurances that the marketing boards would on no account be used as instruments of taxation by withholding money from the producers. Indeed, they were to act as agents and trustees for the producers.[17]

Official statements have rarely been discredited so speedily and completely as were these assurances. From their inception the boards withheld large sums from the producers by paying them far less than market prices, and continued to do so until the end of the colonial period and beyond. They also exercised close control over processors and traders. Neither during nor after

179

colonial rule did the policies of the marketing boards accord in any way with their ostensible objectives.

Between the establishment of the marketing boards (in the 1940s) and 1962, when some of them ceased to publish reports, at least £700 million was withheld from the producers in the form of the surpluses of the marketing boards and by outright export taxes, the very high rates of which were made possible by the operation of the marketing boards. The levies on the producers represented on average between one-third and one-half of the commercial value of the output. They were very much higher still if expressed as proportions of producers' incomes by taking into account costs of production and transport.[18] These levies represented taxation at rates which were borne in Britain only by the very rich people with annual incomes of many thousands of pounds. Most of the producers were small-scale farmers, with modest annual cash incomes of only a few pounds. In addition to the export levies, the producers still had to pay other local taxes, including consumption taxes.

This extremely heavy taxation reduced correspondingly the tax burden on the rest of the population. No other group with similar incomes was taxed at anywhere near such rates. Indeed, throughout British West Africa other people with much higher incomes either paid no direct taxes at all, or paid them at rates which were a small fraction of those paid by these producers. In Gold Coast-Ghana the surpluses of the Cocoa Marketing Board and the export duties in most years far exceeded total government gross capital expenditure. By the mid-1950s even the pretence of stabilization (a meaningless concept unless clearly defined, which was nowhere attempted in the official documents) was abandoned, and monopoly of export came to be used frankly as an instrument of taxation.[19]

9

This heavy taxation of the producers of export crops affected adversely the production and the extension of capacity of the controlled crops.[20] It also inhibited the spread of cash crops, the accumulation of private capital, and the development of a prosperous peasantry and an independent middle class.

The collection of huge sums by the West African governments through surpluses of the marketing boards and the related levies had other effects also. The export monopolies and their funds were the primary power base for a number of politicians. As already mentioned, this was so of Kwame Nkrumah who cut such a figure on the African scene and even beyond it in the 1950s and 1960s. Throughout West Africa, and to some extent also in East Africa, the state export monopolies were a major factor in the politicization of life, and control of funds was a major prize of political power.

The very large sums were handled at first mainly by expatriate civil servants and later by African politicians and civil servants. Few of these men had ever before controlled large sums of money, let alone such huge sums; this was especially true of the African politicians and civil servants. Moreover, in many cases their loyalties and duties were to their families, relatives, friends and political allies. They felt few obligations to abstract entities or nebulous concepts such as the public good of a large area which itself was often an artificial construct, such as Nigeria. Understandably, they often regarded the marketing boards and their funds as instruments for promoting their own personal interests and political power.

The very large sums that accrued to governments and their agencies through the state export monopolies reinforced the effects of other state controls, especially of import licensing, in promoting large-scale corruption. This result was especially evident in West Africa, where both the export monopolies and import licensing were established longest, where their coverage was most comprehensive and the sums at stake the largest. All this helped to turn the West African polities into kleptocracies, in Professor S. L. Andreski's felicitous term.

Even when large-scale government spending was not blatantly political or corrupt it was undertaken with little regard for economic usefulness or popular welfare. It went to prestige projects, or in directions dictated by intellectual fashion such as heavily subsidized industrial or commercial ventures, expensive government buildings and loss-making cooperatives. The sums involved were so huge that politicians and administrators often did not know what to do with the money which kept pouring in. In Sierra Leone, for example, direct spending by the marketing boards out of the funds it has accumulated has generally been wasteful and most of it can be written off as lost.[21] The economic usefulness of the huge expenditure of the Nkrumah government may be gauged from the fact that, after rapid dissipation of the large reserves of the export monopolies which that government inherited and the spending of large current cocoa revenues, the Nkrumah government was bankrupt after several years of acute shortage of consumer goods in the country.

It is not surprising that the sums which accrued to governments from the export monopolies should have been spent with so little regard for the welfare of producers. The politicians and administrators did not have to heed their unorganized and politically ineffective constituents, who were placed at their mercy by the British administrators who established the export monopolies.

181

The politicians and administrators of the marketing boards paid to the farmers as little as they could get away with. The completely open-ended and vague character of the concept of stabilization made this even easier.[22]

A major reason for the extremely heavy taxation of the farmers through the marketing boards was their political ineffectiveness compared with that of the politicians and civil servants. This in turn was an example of the wide difference in effectiveness between the urban population and the rural population which was pronounced in the late colonial period in Africa. A notable shift in British colonial policy in Africa contributed to this situation. Until the 1930s official policy supported the local rulers and the traditional institutions. The objective was to educate and modernize them in preparation for independence. From the mid-1930s, however, official policy changed direction in favour of the articulate Westernized urban groups.

10

The extension of state control, the expansion of government spending in the colonies, and the increase in Colonial Development and Welfare funds in the closing decades of colonial rule are widely regarded as evidence of a newfound concern for the well-being of the local population by the British colonial authorities. The terminal period of colonialism is accordingly often contrasted favourably with the period before the Second World War, allegedly one of neglect or even exploitation.

Some pre-war administrations might perhaps have spent with advantage more on education, health and agricultural extension. They might perhaps have done more to adapt traditional institutions to the needs of an exchange economy – though the merits of such policies would of course have depended on their specific content and circumstances, including the methods for raising the funds required. The financial problems appear much simpler in retrospect than they did before the Second World War, when the market prospects of export crops were much less favourable. And it is all too probable that had the colonial governments vigorously pursued such policies they would have been criticized for disrupting traditional ways of life or wasting resources.

The increased government spending in the African colonies in the final years of colonial rule was financed very largely from local funds, chiefly from taxation of export crops, and to a lesser extent from mining royalties and corporation taxes. Some external funds were available under foreign aid schemes, and also from Colonial Development and Welfare funds. On the other hand, until 1951 the Ministry of Food paid the West African marketing boards much less than the market price for their crops; and the very large export surpluses of West Africa and Uganda were held in sterling which was subject to several devaluations. These transactions represented an enforced transfer of resources from the colonies to the metropolitan country such as had never occurred in British Africa before then.

Some of the greatly increased spending was presumably productive, as for instance that on roads in Northern Nigeria. But as already noted, a large proportion was spent on projects and activities that were uneconomic at best, or total failures, or instruments for personal enrichment and political patronage. It is facile to assume that increased government spending promotes the welfare of the population or even reflects greater concern for it. This assumption confuses the interests of politicians and administrators with those of the public at large. Such an assumption was especially unwarranted in conditions in which there were extremely wide differences in effectiveness and therefore also in power between the politicians and administrators on the one hand, and the taxpayers on the other, as the latter were largely unorganized and inarticulate farmers and expatriate individuals and companies apprehensive about their future.

The departing colonialists bequeathed a political and financial bonanza to the incoming African politicians. Independent African governments would in any case have attempted extensive state economic controls; and in such attempts they would have enjoyed the support of the international organizations. But without the policies of the closing years of colonial rule the incoming governments would not have inherited the effective and comprehensive state controls established in the 1950s, especially the state export monopolies and the large reserves accumulated by them. They would not have inherited the methods, potentialities and wherewithal for establishing quasi-totalitarian polities, nor the same inducement for attempting to do so. Without these controls, and especially the state export monopolies, the prizes of political power would have been far less and there might have been less scope for large-scale organized oppression and brutality.

11

Until the Second World War the official annual reports on the colonial territories as well as the academic literature readily commended the spread of cash crops. They commended also a rise in living standards and an increase in the supply of consumer goods (which indeed were often termed incentive goods). By contrast, the more recent literature has commended such policies as heavy taxation of producers, large official spending unrelated to general living standards, and the establishment of closely controlled economies. The literature correspondingly has condemned popular spending on consumer goods; and the terms incentive goods and inducement goods have largely disappeared from it. The implications of this shift in emphasis stood out starkly in the experience of British colonial Africa.

Modern social and economic life in Africa dates from the colonial period. Colonial rule greatly accelerated material progress and even made it possible. However, because of the wide political, social and economic results of the wholesale establishment of state controls over the last two decades of colonial rule, assessment of the outcome of colonial rule is more equivocal than it would otherwise have been. Nkrumah enjoined African politicians first to seek the political kingdom, because if they attained that, all else would be added unto them. The closing years of colonial rule helped to show the way in this direction, and also provided the resources for the new leaders. I therefore now find the profit-and-loss account of colonialism more difficult to read than I would have a generation earlier.

CHAPTER 10

The Lesson of Hong Kong

How would you rate the economic prospects of an Asian country which has very little land (and only eroded hillsides at that), and which is indeed the most densely populated country in the world; whose population has grown rapidly, both through natural increase and large-scale immigration; which imports all its oil and raw materials, and even most of its water; whose government is not engaged in development planning and operates no exchange controls or restrictions on capital exports and imports; and which is the only remaining Western colony of any significance? You would think that this country must be doomed, unless it received large external donations. Or rather you would have to believe this if you went by what politicians of all parties, the United Nations and its affiliates, prominent economists and the quality press all say about less developed countries. Has not the vicious circle of poverty, the idea that poverty is self-perpetuating, been a cornerstone of mainstream development economics since the Second World War, and has it not been explicitly endorsed by Nobel Laureates Gunnar Myrdal and Paul Samuelson? Have not the development economists of the Massachusetts Institute of Technology said categorically about less developed countries that

the general scarcity relative to population of nearly all resources creates a self-perpetuating vicious circle of poverty. Additional capital is necessary to increase output, but poverty itself makes it impossible to carry out the required saving and investment by a voluntary reduction in consumption.[1]

As we have seen in earlier chapters, according to mainstream opinion on the subject foreign exchange shortages are inevitable concomitants of reasonable development of poor countries, and rapid population growth and colonial status major obstacles or even insurmountable barriers to material advance. Indeed, according to the most respected academic figures in development economics and representatives of so-called world opinion, even one of the half-dozen characteristics with which I began ensures persistent poverty.

But if instead of following fashion you think for yourself and go by obvious evidence, then you will know that Hong Kong, the country in question, has progressed phenomenally since the 1940s, when it was still very poor. And also that it has become such a formidable competitor that the leading Western countries erect barriers to protect their own domestic industries against imports from this distant country. If you enquired further, you would know that incomes and real wages have risen rapidly in Hong Kong in recent decades. And, incidentally, Hong Kong is only an extreme case of a more general phenomenon, because somewhat similar though less pronounced material progress has occurred in a number of countries or areas, South Korea, Taiwan and Singapore among them, when according to the experts this should have been impossible.

If you suspected all along that the established opinion on these matters was patently unfounded, you will welcome a short but instructive monograph, *Hong Kong: A Study in Economic Freedom* (University of Chicago Press) by Dr Alvin Rabushka. Dr Rabushka, an American political scientist turned economist, knows Hong Kong well, and his wife is Chinese. He has an incisive mind. He writes clearly, confidently and indeed with gusto. His principal themes are not difficult, though it needs a firm mind and some courage to set them out so concisely and vigorously.

Dr Rabushka reviews the processes and methods by which, in less than 140 years, a few empty barren rocks grew into a major industrial trading and financial centre of about five million people. He ascribes this economic success story to the aptitudes of the people and to the pursuit of appropriate policies. Enterprise, hard work, ability to spot and utilize economic opportunities are widespread in a population 98% Chinese engaged in singleminded pursuit of making money day and night. Many are immigrants who brought skills and enterprise mostly from China, especially Shanghai, erstwhile centre of skill and enterprise of mainland China. The policies emphasized by Dr Rabushka are fiscal conservatism; low taxation; the charging of market prices for specific government services; liberal immigration policy, at least until recently; free trade in both directions; unrestricted movement of capital into and out of the country; and minimal government involvement in commercial life, including refusal to grant privileges to sectional interests. There are no special incentives or barriers to foreign investment and no insistence on local participation in foreign-owned enterprises. There are also no tax holidays or other special concessions to foreign investment, but equally, there are no restrictions on the withdrawal of capital or on the remission of profits. These liberal policies, notably the freedom to withdraw capital, were designed to encourage the inflow of productive capital and enterprise, which indeed they did.

The lack of natural resources together with colonial rule encouraged both official economic non-intervention and fiscal conservatism. Absence of natural resources has encouraged an open economy with a large volume of exports to pay for the necessary imports. Such an economy requires a wide range of competitive exports, and also competitive domestic markets. Government assistance to particular economic activities diverts resources from more productive uses, and undermines the international competitive position of the economy. Moreover, in an economy as open as Hong Kong, the wasteful results of such subsidies become apparent sooner than elsewhere. Thus the very absence of natural resources has assisted material progress by discouraging wasteful policies. Inappropriate policies are much more likely to inhibit economic advance than does a lack of physical resources. Sustained budget deficits financed by credit creation also tend to bring about wasteful spending, so that poverty of resources discourages deficit finance. In the traditional British colonial accounting system colonies could not run sustained budget deficits, and this tradition was continued after fiscal autonomy in 1958, partly for the reasons just noted. The absence of election promises, together with an open economy and limited government, have much reduced the prizes of political activity and hence the interest in organizing pressure groups. These circumstances encouraged fiscal conservatism, i.e. low taxation, balanced budgets and the charging of market prices for specific public services. The wish to attract foreign capital, the business outlook of a traditional trading community, and the general preoccupation with money making also worked in this direction.

The official policies and the aptitudes and habits of the population have brought about an economy capable of rapid adjustment. This adaptability has enabled Hong Kong to survive and even to prosper in the face of numerous restrictions against its exports, often imposed or increased at short notice. For social reasons the principle of charging market prices for specific government services has for some time been subject to major exceptions. Large-scale provision of subsidized housing for the poor, and the rationing of water by cutting off supplies for certain periods rather than by charging higher prices for a continuous supply, are the two most important exceptions. They were introduced after much heart-searching and with an eye on local social conditions. The subsidies are moreover largely confined to the really poor. In addition to these subsidies in kind there are substantial cash subsidies to the poor to ensure minimum incomes, and there are also various disability and infirmity grants. Comprehensive compulsory primary education, in fact as well as in name, and extensive public health services have operated for many years.

In recent years Hong Kong has come to be much pressed both by the

British government and by various international bodies to move towards a fully-fledged so-called welfare state, complete with trade union privileges, comprehensive social services, far-reaching labour legislation and redistributive taxation. Rabushka rightly notes that these external pressures reflect mainly a wish to serve various Western interests, as for instance by reducing competition from Hong Kong by inflating costs there. Rabushka also refers to the unease, even resentment, engendered in the supporters of state-controlled economies by the rapid rise in general living standards in this and other market-oriented economies. These external pressures may yet gain support within Hong Kong from ambitious administrators, discontented intellectuals and aspiring politicians, all of whom hope for greater scope in a more politicized society. The present Governor, Sir Murray McLehose, is also more concerned with external opinion than were his predecessors. Rabushka believes, I think rightly, that the expiry in 1997 of the lease of much of the territory of Hong Kong from China, or possible hostile action from the People's Republic of China, is less of a menace to the future of Hong Kong than are trade barriers in the West and Western pressures for the intro- duction of further labour legislation, a comprehensive welfare state and other policies which inflate costs and reduce adaptability. It is the policies of the West rather than those of the People's Republic of China which threaten Hong Kong.

Rabushka's unashamed admiration for Hong Kong and for its market economy pervades the book.

Dare I reveal my boorishness by saying that I find Hong Kong's economic hustle and bustle more interesting, entertaining, and liberating than its lack of high opera, music, and drama? East has indeed met West in the market economy. Chinese and Europeans in Hong Kong have no time for racial quarrels, which would only interfere with making money. This prospect of individual gain in the marketplace makes group activity for political gain unnecessary – the market economy is truly color-blind (p. 85).

There is some over-simplification here. For instance, pursuit of money making can readily go together with racial strife in state-controlled economies. The crucial factor is not money making as such but limited government.

Apart from the main themes, there is much informative and unexpected detail in this book. For instance, who would have thought that in 1843 the British Foreign Secretary would have insisted that if as a result of the creation of a free port '... many people were attracted to Hong Kong, then HM Government would feel justified in securing to the Crown the increased values that the land would then have'?

The outstanding lesson of Hong Kong is the overriding importance of personal attributes and motivations, social mores and appropriate political arrangements for economic achievement. Access to markets is also important but less fundamental. Other countries also have had access to outside markets and supplies without producing such an economic success story.

Hong Kong shows again that economic achievement does not depend on having money, or on possessing natural resources. The utilization of natural resources depends entirely on the other factors just noted. In certain market conditions or political situations the possession or acquisition of natural resources can bring windfalls, even large windfalls; witness the gold and silver of the Americas in the sixteenth century and the operations of OPEC in the twentieth century. But hitherto at any rate such windfalls have not led to lasting economic progress, much less to such sustained and spectacular advance as that of Hong Kong. Nor is economic success without natural resources anything new, witness the examples of Venice, the Low Countries, Switzerland and Japan. Conversely, backwardness amidst large natural resources is evident from the American Indians to the present Third World, where many millions of extremely backward people live amidst unlimited cultivable land. As Tocqueville wrote over a hundred years ago:

> Looking at the turn given to the human spirit in England by political life; seeing the Englishman, certain of the support of his laws, relying on himself and unaware of any obstacle except the limit of his own powers, acting without constraint . . . I am in no hurry to inquire whether nature has scooped out ports for him, and given him coal and iron. The reason for his commercial prosperity is not there at all: it is in himself.[2]

Hong Kong bears out that population increase is not an obstacle to progress, that suitably motivated people are assets not liabilities, agents of progress as well as its beneficiaries. It shows also that economic performance owes little to formal education. In Hong Kong as elsewhere in the Far East, the economic performance or success of hundreds of thousands or even millions of people has resulted not from formal education but from industry, enterprise, thrift and ability to use economic opportunity. This is disturbing to professional educationalists, who like to market their wares as necessary for economic achievement.

Hong Kong is yet another evident refutation of the staples of the dominant, mainstream development literature which I have mentioned earlier, such as that poverty must be self-perpetuating; that balance of payments difficulties are inevitable in economic advance from poverty; that comprehensive planning and foreign aid are indispensable or even sufficient for economic progress. Hong Kong experience offends respectable opinion in other ways. It shows that planning teams and advisory groups are unnecessary for development; and contrasts with the experience of other countries, groaning under the policies advocated by the United Nations and by mainstream academic advisors.

Hong Kong is unpopular with the aid lobbies and the politicized charities. These groups are hostile to people who can dispense with their ministrations. Hence the bad press which Hong Kong has in the West and the hostility it encounters from the great and the good. The achievement is ignored or underplayed, and the shortcomings, whether real or alleged, avoidable or inevitable, are prominently featured. Overcrowding and child labour are examples. In all these respects Hong Kong compares very favourably with the rest of Asia. For instance, real wages are the highest in Asia, except for Japan. If a government tries to run a socialist economy, or at any rate a largely state-controlled one, Western politicians, writers, academics and journalists are apt to present hardship or even suffering there as inevitable, or even commend it as a result of laudable efforts to promote progress. But if the government relies on a market economy, then these bien-pensants will condemn any deviation from arbitrary and Western-inspired norms as a defect, or even a crime.

The experience of Hong Kong confirms once again that political sovereignty has nothing to do with personal freedom. This is blindingly obvious and yet often overlooked. The newly independent African states are habitually termed free, meaning by this that their governments are sovereign. But the people there are far from free, much less so than they were under colonial rule. They are also much less free than the people of Hong Kong. Hong Kong is a dictatorship in that people do not have the vote. But in their personal life, especially their economic activities, they are far freer than most people in the West, not to speak of the Third World. Hong Kong should remind us that a non-elective government can be more limited than an elected one; and that for most ordinary people it is arguably more important whether government is limited or unlimited than whether it is elective or non-elective.

CHAPTER 11

Broadcasting the Liberal Death Wish

You taught me language; and my profit on't
Is, I know how to curse: the red plague rid you,
For learning me your language!

The Tempest

1

Liberals, Malcolm Bradbury wrote in *Stepping Westward*, are people who embrace their destroyers. Professor Mazrui's 1979 Reith Lectures confirm this perceptive observation.[1] Formerly at Makerere, Professor Mazrui is now Professor of Political Science at the University of Michigan, a prominent liberal institution. As he himself recounts (p. 16), as a youngster he was taken up and helped by Europeans in East Africa. He was educated in Western-organized and -financed institutions in East Africa, Britain and the United States. Yet hostility to the West pervades the lectures and provides their unifying theme. His view of the recent past is this:

> The Berlin Congress opened in 1884 to help seal the fate of the continent for at least another century. The nightmare of European penetration and colonization of Africa was now truly underway (p. 32).

His vision of the future:

> The decline of Western civilization might well be at hand. It is in the interest of humanity that such a decline should take place, allowing the different segments of the human race to enjoy a more equitable share not only of the resources of the planet but also of the capacity to control the march of history (pp. 86–7).

These assessments explain his proposals for policy, which, as we shall see, are not designed to assist ordinary Africans but to diminish or undermine the West.

In each lecture Professor Mazrui addresses himself to what he considers a paradox. Africa, the first habitat of man, has decayed through human neglect; it is now the least habitable continent because of disease, lack of

191

communications and political instability. Africans, though they have not experienced a holocaust such as that experienced by the Jews, or genocide such as that of the indigenous American Indians or Australians at the hands of white people, have been the most humiliated people in history through the slave trade, colonialism and racial discrimination. African societies are not the closest culturally to the West, yet they have recently been rapidly Westernized. In Africa, immense mineral wealth and agricultural potential coexist with extremely low living standards. Africa, the second largest continent, is the most fragmented, split into more than fifty nations, many of them tiny. Finally, Africa, a large continent centrally and strategically located in the world, plays only a marginal role in world affairs.

The causes of the predicament of humiliation, poverty and political impotence, and the possible remedies, are Professor Mazrui's main concerns. The prime responsibility for this predicament rests with guess whom? The white man, the West. The remedy lies in guess what? The decline of the West and the overthrow of white rule in Southern Africa.

These lectures are thus only another attack on the West by a Western-supported Third World intellectual, one of the most effective I have read. In particular, they are designed to make the greatest impact on Western feelings of guilt.

2

Professor Mazrui writes well. He moves easily between vivid, pertinent episodes and wide political issues. He presents thought-provoking information on various matters as, for instance, the kaleidoscope of African religious belief and the political role of Westernized intellectuals and soldiers. Again, in referring to the brain drain from the Third World, Professor Mazrui rightly notes that this is the result partly of political persecution but mainly of the wish of people to improve their economic position and to explore new vistas. He aptly compares the migration of African intellectuals to the West with that of African traders and workers between African countries for economic betterment. The merits of the book are, however, peripheral. They do not affect the fundamental flaws of the argument.

Professor Mazrui is a skilled political writer. His enterprise involves him in much delicate tightrope walking. He tries to present Africa, as also the Third World, as some sort of actual or potential unity. On his own admission, in Africa there are some 850 distinct ethnic and linguistic groups (p. 92). When talking about Africa he sometimes means the African continent including the Arab north, and at other times he means sub-Saharan Africa; he changes without warning his readers. There is, of course, not even the semblance of unity and uniformity between North Africa and Black Africa. Apart from very limited trade, in historical times their contact was that of intermittent conquest by North Africa of parts of Black Africa, and also the much more lasting contact of slave raiding and trading.

The notion of a broadly uniform or united Third World embracing some two-thirds of mankind is fiction. Its acceptance enables Professor Mazrui to bypass such matters as the brutal persecution on ethnic and cultural grounds of large numbers of people in South-East Asia, the Middle East and, of course, Black Africa itself. In Asia and Africa such large-scale persecution is widespread and evident, including often officially organized and supported racial discrimination. But champions of the Third World, or rather denigrators of the West, such as Professor Mazrui, cannot acknowledge these realities. A united or uniform Africa and a united or uniform Third World are concepts contrived to help to undermine the West and to extract money from it. To present them as anything else involves tergiversation and suppressions.

Professor Mazrui seems anxious to secure the support of the Jewish intelligentsia. He may hope to rebuild the alliance in the United States between the left-liberal Jewish intelligentsia and the black leaders which has disintegrated through the rise of black antisemitism. This latter objective is suggested by his rather forced comparison between Jews and Black Africans, and also by his account of the fate of the Jews in Germany, an account which is misleading and also internally inconsistent, but is phrased for maximum political impact (p. 26).

3

Professor Mazrui's paradoxes are no more than different facets of the generally low level of economic performance in Africa. Professor Mazrui attempts to obscure this central fact and to turn it to political advantage. This endeavour is assisted by ignorance, guilt and confusion in the West. Most people do not appreciate the low level of economic achievement of the indigenous human resources of Africa. If they know it, they tend to feel responsible, or are made to feel responsible, for it.

In historical times the achievement of Black Africa (i.e. most of the continent of Africa) has been negligible compared with that of Asia and Europe. This in no way justifies enslavement or humiliation. But its recognition is indispensable for an understanding of the African scene, and for an assessment of Professor Mazrui's discussion.

The fact that a million or so years ago an important stage in evolution may have taken place in Africa has nothing to do with what has happened there in historical times. If the Garden of Eden has decayed, it is because its inhabitants have neglected it. Before the closing decades of the nineteenth century Professor Mazrui's erstwhile Garden of Eden was without the rudiments either of civilized or of modern life. For instance, before the arrival of Europeans in sub-Saharan Africa all transport was by muscle, almost entirely human muscle, unaided by the wheel. There was no public security, man-made roads or ports, Western-type science or technology. All this and much else came with the Europeans in the nineteenth century or even later.[2] Except for the most cursory mention, unrelated to the central argument, Professor Mazrui does not discuss conditions in pre-colonial Africa or in Liberia, which never was a colony, or social-economic conditions in Ethiopia, independent for thousands of years except for six years as an Italian colony.

Professor Mazrui does not inquire about the personal, social and political determinants of economic achievement and progress. Achievement is somehow visited on some people but not on others. He writes that as a result of the Industrial Revolution ' . . . economic pre-eminence was bestowed upon the countries of Europe and North America' (p. 5). He does not consider the personal attributes and motivations, the social and political conditions, and the many centuries of Western progress before the eighteenth century which were behind the Industrial Revolution. Disregard of background and antecedent history, characteristic of much contemporary social and political discussion, underlies Professor Mazrui's argument and vitiates it.

Why have the Africans not developed their mineral resources? Why did they have to wait for Europeans to explore, develop, process and market them? Contrary to what Professor Mazrui writes, material backwardness amidst ample natural resources is not anomalous, paradoxical or surprising. It is familiar both from history and from the contemporary world – witness the pre-Columbian Indians, and the contemporary aborigines and pygmies, all extremely backward amidst ample physical resources. Conversely, rapid advance and large-scale achievement of societies with negligible physical resources should also be familiar, as for instance Venice, the Low Countries, Germany, Britain, Japan and, more recently, Hong Kong, Singapore and Taiwan. The physical resources of advanced countries were developed by their peoples, as for instance the reclaiming of large parts of Holland and Flanders from the sea and, more generally, the improvement of land. African backwardness amidst ample natural resources is only one conspicuous example of the fact that material progress depends on personal qualities, social institutions and mores, and political arrangements which make for endeavour and achievement, and not simply physical resources.

The relative lack of able and effective people is crucial. This has long been so, although the unpropitious past is no sure basis for predicting the future. What Shiva Naipaul says about Zambia in his recent informative book *North of South: An African Journey* applies widely in Black Africa:

Expatriates staff the mines, the medical services, the factories, the technical colleges, the universities. Without them, the country would fall apart. Zambia makes nothing; Zambia creates nothing. The expatriate lecturer in English waved apologetically at the handful of books, perhaps half a dozen on the library shelf. 'There,' he said, 'that's it. That's all the Zambian literature there is.' For him, the paucity is a source of genuine embarrassment. 'I would dearly love to teach something Zambian to my students. But what can I do if there's nothing'.[3]

Considerations such as these dispose of Professor Mazrui's paradoxes and most of his argument. But there is much else in his widely applauded lectures which deserves comment.

4

The humiliation and suffering of Africa through colonialism, slavery and racial discrimination provide a major theme. Slavery did indeed inflict much suffering; colonial conquest was often attended by bloodshed; and many Africans have experienced galling racial discrimination. But Professor Mazrui's discussion is nevertheless unbalanced and misleading. Like many Third World writers, he endows the West with complete monopoly both of historical injustice and of contemporary misconduct.

Professor Mazrui writes at length about the Atlantic slave trade. He does not say that slavery was endemic in Africa and widespread elsewhere before then (witness the etymological connection between slav and slave), nor that the supply of slaves for that trade was organized by Africans and Arabs, as the Europeans bought slaves principally at the ports. Nor does he tell his readers that slavery among Africans continued long after it was abolished in the West. Most significant and revealing is, however, the absence of any reference to the Arab slave trade, which was dreaded far and wide in Africa. The Arab slave trade long preceded the Atlantic slave trade, far outlasted it, and was suppressed only through Western effort. It was also even more cruel because many young male slaves were castrated, one reason why in the Middle East there are not many more descendants of Negro slaves. In his masterly and justly celebrated Introduction to *West African Explorers* (Oxford University Press, 1951) Professor Plumb quotes Karl Barth's observation on this: 'Allah had been kind if ten out of one hundred boys survived the operation.' Yet Arabs do not feel guilty, nor are they made to feel guilty, about their role in the slave trade. To say anything about the Arab slave trade might be thought to reflect on the solidarity of the Third World; and thus to impair its ability to confront and mulct the West. A feeling of guilt is genuinely a monopoly of the West.

Professor Mazrui must be well-informed about the Arab slave trade and accordingly well qualified to write about it. He comes from Mombasa, a former Arab slave port. The Mazrui of Mombasa were some of the principal slave traders out of that port when Mombasa was part of the dominions of the Sultanate of Oman in the eighteenth and nineteenth centuries.[4]

He also suggests that Western capitalists ceased to support slavery only because hired labour became cheaper and more efficient. Why then did the abolitionists insist on suppressing slavery when it was uneconomic, and therefore indeed doomed to disappear?

Extermination is another Western monopoly. Professor Mazrui cites the treatment of the Jews by the Nazis, and that of the American Indians and the Australian aborigines by the Whites. He does not mention in this context the large-scale massacres in Africa, including the early wars of the Zulus, or the slaughter of the Ibo by the Hausa as recently as 1966. These instances are rather more pertinent to Africa.[5]

We have seen that Professor Mazrui regards the outcome of colonialism as a nightmare. Yet it was under colonial rule that the rudiments of modern economic and social life, including public security, disease control and the suppression of slave raiding were introduced into Black Africa, and which enabled millions of Africans to live longer.[6]

Like so many others, Professor Mazrui interprets colonial experience entirely from the standpoint of the Westernized intellectuals. Many Westernized Africans (whose Westernization by definition came about through the European impact) may have felt humiliated. But may they not have been irked largely because, under colonial rule, they did not enjoy the status, power and jobs which they claimed because they were educated or at any rate articulate? Under colonial rule, especially British colonial rule, there were relatively few jobs for them, partly because the government was alien, but also because government was so light and limited. What most ordinary people must have felt during the colonial period was that their lives and property were much safer than formerly, and that they were much less affected by disease. To most people such matters are of primary, even paramount, concern. Obafemi Awolowo, a prominent Nigerian politician of the early post-war years, recognized this in his book *Path to Nigerian Freedom*:

Given a choice from among white officials, Chiefs and educated Nigerians, as the principal rulers of the country, the illiterate man, today, would exercise his preference for the three in the order in which they are named. He is convinced, *and he has good reason to be*, that he can always get better treatment from the white man than he could hope to get from the Chiefs and the educated elements.[7]

Among the alleged economic ill-effects of colonial rule Professor Mazrui mentions (in a chapter titled 'The Burden of Underdevelopment') the production of cash export crops:

Important biases in the direction of development included, first, the export bias. . . . Cash crops for export were given priority against food for local people. One quarter to one third of the total cultivated areas in some of the more fertile colonies were devoted to the production of such export commodities as cocoa in Ghana, coffee in Uganda, groundnuts in Senegal and the Gambia . . . (p. 78).

These cash crops have always been cultivated on their own properties by Africans. Cash crops sometimes replace food crops, but in Africa they are often added to food crops, as over much of Africa agricultural production is limited not by land but by labour, and farmers can and often do add cash crops to food (subsistence) crops by working more. But whether they replaced food crops or were grown in addition to food crops, the cultivation of cash crops greatly raised African incomes. Indeed, it was a prime instrument of material advance and helped to transform existence over large areas. Before 1886 there was not one cocoa tree in British West Africa. By the 1930s there were millions of acres under cocoa there, all owned and operated by Africans. Nor were the cash crops grown on fertile or often previously cultivated land; large tracts of jungle or semi-desert were turned into productive land. Professor Mazrui does not acknowledge the key role of cash crops in the progress of much of Black Africa, especially West Africa. Africans produce these crops for the same reason that Professor Mazrui, I and our colleagues teach at universities instead of growing corn or planting potatoes. To condemn cash crops is to patronize the producers by saying that they do not know what is good for them, or that they ought not to have higher incomes.

Incidentally, Professor Mazrui fails to mention that in several African states government policies have affected food production so adversely that the countries have become largely dependent on imported food; and it is not because domestic resources have been diverted to more productive uses. Examples include Mozambique, Tanzania and Zaire.

In colonialism also Europeans enjoy a monopoly of evil or misconduct. Professor Mazrui does not even mention the extremely brutal Moslem conquest of the Sudan in the early nineteenth century, long before the

197

Congress of Berlin. This conquest was attended by massive and ruthless maltreatment of the blacks in the Southern Sudan unparalleled in nineteenth century European colonialism, and much of it continued into the 1970s. Nor does Professor Mazrui mention the oppression of the tribal groups, the great majority of the population, by the coastal black rulers of Liberia, nor that of the lording of Amharics over the Galle in Ethiopia, nor the many similar examples of internal tyranny by one African group or another. And further, he fails to note the large numbers of Black Africans who, as we shall see, have been forced to leave their countries.

In the discussion of racism the whites continue as the sole evil-doers. But the villains of racism are of course the whites of Southern Africa. It is not intended as a defence of apartheid to say that his treatment is altogether distorted. Professor Mazrui speaks of ' . . . the martyrdom of Sharpeville and the heroism of Soweto' (p. 39). It is disputable whether the people killed there were martyrs to a cause, or part of an uncontrollable mob looting and burning mostly African properties, rather like the mobs in the riots in Accra (Gold Coast, January 1948) and Enugu (Nigeria, November 1949) in which many people were also killed. But what is not in doubt is that those killed in Sharpeville and Soweto together were a small fraction of the numbers of Ibo massacred in Northern Nigeria in 1966 well before the Biafran war; and a much smaller fraction still of the number of Africans killed in the 1960s and 1970s in the struggles between rulers and ruled, some involving genocide, in Rwanda and Burundi, in the Southern Sudan and the Nigerian Civil War. The casualties in Sharpeville and Soweto together were in the hundreds; those killed in these other struggles numbered in the tens of thousands.

Professor Mazrui speaks of the ' . . . vast numbers that have been running away either from racial discrimination or racial warfare in Zimbabwe, Namibia or South Africa' (p. 13). However, he seems oblivious – at least to judge from his book – of the large numbers of Black Africans who have been forced to leave their newly-independent African countries. Thus in the three Guineas (Guinea, Guinea-Bissau and Equatorial Guinea) high proportions of the population have been obliged to take refuge abroad. According to an article by Antony Delius (*Times Literary Supplement*, 18 February 1977) about one-quarter of the population of Sekou Toure's Guinea have fled the country and live as refugees in other African states. According to an article in *The Times* of 3 November 1978, approximately one-third of the population of Equatorial Guinea 'is in exile, usually in very difficult conditions'. And many people fled from Guinea-Bissau after the post-independence massacres.

On the other hand, until the outbreak of guerilla warfare, the African refugees from the white-ruled areas of Southern Africa were confined to a small number of political activists. The numbers involved were a tiny fraction of those who were affected in the Guineas, and also of those who entered white-ruled Southern Africa from elsewhere in Black Africa, at times from as far away as Nigeria. Many more wished, and still wish, to come. They are stopped by immigration restrictions introduced to prevent South Africa and Rhodesia (Zimbabwe) from being flooded by would-be entrants. They are obstructed also by various restrictions in Black Africa designed to stop people from leaving for Southern Africa, as this is politically embarrassing to the rulers.[8] Africans migrate to Southern Africa, or try to get there, because they earn more; their lives and property are much safer; and often because the health and educational facilities are greatly superior.

Professor Mazrui refers to the position of the blacks of South Africa as akin to slavery. It must be unique in history that large numbers of people from all over a huge area wish to travel long distances in the face of formidable obstacles to become slaves.

Even among intellectuals the movement has not been one way. Professor Mazrui mentions Ezekiel Mphahlele, a former South African political activist. 'He lived and worked in Zambia, Nigeria and Kenya. He left Africa somewhat disenchanted ...' and 'decided it was time to go home – and suffer with the people. He had decided to come to terms with Africa's paradox of habitation' (p. 13). May he not have returned because he found that with all the humiliation of apartheid South Africa was a better place for him than Zambia, Nigeria and Kenya, where he had worked? Miss Noni Jabavu is a black South African woman. She wrote *Drawn in Colour* (London, John Murray 1960), a sensitive and informative description of life in East Africa and Southern Africa, with a faithful account of the humiliations of apartheid, especially petty apartheid. She lived in East Africa. She was married to a prominent English liberal. She was a friend of Andrew Cohen's and his guest when he was Governor of Uganda. She returned to live in South Africa because life for a black intellectual there was so much more varied, rich and safe than in East Africa.

Professor Mazrui is also out of focus in thinking that white rule in Southern Africa is the overriding problem for Africa as a whole. Much less than one-tenth of the population of Black Africa lives there; many other Blacks would like to go there; and the great majority of the rest are quite unconcerned with Southern Africa, about which most of them know nothing, often not even that it exists.

Indeed, even in the African states adjacent to Southern Africa people at large are quite unconcerned about white supremacy and liberation in South Africa. To quote Shiva Naipaul again:

Rhodesia and South Africa arouse more passion in the West than they do among the citizenry of the black 'front-line' states. The shelves of one Lusaka supermarket I went into were laden with South African merchandise – meat, toilet paper, detergents, tinned goods of all kinds. ... As I strolled along the alleyways of the Lusaka supermarket, I reflected ruefully on the crises of conscience occasioned in the past by my consumption of South African oranges (p. 231).

Professor Mazrui believes that the world over, ethnic, tribal and even family ties are on their way out. He regards preferential treatment even of one's close relatives as inappropriate or even improper (p. 44). He ought perhaps to ask the millions of Chinese in South-East Asia and the Indian refugees from Burma, Sri Lanka and East Africa, his home base, whether ethnic discrimination in the Third World is disappearing. He might also put his question to many Indians in India. He ignores the massive and brutal persecutions perpetrated by Third World governments on ethnic grounds, often with popular approval. But he seizes upon even trivial instances of ethnic discrimination by whites.

5

What Professor Mazrui writes about the cultural and political scene of Black Africa is sometimes lively and informative. He describes the synchretistic attitudes and practices which incorporate Christian, Islam and more traditional elements, as for instance in the coexistence of polygamy and monogamy. He also rightly notes important inconsistencies in Western attitudes towards missionary activity. Western missionaries have promoted beliefs and conduct inconsistent with local tradition. But when people from the Third World propagate beliefs and conduct alien to Western mores, they are apt to be ridiculed, persecuted and even subjected to criminal charges.

Professor Mazrui regards missionary activity as an example of Western penetration of Africa, and more generally of the Third World, which he deplores. He also repeatedly puts forward the interesting suggestion that the Third World should dispatch its own counter-missionaries to the West who might engage in diverse activities, including participation in civil wars, for instance in Ireland and Quebec (p. 16). He looks forward to the decline in the economic and political position of the West. He thinks that the ultimate battles against racial injustice and oppression will be fought 'in the streets of Birmingham, ghettos of Detroit, harbours of Marseilles and the motels of the rest of the Western world' (p. 44). These ideas lend particular interest to his proposal. He does not say who is to finance the proposed counter-missionaries from the Third World to the West. Many of them would need to be financed from the West, either directly or through the international agencies. They may well come to be so financed – some of them are already, and perhaps Professor Mazrui would include himself among their number.

Professor Mazrui describes vividly the role of the Westernized groups in political life. His examples of the swings in political power between the intellectuals and the military are informative and telling. But he ignores the two principal and indeed decisive factors behind the political prominence of Westernized Africans. One is the absence of a strongly entrenched local culture, such as Hinduism or Islam, more resistant to Western impact. The second factor was the increasing readiness of the Western powers in the 1940s and '50s to accept the articulate Westernized groups as the representatives of Africa. This was crucial in the political sphere. In British policy this was a complete reversal of the previous practice of trying to build on traditional and specifically local forms of authority in preparation for independence.

The most influential ideologies in the West since the 1930s consistently favoured the articulate Westernized and urbanized groups in Africa. They also favoured extensive economic controls. As a result, closely controlled economies were handed over to the incoming African governments in which these Westernized groups predominated. Since the Second World War these preferences have continued to shape the policies of the official international organizations and aid agencies. Unwilling and powerless populations have thereby come to be placed at the mercy of their unrepresentative rulers.

Professor Mazrui correctly notes that Western-style government was inappropriate to African conditions, even though its debut there was widely applauded in the 1950s and '60s. But he does not seem to remember that Westernized Africans had pressed for these Western-type parliamentary systems. They claimed that other arrangements would have given power to so-called reactionary elements, that is, traditional authorities such as local chiefs and councils. They claimed also that to deny Western-style political arrangements to the incoming independent governments would be evidence of Western feelings of superiority.

The extensive economic controls promoted in the closing years of colonial rule, and subsequently also by various Western aid programmes, vastly increased the gains and losses in the fight for political power. This result in turn provoked conflict and has encouraged centrifugal forces, the suppression of which required much coercion, often accompanied by large-scale civil war and bloodshed. Western policy since the Second World War therefore not only hastened the collapse of Westminster-style government in Africa, but also ensured that it would be succeeded by kleptocracy, conflict and despotism.

Professor Mazrui regrets to some extent the prominence of the Westernized groups in Africa in which he sees yet another example of Western influence. But he nevertheless interprets African experience virtually wholly in terms of their concerns and interests. This is why he says that the European impact on Africa was a nightmare, or that the production of cash crops by Africans harmed them, when in fact these sequences transformed for the better the lives of many millions of Africans.

Like many other Westernized Africans, notably including Kwame Nkrumah, Professor Mazrui attributes the economical and political weakness of Africa largely to its fragmentation into fifty or more different states; and again like others, including Nkrumah, he blames the West for this. This figure includes the North African countries, which have nothing in common with Black Africa, except for occasional concerted action against the West, especially under UN and UNCTAD auspices. The multiplicity of Black African states is the result of ethnic and tribal diversity, which in turn reflects the age-old isolation of small and warring communities, brought about by the absence even of rudimentary transport facilities and public security. By providing transport facilities and public security Western activities have in fact broken down this isolation over large areas, and have thus helped to create larger communities.

The state-controlled economies of recent decades have to some extent worked in the opposite direction. By greatly increasing the prizes of political power, state economic controls encourage separatist tendencies in heterogeneous societies. Simultaneously, they make the rulers more reluctant to cooperate with one another, as such cooperation implies some surrender of their power over their subjects. But the articulate Westernized Africans have consistently pressed for Western help to establish and operate extensive state controls.

6

Professor Mazrui often refers to East Africa where he comes from and where he taught for many years. Dr Nyerere is accorded the usual uncritical adulation. He is, of course, referred to as a front line President (p. 108) although Tanzania has no common frontier with Zimbabwe-Rhodesia. He is described as '... humane, sophisticated and sensitive to the wider implications of every act of policy' (p. 111); and again, 'Julius Nyerere does not believe in summary justice in his domestic policies. He is in reality a liberal democrat with a socialist veneer' (p. 110). During Nyerere's regime there have been numerous political killings in Tanzania. People have been incarcerated without trial for long periods in harsh conditions. Millions of people have been forced into collectivized villages, often mere sites, far from their homes. Those who tried to resist have had their homesteads razed and were themselves deprived of elementary comforts and civil rights.[9] Expropriations are frequent. But all this is forgiven, perhaps because President Nyerere is hostile to the West, to personal freedom and property and to individual farming and private enterprise.

Professor Mazrui also explicitly commends Nyerere's foreign policy, which he regards as the attempted establishment of Pax Tanzaniana, in turn a stepping stone to a Pax Africana. Components of the Pax Tanzaniana, noted on the whole approvingly by Professor Mazrui, have included the support of the bloody coup in Zanzibar with its butchery of hundreds of people; assistance to the left-wing coup in the Seychelles; forcible closure of the border with Kenya, which inflicted much hardship on the local people, but which was apparently intended 'to teach the government of Nairobi a lesson through economic means' (p. 108). What lesson? Perhaps to force the Kenyatta government to adopt internal policies similar to those of President Nyerere.

Establishment of the Pax Tanzaniana involved also the invasion of Amin's Uganda. Professor Mazrui thinks that the original purpose of this exercise was probably modest, no more than to teach Amin a lesson, but that Nyerere was drawn all the way by the lack of effective resistance. Professor Mazrui says nothing about the killing of civilians and the large-scale looting by the Tanzanian troops, long after the overthrow of Amin in April 1979. The Tanzanian army is still (1980) in Uganda. In Tanzania after many years of massive Western aid living standards are lower than they had been even in Amin's Uganda. The troops may not want to return. Perhaps President Nyerere may not be anxious to have them back after their experiences and activities in Uganda. When in 1964 the Tanzanian army mutinied, Nyerere had to appeal to Britain to suppress the revolt with a handful of troops – another piece of history ignored by the Reith lecturer.

Professor Mazrui repeatedly mentions Amin's oppressive dictatorship. But he does not record that the establishment of a totalitarian regime in Uganda ante-dated it. In 1966, shortly before the date of an election which he would have lost, Dr Obote staged an extremely bloody coup followed by civil war, in which, with Western support, he overthrew the popular Kabaka. He promptly suppressed all political parties other than his own, and set up a tyrannical regime, which in turn was overthrown by Amin in a bloodless coup in 1971. According to the blurb of the book Professor Mazrui was an important influence on the national politics of Uganda under President Obote.

In reflecting on the prospects of non-Africans after the confidently expected overthrow of white rule in South Africa, Professor Mazrui writes that in the long run there may well be much scope for them, although this is not certain. In this context he writes:

At least in the urban areas Kenya has successfully maintained a multiracial society. On the other hand, in Uganda Idi Amin ruthlessly threw out thousands of Asians . . . (p. 18).

Many thousands of Asians and Europeans, including groups who had been there for generations, have had to leave Kenya because, not being indigenous Africans, they were denied economic opportunities. Through the length and breadth of Black Africa post-colonial governments have forced out Asians, Europeans, Levantines, and also Black African 'strangers', by refusing to renew employment permits or trading licences.

7

Certain of Professor Mazrui's other themes, which often mirror contemporary ideology and intellectual fashion, bear both on his hopes and proposals and also on their appeal.

In Professor Mazrui's scheme of things, economic achievement and change do not result from people's activities. They simply happen, as did for instance the Industrial Revolution. At times this leads to bizarre statements such as that Zaire ' . . . was among the very first African countries to discover uranium . . . ' (p. 135). What happened was that Westerners explored and discovered uranium there. Total neglect of human achievement, and of the personal qualities and the social and political circumstances behind it, runs through the lectures, from the unexplained decay of the Garden of Eden in the first lecture to Professor Mazrui's vision of the end of the twentieth century in the last.

Professor Mazrui's lecture on the Burden of Underdevelopment should more correctly be entitled Lack of Economic Achievement. But the role of the determinants of economic performance is exactly what he refuses to acknowledge. This is why he harps on the poverty of Africa amidst ample natural resources.

The continent itself seems to be well endowed with resources, but a disproportionate number of people in the continent is undernourished and underprivileged. A situation where a continent is well endowed but the people are poor is a situation of anomalous underdevelopment (p. 72).

There is no anomaly. As I have already insisted, economic achievement depends on people and their arrangements, not on natural resources.

Professor Mazrui would like Africa to modernize, but without

Westernization (pp. 80–82). This is not possible. The concept of material progress, of steadily increasing control of man over his environment, is Western, as are the modes of conduct which derive from it. Progress and its conditions and manifestations may not be laudable or conducive to happiness. But the idea of modernization without Westernization is self-contradictory.

Professor Mazrui regards income differences as a reflection of unjust privileges and exploitation. Poor individuals, groups and societies are underprivileged and deprived. Like others who write in this vein he fails to ask how external forces, especially Western contacts, could possibly have caused the poverty of the poorest, most backward groups in Africa (pygmies, aborigines, desert people) when these have few outside contacts and no commercial contacts with the West. Throughout Africa, as elsewhere in the Third World, the level of economic achievement declines with the distance from the impact of Western commercial contact.

Professor Mazrui's view that poverty means injustice and oppression clearly implies that poverty reflects misconduct by others. Thus if, say, blacks are relatively poor, this is evidence of misconduct by other groups. This corollary lends special interest to his ideas, mentioned earlier, that the struggle for black liberation must extend beyond South Africa to the West; and that his proposed counter-missionaries should participate in civil wars there. On the other hand, the most backward groups in Africa as well as elsewhere in the Third World seem to be doubly afflicted. They are extremely poor. They are also isolated. Thus there is no one from whom they could be liberated.

Professor Mazrui believes that the size of a country, especially when allied to natural resources, confers political power. He envisages that, because of their size and natural resources, by the end of the twentieth century, Nigeria, a liberated South Africa and Zaire will be the diplomatic leaders of Africa, and will also be prominent in world affairs. Size and natural resources are all. But in fact these confer neither riches nor political power without appropriate human resources and the will to use them for these purposes. Neither size nor natural resources conferred power on China or India. Conversely, Venice, Holland and Britain were world powers when they were still small and had few natural resources.

According to Professor Mazrui world-wide exhaustion of natural resources and the population explosion are among the crises which endanger Africa, the Third World and indeed the whole world. The West is again the root of all evil. 'The Western world already consumes far too much of what there is on the planet, without planning for much more' (p. 115). In accordance with pretentious and fashionable jargon, he is apt to refer to the world as the planet, or the planet earth. Here again, he writes as if goods and services somehow just existed when they are, of course, produced by people. He does not say that Western production not only pays for all Western consumption, but in addition provides capital for the Third World. There is no danger from the exhaustion of physical resources. If a resource becomes relatively scarce, this leads to greater economy in its use, and to the development of substitutes. Moreover, with the exception of fossil fuel, all other mineral resources can be largely recovered as scrap. Should all natural resources threaten to give out, which is extremely improbable, human reproductive behaviour will be modified long before their exhaustion.

It is true that the West is behind the population explosion in the Third World. Before the impact of the West, high fertility in the Third World was balanced by correspondingly high mortality. Western science, technology and medicine and Western-induced economic improvement brought about the steep fall in mortality and the corresponding rise in life expectation there. The population explosion reflects, therefore, a large improvement in conditions, because people like to live longer and see their children do so. However, Professor Mazrui somehow manages to connect the population explosion with high child mortality. He presents a harrowing account of half-a-dozen children of one of his friends dying, which forces his friend to have a larger number of children to replace those lost through early death (p. 114). Here again the West is to blame because, according to Professor Mazrui, the high child mortality reflects Western-imposed economic injustice. But of course, mortality, including child mortality, was far higher before the impact of the West. In recent decades it has declined sharply, and this has brought about the so-called population explosion, a change which, as just noted, is an evident and significant improvement.

Professor Mazrui's treatment of Portuguese colonial rule and of its aftermath is again carefully structured for maximum appeal. He argues that it is because British rule was less repressive and terminated sooner that its successor states are less radically Marxist than are Angola and Mozambique. Special condemnation of Portuguese rule is pleasing not only to general anti-colonial sentiment, but perhaps even more to British conservatives, who have always been both baffled and irked by the longer duration of Portuguese rule. The more explicit Marxism of the governments of Angola and Mozambique owes much to such factors as the greater Soviet involvement there, and to the Cuban intervention in Angola. In any case, it is questionable whether Nyerere's policies are less collectivist than President Machel's. It is certainly rather eccentric to suggest, as does Professor Mazrui, that President Nyerere is a bourgeois liberal. He also forgets that Nkrumah, the first president of the first successor state to British rule in Africa, was an avowed and practising Marxist-Leninist. Nor does Professor Mazrui say that the present rulers of Ethiopia, who took over an independent state, are of extreme left-wing persuasion, and pursue communist policies as far as they can. It is also worth remembering that Nehru had to invade Goa, after refusing its population a plebiscite. Portuguese rule in Africa and Asia has always presented a special problem to anti-racists. The Portuguese explicitly encouraged miscegenation and hoped to create mini-Brazils, especially in Angola and Mozambique, a stance which made it difficult to accuse them of racism.

8

Professor Mazrui is an exponent of the economics and politics of resentment. His policy proposals are designed to erode the West and to undermine the whites in Southern Africa, especially in South Africa, rather than to promote the welfare of ordinary Africans. The pursuit of this overriding objective and the disregard of human faculties and mores lead to numerous and evident inconsistencies.

For the time being Professor Mazrui would welcome ' . . . some continuing extravagance in the Western world, but this is only a transitional strategy designed to weaken it sufficiently to make it responsive to the demands of global reform' (p. 115). He hopes for more cartels of the OPEC type to exploit Western dependence on external sources of raw material. However, as is widely and rightly recognized, the effectiveness of OPEC owes much to special conditions which are certainly not present in the case of African primary products. Commodity cartels for other such products could not possibly be effective without Western support, including that of Western-financed official international organizations. But perhaps Professor Mazrui, viewing issues and prospects from an exalted position, is not to be bothered with such practicalities, nor with the major domestic problems of commodity schemes.

Professor Mazrui takes continued foreign aid for granted. He only wishes individual countries to diversify their sources of aid to make them more independent of particular donors. But how is persistent external help consistent with independence and self-reliance? Professor Mazrui does not suggest that the African countries should help themselves, but only that they should help themselves to Western largesse, a practice which does not make for sustained prosperity.

Professor Mazrui proposes extensive replacement of Western imports and foreign personnel, technology and capital by local resources. Where are these to come from, and who is to pay? Ordinary people in the Third World would either have to pay more for locally-produced supplies, or go without the goods and services they desire. But Professor Mazrui is not concerned with the economic costs borne by ordinary people, or their needs, wants and preferences. He wishes to replace Western publications and films by local products because he regards their ubiquity as a form of imperialism. In fact, in Africa as elsewhere in the Third World, the proliferation of Western products reflects the preferences of ordinary people, a preference obnoxious to local intellectuals.

Professor Mazrui advocates what he calls horizontal interpenetration of the Third World. In plain English, this means official restriction of commercial contact with the West. Such restrictions deprive people of what they want and can afford. Mutual trade among the very poor and the bankrupt does not promote prosperity. The restrictions also place people even more at the mercy of the rulers than they already are.

African or Third World unity is pure fiction. Neither the spirit nor the resources for concerted action are available without external help. Systematic replacement of Western commercial and cultural contacts by mutual trade and cultural collaboration presupposes external organization and resources. The same applies to concerted political or military action.

Professor Mazrui complains that African communications, including telephones, are oriented to the outside world. The reason is of course that they have been constructed by Westerners; and are used by them or by Westernized groups. No external force stopped Africans from developing such facilities. That it is easier to telephone from Kenya to the United States than to West Africa shows again that African unity without outside help is fictitious, that concerted action by African states depends on external resources. All this is stubbornly ignored by Professor Mazrui who refuses to recognize the connection between people and achievement.

Professor Mazrui expects much from the development of the mineral resources of Africa. Indeed, as we have seen, he expects that this will confer international importance and power on some African states, including Zaire and liberated South Africa. But mineral development again presupposes external personnel, technology and capital, whether from the West or from Communist countries.

Professor Mazrui's overriding preoccupation is with the undermining of the West, and with the enhancement of the real or illusory political power of the African rulers, and perhaps that of their Western advisers acting as court theologians. The power of these rulers will depend on the readiness of the West to provide resources for the erosion of its own position and for the tightening of the grip of these rulers over their own subjects.

The direction of his argument is evident also in his proposals for a complete Western boycott of South Africa and for Western subsidies to guerilla movements. He admits that many people think that contacts with South Africa, especially inflow of capital, erode apartheid. An inflow of capital also promptly improves the lot of Africans by increasing the demand for labour and reducing the relative scarcity of capital, which is primarily a white asset.

Professor Mazrui does not specify whether his proposed boycott of South Africa is to extend to relations between that country and the black African states. Zambia depends heavily on South Africa for food and other consumer goods. Many thousands of people from Mozambique work in South Africa under a little-publicized agreement between the two governments. The South African Railways and Harbour Board is extensively involved in the administration of the Mozambique railway and the port of Maputo.[10] Professor Mazrui does not acquaint his readers with these realities. Shortly before Professor Mazrui began his lectures, the extensive dependence on South Africa of Zambia, Malawi and Mozambique for technical personnel, food, consumer goods, organization of transport, basic machinery, employment opportunities for black labour, and export routes and facilities was reviewed in an article in the *Financial Times*, 15 August 1979. The population of these countries would suffer much hardship from an effective boycott of South Africa.

It is speculative whether apartheid would be eroded more effectively by the inflow of capital and the extension of commercial contacts, or by complete boycott of South Africa, if this were practicable, and by large-scale financing of guerilla movements. Professor Mazrui regards violent revolution as the solution for South Africa. Unlike a more gradual process, forcible overthrow of white rule necessarily involves violent conflict and bloodshed. It is also much more likely to unleash tribal war and large-scale maltreatment of Asians. This last outcome is likely to be conspicuous because in South Africa, as in Central and East Africa, Africans at large dislike the Asians much more than they do the whites. This is another matter habitually swept under the carpet by exponents of Third World solidarity, and one about which Shiva Naipaul again writes with candour:

As is the case all over East and Central Africa, it is not the whites who arouse the greatest animosity, but the Asians. My stay coincided with a vigorous anti-Asian campaign in the Zambian press. Day after day, in the Times of Zambia, lengthy articles and impassioned letters to the Editor were devoted to this enthralling subject. Asian women were accused of harbouring feelings of superiority because they did not sleep with or marry Zambian men. Photographs were published showing suitcases filled to the brim with bank notes seized from Asians attempting to smuggle currency out of the country. Asian businessmen, predictably enough, were guilty of monopolising the distributive trades and exploiting innocent Zambians. Could Asians, one letter writer wanted to know, ever become patriots? The climax came with the front-page headline which read: 'Asian Doctors Kill their Patients'. . . . Hounding the Asian is a legitimate blood-sport; a national pastime. On another page of the same newspaper there was a photograph of Indira Gandhi, who, a day or two previously, had been in Lusaka preaching the gospel of Afro-Asian solidarity. Afro-Asian solidarity aside, a man from Mars would have no trouble in deducing that Asians, not Rhodesians, not South Africans, were the overriding threat to the security and well-being of the Zambian State and Zambian people (pp. 232–3).

The fate of the Asians after violent revolution in South Africa would not be enviable. But such matters are of little moment to Professor Mazrui. Writings such as Professor Mazrui's Reith Lectures have been helpful to the determined supporters of apartheid within South Africa. They can make political capital out of them by arguing that their critics are ignorant or malicious.

9

The African scene does indeed present a baffling anomaly or paradox. But this is very different from Professor Mazrui's pseudo parodoxes, and is indeed their opposite.

How does it come about that African rulers whose military and economic resources are negligible are yet taken seriously, and exercise such influence as, say, President Nyerere? Why does the West abase itself before him or Mr Kaunda, rulers whose own resources are extremely meagre, and who could not survive without large-scale Western help? One factor is the unfounded but widespread and much articulated feeling of guilt in the West. Conflict and dissension in the West is another. There are many people in the West who have come to dislike, or even to hate, their own society and its institutions, or who long for more money and power or for greater status. They often look to Third World spokesmen and politicians as allies or instruments in a civil conflict. Mere ignorance does not explain prevailing attitudes, because ignorance by itself is neutral and does not therefore account for a particular slant of opinion. Such influences may also explain the adulation of President Nyerere; the references to Dr Ramphal as the man who saved Rhodesia; the commendations of Mr Kaunda, and of his meaningless vapourings about so-called African humanism; and the references to Professor Mazrui as a formidable mind and as an author capable of Byronic presentation. The effectiveness of such praise and flattery is enhanced because those who proffer them act as a claque. The operation of this claque reinforces the impact of the opinions it supports and simultaneously smothers dissenting voices. There are many thousands of people in the West who have heard of Professor Mazrui for every one who has heard of Miss Noni Jabavu, whose book is far more informative than are Professor Mazrui's lectures.

Such forces presumably explain also how he came to be invited to give the Reith Lectures, the most widely publicized lectures in Britain. In this instance they were also particularly expensive to produce because, as Professor Mazrui acknowledges, he received generous financial support from the BBC for two extensive tours in Africa.

10

His book is published under an educational imprint which I first encountered when reading *Africa Must Unite*, a collection of Nkrumah's outpourings. Professor Mazrui is much more sophisticated than Nkrumah was, but his lectures are of no greater intellectual substance. It is misleading to call such books educational. But then this could also be said of expressions such as the United Nations, the British Commonwealth, the German Democratic Republic and many others. Professor Mazrui's book only reconfirms that the world language of the late twentieth century is not English: it is Newspeak.

PART THREE

The State of Economics

The purpose of studying economics is not to acquire a set of readymade answers to economic questions, but to learn how to avoid being deceived by economists.

Joan Robinson
Collected Economic Papers (1960)

12 Economists and the Two Dollar Problems
13 Economic History as Theory
14 The Investment Fetish
15 Reflections on the State of Economics

CHAPTER 12

Economists and the
Two Dollar Problems

It may be, in fact, that the (dollar) problem should not be regarded
as the fruit of aberrations of policy . . . but that it should be looked
upon as the result of a set of economic circumstances never
contemplated by the text-books – namely, the existence of a country
which, all policy apart, needs so little from the rest of the world, while
the rest of the world requires so much from it, that an equilibrium of
accounts can be brought about by no means available to a free, or
even a tolerably free, market.

'The Dollar Problem',
The Economist, 4 December 1943

1

In Orwell's *1984* an orator of the Inner Party of Oceania harangues a crowd with an inflammatory speech extolling Eastasia and reviling Eurasia, respectively the ally and enemy of Oceania. The speech has been proceeding for about twenty minutes when a messenger slips a note to the speaker informing him of a reversal of the alliance. In mid-sentence he substitutes Eastasia for Eurasia, not only without pause but without even breaking the syntax. No one appears to notice.

The treatment of the dollar in much economic literature since the Second World War uncomfortably resembles this episode. In the 1940s and 1950s the dollar problem, occasionally called the long-run chronic dollar problem, was interpreted as a persistent and unavoidable world shortage of dollars. However, some of the publications on this topic were still in the press when the problem assumed the diametrically opposite meaning – namely that of a glut. The flow of publications referring to the dollar problem as a shortage continued for some years after the emergence of other publications interpreting it as a glut, so that, for a period, both interpretations flourished side by side. However, by the second half of the 1960s the problem came to be interpreted as a persistent surplus: the dollar problem remained, but the sign had been changed from minus to plus.[1]

214

According to the shortage literature, the United States damaged the rest of the world by exporting unemployment and forcing deflation on other countries. In the glut literature, it did damage by exporting inflation and buying up capital assets cheaply with its paper dollars. Both a dollar shortage and a dollar glut were adduced to justify far-reaching policies, especially the control of imports, exports and capital movements. The significance and influence of the shortage literature extended beyond the position and prospects of the dollar. Thus suggestions of a dollar shortage led to talk of a general shortage of world liquidity, which would require the continuous creation of new official reserve assets. At the same time, the system of fixed exchange rates was alleged to impart a *deflationary* bias to the international monetary system, since deficit countries were compelled to attempt to contract their economies without a corresponding obligation on the part of surplus countries to try to expand theirs.[2] This allegedly deflationary system was nevertheless soon overtaken by a general and persistent rise in prices which, in turn, evoked complaints of a flood of liquidity and suggestions that there was an inherent *inflationary* bias in the Bretton Woods system of fixed exchange rates. Having been a problem of the world seeking dollars, it became a problem of dollars swamping the world.[3]

We shall now note some of the highlights in the transition from shortage to glut. Much of the detail is not relevant to our discussion, but we wish to emphasize here that the radical divergence between the prognostications of those who wrote about the dollar problem and the actual sequence of events was not the result of unsuccessful forecasts in the accepted sense of the term, but reflected simple shortcomings in analysis and observation. We shall return later to this matter.

The abrupt transformation of the dollar problem from scarcity to glut reflected the acquisition of large supplies of dollars by central banks outside the United States, and the emergence of the Eurodollar market. The relationship between these phenomena is still a subject of debate which for the present purpose is not relevant.

The shortage literature emerged and burgeoned in the later 1940s and early 1950s, at a time when the economies of Western Europe and Japan were disrupted by the war and its aftermath to a much greater extent than was the economy of the United States. By the later 1950s most of the former had recovered and, in some major instances, progressed much more rapidly than the American economy. The effects of differences in the rates of growth of output on the balance of payments and on rates of exchange depend on the monetary and fiscal policies of the trading partners. From the late 1950s monetary and fiscal policies in the United Sates were generally more expansionist and inflationary than those of other major industrial countries. American policies included intermittent restrictions of interest rates to levels lower than would have otherwise prevailed.

The consequences of these policies in promoting an outflow of dollars were magnified by the expansion of military expenditure abroad and by other official outflows. Moreover, many United States corporations found it more profitable to invest abroad, so further increasing the supply of dollars. The transformation from scarcity to glut thus reflected the operation of the basic determinants of the supply of, and the demand for, currencies: a rate of exchange which undervalued the commercial dollar in one set of conditions came to overvalue it when such conditions changed.

2

Transformation of a dollar scarcity into a dollar glut can therefore readily be explained in terms of changes in the basic determinants of rates of exchange. How did the crucial role of the rate of exchange and its determinants come to be so largely overlooked?

Some of the allegations in the dollar shortage literature were simply assertions or crude extrapolations. Others were supported by arguments of apparent sophistication and complexity, such as suggestions of disparate changes in productivity in different countries and groups of industries. The abrupt and conspicuous failure of predictions of a lasting shortage of dollars and of a world-wide shortage of liquidity was not the result of unsuccessful forecasting in the accepted sense of a failure to take into account unforeseeable occurrences. Unsuccessful forecasts in this sense are both frequent and unavoidable in the course of necessary forward planning by governments, business enterprises and private persons. The failure of the predictions in the literature of the dollar shortage was primarily the result of simple neglect of the relevance of price to supply and demand, that is to say, of what was once the first lesson in economics.[4] It is as though modern geographers warned travellers that if they strayed too far they might fall off the edge of the world. The return of the travellers, no matter how far they may have travelled, could not reasonably be said to reflect an unforeseeable occurrence, but only the failure of the geographers to remember the fundamentals of their subject.

Much of the discussion misinterpreted a situation in which official controls regulated exchange rates at levels at which there was an excess demand for dollars as if it were a normal, permanent and largely inevitable market condition. This approach was rather like suggesting that a shortage of rented accommodation is inherent in the nature of housing, rather than the result of rent controls. The dollar problem was discussed substantialiy without examining the rate of exchange, that is, the price of the allegedly scarce commodity, a neglect familiar in political argument and lay discussion. Much of the discussion also neglected such basic determinants of the rate of exchange as changes in the money supply and levels of interest rates, and the pertinence of financial policies and official controls. The simplest implications of the theory of comparative advantage and costs were also ignored. Further, the participants in the discussion do not appear to have given any thought to the ability of markets to develop substitutes and new institutions for existing arrangements as, for instance, the rise of Euro-currency markets. These fundamentals were usually ignored altogether or, at best, mentioned as casual asides without recognizing their central role. Such transgressions were not isolated lapses by a few ill-qualified practitioners. They were widely perpetrated by prominent economists. Indeed, the neglect by leading economists of fundamentals in this area continued after the discussion of the dollar shortage had died down. This neglect then extended to the discussion of the foreign exchange problems of less developed countries.[5]

How can we account for such transgressions? And how is it that, far from these ideas being promptly exposed by other practitioners and commentators, they were permitted to flourish for many years? It was surprising, to say the least, that economists should discuss supply and demand without considering price, or worry about a lasting shortage without realizing that the idea is meaningless without a reference to price. It was also surprising that problems of exchange rates and of international liquidity should be discussed without examination of monetary and fiscal policies and of interest rates. Moreover, all this took place at a time of rapid expansion of economics and of genuine and substantial advances in some parts of the subject, including international economics, monetary economics and the theory of the foreign exchanges. Similar transgressions have continued to be the order of the day in such important areas as, for example, unemployment, the determinants of the balance of payments and the prospects of Third World countries.

3

At a time of genuine advances in the subject the frequency of simple lapses in fundamentals by leading economists makes it difficult to assess the weight to be attached to professional opinion. The lapses we have noted disfigure large areas of economic discourse. We shall now conjecture about some of the reasons behind them, albeit only briefly; parts of the argument are developed at greater length in the last chapter of this book.

In much of the discussion of the dollar problem, both as a shortage and as a glut, a political thrust can be discerned: namely, the emphasis on the need for extensive state control. But some participants in the discussion, including the most distinguished, have had no political axe to grind. The disregard of simple analysis in their writings may have been the result, perhaps, of a desire to be in the swim, to say something on a major issue of the day, even if the attempt lured them onto unfamiliar territory.

Rapid expansion of a branch of knowledge or academic discipline, such as took place in economics after the Second World War, leads to problems of quality control, especially when the absence of controlled experiments makes it difficult to expose even simple errors quickly and convincingly. The political and personal concerns of economists exacerbate this difficulty. These traditional concerns have, it is true, benefited the subject by keeping economists in touch with the real world and by attracting able people and other resources into economics. But they often mean a confusion between the promotion of policy and the advancement of knowledge, and the subordination of knowledge to political purposes. Such confusion and subordination hamper the establishment and maintenance of standards of competence. Advancement of knowledge and pursuit of political and personal objectives are commendable activities, but to mix them up can be extremely damaging to both. For instance, criticism of even simple mistakes can be countered on the ground that it reflects merely ideological differences. Or again, simple lapses can be defended with a show of plausibility by referring to political and administrative objectives or constraints which the authors claim *ex post* to have had in mind.

The rapid expansion of economics in recent decades has owed much to expectations entertained by the public of its practical potentialities. These expectations were encouraged by economists themselves. Both they and their public hoped and believed that the pursuit and application of economics could do much to promote full employment, to accelerate growth both in the West and in the Third World, and to forecast reliably the future course of economic events and market conditions. Many of these hopes and expectations were unwarranted. The public expected too much, largely because the economists claimed too much. The extent of these hopes and claims has in many ways impeded steady progress in economics, by making it more difficult to assess achievement in the subject for instance. In any field of human endeavour unwarranted claims are apt to lead to substandard performance. Achievement may fall short not only of the claims, but also below what could be brought about by established and recognized methods. Such discrepancies between claims and expectations on the one hand, and between performance and achievement on the other, are often encountered in long-range economic forecasting, a popular and profitable activity of economists.

4

Forecasting is part and parcel of politics, administration and business and is therefore appropriately one of the tasks of applied economists. Scientific prediction, however, must be distinguished clearly from forecasts of the future. Scientific predictions specify the consequences of stipulated changes in certain variables. They take the form: 'If A, then B'. Prediction in this scientific sense is indeed helpful to forecasting by improving its reliability. Although forecasting is often necessary it does not add to knowledge, unlike scientific prediction which results from analysis and observation. Often these exercises purport to forecast developments many years ahead. But frequently they are vitiated by the neglect of basic relationships, such as those between prices, supply and demand, recognition of which is indispensable for worthwhile examination of past, present and future economic sequences. The inadequacy of these exercises is at times obscured by the display of a mass of statistics or impressive technical apparatus or jargon serving as a protective facade. All this was much in evidence in the discussions of the dollar shortage and the likelihood of its persistence.

Many academic and official publications of the post-war years reveal in other contexts this combination of neglect of simple analysis with a readiness to produce long-run forecasts. The World Bank's *Report on the Economic Development of Nigeria* (Baltimore, 1955) tried to guess future export earnings decades ahead, but failed to consider the effects of prices on supply and demand, even in the context of proposals for the imposition of import and export duties. The literature on economic planning in poor countries abounds in long-range forecasts which ignore the simplest and most pertinent variables, notably including the effects of prices on supply and demand, and of exchange rates and financial policies on the balance of payments. In the UK in 1965 the National Institute of Economic and Social Research published a large volume on the future of the British economy entitled *The British Economy in 1975* (Cambridge, 1965). The book examined the prospects of the British economy ten years ahead. It did so without discussion of exchange rates or monetary policies.

However, neither exposure of error, even simple error, nor spectacular failure of forecasts seems to affect the standing of the practitioners, the acceptance of these exercises by the profession or the public, or the prestige of economics as a social science. It is not reasonable to expect economists to refrain from activities which accord with their inclinations and interests. The maxim *caveat emptor* and its implications extend beyond everyday markets for goods and services.

CHAPTER 13

Economic History as Theory

1

Sir John Hicks's book *A Theory of Economic History* is an exceedingly bold attempt to present a theory of world economic history.[1] It is certainly the most ambitious such attempt by a twentieth-century economist. The scope of the endeavour and the position of Sir John Hicks as one of the foremost economic theorists of the twentieth century must command the most serious attention for the book and warrant careful scrutiny and analysis. The attempt at a theory of world economic history by a Nobel Laureate in economics also presents an opportunity to examine yet again the potentialities and limitations of general theories of history. I shall try here both to assess his book and to reflect on the time-honoured quest for a general theory of history.

2

In the opening chapter Sir John Hicks sets out the task he proposes for himself, and the methods by which he intends to pursue it. 'Why should we not treat the Economic History of the World as a single process – a process that (at least so far) has a recognizable trend?' (p. 7). The process is to be examined by an enquiry which spans all time and space since it 'extends in one of its dimensions over the whole world; in another, over the whole span of human history, from . . . the earliest ages of which anthropologists and archaeologists have given us some fragmentary knowledge, right up to . . . the present day' (p. 1).

He proposes to go well beyond the use of 'bits of theory to serve as hypotheses for the elucidation of some particular historical processes', and to apply economic reasoning conceived broadly, on a grand scale, ' . . . so that the general course of history, at least in some important aspects, can be fitted into place' (pp. 2–3). By means of a theoretical scheme rooted in economic reasoning he intends to explain the process by which one state of society succeeds another.

Hicks's unifying theme is the transformation of the market in the course of history. He interprets the different economic states of society as stages in its transformation, from the earliest times when the market emerges from what he calls revenue or custom economies, up to the present day. Different phases in this transformation result in the successive economic states of society.

He proposes to generalize about this evolution by means of a ' . . . theoretical enquiry, which must proceed in general terms – the more general the better. We are to classify states of society, economic states of society; we are to look for the intelligible reasons for which one state should give way to another' (p. 6). Effective pursuit of such a programme requires clear definition of the successive states of society, and of the process by which one such state succeeds another. In this book, however, neither the different states nor the different phases of the process through which they succeed one another are clearly specified or defined. Indeed, the distinguishing characteristics of the states of society, economic states of society, that is the crucial entities, are nowhere identified or defined.

The wide scope of the major theme and of the sub-themes is circumscribed by hedging qualifications. Thus he writes, ' . . . it is only a *normal* development for which we are looking, so it [the theoretical schema] does not have to cover all the facts; we must be ready to admit exceptions, exceptions which nevertheless we should try to explain' (p. 6). But the reasons why a particular development is to be considered the norm are nowhere presented, and exceptions are not stated, much less pursued.

It may seem as if these difficulties are met by Hicks's references to statistical uniformities in history. 'Every historical event has some aspect in which it is unique; but nearly always there are other aspects in which it is a member of a group, often of quite a large group. If it is one of the latter aspects in which we are interested, it will be the group, not the individual, on which we shall fix our attention; it will be the average, or norm, of the group which is what we shall be trying to explain' (p. 3).

It may at times be useful to classify historical events and changes into groups. Demographic phenomena and sequences are an example. But Hicks does not proceed in this manner. He does indeed often present individual episodes, but he does not explain or establish, by enumeration or otherwise, why his examples are normal or typical in a statistical, or some other, sense. Nor does he explain on what criteria or on what grounds his 'states of society, economic states of society' are amenable to informative classification. As already noted, Hicks does not define or identify their characteristics.

Thus the avowed organizing principle of the enquiry is not applied to the record of history. The author's approach to the historical process is casual in the extreme. His procedure is mainly to consider why one situation, or state of society, can give way to another; and he does this almost exclusively by examining implications rather than by narrating and analysing historical events and sequences. The references to the averages and statistical uniformities suggest extensive reliance on statistical evidence, perhaps even a largely inductive method. But another passage proposes a procedure which is almost exclusively deductive: 'My plan is that we begin with this transformation [the Rise of the Market], that we seek to define it, and then see, so far as we can, what logically follows from it. We shall look over our shoulders at the historical record, so as to see that we do not put our logical process into a form which clashes with the largest and most obvious facts. (This is only the first stage of fitting, but it is as far as we shall go.) As we continue with the implications, many things, we shall find, will fit into place' (pp. 7–8). This deductive method is adopted practically throughout. References to the historical record are confined to casual glances, to ensure no more than that the results of logical inference should not clash with the 'largest and most obvious facts'. However, since the declared concern is with the normal and the average, even this rough checking procedure is of very little use. This is so because Hicks does not tell us how to establish an average or a norm, or how to decide whether an inconvenient fact is an irrelevant abnormality or a refutation of the theory.

Hicks's concept of the underlying trend poses similar problems. His theory is supposed to explain how the economic states of society logically succeed one another. And yet, 'we are not to think of our normal process as one which, on being begun, is bound to be completed' (p. 6). But again he does not say how we can discern or define the underlying trend or normal process, or what instances of discordant retrogression or divergence should lead us to question the existence of this underlying trend or normal process.

Although described by him as a theory of history, Hicks's theory cannot be checked by confronting it even with 'the largest and most obvious facts', as he does not tell us how to distinguish the normal from the abnormal, the average from the atypical. And while he claims that his theory explains the course of economic history up to the present, he explicitly doubts whether it can predict the future (p. 8). Thus, future events will not be able to refute the theory either, even though it claims to explain an underlying trend (albeit one which is left unspecified).

In his concluding paragraph, Sir John Hicks writes: 'I have tried to exhibit economic history, in the way that the great eighteenth-century writers did, as part of a social evolution much more widely considered. I have tried to indicate the lines that connect the economic story with the things we ordinarily regard as falling outside it. But when one becomes conscious of these links, one realizes that recognition is not enough. There are threads that run from economics into other social fields, into politics, into religion, into science and into technology; they develop there, and then run back into economics. These I have made little attempt to follow out; but I am in no way concerned to deny their existence' (p. 167). This passage confirms again that Hicks does not offer a coherent theory which could be assessed rigorously. It is absolutely impossible to distinguish systematically between failure of the theory to explain what it claims to be able to explain, and inability of the theory to explain what lies outside its apparently restricted scope as delimited by the author.

Hicks claims to interpret economic history broadly, to note the findings of cognate disciplines and to recognize the influence of institutions. But at least from the phase he terms the rise of the market he envisages institutions and institutional change as emerging from economic activity, as serving its purpose, and thus in effect being only dependent variables. Apart from one or two quite perfunctory remarks which refer mostly to pre-classical antiquity, neither religion nor any other belief is mentioned as influencing either conduct or social institutions. Religion and religious differences are ignored as influences on conduct, as agents of history, and as parameters of economic life. In general, in Hicks's account the causal relationship runs almost exclusively from economics to the other social fields, and not in the reverse direction.

Hicks explicitly disclaims affinity with Spengler and Toynbee. He does not intend to present 'a grand design of history'. His theory ' . . . will be a good deal nearer to the kind of thing that was attempted by Marx, who did take from his economics some general ideas which he applied to history, so that the pattern he saw in history had some extra-historical support. That is much more the kind of thing I want to try to do' (p. 2). The theories of history of Marx, Spengler, Toynbee and Hicks all exhibit instances of considerable insight. Economists may prefer Marx and Hicks to Toynbee and Spengler either for political reasons or because of their emphasis on economic factors. But all four share the basic flaws of the use of ill-defined concepts, and of arbitrary choice of examples and periods.

It is not possible systematically to examine Hicks's theory of economic history because, as I have already insisted and as will be evident from what follows, he does not in fact pursue his own declared objective. Hicks's major theme, regarded by him as a theory of economic history, is not susceptible to methodical review. The discussion must therefore focus on specific major issues and events introduced by him in support of this theory. I shall first discuss an illuminating major theme of the book, and a number of other valuable insights. I will then consider part of Hicks's treatment of two phases of history, the 'city-state system' of the 'First Phase of the Mercantile Economy', and the 'Modern Phase'. Thereafter, I will consider his treatment of the Industrial Revolution, and some of his references to the Soviet Union. In the concluding section I will refer to wider questions of a general theory of world economic history.

3

Whatever the shortcomings or limitations of *A Theory of Economic History*, it contains, as one would confidently expect from Sir John Hicks, a number of insights and penetrating observations. I draw attention to three matters on which I found his discussion to be especially useful.

Hicks envisages economic history as a series of transformations of the mercantile or market economy. The process begins with the custom-command economy from which the early market emerges, and extends to the modern phase, where the market is now in retreat before new types of command and revenue economies. This approach may prove a fruitful way of organizing and (possibly) of interpreting much of the material of economic history, and may serve to provide a pattern of its course over large time-spans and areas. It seems distinctly preferable to systems of interpretation which emphasize the role of single variables such as technology, entrepreneurship, social class or capital. Hicks's system can accommodate the phenomenon of economic decline which some of the familiar models cannot do.

In general, Hicks does not trace the interplay between economic forces and political developments. However, he has a thought-provoking discussion of the impact of the transformation of the market economy upon political centralization. Thus he writes: 'The Mercantile Economy, in its First Phase, was an escape from political authority – except in so far as it made its own political authority. Then, in the Middle Phase, when it came formally back under the traditional political authority, that authority was not strong enough to control it. It might destroy, but it could not control. In the Modern Phase, into which we have now passed, that is changed. Largely because of the internal evolution of the Mercantile Economy, control over it has become immensely easier. This is so, whatever is the political structure, and whatever are the ends of the controllers. Their powers will serve them alike for War or Peace, for the solving of social problems or for smothering them' (p. 100).

Hicks reformulates Adam Smith's celebrated maxim that the division of labour depends on the extent of the market by saying that it depends on the concentration of demand (actually, on the extent of demand). Adam Smith's dictum is indeed invalid if the term market denotes organization for the voluntary exchange of goods, or the volume of voluntary exchanges. There can be much highly specialized activity when there is no market in this sense, as is evident both from the relics of antiquity, especially in Egypt, and from the experience of present-day command economies, such as the Soviet Union. Hicks's reformulation is more than semantics. The market in the sense of organization for voluntary exchange is but one method of achieving the necessary concentration of demand. Hicks's concept of the revenue economy likewise is illuminating as a summary description of conditions which make possible the emergence of highly sophisticated specialization, reflected for example in magnificent structures, works of art and artefacts, when most people are very poor.

4

In Sir John Hicks's exposition, the city-state system is crucial for the development of the mercantile economy,[2] and 'is the principal key to the divergence between the history of Europe and the history of Asia. The reason . . . is mainly geographical. The city-state of Europe is a gift of the Mediterranean' (p. 38).

This formulation embodies simple geographical determinism and ignores straightforward historical evidence. The three ethnic groups or nations of classical antiquity which most profoundly affected the evolution of Europe were the Jews, the Greeks and the Romans. The Jews and the Romans formed no mercantile city-states, and some of the major Greek city-states were not mercantile city-states, in Hicks's sense of communities with much external trade and ruled by a trading class.[3] Moreover, the geographical configuration of the Mediterranean played little part in the emergence of some major city-states, such as early Rome. Hicks also explicitly recognizes that in the relevant physical characteristics the coastal areas and islands of South-East Asia are similar to those of the Mediterranean. At this point he calls in aid the explanation that 'opportunities . . . were less and difficulties greater' (p. 39).[4]

Nor is it appropriate to assign a key causal role to the city-state, especially to the commercial city-state, in the evolution of Europe. This is suggested, for instance, by the comparatively small influence of the Phoenician trading cities, including Carthage (certainly a city-state), on the subsequent course of history. They were not centres of intellectual or artistic life, but places where an authoritarian tradition was maintained or even reinforced. The character and influence of the Greek city-states and the different evolution of Asia and Europe are probably better seen as reflections of a greater intellectual enterprise and restlessness, and a less pronounced authoritarian tradition in Europe compared with most of Asia. These differences were already notable by the sixth century BC, and may have originated in various climatic, political and religious influences.

Although Hicks emphasizes the role of the city-states in the evolution of Europe, he does not mention what was probably their most important single contribution in this context, namely their role in promoting and protecting personal freedom and intellectual activity. Of course, the cities could play such a role only in the absence of a strongly authoritarian tradition: witness Athens compared with Sparta (Lakedaimon) or Carthage.

Important as were some commercial city-states in certain periods and in some areas, Hicks greatly overstates their general significance. Many cities, including cities which subsequently developed into city-states, originated in activities other than trade. They began as political, military, administrative or religious centres, including pilgrimage centres or staging-posts for pilgrimages; or as places where life, property and civil and religious activity could best be protected. From these other roles they often developed into trading centres, a development which was facilitated by the relative concentration of population. City-states then developed from trading centres when political and military conditions were favourable. The history of Venice is one example. But many large cities, including cities pre-eminent over long periods, such as Alexandria and Paris, did not become city-states. Not only was Paris never a city-state but its rise to eminence owed little to trade. And several of the major city-states of the classical world were not mercantile city-states, as interpreted by Hicks. Sparta and Thebes were not primarily mercantile communities. Nor was Rome which, as Hicks rightly recognizes, was a non-mercantile city-state until it suddenly expanded into an empire after the Second Punic War. The artistic and literary flowering of Western Europe in the twelfth century, most pronounced in France, owed nothing to city-states. Moreover, commercial city-states emerged in only a handful of instances, primarily classical Greece, medieval Italy, the Low Countries and the Hansa. They played no part in any other major economies, including those of Britain, France and, of course, the United States.

Hicks asserts that city-states and their legal institutions were broadly similar. This generalization covers Carthage and Florence, and the presence or absence of such institutions as slavery and infanticide. Such a historical generalization has little to commend it. He considers also that the establishment of external settlements and colonies from the Phoenicians right up to the seventeenth century was 'the same story, in some essential respects, in each case' (p. 50). Thus he regards as substantially identical the establishment of Greek colonies in Asia Minor in antiquity; of Venetian quarters in the Levant; the conquests of the Dutch in South-East Asia in the seventeenth century; the British settlements in North America in the same period; and presumably the Spanish conquests in America. These countries, colonies and communities differed greatly in their economic and political arrangements, the degree of political subordination to the country or city of origin and in their relations to other communities, and their right and ability to trade independently. Little is gained by regarding either their origin or their activities as similar in unspecified essentials.

Hicks links the Venetian-led sack of Constantinople in 1204 and the exploitation of Bengal in the eighteenth century as 'evils that belong to the [trading] situation' (p. 52). The supposed connection is, however, extremely tenuous. The sack of Constantinople occurred within a few years or decades of such man-made calamities as the devastation of large parts of the Arab world and Europe by the Mongols, and the first French (Angevin) invasion of Italy, which culminated in the Sicilian Vespers. These episodes had nothing to do with 'trading situations'. The sack of Constantinople cannot be understood without its complex political and religious background, especially the enmity between the Greek and Latin churches, a matter not mentioned by Hicks. And Warren Hastings would not have been impeached if his exactions had been inherent in the situation. Moreover, in Bengal such exactions (or worse ones) by the rulers had long antedated the arrival of the British, and were regarded as inherent not in a trading situation but in the nature of things.[5]

In his discussion of the decline of the trading role of the city-states, Hicks writes that 'when the point comes that it [expansion of trade] no longer absorbs the same energy, art can be pursued for art's sake, and learning for the sake of learning. It was at the end of her period of commercial expansion that Athens became the "mother of arts", it was after their commercial expansion was completed that Florence and Venice became the homes of the High Renaissance' (pp. 58–9). Three comments are in order on this treatment of the interplay between trade and art. First, the explanation neglects the long history of major developments in the arts in Italy during the period of trade expansion. Second, the efflorescence of the arts in Holland coincided with the rapid expansion of trade, as it also did in Shakespeare's England. (Hicks claims, incidentally, that the nation-state of Holland 'had much in common with the city-states' (p. 143).) Third, according to Hicks, it was the decline in trading opportunities in the eighteenth century which provided the stimulus towards the development of manufacturing industry in England (pp. 143–4). But it is by no means clear that there was such a decline in trading opportunities, nor why the supposed decline did not lead to a flourishing of the arts.

5

In Sir John Hicks's schema, the modern phase – the second of the two phases I have here selected for detailed consideration – is 'the state the world is in at the present day' (p. 160). In his treatment of history the modern phase is one of the economic states of society. All economies in existence today are to be regarded, it seems, as members of the same analytical category. Yet this category has only one distinguishing feature, namely, that the member-economies all exist now. Hicks here completely abandons the scheme which underpins his treatment of history, and which is the core of his theory. In Hicks's scheme, the Industrial Revolution and the Rise of Modern Industry are economic states which logically precede the modern phase. But he now regards all economies existing in the world today as being in the modern phase, although many of these have not been through the Industrial Revolution or the Rise of Modern Industry. Thus in Hicks's treatment of the modern phase recourse to the calendar has replaced even the semblance of an attempt at analysis or theory. The radical shift in treatment is particularly startling when it is remembered that Hicks's city-state phase of society ranges in time from the Greek city-states through the Italian city-states and the Dutch Republic to contemporary Singapore – the latter belongs simultaneously, it seems, to two different economic states of society, namely the city-state and the modern phase, which are elsewhere widely separated in Hicks's scheme of things.

The sketchiness of treatment and the blurring of relevant differences characteristic of the book as a whole are especially pronounced here. Thus it is the world which is in the modern phase, a phase which embraces aborigines and tribal societies at one end, the highly industrialized societies of North America, Western Europe and Japan at the other. This is abstraction to a point where it is no longer a useful simplification but an unhelpful travesty of reality. It is the outcome of Hicks's bold attempt at historical generalization across the world and across the ages.

Hicks seems to regard the two billion or more people of the less developed countries as if they were both uniform among themselves, i.e. a homogeneous mass, and also similar in culture and conduct to the peoples of the developed world from whom they differ only in being poorer. They are the proletariat of the modern phase, ready to be absorbed into the industrial working class. Malaysian peasants, Chinese millionaires, Indian labourers, Arabs of the Middle East, tribal Africans, Latin American industrialists, aborigines and pygmies, all are much of a muchness, and are seen as being at the same stage as were the people of Britain and Western Europe in the eighteenth and nineteenth centuries. Hicks does not even so much as hint at possible differences in faculties, attitudes, mores and institutions anywhere in the world, either past or present, or in the less developed world, or between developed and under-developed countries. Humanity in total is and was an undifferentiated mass.

Hicks does not, in fact, discuss the so-called modern phase as an economic state of society, but limits his concluding chapter largely to a consideration as to whether the growing 'pre-industrial proletariat' of the present less developed world can be absorbed into the ranks of modern industry. His first answer is that the industrial expansion required for this absorption 'is indeed enormous; but the expansive power of Modern Industry – the fully science-based industry of the twentieth century – is also enormous' (p. 158). He sees only two substantial obstacles to a world-wide expansion of modern industry, namely the restrictive autarkic policies of governments of less developed countries and their proneness to spend lavishly on politically popular purposes.

Hicks thinks that governments of less developed countries pursue restrictive policies because they fear certain economic consequences of more liberal policies, primarily displacement of local labour as a result of the competition from imports.[6] Reality is considerably more complex than this. The economic policies of these governments reflect the play of political forces, especially the views of the rulers about the most effective way of staying in power, controlling their subjects, pleasing their followers and dispensing patronage. They also sometimes reflect the operation of intellectual fashions from abroad. The second obstacle is the readiness of these governments to devote resources to social expenditure, prestige expenditure, 'or to any expenditure for which support can be whipped up' (p. 166). This is true of many less developed countries. But this factor is of minor overall significance for the less developed world as a whole, as is evident from the position of the most backward societies and groups in Asia, Africa and Latin America.[7]

Government policies do indeed obstruct economic progress in most less developed countries. But it is naive to believe that more favourable policies would bring an early, worldwide industrial revolution. Such a belief overlooks the limits to rapid modernization set by parameters usually regarded as non-economic.

6

A major argument of the chapter entitled The Industrial Revolution is that widespread hardship (termed 'pain and grief' by Hicks) is a concomitant of the capital accumulation involved in this process. Much of the chapter deals with the question of the 'lag of [real] wages behind industrialization' and with the reasons why the rise in wages was delayed in the course of the industrialization of England between, say, 1780 and 1840.

It is not clear why a delay in the rise of real wages should bring about 'pain and grief'. A decline in real wages can cause hardship, but a delay in their rise cannot do so. Hicks offers no evidence whatever for the nature, presence and extent of the supposed 'pain and grief'. Nor does he in this context mention the experience of any other country in Western Europe or North America. In these areas industrialization was not accompanied even by the semblance of widespread hardship which is supposed to accompany an industrial revolution.

Hicks suggests two reasons for the alleged pain and grief in England during the industrial revolution. The first is the rapid increase in population. But why did population increase rapidly if there was large-scale hardship? Population increase means a decline in mortality, that is, a rise in life expectation. This is an improvement in conditions, and is generally the result of improved health, nutrition, housing and clothing. As a second reason Hicks suggests that a switch from circulating capital to fixed capital can bring about a fall in the rate of growth of circulating capital, and thus a slowing-down in the growth of the demand for labour. Hicks writes that it 'is not at all unreasonable to suppose that something of this kind did indeed happen in England, during the first quarter, or even the first third, of the nineteenth century . . .' (pp. 152–3). He offers no evidence of any significant switch to fixed capital over this period any more than he does of pain and grief. Nor does he mention findings such as those of Professor Sydney Pollard which suggest that any such switch was relatively unimportant.[8] Hicks attaches particular importance to investment in machinery. This category of fixed investment is a relatively small part of total investment in any country over any period for which reasonably reliable statistics are available. Because this form of investment does not require substantial drafts on real resources, it does not entail a significant sacrifice in living standards. It is a misconception that investment spending on machinery involves heavy sacrifices in the early stages of industrialization. Hicks presents this much-canvassed idea without any examination of its substance. He also ignores the technical advances during the industrial revolution, which were often capital-saving. Thus improvements in transport reduced requirements of circulating capital as, for instance, in the holding of stocks.

7

The unifying theme in Professor Hicks's book, it will be recalled, is the rise and transformation of the market. He promises (p. 8) that as one continues with the implications of this transformation, 'many things . . . will fit into place'.

I will examine here how aspects of the experience of the Soviet Union, as noted by Hicks, are supposed to do just this.

It is one of Hicks's arguments that developments within the mercantile economy have immensely facilitated government control of the economy itself, primarily by making possible what Hicks terms the Administrative Revolution in Government, which can be dated almost precisely to the First World War. The opportunity for control was seized 'with avidity' by the revolutionary governments of Russia, and later of China. Hicks observes that these were countries 'where the Mercantile Economy had not penetrated deeply' (pp. 162–3). He does not attempt to resolve the apparent contradiction that a development that is supposed to depend on the attainment of a high level of market economy occurs in countries 'not deeply' affected by it. Moreover, Hicks does not specify what is the component part of the administrative revolution which is crucial to the power of the Soviet government over its people. No administrative revolution worthy of the name was necessary for the development of a highly disciplined party whose leaders were ready to deal ruthlessly with opposition and dissent, nor for the construction of mine-fields and barbed wire barriers to stop people from leaving the country, or of prisons for the opposition. In short, what can be explained readily in simple terms has been made to 'fit into' Hicks's theory of economic history. The characteristically allusive treatment of specific historical incidents and sequences, however, provides superficial plausibility to the fitting-in process.

As I have noted, Hicks regards protectionism and autarkic policies as one of the major obstacles to the economic growth of the present less developed countries, and he claims that the 'case of Russia is not fundamentally dissimilar . . . . The Russians have made a much better hand at autarkic development than the majority of less developed countries have done, or are likely to do, chiefly because of the greater variety of natural resources that are at their disposal' (p. 164). However, he does not mention the long period of industrial development before 1917. There is here a parallel with his earlier discussion of the industrial revolution in England where he does not refer to the preceding agricultural revolution, nor to the many centuries of development which went before both revolutions. Neither does he instance the well-attested central role of Western science and technology in Soviet technical progress, or the manifold Western contributions to the maintenance of the Soviet economy, which have extended even to the supply of wheat. These facts cast serious doubt on the appropriateness of the term autarky when applied to the Soviet Union. He does not consider the highly pertinent differences between pre-revolutionary Russia and much of the present less developed world in such matters as people's abilities, mores and social institutions. The Russia of 1914 or 1917 was not like, say, Zaire in 1980. Finally, he does not specify the criteria of successful development, such as higher living standards.

Despite its greater endowment of natural resources, Hicks explains that the Soviet Union has 'not been able to avoid going through the pain and grief which is characteristic of the early stage of an Industrial Revolution, when adequate capital cannot be drawn from abroad' (p. 64). Here again Hicks does not specify the nature and extent of the pain and grief. He would presumably agree that much of the loss of life and other forms of suffering in the Soviet Union, especially during the forced collectivization during the purges of the 1930s, cannot reasonably be regarded as the necessary or inescapable corollaries of industrialization.

The remaining reference to Russia occurs in the context of the mercantilization of agriculture. Hicks writes (pp. 108–10) that, compared with Western Europe, the landowners of East-Central and East Europe severely oppressed the peasants over long centuries from the late Middle Ages until recently. 'The decline in population, which was the occasion for this parting of the ways, was itself a transitory phenomenon; in a couple of generations, or a little longer, it had probably been made up. But the habits and the social institutions which had grown up as a reaction to it were not easily eradicated. Prussia and Poland and Russia remained for centuries in the grip of a nobility of landlords, extracting what revenue they could from poor peasants whom they kept dependent upon them, defending as their lifeline an oppressive system which they were unwilling to reform for fear that the house of cards they had built would fall on their heads' (p. 113).

This suggestion of long and severe subjection invites the question why the peasants failed in the seventeenth and eighteenth centuries to escape in order to improve their lot, when much of this region was repeatedly fought over from end to end. However, another aspect of this discussion is of greater interest. In a tantalizing footnote Hicks appears to relate the earlier divisions of Europe into two different agricultural systems to a contemporary division. He writes: 'It is no more than a coincidence that the frontier which so long separated these agricultural systems has so striking a resemblance to the Curtain which is dividing Europe at the present day. It can be no more than a coincidence; yet the long experience that has moulded men's minds in one way on one side, and in another on the other, has an effect that is recognizable today, even when the division is expressed in very different terms' (p. 114).

It is hard to take seriously the suggestion that people's habits and mentalities differ significantly on the two sides of the Curtain, and that these differences somehow explain its emergence and acceptance. The very existence of the Curtain and the barriers to exit from one side are clear evidence that mentalities do not differ greatly. If people's mentalities did differ greatly, it would not be necessary to use force to prevent people leaving the eastern bloc countries. Thus the Curtain by itself is an immediate and direct refutation of Hicks's fanciful speculation. Moreover, the region east of the Curtain includes Bohemia and Central Germany, which were highly commercialized and industrialized for centuries, and not simply societies ruled by landowners. In fact, explanation of the existence and location of the Curtain does not call for a theory of economic history or recourse to historical continuities. The Curtain represents a division agreed by the Allies in the latter stages of the Second World War. Had the Soviet forces occupied France, Italy or Austria, the Curtain would have been drawn that much further west. Indeed, in so far as mentalities and preferences are relevant, it is notable that in France and Italy in open elections now the Communist parties enjoy much greater popular support then they ever did east of the Curtain (or seem to do now, for that matter). It is not only unnecessary but also misleading to look beyond political forces for the establishment of the Curtain, and beyond coercion for the maintenance of a political system on one side of it.[9]

Altogether, Hicks's treatment of the Soviet experience and the industrial revolution shows all too clearly the outcome of attempting to write history without examining the evidence, and of neglecting the time-dimension in an apparently historical enquiry. Such an approach invites uncritical acceptance of fanciful and fashionable notions which may be totally without substance. Hicks's treatment of these topics also makes it clear that even foremost economic theorists may be prone to such practices, and thereby vulnerable to the seductive influence of even trivial intellectual fashion and political prejudice.

8

In his first chapter Hicks not only promises to present a discernible or definable theory of world economic history, but he even specifies two distinct though related methods by which he proposes to pursue his quest. The first method is that of inference from statistical uniformities of some aspects of historical events. The second is examination of the implications of particular phenomena in order to deduce how one situation leads predictably to another. But as we have seen, he does not in fact present a general theory of economic history. Hicks is right in abandoning his announced quest since its objective is unobtainable by either of his two methods, or indeed by any other.

There are various reasons why the search for statistical uniformities is of little use for the explanation and prediction of the general course of history. It is generally difficult or even impossible to specify the class or category of events from which examples should be selected, or for that matter have been selected. And even if certain statistical uniformities have been discerned between clearly defined and probably limited phenomena, we often cannot tell whether these uniformities reflect functional relationships between the variables examined. Nor is it possible to predict with confidence whether the uniformities or relationships will persist because the parameters or their interaction with the phenomena and relationships under observation shift and vary.[10] Finally, the influence of chance, including the operation of factors external to the society or activity under observation, is so frequent and potent that it often swamps the operation of the variables in which one is interested, and which may often have been decisive in the past.[11]

The disproportionate impact of some people on the course of events, and also significant characteristics of people's motivations and conduct, much restrict, or indeed negate, the usefulness of statistical uniformities for explaining and predicting the course of history. To begin with, some individuals affect the course of history, including economic history, far more than the rest of mankind. Obvious instances include Julius Caesar, Christ, Mohammed, Charlemagne, Luther, Marx, Lenin, Stalin, Mao Tse-tung and Hitler.[12] Their emergence, motivations, actions or people's response to them cannot be explained in terms of statistical uniformities, nor generally in terms of economic factors. Statistical uniformities or economic factors would not have helped in forecasting Caesar's decision to cross the Rubicon, or Ludendorff's action in sending Lenin to Russia, or that of the majority of the British government to declare war in 1914, or for that matter the policies of the Federal Reserve Board in the 1930s. And the same individual's response to apparently similar situations varies greatly at different times: witness Chamberlain's reaction to the international political situation in 1938 and 1939 respectively; and Roosevelt's support of the different responses on the two occasions. Much the same applies to the conduct of groups and collectivities. For instance, German university students reacted very differently to prosperity in the late-nineteenth century and in the mid-twentieth century.

Retrospective explanations and interpretations can be offered about the sequence of events and the conduct of persons and groups. But even in conditions which are as nearly identical as we can make them, we cannot foretell either the sequence of events or the conduct of persons in contexts of historical importance. There are many valid generalizations which can be made about the physical, psychological, material and spiritual conditions of man throughout the ages. But these generalizations are not about variables which predictably affect the course of history, or whose operation is sufficiently powerful to resist the impact of mere chance, or external factors. In the field of human conduct statistical uniformities are useful for prediction only at levels which are trivial in the context of the historical development of societies, such as that most people will continue to get married. Outside such trivialities, few forecasts and predictions of historical processes based on statistical uniformities have succeeded. Even demographic forecasts have often failed, from the time of Malthus to the present day. Yet demographic forecasters enjoy exceptional advantages. In their field statistical analysis is highly advanced; it also relates to large numbers of instances, and what is perhaps most distinctive and significant in demography, statistical techniques can take advantage of firmly based biological categories such as the limits of the child-bearing age. In social studies, this latter advantage is most unusual because the distinctions and categories on which they rely are rarely so clearly defined and stable.

Like many social scientists and some historians, especially Marxist historians, Hicks often personifies collectivities such as city-states or underdeveloped countries, and endows them with powers to make decisions, express sentiments and pursue courses of action. This familiar practice obscures the fact that these decisions are taken by persons either individually or in groups, who face choices, and who *ex ante* have to weigh costs, risks and results. They normally do not know what the outcome will be, and observers cannot normally predict their decisions.

Hicks's other suggested method, the examination of the implications of situations to predict the sequence of events, is primarily deductive. Unfortunately, this method does not provide a worthwhile theory of economic history either.

Most historical events and sequences do not issue in unique and unambiguous results. Widely different results can emerge from given initial conditions. Close enquiry of the *ex post* situation is necessary to find out which of several and often numerous possible results have actually issued from a particular antecedent situation. And even the definition or interpretation of the initial conditions, as well as the assessment of large and apparently obvious facts, requires more than a casual glance over one's shoulder. To speculate about situations and processes without looking at actual experience is to risk losing touch with reality.

Anyone presenting a theory of history is confronted by countless events and sequences from which he perforce must choose. Supporters of a particular theory can always find events and interpretations in support of that theory.

They can do so whether they think their generalizations (the uniformities they claim to have discerned), i.e. the so-called laws of history, reflect the unfolding of God's will or the influence of economic determinism. That way lies arbitrariness, both in the choice of events and in their interpretation. These considerations apply generally to theories of history, and also to attempts to divide its course into specific stages. Successful division of a sequence into distinct stages requires that the stages themselves, the turning points and the processes by which one stage leads to another, are distinct and definable. The life cycles of living organisms satisfy these criteria. So-called stages of history generally do not.

Neither statistical inference nor the examination of the implications of situations can serve as basis for a worthwhile theory of history. This is the reason for the inadequacy of economic determinism as the explanation of world economic history. The explanation and predictions of the course of history derived from economic determinism have been spectacularly unsuccessful, without affecting its appeal. Nor has this appeal been diminished by frequent exposure of its shortcomings, such as its evident irrelevance to major decisions which have shaped historical events; or the many obvious instances when people have taken decisions contrary to their material interests. Indeed, economic determinism has often led its exponents to diametrically opposite inferences from what they thought passed as analysis of a particular situation. In the 1930s some adherents of economic determinism argued that capitalism must necessarily lead to war, on the ground that only large-scale production of arms or even outright war can prevent the collapse of the capitalist system. Other economic determinists insisted that capitalism must lead to appeasement or even to total surrender by the West, because the capitalists could not tolerate the disruption of the profit system.

Although Hicks does not pursue systematically his quest for a general theory of history, the familiar characteristics of such attempts are conspicuous in his book. Heroic abstraction and aggregation and the personification of collectivities (i.e. treating them as if they were single decision-making units) are instances.

Like other architects of general theories of history, Hicks envisages that the relationships between specifically economic activities on the one hand, and such factors as people's attitudes and social institutions on the other, are largely one way. He regards the causal relationship as running almost entirely from the former to the latter, even when the reverse relationship would seem to be far more significant.

Construction of a general theory of history to cover all ages and all mankind

237

is a will-o'-the-wisp. The attempt is both sterile and damaging. It generally diverts attention and effort from more modest but much more informative and intellectually rewarding endeavours. Worthwhile study of history requires the patient and systematic collection of material, and correspondingly methodical examination at some depth of evidence drawn from the actual record of history. It requires also the drawing of inferences from the various sources of evidence, and subsequent comparison of results with the findings of other such exercises, including those in cognate fields of study.

Economic reasoning can play a useful and indeed significant part in such activities, though it may be no more than the use of 'bits of theory to serve as hypotheses for the elucidation of some particular historical processes', in Hicks's rather dismissive formulation. Such endeavours may well appear pedestrian beside the attempts to construct a general theory of history, but they are likely to tell us far more about reality, either past or present. The quest for a general theory of history can also have more widely damaging results. Many of those who have claimed to have discerned the laws of history have simultaneously claimed it as their right, or even as their duty, to interpret and to enforce these laws. They have claimed it as their mission to bring about and hasten an outcome which was in any case inevitable. And in the pursuit of this march the proponents of these ambitious claims have been ready to tolerate or to perpetrate large-scale and lasting brutality. The pretence of having successfully discovered such laws has served as spurious moral or intellectual justification for such conduct. For instance, it has served to underpin the Marxist-Leninist position at popular, academic and political level.

Outstanding scholars, among them Pieter Geyl, Sir Karl Popper and Professor G. R. Elton, have exposed the futility of attempts to construct general theories of history. But the intellectual and political appeal of these endeavours is such that it is safe to predict that there will always be those who are willing to attempt them.

CHAPTER 14

The Investment Fetish

1

Sellers of durables, antiques and jewellery have long known that to tell people they are investing rather than spending is an effective way of making them part with their money. 'You buy a car but you invest in an Austin', said an advertisement of the 1930s.

Since the Second World War an investment fetish has emerged in the West and in Westernized parts of the Third World. It has come to be widely argued and believed that increased investment is necessary or even sufficient to remedy a wide range of real or alleged economic ills, including stagnation, slow growth, sustained unemployment, social discontent, a weak currency and balance of payments problems in the West, and backwardness and poverty in the Third World.

The efficacy of a fetish is taken for granted. Much spending in the West and in the Third World is uncritically accepted as desirable or even as necessary, simply when those who favour it can call it investment. In the same way drastic policies have been justified or rationalized as being of crucial importance because they are said to be designed to promote investment.[1]

2

Discussion of investment has been obfuscated by widely differing interpretations of the terms. Technical advance is often regarded as synonymous with investment, or at any rate as requiring investment. Indeed, technical advance and increase in physical capital are often confused in both professional and lay discussion. But much technical advance requires no net investment as the new or improved equipment can often be financed from funds set aside to provide for replacement. Further, much technical advance is capital saving. It has even been suggested that any social or economic change which raises productivity or otherwise increases incomes should be termed investment. On this interpretation a change in mores and attitudes leading to higher income, say by relaxing constraints on women's work outside the home,

239

would qualify as investment. The misleading character of these instances of loose terminology is evident, and therefore need not be spelt out. Moreover, they are not of primary importance in the advocacy of investment spending, except perhaps that they lend superficial plausibility to the idea that more investment is the same as higher productivity. The wide acceptance of this idea has encouraged the advocates of any form of spending to call this investment, regardless of whether it yields an economic return, and regardless also of the alternative uses of the money.

More important has been the confusion between two substantially different meanings of investment rife since the 1930s. This is the confusion between spending to increase demand, output and employment, and spending designed to increase the stock of productive assets or to improve their quality.

The former interpretation derives from Keynesian macroeconomic theory, which emphasizes investment as an instrument for expanding effective demand and thus for reducing unemployment. However, in that analysis *any* increase in aggregate spending serves this purpose. The analysis does, however, emphasize investment; but it does so primarily because this form of spending generates additional income ahead of the output of consumer goods produced by the capital goods resulting from the investment. The spending of this additional income is thought to raise total spending (and therefore activity and employment) by more than the initial investment.

In the present context the validity of the Keynesian analysis is immaterial. What is pertinent is that it is preoccupied primarily with the effects of spending on the level of activity and employment, and with investment as one form of spending. The primary concern is not with the productivity of the expenditure. Thus digging holes and filling them up again is a form of spending alternative to spending on productive assets.

Since the early 1960s a cognate interpretation of investment has sprung up in Britain and elsewhere in Europe. Any form of official subsidy to maintain employment in particular enterprises, locations and activities is termed investment. This practice disregards not only the real productivity of the spending but also its effects on total activity and employment. Employment or wage subsidies have thus come to be called investment. This usage would have treated as investment the public spending involved in the Speenhamland System of the late eighteenth century, when employers were subsidized from local rates (property taxes) to employ labourers to keep them out of the workhouse.

The confusion between investment as an instrument for maintaining employment (including employment in particular activities, locations and enterprises) and investment designed to increase the productivity of resources has helped the investment fetish in various ways. It has made it easier for the advocates of any spending termed investment to shift the grounds of their advocacy. It has helped also to obscure the wasteful character of much so-called investment spending. In particular, it has made it easier to argue that the spending was not only humane and productive, but that it was also costless, because it used resources which otherwise would have remained idle. This last contention is rarely substantial. It was plainly insubstantial in the 1960s and 1970s when there was no general unemployment or underemployment of resources resulting from lack of aggregate demand. Hence the spending absorbed real resources diverted from other uses. Moreover, investment financed or subsidized by the government has contributed to persistent inflation and to the attendant anxieties and tensions. Of course, if unemployment can be reduced by increasing spending without cost, the spending need not be camouflaged as investment.

The productivity of investment depends on technical and market conditions in the widest sense, including the demand for its output, the supply of complementary resources, and often also the institutional and political background. The productivity of investment is its net contribution to output; net, that is, after taking into account the cost of the additional output, including the cost of capital itself. This contribution can therefore be ascertained only after a time-span long enough for the streams of output and cost to be established. This span of time may run from a few months to much longer periods, according to the nature of the investment. It may extend to many years for buildings, railways, roads, ports, ships or large-scale water control systems. These forms of investment are usually expensive and absorb much monetary saving; and some of them are major components of monetary investment almost everywhere. It follows that the contribution of investment to the growth of the national income through increased productivity cannot be assumed by relating investment to broadly simultaneous changes in the national income.

3

It is clear from much and varied evidence that investment spending is not the primary, much less the decisive, determinant of economic performance. Although widely ignored in public and academic discussion, much of this evidence is readily accessible. It is familiar to many applied economists and statisticians. I shall therefore touch on it briefly. Some of the less familiar or forgotten evidence deserves more extended notice.

Since the early 1950s a number of studies by leading economists and statisticians have shown that the growth of the capital stock cannot explain most of the secular increase in output in the West. Such findings include among others those of Abramovitz, Cairncross, Denison, Kuznets and Solow and are indeed major themes of their publications.[2]

The following passage epitomizes Kuznets's important findings:

> While various modifications can be introduced into this statistical allocation, and while the results clearly vary among individual countries, the inescapable conclusion is that the direct contribution of man-hours and capital accumulation would hardly account for more than a tenth of the rate of growth in per capita product – and probably less. The large remainder must be assigned to an increase in efficiency in the productive resources – a rise in output per unit of input, due either to the improved quality of the resources, or to the effects of changing arrangements, or to the impact of technological change, or to all three.[3]

The long-term economic advance in the West has been the result of factors such as technical advance, changes in habits, changes in the occupational and geographical distribution of the labour force, advances in education and other influences. Thus even real capital formation is not the primary or decisive determinant of long-term growth; and much spending habitually termed investment does not increase or improve the stock of such capital.

Cross-country statistical comparisons of the volume of investment and the increase in gross domestic product are subject to conceptual and statistical limitations so serious as to be of little use for establishing functional relationships between these magnitudes. For instance, differences in the composition of economic activity or in the rate of migration from the country to the towns or from agriculture to industry affect the amount of capital formation necessary for a specified volume of economic activity. The lag between investment and the resulting growth of output also affects the significance of such comparisons, especially as a basis for functional relationships. For what it is worth, I may note that since the Second World War gross investment in Britain has not been low, either by historical standards or by comparison with the United States where incomes and living standards have on the whole risen faster. For instance, between 1963 and 1972 gross fixed investment in the United Kingdom was slightly higher (as a percentage of national income) than in the United States, where over this period the rate of increase of gross national product (in real terms) was about half as much again as in the United Kingdom.

Recent British experience underlines the unwisdom of focusing on the amount of investment rather than on its quality. As just noted, in recent decades investment in Britain has not been particularly low, by historical or American standards. But the return even on business investment has been modest over much of the post-war era, and has declined more or less steadily since the mid-1960s. This decline has been widely recognized. It has also been welcomed by Marxist economists as heralding the demise of private industry in Britain because of an inability to generate sufficient capital funds for its survival.

The low and declining rate of return in British industry was discussed in an article, 'Trends in Company Profitability', in the *Quarterly Bulletin of the Bank of England*, March 1976. The introduction summarizes the argument:

It has already been shown elsewhere that, before tax, the rate of return on industrial and commercial companies' physical capital appears to have fallen from 13 per cent per annum in 1960 to only 4 per cent in 1974 . . . . The post-tax rate of return in 1960 is estimated to have been around 8 to 9 per cent, and would have fallen to zero by 1974 but for tax relief on increases in the value of the stocks: if all companies had been able to take advantage of this relief, the post-tax rate would have been about $3\frac{1}{2}$ to 4 per cent, but with many companies earning insufficient profits against which to set tax allowances, the average rate of return must in fact have been somewhat less.

These observations refer to private industry and commerce. The productivity of government expenditure termed investment is far lower still, as much of it is undertaken on political grounds (often termed social reasons) regardless of economic return. The readiness to undertake public investment without regard to economic return is familiar as a general phenomenon. It is particularly significant in Britain, where the investment undertaken by the government or directly financed by it is large, much larger than, say, in the United States. Moreover, official subsidies to business to prevent even local unemployment seem also to be taken for granted more readily than elsewhere, possibly because comprehensive rent controls, trade union practices, minimum wages and various other restrictions on entry into particular activities often make it difficult to absorb the unemployed.

In Britain, and to some extent elsewhere in Europe also, much private investment is undertaken to maintain employment in particular enterprises rather than for a direct commercial return. (It may yield indirect returns through improved relations with government or union leaders.) In Britain the Employment Protection Act, the requirement for firms to make substantial redundancy payments, and various forms of official pressure and inducement encourage spending to maintain employment. Companies in receipt of government contracts or subsidies, or enterprises in which part of the capital is government-owned, are particularly liable to such pressures though the firms may be in the private sector. Moreover, when spending to maintain employment is regarded as laudable *per se*, it may sometimes be undertaken even without official pressure.

Housing is another major category of investment where the volume of spending misleads about its economic contribution. House building is a significant component of fixed investment practically throughout the West. For instance, in Britain in 1975 housing represented about twelve per cent of gross fixed investment, over half of it by the government. However, rent controls and the public provision of a large part of the housing stock together have produced the available volume and quality of accommodation at a much greater cost than would have been the case with other arrangements. Moreover, the policies pursued have severely inhibited the mobility of people between places and jobs, with adverse effects on national output and employment. Thus much investment in housing in Britain, including public investment, is not an instrument of material progress, but part of a policy that has obstructed it.

Housing should serve as a reminder that much spending classified as investment is in practice also a form of spending on consumer durables. In other words, it is quite as much spending out of income as it is an instrument for promoting growth of income.[4] The same applies to some other quantitatively less important categories of investment, such as museums and churches.

Under-utilization of equipment and wide differences in output per worker with the same equipment and amount of power also refute the notion that economic achievement and progress depend on the amount of investment. For instance, in Britain since the early 1960s very large sums have been spent on expensive and up-to-date equipment which was then left unused for long periods and under-utilized for even longer periods, primarily because of trade union resistance to more effective use. Well-worn examples include the nationalized ship-building and steel industries, and also the ports. The British Steel Corporation has spent huge sums on the construction of blast furnaces which were among the most up-to-date in the world and which were then left under-utilized. Thus if investment had been less, this would have had little or no effect on output and income.

The familiar features of the British industrial scene are rarely examined in official reports, and their implications are even less often spelt out. A notable and informative exception was a report on the British motor car industry by the Central Policy Review Staff (known as the Think Tank) published in November 1975.[5] Even though its principal findings should not have come as a surprise, at first the report attracted considerable attention. It was soon forgotten and has had no perceptible effect on public discussion of policy. The following passages which refer to mass-produced cars summarize the principal findings, the pertinence of which extends far beyond the British motor car industry.

With the same power at his elbow and doing the same job as his continental counterpart, a British car assembly worker produces only half as much output per shift (p. v).

It takes almost twice as many man-hours to assemble similar cars using the same or comparable plant and equipment in Britain as it does on the Continent .... To check the data obtained from the manufacturers, members of the CPRS team, including two engineers, examined all the plants involved in assembling the models used for these productivity comparisons to ensure that production facilities, including capital equipment, age of equipment and plant layout, were comparable. In the comparisons of identical models most of the capital equipment used was identical (p. 79).

Heavy capital expenditure simply increases production costs unless manning levels and work practices change .... Fundamentally, these problems reflect prevailing attitudes of management and labour towards each other, towards productivity and towards work (p. 119).

The report also noted that much of the equipment in the industry was among the most modern in Europe.

In such conditions, which are not exceptional, the spending termed investment is not an instrument of economic advance but an evident waste of resources. In public sector investment the results of the waste are often compounded by the repercussions of the taxation, inflation or controls introduced or promoted by the need to finance it.

Although not confined to the public sector, wasteful spending protected and promoted by the investment fetish and its terminology is most likely to be pronounced in government and quasi-government activities. Politicians and civil servants do not spend their own money or that of their backers. Indeed their prestige, influence and power often benefit from large-scale spending. Moreover, in public or quasi-public investment economic productivity is often impossible to assess, and this makes it easier to conceal wasteful spending or to rationalize it. But the belief that investment is desirable *per se* leads to waste in the private sector also. Much investment classified as private is subsidized by public funds, or is undertaken to retain the goodwill of politicians and civil servants. Again, shareholders cannot easily restrain large-scale spending termed investment when it suits the personal interests and inclinations of directors or senior managers of large public companies. Large-scale, patently uneconomic investment has contributed to the difficulties or even demise of major British companies in the private sector, including AEI, Rolls Royce and British Leyland.

Wasteful spending in the business sector is of course especially likely when directors pay little attention to shareholders and prefer doubtful investment to the payment of dividends. It is difficult to estimate how important this is in practice, but it seems to be frequent, and is helped along by an uncritical attitude to forms of spending which can plausibly be termed investment. In some Western countries, including Britain, the practice is encouraged also by various aspects of the fiscal system which favour retention of profits rather than their distribution. Such measures include tax incentives to spending on buildings or plant, and higher rates of taxes on income compared with capital gains.

4

Spending financed or induced by the government confers direct political and financial benefits on some people, who can therefore be expected to support it. The costs and possible unfavourable repercussions of specific expenditure are often widely diffused, and people affected adversely frequently do not perceive the costs. Moreover, even if such people do perceive the costs and the possible other repercussions, they are unable individually to influence the course of events, and concerted action is often difficult and expensive to organize. This difference in effectiveness and influence between the beneficiaries of public spending programmes and those who bear the cost is a familiar theme of public sector economics.

The investment fetish has enjoyed the support of commercial interests which have benefited from the spending. For a variety of reasons it has also enjoyed extensive support in the academies and the media. Without this latter kind of support the fetish might not have been accepted so uncritically. Academic economists in particular might have been expected to insist that investment spending is a cost and not a benefit. They might also have been expected to note that the distinction between consumption and investment is in practice often altogether arbitrary; and also that employment subsidies differ from productive investment.

Thus, such basic distinctions as that between spending to maintain employment and spending to increase productivity, or that between increase in capital and technical progress, have come to be blurred.

5

As applies so widely, phenomena and influences operating elsewhere are also particularly evident in the Third World. The implications and results of the investment fetish stand out in especially clear relief there. The fetish is accepted even more uncritically in the Third World, and in discussions on its prospects, than it is in other contexts in the West. In political debate in the Third World and in discussions about its development, practically any spending favoured by its proponents is apt to be termed investment and regarded as by definition helpful to economic advance, or even as necessary for it. Similarly, the most diverse activities and policies are apt to be supported and rationalized as required for more investment, which in turn is regarded as necessary or even sufficient for economic development.

Since the Second World War the mainstream development literature, as well as Third World politicians and academics influenced by it, has taken for granted that economic progress depends on expenditure called investment, or is even determined by it. It is widely and influentially urged that, in order to increase investible funds, consumption and general living standards in many ldcs should be restricted, forcibly if necessary.

Professor Gunnar Myrdal said in his much-publicized Cairo lectures:

> There is no other road to economic development than a forcible rise of the part of the national income which is withheld from consumption and devoted to investments, and this implies a policy of utmost austerity .... This frugality must be applied to the level of living of the masses of the people for the simple reason that they are the many ....[6]

As noted in chapter 10 above, the Center for International Studies of the Massachusetts Institute of Technology stated unequivocally that in ldcs ' . . . poverty itself makes it impossible to carry out the required saving and investment by a voluntary reduction in consumption'. Yet if poverty is caused by a general scarcity of resources, the scarcity cannot be removed by compulsion. Insistence that compulsion is necessary therefore means that resources are available, but the people are not prepared voluntarily to supply them to finance so-called investment spending.

Academic opinion on this subject has entered wider discussion and has influenced opinion at large. A characteristic instance is an article 'The Costs of Growth' in the *New York Times*, 26 July 1979. It deserves to be quoted extensively as a typical example both of the investment fetish and of the readiness to whitewash brutality by Third World governments.

> In the late 1970s it is no longer possible to ignore the evidence of deepening poverty and increased repression in the newly dynamic economies of the underdeveloped

world: escalating rates of infant mortality, increasing incidence of disease and malnutrition, *coups d'état*, torture and arbitrary imprisonment. Analysts are beginning to suspect that there may be an organic link between contemporary growth processes and social and political oppression . . . .[7]

At the root of the dismal trade-off between growth and equity are the investment needs of economic development. The transformation of economic structures so as to propel society to a new level of productive capability requires unprecedented levels of saving and investment. This normally means the forced restriction of consumption for the mass of the people.

The resulting oppression takes two forms: social injustice (severe and deepening poverty) and political repression (authoritarian rule and the loss of civil liberties). The former is a direct result of the capital-accumulation process, the latter is the apparatus of control necessary to prevent revolt . . . .

Capitalist strategies, for example, in Nigeria, the Philippines and Brazil, have achieved rapid rates of economic growth, but such economic dynamism has rested on mass misery. In these countries, at least half of the citizenry has been excluded from the modernizaton process and remains in abject poverty. Some of these nations have maintained individual freedom for the elite classes, but most civil and political rights are incompatible with the mass exploitation typical of the capitalist underdeveloped world.

In the passage already quoted, Professor Myrdal wrote that economic development ' . . . implies a policy of utmost austerity'. This is simply untrue. Enforced austerity has not been necessary for the economic advance of Western countries, nor for that of many Third World countries.[8]

Earlier in this chapter I quoted Simon Kuznets and referred to studies by other leading scholars who found that capital formation has played a very small part in long-term development in the West. The same applies to the contemporary Third World. Emergence from poverty there does not require large-scale capital formation. It requires changes in attitudes and mores adverse to material improvement, readiness to produce for the market instead of for subsistence, and the pursuit of appropriate government policies. Much of capital formation is not a pre-condition of material advance but its concomitant. Housing is one example of those categories which absorb substantial savings. Much of the so-called infrastructure (roads, railways and the like) is also a collection of assets and facilities which do not precede or determine development, but are largely developed in the course of it. And in the Third World especially much public spending routinely termed investment has nothing to do with productive capital formation. Familiar examples include prestige projects of all kinds, the creation of brand new capital cities, collectivized villages, military barracks or political prisons, or the establishment of expensive and uneconomic domestic capital goods industries.

The realities of investment spending are often obscured by statistical convention. The celebrated East African Groundnut Scheme was wound up after £35 million was spent on it, without producing any groundnuts at all. This spending was included in statistics of gross investment. At the same time the establishment and improvement of hundreds of thousands of small-scale African agricultural holdings, producing in the aggregate a huge volume of groundnuts, was not included in the statistics. These anomalies persist. For instance, successive Nigerian governments have spent millions of pounds and nara (the local currency) on totally uneconomic projects, and called this spending investment. At the same time the extremely heavy taxation of the producers of cash crops inhibited the establishment and improvement of farms, and the increases and improvement of traders' stocks and equipment. These latter types of capital formation are often provided by direct investment, meaning investment not financed through conventional monetary channels. They are often not recorded in the statistics, or recorded incompletely. The repercussions of official policies on these types of capital formation are apt to be neglected. Yet such capital formation promotes economic advance, especially in economies emerging from subsistence production. This capital formation is also likely to be productive because it is undertaken by those who bear the cost and receive the return.

Even if large-scale investment is highly productive, or regarded as indispensable for substantial progress, its financing would not require coercion. When the proposed spending is productive, government or business can borrow either locally or from abroad, which obviates the need for coercive measures. If neither government nor business can borrow, this suggests that for various reasons (which can include inappropriate policies) the funds cannot be used productively.[9]

The pervasive material progress of the West in the eighteenth and nineteenth centuries was not accompanied by enforced austerity. Even the two often-quoted examples to the contrary, namely, the British industrial revolution and the Soviet experience, are only apparent exceptions. The financing of the industrial revolution did not require expensive investment. It involved technical advance together with the construction of machinery. These processes did not require substantial drafts on total savings. The extent of the hardship which attended the process is much disputed among historians. But what hardship there was resulted from causes which had nothing to do with enforced saving.[10] The hardships and extensive coercion in the Soviet Union resulted from the pursuit of various political objectives. The persistent lack of consumer goods and of low general living standards in the Soviet Union suggest that higher living standards had no high priority among these objectives.

The habitual references to the Industrial Revolution and to Soviet experience as examples of austerity necessary for material progress often reflect a misreading of history. But they are also often attempts to rationalize or explain away a decline in living standards or a persistence of low living standards, lack of simple consumer goods, or even recurrent famines in the contemporary Third World. However, these conditions are usually brought about by such policies and circumstances as the persecution of productive people, expulsion of minorities, suppression of trade, restriction of external commercial contacts, neglect of basic transport facilities, special taxation of farmers, or sheer official ineptitude. Inept, inappropriate and even brutal policies are spuriously justified by attributing their results to the austerity dictated by the supposed capital requirements of development, even when the policies have nothing to do with productive capital formation and indeed evidently obstruct it.

6

It is widely believed in the Third World that economic progress requires domestic production of capital goods. The example and prestige of the Soviet Union are behind this belief. This idea was a major theme of the Second Indian Five Year Plan (1956–61), which much influenced subsequent policy in India and has served also as a model for the planning policies of many other governments.

The need to develop domestic production of capital goods underlies the priorities of the Second Five Year Plan, as shown in the following passages:

The expansion of the iron and steel industry has obviously the highest priority since, more than any other industrial products, the levels of production in these materials determine the tempo of progress of the economy as a whole. . . . Heavy engineering industries are a natural corollary of iron and steel works. The high priority accorded to them arises both on this account and from the fact that they will provide from within the country a wide range of industrial machinery and capital equipment, such as locomotives for railways and power plants for the generation of electricity. In the absence of facilities for their manufacture, a developing economy has to depend on foreign sources of supply with attendant difficulties and uncertainties. To facilitate the production of a wide range of items going into the manufacture of plants intended to turn out a product like steel, diverse types of fabricating facilities have to be created in a large number of establishments. In other words, heavy engineering industries and workshops in the country have to be generally strengthened for undertaking such tasks as the construction of steel plants, fertilizer factories, etc. In this context the creation of basic facilities such as the establishment of heavy foundries, forges and structural shops is absolutely necessary. It is, therefore, proposed that the establishment of these facilities, which constitute an essential and primary phase of development for the manufacture of heavy industrial machinery in the country, should be undertaken at an early date. These developments have a priority second only to that of expansion of the steel industry.[11]

These priorities have been widely accepted in the Third World. Governments there spend lavishly on the establishment of capital goods industries such as iron and steel, heavy engineering and petrochemicals on the argument that these are necessary for economic advance.

Local production of capital goods is certainly not necessary for development. Both in the West and in the Third World many countries have progressed rapidly without first developing such activities. Indeed, it is hard to think of examples where a local capital goods industry preceded material progress or 'determined the tempo of progress of the economy as a whole'. To suggest that such activities must be economically effective or desirable is to ignore prices, costs and consumer demand in assessing the economic merits of an activity. Advocates of government-operated or government-supported heavy industry do indeed habitually ignore prices, costs and demand when pressing their case. For instance, these are not mentioned in the passages in the Second Indian Five Year Plan just quoted.

Demands for more investment and for the local production of capital goods are logically quite distinct. They are, however, closely linked both in Third World policies and current development ideology. For instance, both serve as justification for increased taxation or for specific controls. Advocacy of large-scale government-operated or -supported local capital goods industries can be seen as a component, or a local variant, of the investment fetish. The Third World is littered with uneconomic capital goods industries, established with little or no regard to current or prospective consumer demand.

The development plans of many Third World governments rely extensively on estimates of capital-output ratios in calculating the investment required. A common practice is to postulate a specified future level of output, or a prospective rate of growth of output, and then to estimate the capital required for these objectives on the basis of total or incremental capital-output ratios. In spite of their ostensible sophistication, these exercises are useless for their proclaimed purposes. The procedures usually overlook that neither the level nor the growth of income depends on capital alone, but also requires other factors of production, including labour. They are based on capital-output ratios observed in conditions which differ widely from those prevailing in the countries to which these exercises are applied (e.g. the use of Soviet capital-output ratios for estimating the capital requirements of the growth of output in India); they habitually confuse a statistical association with a functional or causal relationship; they ignore basic problems of the measurement of capital, and also the wide errors and biases in statistics both of capital and of income, particularly in the Third World and in Communist countries; they involve the aggregation of activities which use productive resources in widely different proportions; and they usually ignore the problems of putting current values on uncertain future output.[12]

It is not clear how far these much-publicized exercises actually affect what governments do. The conduct of governments is apt to be influenced more by the play of political forces than by calculations of capital-output ratios. But these exercises have helped to confuse issues and to make it difficult, even impossible, to assess systematically the merits of proposals for publicly supported investment programmes. This confusion makes it easier to invoke the investment fetish on behalf of policies with objectives altogether different from those proclaimed for them.

Advocates of public investment projects in the Third World often predict very high rates of return on these projects, whether on the basis of estimated capital-output ratios (which, as already noted, do not normally take into account the cost of resources other than capital) or on some other basis. The unreality of many of these predicted rates of return is evident when they greatly exceed prevailing rates of interest, including those at which the governments themselves are prepared to lend abroad. Thus in 1975 a study organized by the International Labour Office dealing with a public investment project in Iran expected a marginal social rate of thirty-three per cent on investment at a time the government was lending abroad at under nine per cent.[13]

7

In the Third World the investment fetish is very damaging. The enforced enlargement of investment expenditures and the need to secure particular components of investment projects (e.g. foreign exchange required for imports of capital goods) involve additional taxation and the imposition of controls. These extensions of state economic control damage material progress and often provoke acute political and social conflict in the heterogeneous societies of the Third World. I mention these results first because they are a specifically significant outcome of the investment fetish in the Third World. But I need not develop this matter here, as the politicization of life has been covered in earlier chapters.

Although Third World poverty is often much exaggerated, it is nevertheless true that people at large are much poorer than in the West. They are correspondingly hit harder by economic waste, such as that brought about by the uncritical acceptance of the case for more investment or for domestic production of capital goods.

Some of the poorest groups, such as the poorer sections of ethnic minorities and the rural poor, are much harmed by the repercussions of political conflict and of the restriction of external contacts. The burden of the taxation and of the controls to collect resources for publicly supported investment also falls disproportionately on the poor, notably on small-scale producers of cash crops. Such effects have been conspicuous in the operation of the state export monopolies of Burma, East Africa and West Africa.

In most Third World countries the difference in political effectiveness is very wide between those who benefit from public spending and those who pay for it. This situation reinforces the appeal of the investment fetish, because the benefits of the spending are exaggerated and the costs understated. The uncritical attitude to the Soviet Union also works in this direction. Its political, military, scientific and economic achievements are widely acclaimed. Indeed, they are often overstated. The role of large-scale investment and of domestic production of capital goods in these achievements is also apt to be exaggerated, while the costs of these policies are ignored or underestimated.

The distinction between investment and consumption is even more tenuous in ldcs than in the West. Much expenditure classified as consumption sustains or increases current productivity by maintaining the health of people and of animals, or by preserving crops or stocks of goods (e.g. spending on insecticides, pesticides and hardware). Moreover, consumption widely serves as inducement for higher economic performance. Especially in the course of emergence from subsistence activity to production for the market, a higher or more varied actual or prospective level of consumption promotes improved economic performance, such as more work (in replacement of leisure), greater readiness to produce for the market instead of for subsistence, more direct investment, and greater saving out of higher cash incomes. Until the Second World War these sequences were readily recognized in the concept of incentive goods, an expression which has largely disappeared from the development literature.

Thus over a wide range of activity consumption and investment in ldcs are complementary rather than competitive. (This applies at times also in advanced countries in certain conditions of unemployment, or when taxation has major disincentive effects.) It is then inappropriate to treat consumption and investment as mutually exclusive alternatives. Enforced restriction of consumption is therefore likely to inhibit material progress and productive capital formation. This applies particularly in much of Asia and Africa where subsistence production is still important.

Sir Arthur Lewis has been among those who have argued that extension of human choice is the very essence of economic development. Enforced austerity is proposed and imposed on the ground or pretext that it is necessary for a promised increase in output. The increase is to take place in the unspecified future, and in a form only tenuously related to general living standards. What right have the rulers to coerce their subjects for this purpose?

CHAPTER 15

Reflections on the
State of Economics

1

The argument of much of this book is critical of the methods and findings of contemporary economics, especially development economics. The reader should not be led to suppose, however, that the disquiet expressed in earlier essays at the present state of economics is so peculiar to me as to be idiosyncratic.

In the early 1970s, after several decades of rapid expansion of the subject, prominent economists in major addresses expressed serious doubts about its intellectual position and prospects. Professor Sir Henry Phelps Brown entitled his presidential address to the Royal Economic Society in 1971 'The Underdevelopment of Economics'[1]; in the same year Mr G. D. N. Worswick addressed the British Association under the title 'Is Progress in Economic Science Possible?'[2]; and Nobel Laureate Professor Wassily Leontief delivered his presidential address to the American Economic Association in December 1969 under the heading 'Theoretical Assumption and Non-observed Facts'.[3]

Such pessimism in major academic addresses is certainly unusual, and may even be unique when expressed in the midst of a period of rapid expansion of a discipline.

Criticism of the methods or preoccupation of economists is at times dismissed as evidence of failure to keep up with recent advances, or of political bias or obscurantism. But such suggestions would hardly be appropriate in the case of addresses by a Nobel Laureate in Economics, the President of the Royal Economic Society and the Director of the National Institute of Economic and Social Research. Serious suggestions that their opinions reflected lack of professionalism or sloth would indeed justify their apprehensions, because it would establish that there were no standards in economics.

The bewilderment and discontent of many economists, including leading economists, in the face of recent developments in their subject are not inevitable results of the growth of specialization. A biochemist may not understand the work of a physical chemist, still less that of a mathematical physicist, but this will not lead him to question the reality or possibility of progress in chemistry or physics.

It should and will be evident that my critical comments do not apply to the work of all economists. But the practices and analyses I consider are nevertheless more than incidental lapses by a few slipshod or incompetent practitioners, as can be verified from examination of leading journals and other easily accessible publications.[4]

2

Neither progress nor stagnation describes adequately the condition of economics since the 1930s. There seems to have been a curious coexistence of rapid and substantial progress in some respects and of retrogression in others, including decay at the core of the subject. This confused state of economics may explain the bewilderment or scepticism of prominent economists.

There have been major, genuine and undisputed advances in recent decades. They have been genuine in that they have helped us to understand real phenomena and sequences. They are undisputed, in that their significance is recognized regardless of differences in political position or in preferred methodology. An incomplete list of such areas of progress would include advances in price theory, including its application to the incidence of taxation and determination of foreign exchange rates; the analysis of the interaction of monetary and fiscal policies; the economic analysis of major political and administrative processes; and the examination of the economic implications of different kinds of property rights. There is no need to elaborate on these well recognized advances, since improvement in understanding is an accepted and expected condition of an expanding discipline. The advances may have fallen short of some claims or expectations, but their reality is not in serious dispute.

Simultaneously, much of the subject has come to be disfigured on a large scale by the crudest transgressions, perpetrated sometimes even by prominent practitioners. Emphatic statements, expressions of opinion and methods of reasoning which go counter to well-established propositions of the subject, or to simple logic or obvious evidence, abound in the academic literature. Some of the transgressions are novel, in that they have emerged only recently; others represent re-emergence of errors exposed long ago. It is therefore appropriate to talk of erosion at the core of the subject at a time of rapid advances in many directions.

3

As noted in chapter 12 in the discussion of the so-called dollar problem since the Second World War, acknowledged leaders and spokesmen of the profession, and not just a few careless or eccentric practitioners, neglected that supply and demand depend on price; that a shortage cannot be discussed sensibly, except as an excess of demand over supply at a price; and that trading patterns and prospects are much affected by comparative advantage and costs. They neglected these fundamentals in contexts in which they often were regarded as experts; and they did so at a time when both economics as a whole and the theory of foreign exchanges had advanced greatly. The discussion was an unambiguous example of retrogression. Before the Second World War the role of the rate of exchange and its determinants were noted as a matter of course in discussion of external payments: witness the literature on the British return to the gold standard in 1925. Similarly, the role of comparative costs in the long term pattern of international trade (a role which makes it impossible for one trading partner persistently to undersell others over the entire range of traded goods) had been a staple of textbooks since the nineteenth century.

The notion of a lasting dollar shortage soon grew into that of a persistent foreign exchange shortage of underdeveloped countries. By the mid-1950s a number of leading economists wrote that the progress of these countries was constrained not only by domestic resources but also by a shortage of foreign exchange; and also that payments difficulties were an inevitable concomitant of a reasonable rate of development. These ideas were again canvassed without reference to the rate of exchange and of its determinants, including domestic financial policies.[5]

These discussions frequently instanced the decline in exports of particular commodities from a country as evidence of a fall in the demand for that product. Such suggestions confuse changes in the amount supplied from one source with changes in world demand. When they referred to prices at all, the proponents of the idea of a persistent shortage of foreign exchange frequently argued that a low price elasticity of demand made it impossible for an underdeveloped country to increase its foreign exchange earnings by exporting more. However, if such an improbable situation existed in real life, it would be beneficial rather than damaging. In such a situation, a country could increase its foreign exchange earnings simply by exporting less, saving resources at the same time.

Neglect of the role of prices and an inability to handle elementary price theory have not been confined to discussion of external payments. In much of labour economics, the familiar projections of long term labour requirements freely ignore both the general level of wages and also relative wages. Unemployment is also often discussed without making it clear that it represents an excess of supply over demand at particular wage rates. The concept of unfilled vacancies also reflects disregard of prices, since the number of vacancies must depend on wage rates; that is, the price of labour. The concept of unfilled vacancies may have administrative uses. But it is inappropriate for economists to use so readily in academic discussion a concept which implies fixed relative factor prices, as well as given wages and methods of production.

Prices are neglected frequently in discussion of the effects of taxes on supply and demand, and this in spite of the important recent advances in the analysis of the incidence of taxation. A notable example, one of many, was the discussion by prominent development economists of the operation of state export monopolies in less developed countries, without noting the effects of the underpaying of producers on the output and long term supply of the commodities affected.

Development economists almost routinely propose heavy taxation to promote public investment spending. They often do so without taking account either of the direct effects of the additional taxes on supply or demand, or of the wider political and social repercussions of heavy taxation.[6]

The treatment of an activity or of its output as an addition to welfare or to total output without considering alternative uses of the resources employed, i.e. the cost, is another practice which in recent years has found its way into much technical economic writing, notably so in the literature on development and planning. Paradoxically, these lapses have occurred simultaneously with the upsurge of the literature on shadow prices, i.e. prices estimated and introduced to correct for real or alleged differences between market prices and social opportunity costs, and designed to affect production and consumption decisions.

To ignore the cost of an activity is to treat scarce resources as if they were free goods. A bizarre instance of this practice was the widely canvassed proposal by leading American academics in the 1950s, that the United States should undertake to supply all the finance which any underdeveloped country anywhere could use productively.

Such transgressions have long been familiar in non-technical discussions. Laymen are prone to envisage economic phenomena as given magnitudes rather than as functional relationships. Professional economists on the other hand have traditionally recognized them precisely as such relations. This indeed was a major pillar of the claim that economics was the queen of the social sciences.

Such practices obliterate the distinction between lay and expert treatment. An effortless, firm grasp of fundamentals is a recognized hallmark of expert knowledge. The transgressions which I have noted have been freely perpetrated by world figures in economics[7]. Thus, on this accepted criterion of expertise these leaders of the profession do not qualify as experts. This curious situation also explains the wide differences of opinion among economists about the competence or significance of the work of their colleagues, differences which are far wider than they are in most other fields of academic study.

4

The shortcomings prevalent in much of economics generally are especially prominent in development economics. In the mainstream development literature they have been combined with disregard of evident determinants of economic achievement, such as personal qualities and social and political arrangements. The role of external contacts in extending markets and widening horizons has also been largely ignored. Indeed, the emphasis now is on influences such as the volume of investment spending and the supply of foreign exchange. However, the analysis of these variables is also often quite inadequate even when formally competent. In any case, such analysis focuses on factors chosen because of their suitability for treatment by the methods of conventional economic theory rather than because of their significance for economic development, which the discussants claim to explain.

Moreover, changes in the variables which are examined react on the determinants of development which are ignored. These repercussions affect development much more than do the variables which are being examined, yet they are ignored. For instance, large-scale taxation or extensive specific controls in order to increase investment spending affect determinants of development such as the overall political situation and temper, the range of external contacts, the spread of new ideas and methods, the supply of incentive goods, and the volume of direct investment in agriculture. Such repercussions are perforce overlooked if these determinants themselves are ignored. These lapses are not merely of academic interest. The analyses or studies lead to the espousal and implementation of policies which are inappropriate in terms of their proclaimed objectives. Similar criticisms apply to much of the literature on planning in both market economies and socialist economies in advanced countries, though the results of the transgressions may be less pronounced.

Books published a generation or two ago by Vera Anstey, Allan McPhee or Sir Keith Hancock are far more illuminating and of greater predictive usefulness than the ostensibly more sophisticated recent literature. Similarly, the writings of many novelists, anthropologists, historians and administrators are far more informative about the Third World and about development than is much of mainstream development economics.

5

What explains the curious situation of contemporary economics, especially the acceptance of evidently insubstantial, even bizarre, notions?

The expansion of the subject since the Second World War and the circumstances surrounding it must here be considered together. Unlike the expansion in the natural sciences in recent decades, especially in physics and chemistry, the expansion in economics (and in other forms of social study) was not an instance of the growth of knowledge leading to a quantum jump in the number of people and the money attracted. The expansion resulted from the belief that economists could help significantly in solving social and political problems; and that their capacity to do so depended largely on their numbers and on the money at their disposal. The belief in the efficacy of numbers and money was encouraged by what happened in other fields of endeavour, especially the natural sciences. More scientists and more money usually help to advance knowledge, and thereby to clarify previously unsolved problems. But, as the term is usually understood, economic problems are different. Economic problems typically do not present themselves because of perceived gaps or inadequacies in knowledge. Rather, economic problems are said to exist wherever there are differences between proclaimed norms and observed reality. Such problems evidently cannot be solved by improvements in knowledge alone. Indeed, as already suggested in chapter 1 (and noted repeatedly elsewhere), economists and other social scientists generally create problems rather than solve them.

In academic study unwarranted claims are apt to inhibit the advance of understanding. Attempts to justify unfounded claims, or to mask the failure to live up to them, encourage the proponents of such claims to shift their ground. For example, when certain policies widely canvassed by development economists as necessary for raising living standards, such as large-scale public investment, domestic production of capital goods or the collectivization of agriculture, fail to bring about the expected results, the policies themselves come to be regarded as the very stuff of progress rather than as what they are, unsuccessful instruments for its promotion.

In principle, the distinction between the advancement of knowledge and the promotion of policy is as clear in social study as it is in other disciplines. But many economists have always disputed this distinction and the public even more so. The recent rapid expansion of economics has been largely propelled by the expectation of practical results, notably results helpful for policy. This influence has served further to confuse the promotion of knowledge with the promotion of policy. In major branches of economics some economists and their customers do not even seem to know of these distinctions.

The rapid expansion of the subject, the flood of publications it has generated, and the confusion between the promotion of knowledge and of policy have made it difficult to expose even simple transgressions. Economists who have perpetrated them may not even know of criticisms which have been advanced. And even if they do, they can often safely disregard them or dismiss them as being politically motivated. The transgressions have also been protected by a facade of technique and jargon, a matter to which I return later. The prestige of the authors and of the academic institutions supporting them have also served to protect even crude lapses. Both fellow academics and members of the public find it difficult to believe that well-known economists, enjoying much prestige and financial support, could have perpetrated such simple and readily demonstrable errors. They are therefore apt to believe that the critics have misrepresented these prominent figures. The official bodies and the academic institutions which have supported the authors of the lapses have a vested interest in protecting them; and the larger and more prolonged the support, the greater becomes this interest. Moreover, the transgressions often embody conclusions, or clearly imply conclusions, which are congenial to influential groups of economists and their supporters. These various groups often act as a claque or effective phalanx ready to shield the perpetration of even the crudest lapses.

A few examples will illustrate the effectiveness of these protective barriers. As instanced in the immediately preceding chapter, leading economists, statisticians and econometricians established in the 1950s and '60s that the growth of the capital stock cannot possibly account for the long-term development that has occurred in the West. However, their findings are largely ignored in the mainstream literature of development and planning, and in the policies based on it. The discussion of the dollar shortage remained quite unaffected by the writings of a few critics who quite early on exposed the simple misconceptions of the central idea. Again, more than fifteen years ago Professor Usher first demonstrated that, relatively to the national incomes of more advanced economies, the national income estimates for Third World countries are grossly understated (the degree of understatement differing from one country to another). Yet such estimates continue to be published (sometimes expressed to the nearest dollar), and continue to be used in academic studies and in policy documents.[8]

The natural sciences have also expanded greatly under the impetus of

261

practical concerns without such results. Much of their expansion occurred after a period of rapid progress of knowledge leading to well-established propositions helpful to these practical concerns. Moreover, standards in these disciplines benefit from certain bonding agents or other forms of protection from disintegration. For instance, the distinction between knowledge and policy is usually more readily accepted. Again, the reproducible experiment, the firmness of distinctions between various concepts and the much greater constancy of parameters, all make easier the immediate exposure of simple transgressions. In a period of rapid expansion one would not find prominent scientists disputing the reality or even the possibility of progress in their subjects, nor lapses in them as crude as those I have mentioned.

6

The spread of mathematical methods in economics has not averted the coexistence of rapid advance and erosion. It has not made easier the effective exposure of egregious transgressions. This outcome is both unexpected and disappointing. Mathematical methods might have been expected both to raise the general level of performance and to result in greater consistency in standards. New methods should benefit a discipline by extending its potential. This presumption could have been expected to apply strongly to the adoption of mathematical methods in economics. The principal phenomena studied by economics are multivariate functional relationships. Some knowledge of mathematics should make it easier to recognize this characteristic. It should also make it easier to understand or examine simple but basic matters such as the difference between average and marginal quantities, or that between levels and rates of change, and to recognize the operation of feedback effects. The use of mathematical methods could also be expected to encourage economists to specify their assumptions precisely, and to consider the consistency of different assumptions underlying their arguments. It is therefore not surprising that economists trained in mathematics have played a large part in the many genuine recent advances. Economics has also benefited from recent advances in related disciplines such as statistics and demography, advances to which mathematical methods have contributed greatly.

In economics these benefits have, however, been bought at a heavy cost. An uncritical attitude to mathematical methods has inhibited understanding, and obscured or confused basic issues. It has thereby contributed to the survival or spread of simple transgressions. As a result substantial areas of economics have become less informative than they were before this burgeoning of mathematical methods. Such an untoward and unexpected outcome is not a consequence of the adoption of mathematical methods but only of their inappropriate employment. The inappropriate uses and the untoward consequences could be classified under various headings: provision of a protective facade for misleading ideas or methods; encouragement of inappropriate habits of mind; promotion of unwarranted claims and expectations; and perhaps others as well. In practice, however, these various influences and results are intertwined.

7

A critical or even questioning attitude towards mathematical methods in social study almost routinely elicits the response that the critical observer is insufficiently qualified. In particular, it is apt to evoke the response that the critic does not know enough mathematics, especially modern mathematics, or does not grasp the potentialities of the computer. I shall therefore now quote some outstanding scholars whose qualifications are not open to legitimate doubt. And I shall do so at length to make clear that the passages are not quoted out of context or are otherwise untypical.

Norbert Wiener was full Professor of Mathematics at the Massachusetts Institute of Technology. He created cybernetics and he was indeed one of the makers of modern mathematics since the Second World War. He had a life-long interest in the application of mathematics to economics. He expressed his disenchantment primarily in a book published after his death. His highly pertinent remarks seem to be largely unfamiliar to economists, although the book is readily accessible.[9] Here are some of his observations:

> I have found mathematical sociology and mathematical economics or econometrics suffering under a misapprehension of what is the proper use of mathematics in the social sciences and of what is to be expected from mathematical techniques, and I have deliberately refrained from giving advice [on the application of Cybernetics to economics] that, as I was convinced, would be bound to lead to a flood of superficial and ill-considered work . . . (p. 88).
>
> The use of mathematical formulae had accompanied the development of the natural sciences and become the mode in the social sciences. Just as primitive peoples adopt the Western modes of denationalized clothing and of parliamentarism out of a vague feeling that these magic rites and vestments will at once put them abreast of modern culture and technique, so the economists have developed the habit of dressing up their rather imprecise ideas in the language of the infinitesimal calculus (pp. 89–90).
>
> In doing this, they show scarcely more discrimination than some of the emerging African nations in the assertion of their rights. . . . Very few econometricians are aware that if they are to imitate the procedure of modern physics and not its mere appearances, a mathematical economics must begin with a critical account of these

quantitative notions and the means adopted for collecting and measuring them . . . (p. 90).

To assign what purports to be precise values to such essentially vague quantities is neither useful nor honest, and any pretence of applying precise formulae to these loosely defined quantities is a sham and a waste of time (p. 91).

These highly critical remarks are not directed at economics, much less at mathematical methods; they are directed at the inappropriate application of the latter by practitioners of the former.

Economists of world stature, including indeed some of the makers of modern economics, highly qualified in mathematics, have been extremely critical of mathematical economics. In a letter to Bowley, Marshall wrote in 1901:

In my view every economic fact whether or not it is of such a nature as to be expressed in numbers, stands in relation as cause and effect to many other facts, and since it NEVER happens that all of them can be expressed in numbers, the application of exact mathematical methods to those which can is nearly always a waste of time, while in the large majority of cases it is positively misleading; and the world would have been further on its way forward if the work had never been done at all.[10]

Keynes in *The General Theory* was even more explicit and critical.

Too large a proportion of recent 'mathematical' economics are mere concoctions, as imprecise as the initial assumptions they rest on, which allow the author to lose sight of the complexities and interdependencies of the real world in a maze of pretentious and unhelpful symbols.[11]

Keynes here emphasizes the imprecision of the assumptions. The imprecision of the basic concepts is perhaps even more significant. Keynes's contentions apply as much in 1980 as they did in 1936.

Once mathematical methods have become fashionable, the desire to be in the swim and the operation of established interests set up forces of self-perpetuation. Professor Leontief has specified some of these.[12]

Continued preoccupation with imaginary, hypothetical, rather than with observable reality has gradually led to a distortion of the informal valuation scale used in our academic community to access and to rank the scientific performance of its members. Empirical analysis, according to this scale, gets a lower rating than formal mathematical reasoning. Devising a new statistical procedure, however tenuous, that makes it possible to squeeze out one more unknown parameter from a given set of data, is judged a greater scientific achievement than the successful search for additional information that would permit us to measure the magnitude of the same parameter in a less ingenious, but more reliable way. . . . A natural Darwinian feedback operating through selection of academic personnel contributes greatly to the perpetuation of this state of affairs. Thus, it is not surprising that the younger economists, particularly those engaged in teaching and in academic research, seem by now quite content with situations in which they can demonstrate their prowess (and incidentally, advance their careers) by building more and more complicated mathematical models and devising more and more sophisticated methods of statistical inference without ever engaging in empirical research.

Almost every issue of the leading journals will yield a crop of examples of the habits of mind emphasized and criticized in this section, notably the interest in form rather than substance. It is indeed evident from the textbooks, journals and the contents of curricula that the criticisms by Marshall, Keynes and Wiener have been ignored. They were echoed and brought up to date in the addresses by leading economists noted at the beginning of this chapter, again without perceptible results.[13]

The adoption of mathematical methods as the standard form in economics has had serious untoward effects. The use of these methods has even come to serve as a barrier to criticism of a wide range of transgressions. Many of the lapses in analytical and applied economics considered in this book have at various times been surrounded protectively by a facade of technique and jargon which is apt to obfuscate the discussion and so to deter and blunt criticism. A list of these transgressions which at times have been buried in a welter of mathematical formulae and manipulations would include the following: that export earnings are independent of exchange rates and of supply conditions; that population growth produces unemployment; that economic development can be discussed on the basis of fixed factor proportions, or unemployment without reference to wage rates; and that increases in national income depend on the volume of investment.

Apart from the shielding of specific lapses, emphasis on the use of mathematical methods has contributed more pervasively to inappropriate practices and habits of mind. Possibly the most important of these inappropriate or even misleading practices is the tendency to elevate technique above substance, form above content. Others include preoccupation with economic phenomena and factors which can genuinely or spuriously be quantified, and consequent neglect of those which cannot be so treated but frequently are more germane;[14] the application of concepts which, even when they are capable of precise expression in the abstract, are in practice necessarily vague, so much so that they are habitually subject to different or even conflicting interpretation; the neglect of observation of economic phenomena or processes except those expressed quantitatively in readily available statistical sources; and the neglect of the historical and institutional background. The availability of computers has put a premium on an often rather mechanical application of mathematical methods in the examination of social and economic sequences. It has helped to divert attention from their limitations in economic reasoning and in its applications. It has correspondingly downgraded direct observation, simple reflection, investigation of the background, the critical examination of sources, and other processes indispensable for informative inference in social studies.

The uncritical approach to mathematical methods in economics and its untoward results are likely to persist. The forces of self-perpetuation perceptively noted by Professor Leontief are likely to continue, just as they are likely to continue to draw strength from other sources. One of these sources is the prestige which mathematical methods derives from their indisputable success in major branches of natural science. Economists and their audiences are apt to ignore, or to underrate, the differences between the natural sciences and economics relevant to the usefulness of mathematical methods in much of economics. Objective and conclusive reasoning is just as possible in economics as it is in the natural sciences, but there are nevertheless significant differences between these two fields of study and these limit the applicability of mathematical methods in economics.[15]

8

Many characteristics of current economic discourse, such as equating the quantifiable with the significant or the display of sophistication together with inability to note obvious evidence, are commonplace also on the larger contemporary scene. Economics is so close to politics and other practical matters that it can be expected to mirror wider influences. The subject is also porous in the sense of an inability to resist intellectual and political fashion, whether emanating from within the subject or from outside.

It is conjectural how far the difficulty of exposing crude lapses reflects the rapid growth of the subject, or the protective facade provided by mathematical methods, or refusal to distinguish between knowledge and policy, or other influences. Whatever the reasons, the difficulty of effective exposure of simple transgressions has much increased the difficulty of maintaining standards. The exposure of economics to political influences and to intellectual fashion is likely to ensure the persistence of its confused state, in which there will continue to flourish side by side genuine advances of knowledge, meretricious displays of technique, and crude lapses which acquire a life of their own.

Notes

Part One · Equality

1 · The Grail of Equality

1 For reasons I shall go into later, I use the term differences rather than inequalities – except in the context of political power. Also, I use differences in income and wealth, or more simply income differences, interchangeably with economic differences.

2 A full assessment of changes in income differences over time is a complex exercise which requires examination of inter-generation as well as intra-generation changes, that is, changes in income differences between generations as well as those within a generation. The introduction of more than one generation into the analysis also implies that the income-receiving group must be thought of as extending beyond the family. (Otherwise consideration of more than one generation would imply marriages between brothers and sisters.) Take the case where group A and group B are drawn from the same generation; and let us assume that, whatever the relative position of A and B in any single year, the aggregated lifetime income of A exceeds that of B. In other words, there is a clear intra-generation difference. Now let us contrast two opposing situations; in the first, group A descendants have larger incomes than group B descendants but in the second the reverse is the case. We need not concern ourselves at this stage with the reasons why differences in incomes between specified groups may continue between generations or be reversed. But we can already note certain consequences. Taking first and second generation circumstances together, we clearly have a far less unequal income situation in the second case than in the first. Or, putting the same argument in another way, it is not sufficient to confine oneself to lifetime income comparisons: one needs also to know whether such differences are perpetuated or reversed over the generations if we are to have a fully rounded view of income differences or inequalities in a society. (In the same way, unemployment statistics mean very different things if they relate to two people being out of work for short periods rather than to one for a long period.)

3 Certain specific exceptions which do not affect the substance of the argument are noted later in this section.

4 'Now, what I want is, Facts. Teach these boys and girls nothing but Facts. Facts alone are wanted in life. Plant nothing else, and root out everything else. You can only form the minds of reasoning animals upon Facts: nothing else will ever be of any service to them. This is the principle on which I bring up my own children, and this is the principle on which I bring up these children. Stick to Facts, sir!'

5 The antiquity and ubiquity of envy is the major theme of Professor Helmut Schoeck's massive treatise *Envy: A Theory of Social Behaviour*, London, Secker and Warburg, 1970.

2 · Class on the Brain

1 Berkeley and Los Angeles, University of California Press, 1959.

2 S. J. Chapman and F. J. Marquis, *Journal of the Royal Statistical Society*, February 1912, pp. 293–306. Chapman was Professor of Political Economy in the University of Manchester. Marquis, a Lancashire man of modest background, subsequently became Lord Woolton, Cabinet Minister and Chairman of the Conservative Party. Professor D. A. Lury and Mr John Wood suggested, independently of each other, that I should note this example of social mobility.

3 D. V. Glass: *Social Mobility in Britain*, London, Routledge and Kegan Paul, 1954; J. Westergaard, *Class in Capitalist Society* (with H. Resler), London, Heinemann, 1975.
4 *The Daily Telegraph*, 19 November 1975.
5 *The Observer*, 28 April 1976.

Part Two · The West and the Third World

3 · *The Population Explosion: Myths and Realities*

1 *Report of the Commission on International Development*, New York, Praeger, 1969, p. 55.
2 Robert S. McNamara, *One Hundred Countries, Two Billion People: The Dimensions of Development*, London, Pall Mall Press, 1973, pp. 31, 45–6.
3 The Malaysian census for 1970 includes a breakdown of household incomes by ethnic groups. The averages are reported as follows, in Malaysian dollars per month: Chinese, 394; Indian, 304; Malay, 172.
4 A recent survey of statistics of availability of land and also of the prevailing mis-information on this subject will be found in an article by Professor Julian L. Simon, 'Resources, Population and Environment: An Over Supply of False Bad News,' *Science*, 27 June 1980.
5 Robert McNamara, op. cit, pp. 35–6.
6 This particular point is developed at length in chapter 14 below; cf. also P. T. Bauer, *Dissent on Development*, London, Weidenfeld and Nicolson; and Cambridge, Harvard University Press, 1971, especially pp. 136–42.
7   The weariest and most loathed worldly life
    That age, ache, penury, and imprisonment
    Can lay on nature, is a paradise
    To what we fear of death.
                (*Measure for Measure*, III,1)
8 The argument is not affected by the import of minerals and some foodstuffs from ldcs: these supplies are fully paid for by the users.
9 T. W. Schultz, 'The Food Alternatives Before Us: An Economic Perspective', University of Chicago mimeograph, 1974, p. 21.
  In Britain farmland rent represented about 40% of the value of agricultural output in the 1880s, and under 10% in the 1960s.
10 W. David Hopper, 'Distortions of Agricultural Development Resulting from Government Prohibitions', in T. W. Schultz (ed.), *Distortions of Agricultural Incentives*, Bloomington, Indiana University Press, 1978, p. 72. The rationalization for these prohibitions is usually the maintenance of employment opportunities for rural people. Hopper shows that this argument and other rationalizations are specious.
11 See, for example, *Financial Times*, 10 November 1980, p. 17.
12 The experience of Hong Kong is discussed at greater length in chapter 10 below.
13 The rapid population growth in ldcs in recent decades is discussed in many publications on demography and development. Convenient, easily accessible publications include William Petersen, *Population*, Third Edition, New York, Macmillan, 1975; Julian L. Simon, *The Economics of Population Growth*, Princeton, Princeton University Press, 1977; Michael P. Todaro, *Economic Development in the Third World*, London Longman, 1977; and UN Department of Economic and Social Affairs, *The Determinants and Consequences of Population Trends*, New York, 1976 (subsequently cited as UN study). The books by Professors Petersen and Simon are more reflective than other publications noted here. A recent and informative article is Eric M. Breindel and Nick Eberstadt, 'Paradoxes of Population', *Commentary*, August 1980.
14 Cf. UN Study, chapters V and XIV; D. M. Morawetz, *Twenty-five Years of Economic Development 1950 to 1975*, Baltimore, World Bank, 1977, pp. 24–5; and Deepak Lal, *Poverty, Power and Prejudices*, Fabian Research Series, No. 340, p. 2.
  Unless stated otherwise references in this essay are to unstandardized (crude) birth rates and death rates. For many purposes of demographic analysis it is of course necessary to use standardized rates. But this is not required for the central themes of this essay.
15 Statistics of life expectation in India between 1951 and 1971 at various ages from ten years to sixty years are

presented by Rati Ram and T. W. Schultz, 'Some Economic Implications of Increases in Life Span with Special Reference to India', University of Chicago, 1977, mimeographed.

16 The theory of demographic transition is outlined in most modern textbooks on population. There is a convenient summary with extensive quotations in John C. Caldwell, 'Towards a Restatement of Demographic Transition Theory', *Population and Development Review*, September-December 1976; see also Michael P. Todaro, op. cit.

17 Cf. Alan Sweezy, *Recent Light on Relations between Socio-Economic Development and Fertility Decline*, Pasadena, California Institute of Technology, 1973.

18 J. Hajnal, 'European Marriage Patterns in Perspective', in D. V. Glass and D. E. C. Eversely (eds.), *Population in History*, London, Edward Arnold, 1965.

19 Instances of increases in birth rate accompanying economic improvement in ldcs are noted in the UN Study, p. 72, and at greater length in Petersen, op. cit., chapter 16.

20 James E. Kocher, 'Social and Economic Development and Fertility Change in Rural Africa', Harvard Institute for International Development, December 1976, mimeographed.

21 John C. Caldwell, op. cit. Fertility may even be higher in the cities.

22 Petersen, op. cit., especially pp. 636–7.

23 For example, systems of land tenure may influence family size. A recent study has shown that in Mexico members of an *ejido* (an agrarian community that has received and continues to hold land in accordance with agrarian laws following the Revolution of 1910) tend to have more children than private farmers or paid farm workers. The constant competition for better land within the *ejido*, the desire to secure a legal renter or inheritor for the land, and considerations of labour supply seem to contribute to this demographic difference. A. De Vany and N. Sanchez, 'Land Tenure Structures and Fertility in Mexico', *Review of Economics and Statistics*, February 1979.

24 The theory helps to explain the often observed effects of increases in income on fertility in Western countries. In the short term an income effect operates: parents can afford more of the good things in life, including children. In the long run substitution effects may swamp the income effect. The relative costs of raising children may increase; their contributions of income to their parents may decline; and with greater affluence parents may discover other outlets for expenditure.

25 Caldwell quotes from a study of the Fulani of Northern Nigeria: 'The prospect of a secure and relatively care-free old age under the care of their sons will often restrain young women from deserting or divorcing their husbands. Both men and women in many respects show a remarkable disposition to forgo present convenience (or pleasure) in the interests of future benefits'. Caldwell adds: 'Such attitudes are universally reported by field researchers, even among the businessmen of Ghana's capital Accra'.
A Punjabi water carrier, mistaking an anththropologist for a family planner who had visited him many years earlier, is reported to have said: 'You were trying to convince me . . . that I shouldn't have any more sons. Now, you see, I have six sons and two daughters and I sit at home in leisure. They are grown up and they bring me money. One even works outside the village as a labourer. You told me I was a poor man and couldn't support a large family. Now, you see because of my large family, I am a rich man'. Quoted in A. MacFarlane, 'Modes of Reproduction', in G. Hawthorn (ed.), *Population and Development*, London, Frank Cass, 1978, p. 108.

26 Self-perpetuation as motive for procreation has been recognized from antiquity to the present day. It was explicitly noted by Plato. It is one of the themes of a bold and original book by Richard Dawkins, an Oxford biologist, *The Selfish Gene*, Oxford, Clarendon Press, 1976. Conversely, a lack of interest in the continuity of society and an inability or unwillingness to procreate may go together. Perhaps the most familiar explicit expressions of lack of interest in the more distant future are Mme. de Pompadour's observation 'Après nous le déluge', and Keynes's remark that in the long run we are all dead. Both were childless.

27 'In many parts of Africa a marriage is not regarded as properly established until the birth of the first child, when the supreme purpose of marriage, which is procreation, is practically and symbolically affirmed. As is well known, it is in the interval between the beginning of conjugal relations and the evidence of first conception that apprehension of sterility is most acute, and remedies ranging from traditional medicine and magic through modern patent medicines, new religious cults, and Western-trained doctors are anxiously sought. We must bear in mind that such a first pregnancy is anxiously awaited not only by future parents but

also by kinsfolk concerned with the continuation of the joint family and descent groups'. Meyer Fortes, 'Parenthood, Marriage and Fertility in West Africa', in Hawthorn (ed.), op. cit., p. 132.

28 On at least one occasion Queen Elizabeth I contrasted her lot unfavourably with that of her prisoner, Mary Queen of Scots, because the latter had been delivered of a bonny baby while she was barren stock.

29 It is sometimes said that parents in the less developed world, especially in Africa, do not love their children in the way parents do in the West, and are unwilling or incapable of caring for them. This attitude is again unfounded. To the extent that such comparisons are sensible, African parents seem to love their children as much as do parents in the West. A vivid account of the reaction of an African mother to the death of one of her five children is presented in Julian L. Simon's book, op. cit., p. 315.

It is also pertinent that white families in Southern Africa habitually employ African women to look after their children.

30 James E. Kocher, op cit., p. 5.

31 Mead T. Cain, 'The Household Life Cycle and Economic Mobility in Rural Bangladesh', *Population and Development Review*, 1978, New York.

32 Young girls play an important role in the trading activities of secluded Moslem women in parts of West Africa. The women are confined to their homes, and young girls go about buying and selling for them. A housewife can mobilize female child labour in three ways: by bearing and raising her own children; by fostering children of members of her family; and, failing these, by hiring young girls. Cf. Abner Cohen, *Custom and Politics in Urban Africa*, Berkeley and Los Angeles, University of California Press, 1969, chapter 2.

33 Children are a higher proportion of the population in the Third World than in the West, and the economic contribution of children is greatly under-stated in national income statistics. For this reason, among many others, the so-called income gap between the Third World and the West is exaggerated.

34 According to a recent report, in parts of Indonesia each local authority now keeps an 'up-to-date map showing the contraceptive practice of every fertile couple, so that fieldworkers can concentrate their efforts'. And there is an experimental programme to provide 'awards to villages with good records in family planning'. The various activities have been supported by the World Bank and by the United Nations Fund for Population Activities. *The Times*, London, 7 June, 1978.

35 See J. Hanlon and A. Agrawal, 'Mass Sterilisation at Gunpoint', *New Scientist*, London, 5 May 1977. This article is based in large part on the report of a team headed by Professor D. Banerji. Hanlon and Agrawal write: 'The Western aid agencies . . . either kept quiet or applauded the sterilization programme. World Bank President Robert McNamara took time off his busy schedule during his Indian visit to call upon the Indian Health and Family Planning Minister to congratulate him for the Indian Government's "political will and determination" in popularizing family planning. This was during November 1976, at the height of the compulsory sterilization campaign'. See also *Washington Post*, 4 July 1977, for an account of forcible mass sterilization in India.

4 · *Western Guilt and Third World Poverty*

1 In current usage the Third World means most of Asia except Japan and Israel, most of Africa except white southern Africa, and Latin America. Classification of the oil-producing countries is often vague – sometimes they are included in the Third World, sometimes not.

2 Throughout this chapter, Western responsibility refers to the accusation that the West has inflicted backwardness or poverty on the Third World. This usage again accords with standard practice. The different question of moral responsibility for the relief of poverty is examined in the next chapter.

3 Paul A. Baran, *The Political Economy of Growth*, New York, Monthly Review Press, 1957, p. 177.

4 Peter Townsend, *The Concept of Poverty*, London, Heinemann, 1970, pp. 41–2.

5 Kwame Nkrumah, *Towards Colonial Freedom*, London, Heinemann, 1962. Cf. also P. T. Bauer, *Dissent on Development*, op. cit., chapters 3 and 4.

6 An adulatory profile in *The Observer* (23 November 1975) cosily referred to Nyerere as 'St. Julius'. An article in the *Financial Times* (11 August 1975) described him as 'Africa's senior statesman and a man of formidable intellect'.

7 I. Potekhin, *Problems of Economic Independence of African Countries*, Moscow, Academy of Sciences, 1962, pp. 14–15.

8 A list of such warnings and objections will be found in *Dissent on Development* op. cit.

9 In fact, the areas most involved in the Atlantic slave trade, particularly West Africa, have become the economically most advanced areas in Black Africa. A recent study of pre-colonial South-Eastern Nigeria examines the economic development promoted by the slave trade which '. . . led to sufficient economic development of the region' to enable the profitable trade in palm-oil to burgeon in the early nineteenth century. David Northrup, *Trade Without Rulers: Pre-colonial Economic Development in South-Eastern Nigeria*, Oxford, Clarendon Press, 1978, p. 176.

10 This extension of Marxist-Leninist ideology is reflected, for instance, in the passage from the Soviet Academician Potekhin, section 2 above. Marxist-Leninist statements are apt to be designed for political purposes. Thus, in Potekhin's booklet, the passage I have quoted is followed immediately by the injunction that Western enterprises in Africa should be expropriated and economic activity collectivized. This injunction is now accepted by a number of African states.

11 This relationship was noted in chapter 1 above.

12 Underprivileged is a nonsense expression akin to under- or overfed. Privilege connotes special advantages conferred on some people and denied to others.

13 See chapter 10 below.

14 A convenient recent example is a statement by the Ayatollah Khomeini in January 1979: 'Our people are weary of it (colonial domination). Following their example other countries will free themselves from the colonial grip.' *Daily Telegraph*, 10 January 1979. In its long history Iran never was a Western colony. Further examples of this usage are noted in *Dissent on Development*, chapter 3, 'The Economics of Resentment'.

15 These allegations and the demand for a New International Economic Order are discussed at some length in several essays in Karl Brunner (ed.) *The First World and the Third World*, University of Rochester, N.Y., 1978. See especially essays by Karl Brunner, Harry G. Johnson, Peter T. Bauer and Basil S. Yamey.

16 When some ostensible evidence is produced in support of these allegations, it usually turns out to involve shifts in base periods or in the aggregates under discussion. I have examined these matters in some detail in *Dissent on Development*, chapter 6: 'A Critique of UNCTAD'.

17 Even if the West had the market power implied in many of these discussions, this would not account for a deterioration of the terms of trade, unless the effectiveness of this power increased persistently. Any such idea would be quite unrelated to reality.

18 An article in *The Observer* (22 July 1979) was entitled 'The boat people's "brain drain" punishes Vietnam'. The article suggested that the refugees from Vietnam were selfish and unpatriotic people who left because they could earn more elsewhere, and because they would not accept the new socialist order. It suggested further that this brain drain deprived the country of much-needed skills, especially medical skills. The article used the terms *brain drain, exodus* and *loss* to describe what was in fact a well-documented example of a huge mass expulsion – a revealing misuse of language.

19 The distinction which applies in many contexts is pertinent also to an assessment of changes in a country's terms of trade. As noted earlier in this section, changes in the terms of trade do not necessarily correspond to the ability of people to buy imports.

20 At the official level, a damaging international demonstration effect may indeed operate by encouraging show projects and unsuitable technologies financed with public funds. But this is not usually what the exponents of the international demonstration effect have in mind. Nor is it appropriate to blame the West for the policies of Third World governments in their adoption of unsuitable external models.

21 Quoted by Daniel P. Moynihan, 'The United States in Opposition', *Commentary*, March 1975.

22 The article, written by Ngugi wa Thiang'O, opened a special survey of Kenya.

23 These implications and results of official foreign aid are examined at greater length in the next chapter.

24 Cf. chapter 5, section 13.

5 · *Foreign Aid and Its Hydra-Headed Rationalization*

1 References to aid and foreign aid throughout are to official government-to-government economic aid,

whether bilateral or channelled through international organizations. Besides direct grants in cash or kind, foreign aid appropriately also includes the grant element in subsidized loans and debt cancellation. It excludes military aid, private investment and voluntary charity. Precise coverage of the concept does not affect most of the argument of this chapter; when it is pertinent, this will be specified or will be clear from the context. References to the amounts of aid are to flows of official economic aid as shown in the annual reports of the Development Assistance Committee of the OECD, in the official *British Aid Statistics*, and in the Annual Abstract of Statistics of the United States.

I shall use interchangeably the broad terms foreign aid and international wealth transfers, though in accordance with common practice I shall refer more often to foreign aid when the primary emphasis is on development or the relief of poverty and to wealth transfers when it is to global redistribution and restitution. The discussion also covers much of the New International Economic Order and the North-South dialogue, as these are mostly demands for large-scale aid.

2 Edward Luttwak claims, indeed, that the only common theme in the 'variegated assemblage' called the Third World is 'a profound and utterly incurable resentment of the Western industrial democracies'. E. N. Luttwak, letter, *Times Literary Supplement*, 18 January 1980.

3 The following passage is from a text-book by a well-known economist:

> 'The underdeveloped nations happen to be overwhelmingly non-white. The biased allocation of world affluence to the white race lends an ugly and dangerous accent to a situation that is explosive enough in itself.'

Jagdish Bhagwati, *The Economics of Underdeveloped Countries*, Weidenfeld and Nicolson, London, 1966, p. 36.

4 The Corporation operates in over fifty countries, including a number outside the British Commonwealth. When the Prince of Wales joined the Corporation, the countries in which it operated included not only countries such as Ethiopia and Tanzania, but also Uganda, then ruled by President Amin.

5 A report in the *Financial Times*, 10 July 1979, was headed 'UK aid down by £50 million'. It referred to the budget of June 1979. In fact United Kingdom aid for 1979–80 announced in that budget represented an increase in official aid of two per cent in real terms over the previous year; the so-called cut was from a planned increase of six per cent to one of two per cent in real terms.

6 According to an official statement by the Bank, the disbursement was suspended because the invasion of Kampuchea showed that the government of Vietnam was not concerned with the promotion of development. But on that argument the Bank should have withdrawn its support from the government of Tanzania when Nyerere's army invaded Uganda. Indeed, the argument that military aggression or other policies patently incompatible with the promotion of development disqualified a government from World Bank aid would require the abandonment of World Bank assistance to most Third World governments.

7 Reports on the butcheries in Ethiopia included items in *The Times* (London), 22 and 23 March 1978; on political executions in Tanzania under President Nyerere's rule, items in *The Times*, 28 November 1969, 8 March 1973, 9 March 1973; on forcible collectivization in Tanzania, items in the *Washington Post*, 6 May 1975, 7 February 1977, *Financial Times*, 7 January 1975, *The Times*, 17 November 1975, and the *New Statesman*, 13 October 1978.

8 'That India has directed some of its precious resources into nuclear development (for military purposes) may dismay many in this country; but this is no excuse for ignoring the legitimate agricultural and monetary needs of the Indian government.' *New York Times*, 8 June 1974. 'Legitimate' here suggests that India, or rather the Indian government, has a right to foreign aid.

9 Yet in the 1950s, many prominent economists endorsed this notion, including Professors Samuelson, Myrdal, Nurkse, Millikan, W. W. Rostow and Rosenstein-Rodan. I have quoted some uncompromising expressions of this notion and examined them at some length in my book *Dissent on Development*, especially pp. 31–38.

10 Even if it were true, which it plainly is not, that the Third World could not progress without external donations, it is not clear why these should be provided by Western taxpayers.

11 '. . . there must be something wrong with an underdeveloped country that does not have foreign exchange difficulties.' Gunnar Myrdal, *An International Economy*, London, Routledge and Kegan Paul, 1956, p. 270.

12 An exception which, however, is only apparent could be provided by the case of a newly independent

country, the political survival of which is doubtful, so that government or business may not be able to borrow abroad even if it could use capital productively. Taiwan or Israel (or West Germany immediately after the war) may have provided such an exception. How unusual are such circumstances is shown by the ability of Hong Kong and South Korea to secure foreign capital. The exception is in any case apparent rather than real, since the need for external support derives from the doubt of political survival. The exception is evidently irrelevant to the case for wealth transfers to the present Third World.

13 Cf. for instance the comparison of real GDP per capita for India (and many other Third World countries) with that of the United States, in Irving B. Kravis, Alan W. Heston and Robert Summers, op. cit., especially Table 4. The World Bank in its *World Development Report 1978* estimates that the official figure of per capita income for India should be raised by a factor of more than three to make it more nearly comparable with the corresponding figure for the United States.

14 G. F. Papanek, 'The Effect of Aid and Other Resource Transfers on Savings and Growth in Less Developed Countries', *Economic Journal*, September 1972, pp. 934–50.

In a later study the same author comments as follows on his statistical analysis: 'However, it suffers from all of the problems of cross-country analysis. Above all, there is of course no assurance that the model tested is not misspecified. The correlations found may be due to excluded variables and may be quite unrelated to causality.' G. F. Papanek, 'Aid, Foreign Private Investment, Savings and Growth in Less Developed Countries', *Journal of Political Economy*, January–February 1973, pp. 120–30.

15 'The correlation between the amounts of aid received in the past decades and the growth performance is very weak.' *Report of the Commission for International Development*, New York, 1969, p. 49.

16 The link between aid and the maintenance of a policy of collectivization, adverse to the improvement of living standards, is especially clear in Tanzania. According to W. David Hopper, of the World Bank,

'Government attempts to bring about a social transformation . . . have been responsible for a major decline in national food output. . . . In this case, the ideology of social reform has fully replaced any drive for economic growth. As long as food aid (or long-term loans for food purchases) is supplied to Tanzania by the industrial nations, the social experiment will continue.'

W. David Hopper, in T. W. Schultz (ed.), op. cit., p. 76.

17 Examples of such sustained waste abound in Third World countries, the governments of which have received large-scale Western aid.

18 'For the new urban dweller, especially the industrial worker whose memories of tranquil, slow-moving village life are still fresh, the pace of change has been upsetting and alarming. Thus the anti-Shah rampage in Tabriz a few weeks ago rapidly took on an anti-secular character. Eye-witnesses spoke of villagers pouring into town with their "martyrs' shirts" on, ready to die, furious at examples of Western permissiveness.' *Financial Times*, 15 March 1978.

19 Allan McPhee, *The Economic Revolution in British West Africa*, London, P. S. King, 1926, p. 8.

20 Some influential aid advocates and administrators are prepared to accept or encourage the attempted wholesale remoulding of societies and people. We will note Professor Myrdal's advocacy of coercive transformation of existing societies (section 11) and will refer to the World Bank's support for mass collectivization in Tanzania (section 16) and forcible sterilization in India (section 15).

21 This effect of aid is discussed in a rarely noted article by Dr Hans O. Schmitt, 'Development Assistance: A View from Bretton Woods', *Public Policy*, Fall 1973.

22 Cf. section 3 above, and chapter 7 below.

23 Professor Myrdal is among those who have recognized these matters. In his book *Asian Drama* (London, Allen Lane, Penguin Books, 1968) he specified some of the policies he thinks necessary in India if 'the government were really determined to change the prevailing attitudes and institutions and had the courage to take the necessary steps and accept their consequences [including] . . . the abolition of castes, a rational policy for husbandry, including the killing of cows, (and) in general, enactment and enforcement, not only of fiscal, but also of all other obligations on people that are required for development' (pp. 1909–10). And he also notes in the book that '. . . institutions can be changed only by what in the region is called compulsion – putting obligations on people and supporting them by force' (pp. 115–16).

Wide moral issues are raised by the claim of élite groups to attempt forcibly to transform their fellow men. I have attempted to set out some of these issues in 'Asian Vistas', in *Dissent on Development*, essay 5.

24 Cf. chapter 3 above.

25 In a well-publicized speech in London, President Julius Nyerere urged the 'eradication of poverty' which would involve 'a ceiling on wealth for individuals and nations, as well as deliberate action to transfer resources from the rich to the poor within and across national boundaries'. J. Nyerere, 'The Economic Challenge – Dialogue or Confrontation', *African Affairs*, April 1976, p. 247.

    The Brandt Commission has made proposals to enlarge the 'flow of official development finance'. These include 'an alternative system of universal revenue mobilization, based on a sliding scale related to national income', and 'automatic revenue transfers through international levies on some of the following: international trade; arms production or exports; international travel; the global commons, especially sea-bed minerals'. *North-South: A Programme for Survival*, London, Pan Books, 1980, pp. 290–1.

26 Cf. chapter 1.

27 This is clear from the limiting case such as a country with no foreign trade whatever, so that the application of international prices and rates of exchange must be arbitrary. In fact, much of the output of many Third World countries, especially the largest (India, Pakistan, Bangladesh, Indonesia, Burma, Nigeria, Zaire), is outside the orbit of international trade, and often also of local trade, which undermines comparisons of their incomes.

28 Dan Usher, *The Price Mechanism and the Meaning of National Income Statistics*, Oxford, Clarendon Press, 1968. The book was favourably reviewed in the *Economic Journal*, September 1969 by Miss Phyllis Deane, pioneer of national income accounting in tropical countries. Professor Dan Usher's methods were commended by Professor P. A. Samuelson; 'Professor Dan Usher's Contribution to National Income Comparison', *Economic Journal*, September 1975.

29 For instance, Nigeria's official 1963 census put the country's population at 55.6 million. In his book, *Industrialization in an Open Economy* (Cambridge, Cambridge University Press, 1969), Professor Peter Kilby estimated it at 37.1 million. Such discrepancies persist. Yet the Nigerian statistical service is far more advanced than those of, say, Ethiopia, Liberia or Zaire.

30 Thus Sir Arthur Lewis said at a conference a few years ago: 'What will happen to the gap between the rich and the poor countries? . . . I do not know the answer and . . . since I think that what matters is the absolute progress of the ldcs and not the size of the gap, I do not care.' Quoted in David Morawetz, op. cit., p. 30.

31 The wide and widening gap as an argument for aid is considered further in the Appendix to this chapter.

32 It is doubtful whether many of the rest would have preferred the short span of life, poverty, disease and recurrent tribal wars in order to retain control of their countries, the resources of which they were unable to develop.

33 In 1977, the last years for which official figures were available in 1979, the share of multilateral aid in total Western aid was just over 31%. For the United Kingdom, the corresponding figure for 1977 was about 38%.

34 Contrast this disregard of the United States with the experience sixty years earlier, when Russia and Japan turned to the United States for mediation after the Russo-Japanese War. This was before foreign aid.

35 Population pressure and population growth in the Third World have been examined in detail in chapter 3. Only a short discussion is presented here.

36 See chapter 3, section 9.

37 These matters are discussed in a recent and informative article by Lawrence J. Brainard, 'Oil and the OPEC Surplus: New Patterns of Growth and Adjustment in the World Economy', *Bankers Trust Company Economic Benchmarks*, May 1980.

38 According to the heading of a feature in *U.S. News and World Report*, 1 November 1976: 'Foreign Aid Keeps Growing – Despite all the Complaints; After spending $221 billion in 31 years to help other countries, US finds it is a habit hard to break.'

39 Even distribution of disaster relief supplies is best left to the voluntary agencies, like the Red Cross, which have both the organization and experience in these situations.

40 Some soi-disant charities now have primarily political aims, such as international redistribution or so-called liberation; they are thus best regarded as political parties or front organizations.

41 As Dostoevsky made one of his characters say in *The Possessed*, '. . . the enjoyment derived from charity is a haughty and immoral enjoyment. The rich man's enjoyment (lies in) his wealth, his power, and in the comparison of his importance with that of the poor. Charity corrupts giver and taker alike; and, what is more, (charity) does not attain its objects as it only increases poverty.'

274

42 M. Bronfenbrenner, 'Predatory Poverty on the March: The UNCTAD Record', *Economic Development and Cultural Change*, July 1976, p. 829.

43 A more detailed discussion of the concept and its limitations will be found in *Dissent on Development*, chapter 1, and in an article 'N. H. Stern on Substance and Method in Development Economics', *Journal of Development Economics*, December 1975.

44 D. Morawetz, op. cit.

6 · Background to Aid

1 Here are some key passages from President Truman's Point Four:

> 'More than half the people of the world are living in conditions approaching misery. . . . Their economic life is primitive and stagnant. Their poverty is a handicap and a threat both to them and to more prosperous areas. . . . '

> 'I believe we should make available to peace-loving peoples the benefits of our store of technical knowledge in order to help them realize their aspirations for a better life. And in cooperation with other nations, we should foster capital investment in areas needing development. . . . '

> 'This should be a cooperative enterprise in which all nations work together through the United Nations and its specialized agencies whenever practicable. It must be a worldwide effort for the achievement of peace, plenty, and freedom.'

2 Connoisseurs of the role of chance in history will relish the account of the origins of Point Four in Helmut Schoeck, *Entwicklungshilfe: Politische Humanität*, Munich, Langen Muller, 1972.

3 The peroration of Professor Bhagwati's book, *Economics of Underdeveloped Countries* (mentioned in the previous chapter) aptly illustrates two themes often discernible in discussions on international transfers: first, that of the less developed world as an outlet in the search of new causes, and second, the attraction of the Soviet system for many advocates of aid and development:

> 'Indeed, for the idealists among us, the challenge of development represents today the kind of invigorating stimulus for sustained action that the Soviet revolution was for progressive opinion after the first world war. This itself constitutes the surest guarantee of a continual, even though halting, transition to an international framework favourable for rapid economic growth in the underdeveloped world.'

4 The role of the Alliance for Progress in the promotion of these aims in Latin America has often been noted. An instructive document on this subject is a long letter from a group of Guatemalan citizens, submitted in 1967 to the Appropriations Committee of the United States House of Representatives, and printed in the Congressional Record 1967–8, pp. 292–6. The letter argued at length and in detail that the activities of the Alliance for Progress in Guatemala did not serve to promote development or to help the poor, but only to encourage confiscation of property and to assist in the establishment of a state-controlled economy.

5 John A. Pincus, *Trade, Aid and Development*, New York, 20th Century Fund, 1967, p. 353.

6 Robert S. McNamara, op. cit., p. 30.

7 J. Bhagwati, op. cit., p. 36.

8 Mahbub ul Haq, *The Poverty Curtain: Choices for the Third World*, New York, Columbia University Press, 1976, p. 181.

9 *New York Times Magazine*, 6 August 1976. A London vagrant whose qualifications differ from Professor Sowell's also put the same point rather pithily in conversation: 'There is much money in poking and prodding us poor.'

10 It is sometimes argued that development economics or the economics of underdeveloped countries represents a reversion to the interests of the classical economists who addressed themselves to issues of long-run social and economic development. Although there is some substance in this contention, nevertheless there are radical differences between the preoccupations of the classical economists and those of the latter-day development economists. For instance, the classical economists did not think of economic achievement as being determined by physical and financial factors. Nor did they divide the world into two global aggregates or insist that the more advanced countries should support the rest.

11 *Financial Times*, 12 February 1976. This was written at a time when the sharp decline of the pound inflicted heavy losses on many Third World governments and individuals who held their reserves in sterling.

12 Cf. a dispatch from Brussels in the *Financial Times*, 12 October 1978.

13 In July 1979, the Prime Minister said in the House of Commons that the construction of four ships provided to Vietnam under British aid had proceeded so far that to cancel the ships would be more expensive than to complete them. This answer illustrates the momentum of aid. It left unanswered the question why these ships when completed could not have been supplied to a British company or to another government, including one of the governments embarrassed by the flood of refugees from Vietnam.

14 'Myths about Minorities', *Commentary*, August 1979. It has long been recognized that many reformers and humanitarians are interested primarily in groups who can be declared or classified as helpless, and are often indifferent, even hostile, to those who are self-reliant and competent, even if they are victims of persecution. Such attitudes are not surprising. Competent and self-reliant people endanger the emotional and financial security, and also the jobs of many reformers and humanitarians.

As early as the eighteenth century the celebrated Madame de Deffand observed: 'Il me faut absolument des malheureux pour en faire des heureux.'

15 It seems necessary to say that the claque was a group of professional applauders prominent in nineteenth-century French theatre. Claque and clique are different concepts, even though the similarity between them extends beyond the merely phonetic.

16 In Britain War on Want is one of the organizations participating in officially financed aid propaganda. The prime platform of this organization is insistence that the poverty of the Third World is the result of Western exploitation (cf. chapter 4, above). This opinion encourages attitudes and policies in the Third World which greatly damage economic advance and also promote conflict in Third World countries as well as internationally.

17 There are many examples to substantiate these statements about the publications of the Bank. An early instance was *The Economic Development of Nigeria* (Baltimore, Johns Hopkins Press, 1955), a report which, according to the Bank, was to serve as a model for subsequent reports. I examined the report in the *Journal of Political Economy*, June 1955, and in *Dissent on Development* (1972 edition), chapter 11. A recent instance, a Bank study on Romania, was the subject of a serious yet entertaining editorial in the *Wall Street Journal*, 10 August 1979, entitled 'Resurrection of the Dead'. The Bank study accepted the claim of the Romanian authorities that GNP there had increased by 9.6 per cent a year compound over the last 25 years. If this had been true, income at the beginning of the period would have been too low to sustain life. Hence the title of the article.

8 · *Cost and Risks of Commodity Stabilization*

1 The complexities of stabilization are examined more fully in P. T. Bauer and B. S. Yamey, *Markets, Market Control and Marketing Reform*, London, Weidenfeld and Nicolson, 1968, especially essays 7 and 9, the latter by P. T. Bauer and F. W. Paish. Stabilization without controls is considered in detail in essay 6 in Bauer and Yamey, ibid.

2 Lim Teck Ghee writes of the ability of peasants in pre-war Malaya to 'adjust quickly to new conditions. The period of rubber depression, for instance, saw many peasants planting subsistence food crops, thereby reducing their dependence on food purchases and conserving the income obtained from the cash crop. Although some old and unproductive (rubber) trees were cut down and replaced with food crops, the smallholder did not give up rubber cultivation to revert to subsistence cultivation of food crops alone. The peasants also diversified by cultivating miscellaneous cash crops which brought in quick returns, or by engaging in activities which supplemented the income obtained from commercial cultivation'. Lim Teck Ghee, *Peasants and the Agricultural Economy in Colonial Malaya 1874–1941*, Kuala Lumpur, Oxford University Press, 1977, p. 234. These observations refer to pre-war Malaya, the economy of which was often instanced as an extreme example of vulnerable monoculture.

There are many other instances to show that farmers in poor countries, thought to be heavily dependent on a single export crop, can readily shift to other products. The ability of the cocoa farmers of the Gold Coast in 1937–38 to withhold supplies from merchants for over six months provides another example.

3 In principle, a specified restriction of output or transfer of resources could be effected by concerted export taxes rather than by quota schemes. These various arrangements are rarely applied in practice and do not affect the general argument.

4 Thus in 1969 Sir Arthur Lewis wrote that 'nowadays commodity agreements tend to be an international

conspiracy against Africa, since it is the expansion of her output which tends to cause much of the trouble'. W. Arthur Lewis, *Aspects of Tropical Trade 1883–1965*, Stockholm, Almqvist & Wicksell, 1969, p. 26.

5 Under some commodity agreements output is not restricted formally, but part of it is diverted to secondary markets, destroyed, or accumulated and withheld from the market for long periods.

9 · *British Colonial Africa: Economic Retrospect and Aftermath*

1 Kwame Nkrumah, *Africa Must Unite*, London, Heinemann, 1963, p. xiii.

2 *Report of the Commission for International Development*, New York, Praeger, 1969, annex.

3 W. Arthur Lewis, op. cit., pp. 9, 15. This book was published in the same year as the Pearson Annex, with the passage just quoted. Sir Arthur Lewis was a member of the Pearson Commission.

4 S. Herbert Frankel, 'The Tyranny of Economic Paternalism in Africa', *Optima*, December 1960.

5 Elizabeth Colson, 'The Impact of the Colonial Period on the Definition of Land Rights', in Victor Turner (ed.), *Colonialism in Africa 1870–1960*, Cambridge, Cambridge University Press, 1971.

6 Cf. Mary Kingsley, *West African Studies*, New York, Macmillan, 1901, *passim*.

7 A. McPhee, op. cit., p. 8.

8 W. K. Hancock, *Survey of British Commonwealth Affairs*, Vol. 2, *Problems of Economic Policy 1918–1930*, London, Oxford University Press, 1942, Part 2, p. 283.

9 Human porterage, the principal means of transport in pre-colonial Africa, was prodigal in the use of labour and also took a heavy toll of life.

10 The railways and roads of the colonial period are now so much taken for granted that their role as agents of change has come to be ignored. McPhee, who wrote in the 1920s, was well aware of their significance. He discusses in detail the cost and difficulties of the construction of roads and even more of railways. He also examines their role in public security, the development of cash crops and the suppression of slavery.

11 The magnitude and significance of this form of investment is a major theme of S. H. Frankel's *Capital Investment in Africa 1870–1938*, London, Oxford University Press, 1938.

12 Some of these controls are discussed in the *Report of the East Africa Royal Commission 1953–55*, London, HMSO, 1955; and in P. T. Bauer, *West African Trade*, Cambridge, Cambridge University Press, 1954; London, Routledge and Kegan Paul, 1963; P. T. Bauer and B. S. Yamey, op. cit., especially essay 15. Cf. also, C. Ehrlich, 'Building and Caretaking: Economic Policy in British Tropical Africa', *Economic History Review*, November 1973.

13 For instance, in the late 1940s the controlled retail price of Raleigh bicycles in Accra (Gold Coast) was £13. This price was largely enforced in the stores of the import merchants. In the neighbouring retail markets the bicycles sold at £18.

14 The operation of price controls in the conditions noted in the text is discussed in some detail in P. T. Bauer, *West African Trade*, especially chapters 6, 13 and appendix 5, and also P. T. Bauer and B. S. Yamey, op. cit., essay 12, 'Price Control in Under-developed Countries'.

15 P. T. Bauer, *West African Trade*, Part 5; P. T. Bauer, *Dissent on Development*, chapters 11 and 12; P. T. Bauer and B. S. Yamey, op. cit., essays 8 and 9; G. K. Helleiner, 'The Fiscal Role of Marketing Boards in Nigerian Economic Development, 1947–61', *Economic Journal*, September 1964; and A. T. Killick, 'The Economics of Cocoa', in W. B. Birmingham, I. Neustadt and E. N. Omaboe, *A Study of Contemporary Ghana*, Vol. 1: *The Economy of Ghana*, London, Allen and Unwin, 1965.

16 The organization responsible was first the Cocoa Control of the Ministry of Food, and subsequently the West African Cocoa Marketing Board, which in turn became the West African Produce Control Board when monopoly of export was extended to other products. In 1947 the West African Produce Control Board gave way to separate marketing boards in the different West African colonies.

17 The principal documents were two British Government White Papers, *Report on Cocoa Control in West Africa 1939–1943 and Statement on Future Policy*, Cmnd. 6554, 1949; *Statement on Future Marketing of West African Cocoa*, Cmd. 6950, 1946. Cf. also *Statement of the Policy Proposed for the Future Marketing of Nigerian oils, oil seeds and cotton*, Nigerian Sessional Paper No. 18, Lagos, Government Printer, 1948. The text of the official guarantee is reproduced in *West African Trade*, chapter 20.

18 See also P. T. Bauer, *Dissent on Development*, chapter 12.

19 Before decolonization, the Colonial Office, the colonial governments and the academic supporters of the

marketing boards persisted in denying that these organizations levied taxes on the producers. However, by the 1960s the academic supporters argued that it was self-evident that from their inception these boards were instruments of taxation and should be welcomed as such.

20 These effects have been noted by a number of economists not involved in the controversies over the marketing boards. Examples include J. Clark Leith, *Foreign Trade Regimes and Economic Development: Ghana*, New York, Columbia University Press, 1974; Theodore W. Schultz, 'On Economics and Politics of Agriculture', in T. W. Schultz (ed.), op. cit.; John Levi, 'African Agriculture Misunderstood: Policy in Sierra Leone', *Stanford Food Research Institute Studies*, vol. 13, 1974.

21 John Levi, op. cit., p. 257.

22 The price policies of the marketing boards are examined in some detail in G. K. Helleiner, op. cit; P. T. Bauer, *Dissent on Development*, especially chapters 11 and 12; P. T. Bauer and B. S. Yamey, op. cit., especially essay 9.

10 · The Lesson of Hong Kong

1 *Study submitted by the Center for International Studies of the Massachusetts Institute of Technology to the Senate Committee investigating the operation of Foreign Aid*, Washington, Government Printing Office, 1957, p. 37.

2 Alexis de Tocqueville, *Journeys to England and Ireland* (1833) (ed. J. P. Mayer) London, Faber and Faber, 1958.

11 · Broadcasting the Liberal Death Wish

1 *The African Condition*, The Reith Lectures, London, Heinemann Educational Books, 1980.

2 Cf. chapters 4 and 9.

3 'The man who writes a book in Zambia – usually a simple tale of tribal life – is immediately whisked away into the higher reaches of the administration. One of the writers represented on the shelf had become a member of the Central Committee of the Party; another had been put in charge of a large state-owned organization. But with the fruits of high office dangling so alluringly before them, Zambia is by no means short of would-be writers'. Shiva Naipaul, *North of South: An African Journey*, London, André Deutsch, 1978, pp. 233–4.

4 See a communication on this subject by Dr J. B. Kelly, *Encounter*, August 1980.

5 Professor Mazrui does mention the genocidal wars between the Hutu and the Tutsi in Rwanda and Burundi. But even for these he blames the Europeans for not having incorporated these countries into Tanganyika after the First World War (p. 107).

6 Cf. chapters 4 and 9.

7 Quoted in Frederick Pedler, *Main Currents of West African History 1940–78*, London, Macmillan, 1979, p. 265 (italics added).

8 Such restrictions which I have not seen mentioned in the Western press have been enforced in some black African states since the 1960s. On this subject again Shiva Naipaul is informative: 'Many of the youthful unemployed and under-employed of Lusaka gaze with longing towards Rhodesia and South Africa. Several of those I spoke to said they would, if they could, go to these countries to seek work. Naturally, the Zambian government cannot allow that to happen' (ibid., p. 232).

9 See chapter 5, footnote 7. A report in the *Washington Post*, 6 May 1975, put the numbers who had to leave their traditional villages at between six and eight million. According to the report this was the largest migration in African history.

10 The economy of Mozambique would probably collapse if it did not allow South African technicians to operate its ports and railways and encourage substantial numbers of its citizens to work in the mines of the 'enemy'. S. Naipaul, op. cit. p. 232.

Part Three · The State of Economics

12 · Economists and the Two Dollar Problems

1 The major contributions to the literature on the dollar problems are listed in P. T. Bauer and A. A. Walters, 'The State of Economics', *Journal of Law and Economics*, April 1975.

2 This was the rationale for the scarce currency clause of the Bretton Woods agreement.

3 We may note in passing that the misconception of a persistent dollar shortage has lent a helping hand to the fallacy that an inevitable shortage of foreign exchange is a concomitant of the development of poor countries.

4 The neglect of the exchange rate has at times been rationalized *ex post* by suggesting that the maintenance of a fixed rate of exchange ruling at the time was taken for granted, and that this approach was appropriate in the circumstances. This defence is inadmissible. Excess demand is meaningless without specifying the price at which the quantity demanded exceeds the quantity supplied. Moreover, the assumption of a fixed rate of exchange was not stated clearly and in any case conflicted with the numerous alterations in exchange rates in the years before the discussion of the dollar shortage, and even during the period of the discussion.

5 References will be found in Bauer and Walters, op. cit.

13 · Economic History as Theory

1 John Hicks, *A Theory of Economic History*, Oxford, Clarendon Press, 1969. Page references are to this book.

2 Hicks uses the term mercantile economy to cover the market (exchange) economy generally, and also economies or polities with much external trade. This ambivalence blurs the argument in some contexts, but not in this particular instance.

3 In his observations on the early history of the Greek city-states Hicks concedes that the ruling classes were landowners and not merchants. He argues, however, that once trade was active 'even a landowning class is likely to have been engaged in trade to an extent which is sufficient for the trade orientation' (p. 40). But this attempt at reconciliation contradicts Hicks's emphasis on the key role of the specialized merchant in the earlier development of the mercantile economy (pp. 27–9).

4 Hicks writes that 'until the rise of Singapore in very recent times', South-East Asia 'has not been a place for city-states' (p. 39). This formulation suggests that by declaring itself independent of Malaysia, Singapore overnight became a city-state. It is rather baffling that a city can overnight become a city-state, and thus enter one of Hicks's 'economic states of society'. It is not clear how Hong Kong, Penang and some other contemporary trading centres would fit into this scheme of things.

5 In 1527, about the mid-point between the sack of Constantinople and the trial of Warren Hastings, Rome was sacked by the Imperial forces led by the troops of the Most Catholic King in the course of a triangular struggle with the Most Christian King and the Pope. This sack, the worst ever experienced by Rome, had nothing to do with what Hicks would call the trading situation. The sack of Rome bore a much closer family resemblance to the sack of Constantinople than did the latter to the activities of British merchants and civil servants in eighteenth-century Bengal.

6 In Hicks's rationalization of these restrictive policies, there is a curious reference to the displacement of Indian handloom weavers as a result of the import of textiles. Hicks notes that from this development 'there would be a favourable effect, somewhere; but it might be anywhere; there would be no particular reason why it should be in India' (p. 165). This formulation ignores the fact that the consumers of the cheaper textiles obviously were Indians, who must have benefited from lower prices or improved quality. Moreover, even if they did not spend the increase in their real incomes on other Indian products, somebody else must have spent more on them, because otherwise the country could not have paid for the imports – payment certainly was not in bullion.

7 The modern phase is the only period in history in which Hicks ascribes a central influence or role to government policies as such. Thus in his discussion of the industrial revolution in eighteenth-century England, Hicks does not mention the propitious circumstances of limited government, moderate taxation dependent on the approval of a Parliament made up largely of property owners, and a legal system and judiciary favourable to the rights of property owners. Nor, incidentally, does he refer to other aspects of the social and political background which encouraged the taking of long views and the experimental outlook, and promoted long-term investment in agriculture and industry.

8 Sydney Pollard, 'Fixed Capital in the Industrial Revolution in Britain', *Journal of Economic History*, September 1964.

9 In 1948, the Minister of Propaganda in one of the East European countries was asked privately for his opinion about the percentage his government would poll in a free election. He put it at between five and ten per cent. He predicted, however, that twenty years of consistent political education would serve to obliterate the past sufficiently to enable the Communist Party to secure a majority in a free election. The Minister's views and the reason for his long-term optimism, namely that the past would have been forgotten in twenty years, furnish an interesting comment on Hicks's opinion on the persistent differences in mentality on the two sides of the Curtain.

10 The central issue in this range of problems has been summarized by Sir Karl Popper in his phrase 'But trends are not laws'. *The Poverty of Historicism*, London, Routledge and Kegan Paul, 1957.

11 The influence of mere accident on the course of history is large, though many people, especially those with a religious or Marxist turn of mind, are reluctant to admit this.

12 There are no scientists in this list. Sir Peter Medawar has argued that a scientist is aware that if he himself does not make a particular discovery, some other scientist is bound to, and probably reasonably soon. This contention is a theme of his book, *The Art of the Soluble*, London, Methuen, 1967. If this is accepted, then even the most outstanding scientist only anticipates the findings of others. To some extent the same may be true of those who apply the findings of scientists. But it cannot be said of the activities of the people listed in the text.

14 · *The Investment Fetish*

1 In public and academic discourse, the advocacy of investment always refers to expenditure on real resources, that is, on labour or physical resources, and not to financial investment in the sense of acquisition of financial assets. Throughout this chapter also investment refers to spending on real resources.

2 M. Abramovitz, 'Resource and Output Trends in the United States since 1870', *American Economic Review*, Papers and Proceedings, May 1956; A. K. Cairncross, *Factors in Economic Development*, London, Allen and Unwin, 1962; E. F. Denison, *Accounting for US Economic Growth 1929–69*, Washington, Brookings Institution, 1974; Simon Kuznets, *Modern Economic Growth: Rate Structure and Spread*, New Haven, Yale University Press, 1966; and Robert M. Solow, 'Technical Change and the Aggregate Production Function', *Review of Economics and Statistics*, August 1957.

3 Op. cit. pp. 80–81.

4 Analytically and conceptually it is possible to distinguish between spending on current consumption and spending which encourages the future flow of income. But this possibility does not affect the argument of the text.

5 ˙Central Policy Review Staff, *The Future of the British Motor Car Industry*, London, HMSO, 1975.

6 *Development and Underdevelopment*, Cairo, National Bank of Egypt, 1956, p. 64.

7 The statements in this article about infant mortality and diseases are the opposite of the truth. It is precisely the reduction in mortality which is behind the rapid increase in population in the Third World.

8 Soviet history and the Industrial Revolution in Britain are often cited as examples that forcible depression of living standards is necessary for economic progress. For reasons set out later in this section, neither of these experiences provides an example of enforced austerity for economic development.

9 It is sometimes argued that the financing of infrastructure for development requires enforced austerity because the output of these facilities cannot be marketed. This reasoning is invalid. If the infrastructure is necessary for development or even helpful to it, this will increase incomes and taxable capacity, and this should enable the government to service capital borrowed for this purpose.

10 Cf. chapter 13, section 6, above.

11 Government of India, *Second Five Year Plan*, Delhi, 1956, p. 394.

12 In some of these respects, the concept of the incremental capital-output ratio widely used in the planning literature differs from the Keynesian concept of the marginal efficiency of capital. Whatever its shortcomings, the latter concept envisages a functional relationship between increments of capital and output, and not merely a statistical association; and it also recognizes the need to take into account the cost of other resources required for additional output.

13 Cf. A. A. Walters, 'Roads and Redistribution: A Comment', *Journal of Development Studies*, October 1976.

15 · *Reflections on the State of Economics*

1 E. H. Phelps Brown, 'The Underdevelopment of Economics', *Economic Journal*, March 1973.

2 G. D. N. Worswick, 'Is Progress in Economic Studies Possible?', *Economic Journal*, September 1972.

3 Wassily Leontief, 'Theoretical Assumptions and Non-observed Facts', *American Economic Review*, March 1971. Cf. also Axel Leijonhufvud, 'Life Among the Econ', *Western Economic Journal*, September 1973.

4 In this chapter I have only a few references to particular publications, because my purpose is to offer reflections of a general nature rather than to engage in controversy over particular economic issues. An article by Professor A. A. Walters and myself, 'The State of Economics', op. cit., provides many specific references to the practices referred to in the present chapter. That article also discusses on a somewhat more technical level some of the issues examined here.

5 According to a major variant of this idea, the foreign exchange earnings of the ldcs were rigidly constrained by external market conditions and could not be increased, whether the country exported more or less. This notion is fanciful, even though it has been advanced by leaders of the profession in serious journals. (For example, see Bauer and Walters ibid.) It would hold only if the price elasticity of demand for every single export were exactly unity over the entire range of the demand curve.

6 Neglect of the effect of prices even when the effect is patently significant is frequent in studies which claim to project output and demand decades ahead. World Bank studies on particular countries are examples. Cf. a review article of a major World Bank report on Nigeria in *Dissent on Development*, essay 11, and also Bauer and Walters op. cit. p. 3.

7 See *Dissent on Development*, chapter 1, and Bauer and Walters, ibid. p. 3.

8 A depressing list of extremely crude transgressions by leading economists will be found in *Dissent on Development, passim*; in Bauer and Walters ibid. pp. 3–6, and also in P.T. Bauer, 'Development Economics: Intellectual Barbarism', in Karl Brunner (ed.), *Economics and Social Institutions*, The Hague, Martinus Nijhoff, 1979. This last-named essay also considers the political direction of some of the lapses examined there.

9 Norbert Wiener, *God and Golem Inc.*, Cambridge, Mass., MIT Press, 1964.

10 A. C. Pigou, *Memorials of Alfred Marshall*, London, Macmillan, 1928, p. 422.

11 *General Theory*, London, Macmillan, 1936, p. 298. Both Marshall and Keynes were mathematicians before they became economists.

12 W. Leontief, op. cit., p. 3.

13 Professor George J. Stigler has forcefully restated some of these criticisms in his thoughtful essay, 'The Mathematical Method in Economics' in *Five Lectures on Economic Problems*, London, London School of Economics, 1949.

14 It should be obvious that knowledge of economic magnitudes is an essential part of an economist's tools of trade. But this is very different from the practice, encouraged by the vogue for mathematics and econometrics, of treating the quantifiable aspects (whether genuinely quantifiable or only ostensibly so) of a situation, factor or process as if they were the most important or representative characteristics.

15 Cf. Bauer and Walters, op. cit., pp. 17–18. The relevant differences and similarities between the natural sciences and the study of society are the subject of a large literature, much of which is familiar to economists interested in this subject. I may however mention two publications with which economists may not be familiar. One is an illuminating article by Professor Michael J. Moravcsik, an American physicist, 'Scientists in Politics and Out', *Bulletin of the Atomic Scientists*, January 1966; the other is the title essay of Sir Peter Medawar's book, *The Art of the Soluble*, op. cit. Both authors emphasize that, because natural scientists are concerned with establishing uniformities about unchanging reality, there are certain basic differences between their methods and those appropriate to the study of society. Professor Moravcsik writes at length about the pitfalls of the quest for simplicity and elegance in the study of society.

Index

aborigines, 70, 74, 79, 88, 96, 111, 135, 194, 205, 229; Australian, 196

Abramovitz, M., 242, 280n

Addison, Joseph, 32

Afghanistan, 67, 75, 88, 94, 112

Africa, 4, 22–3, 45, 50, 51, 53, 54, 57, 58, 66, 70–5 *passim*, 79, 82, 84, 88, 106, 107, 112, 117, 121, 122, 126, 127, chapter 9 *passim*, 190, chapter 11 *passim*, 229, 230, 249, 254, 263, 269n, 270n, 277n; Black Africa, 70, 72, 164, 166, 169, 176, 193 195–200 *passim*, 202, 204, 271n, 278n; Central, 44, 73, 112, 174, 177, 209; East, 71, 73, 74, 94, 106, 112, 157, 170, 174, 177, 181, 191, 199, 200, 209, 249, 253; North, 112, 193, 202; sub-Saharan, 57, 165, 167, 192, 194; South/Southern, 71, 73, 84, 171, 192, 198, 199, 200, 203, 205, 207–10 *passim*, 270n, 278n; West, 49, 57, 59, 63, 70, 71, 72, 74, 99, 108, 112, 157, 159, 163, 165, 166, 167, 169, 170, 174, 177, 178–83 *passim*, 197, 208, 253, 270n, 271n; apartheid, 198, 199, 209, 210; native reserves, 166, 167; *North of South: An African Journey,* 195, 278nn; Pax Africana, 203; Sharpeville, 198; Soweto, 198; United Africa Company, 173; Zulus, 196

aggregate spending, 153, 240

Agrawal, A., 270n

agriculture, 22, 43, 47, 49, 50, 51, 52, 57, 63, 64, 67, 82, 99, 114, 117, 126, 162, 167, 174, 176, 177, 178, 182, 192, 197, 232, 233, 242, 249, 259, 260, 268n, 269n, 279n

aid, 3, 5, 82, 83, 84, chapter 5 *passim,* chapter 6 *passim,* chapter 7 *passim,* 161, 182, 189, 203, 207, 271n; agreements, 78, 96; lobbies, 93, 138, 142, 147, 190; tied, 123, 131, 146, 147; bilateral, 123, 131, 132, 133, 151–2, 272n, 274n; multilateral, 92, 109, 122, 124, 132, 133, 151, 152, 274n; the term 'aid', 141; principal declared objective of, 134; international/official wealth transfers, 20, chapter 5 *passim,* 139–45 *passim,* 148, 149, 150, 272n, 273n, 275n; aid agencies/ organizations, 86, 90, 91, 93, 97, 105, 109, 111, 116, 123, 124, 132, 134, 139, 141, 144, 149, 150, 151, 153, 154, 200, 201, 207, 272n; voluntary agencies, 128, 129

Algeria, 57, 88, 94, 123

America, *see* United States of; South; Latin; North

Americas, the, 46, 189

American Economic Association, 67, 255

Americans, 69, 73, 81–2, 114, 117, 122

Anderson, Sir John (Viscount Waverley), 29

Andreski, S. L., 181

Angola, 88, 123, 206, 207

Anstey, Vera, 259

Arabia (UAR), 164, 228; Arabs, 70, 73, 192, 196, 229; slavers/slave trade, 70, 73, 195, 196

Argentina, 71

Asia, 22 50, 54, 66, 68, 70, 73, 75, 79, 84, 88, 112, 121, 171, 185, 190, 193, 226–7, 230, 254, 270n; Asians in Africa, 44, 51, 74, 79, 94, 106, 112, 175, 204, 209, 210

Australia, Australasia, 54, 75, 164, 192, 196

Austria, 234

Awolowo, Obafemi, 196

Bahrain, 95

balance of payments, 26–7, 78, 109, 122, 127, 189, 215, 217, 219, 239, 257

283

Banerji, D., 270n
Bangladesh, 63, 82, 270n, 274n
Bank of England, 28, 29; *Quarterly Bulletin of the*, 243
Baran, Paul A., 66, 67, 270n
Barth, Karl, 195–6
Bauer, P. T., 268n, 270n, 271n, 276n, 277n, 278n, 279n, 281nn
Belgium, 44; *see also* Low Countries
Belize, 88
Bendix, Reinhard, 29
Bengal, 29, 228, 279n
Berlin Congress (1884), 191, 198
Bhagwati, Jagdish, 272n, 275nn
Bhutan, 67
Birmingham, W. B., 277n
Boot, Thomas, 28
Borneo, 44
Bowley, Sir Arthur, 264
Bradbury, Malcolm, 191
brain drain, 79, 192, 271n; *see also* migration
Brainard, Lawrence J., 274n
Brandt Report, 140, 274n
Brazil, 68, 71, 111, 127, 207, 248
Breindel, Eric M., 268n
Britain/British, 14, 18, 20, 22, 26–39 *passim*, 48, 68, 75, 78, 88–92 *passim*, 95, 96, 117, 124, 129, 136, 141, 146, 149, 150, 154, 172, 173, 180, 188, 189, 191, 194, 196, 200, 203, 205, 206, 211, 219, 227, 228, 229, 231, 232, 235, 240, 242–3, 244–5, 246, 249, 268n, 279n, 280n
British aid, 91–5 *passim*, 99, 146; dependencies, 159, 188; colonies (*see also* colonialism), 83, 172, 174, 182, 187; Br. Colonial Africa, chapters 9 and 11 *passim*; local authorities, 95, 134; Br. Association for the Advancement of Science, 255; motor-car industry (Think Tank Report), 245
Bronfenbrenner, Martin, 132, 275n
Brunner, Karl, 271n, 281n
Bullard, Sir Reader, 29
Burma/Burmese, 44, 112, 157, 200, 253, 274n
Burundi, 67, 104, 198, 278n
Bury, J. B., 71

Cain, Mead T., 270n
Caine, Sir Sydney, 36
Cairncross, Sir Alec, 242, 280n
Caldwell, John C., 57–61, 269n
Callaghan, James, 29
Cambodia, *see* Kampuchea
Cambridge University, 28, 29, 32, 36, 37, 38, 67, 219
Canada, 117, 164, 200; *see also* North America
cannibalism, 82
capital, 45, 46, 49, 51, 52, 70, 71, 74, 78, 94, 96–103 *passim*, 105, 106, 107, 109, 110, 112, 120, 132, 134, 169, 180, 185, 186, 187, 206–9 *passim*, 215, 225, 230, 231, 239, 241–6 *passim*, 248–53 *passim*, 260, 261, 273n, 280n
capital formation 47, 101, 174, 242, 248, 249, 250, 254; capital goods, 72, 240, 250–3 *passim*
capitalism, 67, 69, 99, 237, 248
Caribbean, the, 44, 54, 57, 70, 117, 127, 171
cash crops, 49, 59, 64, 70, 98, 112, 157, 167, 169, 180, 183, 197, 202, 249, 253, 276n, 277n
Catto, Lord, 28
Chad, 67, 88, 89
Chadwick, Sir James, 29, 36
Chapman, S. J., 267n
charities, 20, 68, 97, 129
charity, voluntary, 117, 129, 140, 272n, 274n
Chile, 71, 88
China, 171, 186, 188, 205, 232; communist, 38, 68; People's Republic of, 135, 137, 188; Shanghai, 186; Mao Tse-tung, 235
Chinese, the, 10, 16, 38, 44, 51, 54, 71, 73, 74, 79, 94, 106, 112, 186, 188, 200, 229, 268n
churches, 3, 24, 32, 37, 68, 69, 90, 129, 141, 149, 150, 228, 235, 244
civil service, 29, 33, 34; civil servants, 104, 109, 111, 158, 174, 175, 176, 181, 182, 245, 279n
Clarke, Charles, 68
class, class system, chapter 2 *passim*
Clore, Sir Charles, 28
cocoa, 68, 69, 72, 159, 160, 161, 171, 177–81 *passim*, 197, 276n, 277n

coffee, 68, 160, 161, 162, 197
Cohen, Abner, 270n
Cole, Lord, 28, 36
collectivization, 51, 94, 105, 126, 203, 206, 233, 248, 260, 272n, 273nn
colonies/colonialism, 4, 67, 69, 75, 76, 95, 121, 148, 163, 164, 167–70 passim, 172, 173, 177, 182–5 passim, 190, 192, 195–8 passim, chapter 11 passim, 228; British col. rule, 83, 172; in Africa, chapter 9 passim; Colonial Office, 174, 178; Portuguese col. rule, 206, 207; see also exploitation
Colombia, 68, 71, 127
Colson, Professor Elizabeth, 166, 167, 277n
Commentary, 271n, 276n
commodity/commodities, 127, 146, chapter 8 passim, 169, 173, 174, 257, 258; com. agreements, 96, 112, 131, 156, 160, 161, 162, 276n, 277n; com. cartels, 157, 207; crude com. terms, 77; com. stabilization, chapter 8 passim, 179, 180, 182; international buffer stocks, 157, 158; see also marketing boards
Commonwealth Development Corporation, 89
communism, 124, 207, 234, 280n; communist countries, 15, 70, 208, 252; communist bloc, 66, 105
Connolly, Cyril, 69
cooperatives, 173, 176, 181
copper, 160, 162, 171
cotton, 30, 72, 162, 175, 176
crops, 79, 105, 159, 169, 173, 179, 180, 182, 183, 253; cropping, double, treble, 52; see also cash crops; subsistence production
cybernetics, 263
Cyprus, 44

Daily Telegraph, The, 33, 268n, 271n
Dawkins, Richard, 269n
Dawson, Christopher, 71
Deane, Phyllis, 274n
debt cancellation, 95–7, 131, 272n
deflation, 214
demographic transition, 55, 56, 60, 61, 269n; dem. phenomena, 222; dem. forecasts, 236; demography, 262, 268n
Denison, E. F., 242, 280n

desert peoples, 70, 74, 79, 88, 111, 205
determinants of economic development, 64, 73, 100, 103, 105, 113, 118, 119, 125, 130, 166, 189, 194–5, 204, 241, 242, 259
developing countries, see ldcs
development economics/economists, 67, 145, 146, 185, chapter 15 passim, 275n; see also aid
development literature, 47, 63, 80, 81, 105, 111, 137, 167, 184, 189, 247, 253, 256, 258, 259, 261
Diamond Commission (Standing Royal Commission on the Distribution of ·Income and Wealth), 8
discrimination, 79, 84, 95, 97, 195, 198, 200; see also ethnic groups
disdevelopment, 102
disease, 113, 121, 165, 191, 196, 248, 280n
Disraeli, Benjamin, 29
distribution, economic theory of (terminology), 12
dollar problem(s), chapter 12 passim, 214, 256–7; dollar shortage, 261, 279n
Dostoevsky, Fedor, 274n
Dumont, René, 82, 126
Dzerzhinski, 19

Eberstadt, Nick, 268n
econometrics, 263, 281n
economic control(s), see state economic control
economic determinism, 237
economic history (theory of), chapter 13 passim
economics, state of, chapter 15 passim
economic states of society, chapter 13 passim
economic differences, 13, 16–22 passim, 24–5, 69, 71, 219; see also income, differences in
economies, emerging, 105
Economist, The, 214
Edison, Thomas, 10
egalitarianism, chapter 1 passim, 74, 116, 118, 119, 120, 134, 142; global egal., 118, 119, 134
Egypt, 57, 226, 227, 247, 280n
Ehrlich, Cyril, 277n

Ellerman, Sir John, 28
Elton, G. R., 238
Encounter, 278n
England, *see* Britain
Ethiopia, 49, 75, 82, 88, 93, 94, 104, 123, 150, 164, 165, 169, 194, 198, 207, 272n, 274n; Mengistu, 93
ethnic groups, 9, 16, 44, 106, 175, 192, 193, 198, 200, 226, 230; minorities, 9, 44, 51, 70, 74, 79, 84, 94, 106, 112, 250, 253; e. and tribal diversity, 175, 202; *see also* discrimination, Jews, Indians, Chinese, Asians, etc.
Eurocurrency/Eurodollar markets, 215, 217
Europe, 11, 31, 32, 45, 55, 56, 70–1, 75, 78, 82, 89, 100, 110, 146, 167, 168, 170, 171, 193, 194, 202, 215, 226–7, 228, 229, 231, 233, 240, 243, 245; Central, 71; Eastern, 54, 71, 233; Southern, 135, 171
Europeans, 11, 17, 54, 56, 70, 73, 75, 79, 84, 106, 112, 175, 188, 191, 194, 195, 196, 197, 198, 204
European Economic Community (EEC), 92, 146
exchange controls, 109, 173, 185; ex. economy, 93, 96, 102, 182; foreign exchange, 96, 103, 153, 159, 185, 217, 252, 256, 257, 259, 279n, 281n; theory of the foreign exchanges, 217; ex. markets, 91; ex. rates, 78, 92, 109, 215, 216, 217, 219, 265, 274n, 279n; Bretton Woods system, 215, 273n, 279n
exploitation, 4, 12, 25, 27, 63, 68, 69, 70, 74, 75, 76, 78, 84, 107, 118, 120, 121, 145, 149, 163, 177, 182, 205, 228, 248, 276n
exports, 50, 69, 70, 72, 77, 78, 79, 80, 96, 98, 122, 123, 130, 131, 146, 152, 158, 159, 160, 161, 164, 173–9 *passim*, 182, 183, 185, 187, 197, 215, 219, 257, 265, 274n; quotas, 161, 162, 173; *see also* trade; monopolies
expulsion(s), 93, 94, 104, 112, 146, 271n, 276n

Fabians, 15, 30; F. Research Series, 268n
factoral terms of trade, 77
famine, 49, 73, 82, 102, 112, 145, 165, 250
Far East, 54, 83, 112, 130, 147, 189

fertility, 53–65, 124–5, 149, 206, 269n, 270n; *see also* population; mortality
Financial Times, 26–7, 126, 146, 209, 268n, 270n, 272n, 273n, 275nn
First World War, 29, 30, 72, 232, 235, 278n
fiscal autonomy, 187; fiscal conservatism, 186, 187; (monetary and) fiscal policies, 152, 158, 215, 217, 246, 256
Flanders, 194; *see also* Low Countries
Ford, Henry, 10
foreign aid, *see* aid
Forte, Sir Charles, 28
Fourth World, 67
France, 71, 136, 227, 228
Frankel, Professor, 166, 167, 277nn
free trade, *see* trade

Gambia, 173, 197
Gandhi, Mrs Indira, 93, 210
Germany, 26–7, 44, 90, 110, 136, 150, 193, 194, 235, 273n; Federal Republic of, 89; Democratic Republic, 211, 234
Geyl, Pieter, 238
Ghana, 62, 69, 97, 108, 123, 163, 180, 197, 269n, 277n, 278n; Gold Coast, 69, 72, 163, 164, 165, 171, 179, 198, 276n, 277n; G. C. Marketing Board, 177, 180; Accra (riots), 177, 198, 269n; Ashanti, 170; *see also* Nkrumah
Ghee, Lim Teck, 276n
Glass, D.V., 30, 268n
global redistribution, 22, 89, 116, 118, 133, 272n
Gluckstein (family), 28
Goa, 207
Goldthorpe, John, 30, 31
Gold Coast, *see* Ghana
Gombrich, Sir Ernst, 11
Greece/Greeks, 44, 112, 226–9 *passim*
groundnuts, 72, 165, 178, 197, 249; East African Groundnut Scheme, 249
Guardian, The, 82
Guatemala, 71, 88, 275n
guilt, 66, 71, 73, 81, 83, 84–5, 88, 98, 122, 123, 124, 141, 146, 147, 164, 192, 193, 196, 210; guilt literature, 69, 84
Guinea/Guinea–Bissau/Equatorial Guinea,

198, 199; New Guinea, *see* Papua–New Guinea

Hajnal, John, 56, 269n
Hancock, Sir Keith, 167, 259, 277n
Hanlon, J., 270n
Haq, Mahbub ul, 144, 275n
Hartwell, R. M., 24
Hawthorn, G., 269n, 270n
Hay, Sir John, 28, 36
Healey, Denis, 29, 37
Heath, Edward, 29, 37
Helleiner, G. K., 277n, 278n
Heren, Louis, 33
Heston, Alan W., 273n
Hicks, Sir John, chapter 13 *passim; A Theory of Economic History*, 221, 225, 279n
Hinduism, 61, 201
Holland, 44, 45, 89, 194, 205, 228, 229; *see also* Low Countries
Hong Kong, 43, 44, 49, 51, 75, 127, 164, chapter 10 *passim*, 194, 268n, 272n, 279n
Hopper, W. David, 268n, 273nn
Huguenots, 16, 44
Hungary, 121

imports, 50, 77, 78–80, 130, 147, 160, 161, 174–7 *passim*, 181, 185, 186, 187, 207, 215, 219, 230, 271n
incentive goods, 80, 183, 184, 253
income(s), of children, 21; conventional comparisons, 21; differences in, chapter 1 *passim*, 105, 115, 116, 118, 119, 120, 124, 135, 136, 137, 205, 267n; distribution, 23, 48; national estimates, 4, 136, 261; international comparisons, 120, 121, 135; world income (definition), 116, 119
India, 11, 44, 57, 61, 62, 65, 67–8, 78, 79, 81, 88, 93, 94, 96, 101, 107, 115, 117, 123, 123–4, 125–6, 127, 146, 171, 200, 205, 207, 250, 252, 261n, 270n, 272n, 273n, 274n, 279n
Indians, 73, 82, 200, 229, 267n; in Burma, 112, 200; in Malaysia, 44, 71; in South-East Asia, 79, 106, 200; in Uganda, 175; North American, 45, 122, 189, 192, 196; Navajo, 113; pre-Columbian, 194

Indonesia, 44, 45, 88, 89, 93, 104, 270n, 274n
inequality, definition of, 10–11
inflation, 78, 90, 92, 96, 109, 122, 132, chapter 7 *passim*, 161, 188, 215, 241, 245
inter-generational flow of wealth, 58, 59–61; int.-gen. differences, 267n
international demonstration effect, 81, 271n
International Development, Agency for, 141
International Development Association, 94, 95, 129, 150, 151; *see also* World Bank
International Labour Office, 51, 252
International Monetary Fund (IMF), 92, 151, 153
international monetary reform, 154, 155
international monetary system, 215
international money, 153
international/official wealth transfers, *see* aid
investment, 76, 81, 82, 91, 98, 101, 109, 130, 133, 142, 159, 173, 185, 186, 216, 231, chapter 14 *passim*, 258, 259, 260, 265, 277n; inv. fetish, 142, chapter 14 *passim*; investible funds, 99, 101, 102, 103, 247, 272n, 280n
Iran, 29, 88, 95, 108, 252, 271n, 273n; *see also* OPEC
Iraq, 95, 96, 104; *see also* OPEC
Ireland, 200
Israel, 270n, 273n
Islam, 200 201
Italy, 71, 75, 129, 194, 226, 227, 228, 229, 234, 279n; *see also* Venice
Ivory Coast, 127, 164; *see also* Africa

Jabavu, Noni, 199, 211; *see also* Africa, South
Japan, 44, 54, 78, 82, 84, 136, 164, 173, 189, 190, 194, 215, 229, 270n
Jews, 16, 32, 44, 112, 192, 193, 196, 226
Johnson, Frank, 33
Johnson, Harry G., 271n
Johnson, Dr Samuel, 9
Journal of Political Economy, 273n, 276n
Journal of Development Economics, 275n

Kampuchea (Cambodia), 88, 94, 104, 139, 272n
Kaunda, Kenneth, 210

Kelly, John B., 278n
Kenya, 127, 164, 199, 203, 204, 208, 271n;
see also Africa
Keynes, John Maynard, 9, 51, 240, 264, 265,
269n, 280n; General Theory, 9, 264, 281n
Kilby, Peter, 273n, 274n
Killick, A. T., 277n
Kingsley, Mary, 167, 277n
Kocher, James, 57, 269n, 270n
Korea, 38; South, 127, 186, 273n
Kravis, B., 273n
Kuwait, 88, 95; see also OPEC
Kuznets, Simon, 99, 242, 248, 280n

Lal, Deepak, 268n
Lancashire, 28, 30; Spinners' Union, 30
Latin America, 45, 46, 54, 57, 58, 62, 66, 70,
71, 72, 88, 97, 99, 127, 130, 146, 229, 230,
270n, 275n
ldcs (less developed countries), 1, 42, 45–59
passim, 61–5 passim, 68, 87, 132, 135–7,
142, 144, 145, chapter 7 passim, 159–60,
185, 229, 230, 232–3, 247, 253, 258, 268n,
270n, 274n, 281n
Lebanese/Lebanon, 44, 89, 139
Leijonhufvud, Axel, 281n
Leith, J. Clark, 278n
Leontief, Wassily, 255, 264, 266, 281nn
less developed countries/world, see ldcs
Lesotho, 88
Levant, the, 44, 228; levantines, 73, 74, 112,
175, 204
Levi, John, 278n
Lewis, Sir Arthur, 136, 164, 165, 254, 274n,
276n, 277nn
Liberia, 75 164, 165, 169, 194, 198, 274n
Libya, 94, 95, 96; see also OPEC
Link Scheme of Aid, chapter 7 passim; see
also SDRs
Lipset, Seymour Martin, 29
Lloyd George, 29
Low Countries, 71, 189, 194, 227; see also
Belgium; Holland
Lury, D. A., 267n
Luther, Martin, 235
Luttwak, Edward, 272n
Lygo, Admiral Sir Raymond, 33
Lyons (family), 28

MacDonald, Ramsay, 29
MacFarlane, A. 269n
McNamara, Robert, 42, 46, 106, 140, 144,
268n, 270n, 275n
Macrae, Donald, 31
McPhee, Allan, 108, 167, 259, 273n, 277nn
macroeconomics, 240
Malawi, 111, 209
Malaysia, 11, 43, 44, 45, 49, 51, 57, 71, 88,
89, 93, 159, 164, 268n, 279n; Malaya, 67,
71–2, 276n; Malays, 11, 43, 44, 45, 71,
229
Malik, Charles, 139
Malthus, Thomas, 48, 236
market(s), chapter 8 passim, 174–7, 259;
market economies, 10, 12, 13, 15, 17, 37,
142, 188, 190, 232, 279n; m. forces, 69;
market-sharing (pools), 179; m. societies,
89; m. system, 105, 132, 142;
transformation (rise of), 221, 223–5, 231–2
marketing boards, 157, 158, 159, 177, 178,
179, 180, 181, 182, 183, 277n, 278n; Gold
Coast Marketing Board, 177
Marquis, F. J. (Lord Woolton), 267n
Marshall, Alfred, 264, 265, 281n
Marshall Plan, 100, 110
Marxism, 69, 74, 76, 143, 206, 207, 236, 238,
243, 271n; 280n
Marx, Karl, 80, 224, 235
Massachusetts Institute of technology
(MIT), 185, 247, 263, 278n
mathematical methods in economics, 262–6
Mauritius, 54, 57
Mazrui, Ali, chapter 11, passim, 278n
Medawar, Sir Peter, 280n, 281n
media, 3, 24, 31, 61, 66, 75, 111, 129, 138,
141, 145, 146, 150, 168; press, 185, 190,
214, 246
Mediterranean, the, 226
Mende, Tibor, 81
mercenary soldiers, 171, 192
Mexico, 71, 88, 269n
microeconomics, theory of fertility, 58, 61
Micronesia, US Trust Territory of, 113–14
Middle East, 36, 46, 54, 61, 62, 70, 71, 72,
73, 88, 112, 193, 195, 229
migration, 52, 73, 79, 106, 145, 171, 172,
173, 192, 242; immigration, 44, 45, 79,

130–1, 185, 186, 199; 'strangers', 174, 204; *see also* brain drain

Mill, John Stuart, 80

Millikan, Professor, 272n

minerals, 50, 51, 67, 70, 192, 206, 208, 268n; mining, 51, 77, 160, 169, 182, 194, 195; metals, discovery of, 100, uranium, 204

Ministry of Food, 178, 182

minorities, *see* ethnic groups

Mombasa, 196

money, 14, 99, 109, 116, 117, 122, 123, 145, 147, 148, 150, chapter 7 *passim*, 156, 166, 167, 168, 179, 181, 186–9 *passim*, 193, 210, 217, 240, 241, 245, 260; *see also* international monetary reform, fiscal

Mongolia/Mongols, 121, 228

Moravcsik, Michael J., 281n

monopoly/monopolies, 37, 67, 178, 180, 195, 196; state and export, 105, 157, 158, 159, 173, 174, 176, 177, 181, 182, 183, 253, 258, 277n

Morawetz, D. M., 268n, 274n, 275n

Morocco, 88, 94

mortality, 53–5, 59, 63, 72, 83, 136, 137, 165, 206, 231, 248; *see also* population; fertility

Moynihan, Daniel P., 271n

Mozambique, 123, 139, 197, 206, 207, 209, 278n; President Machel, 206

Mphahlele, Ezekiel, 199, *see also* South Africa

multinational companies, 75, 76, 145, 146–7

Muslims, 22, 61, 197

Myrdal, Gunnar, 185, 247–8, 272nn, 273n

Naipaul, Shiva, 195, 199–200, 209, 278nn

Namibia, 198

Nasser, Gamal Abdel, 19

National Institutes of Economic and Social Research, 219

Nature, 90

Nepal, 67, 75

Nerval, Gerard de, 2

Netherlands, the, *see* Holland

Neustadt, I., 277n

New International Economic Order,, 19, 76, 95, 119, 140, 272n

New Scientist, 270n

New Society, 31

New Statesman, 272n

Newsweek, 81

New York Times, 247, 272n, 275n

New Zealand, 164

Nigeria, 44, 51, 57, 60, 72, 89, 94, 104, 164, 170, 173, 174, 181, 196–7, 274n, 277n, 281n; *Report on the Economic Development of* (World Bank), 219; *Path to Nigerian Freedom* (Obafemi Awolowo), 196; Northern, 165, 170, 183, 198, 269n; Southern, 60, 62, 165; the Ibo, 44, 51, 106, 112, 196, 198, 199, 205, 219, 248, 249, 271n; the Fulani, 269n; the Hausa, 196; the Tiv, 165; the Yoruba, 57; Biafran War, 198; Enugu riots, 198

Nkrumah, Kwame, 69, 163, 164, 177, 180, 181, 184, 202, 206, 211, 270n, 277n; *Africa Must Unite*, 163, 164, 211, 270n; *see also* Ghana

nomads, 79, 96

Nonconformists, 16, 32, 44

North America, 45, 74, 228, 231; N. A. Indians, 45, 113, 122, 189, 192, 196; *see also* United States of America

North-South dialogue, 272n

Northcliffe, Lord, 10

Northrup, David, 271n

Nuffield, Lord, 28; College, 28, 31

Nurkse, Professor, 272n

Nyerere, Julius, 19, 69, 94, 106, 144, 202, 203, 206, 210, 270n, 272n, 274n

Observer, The, 31, 33, 268n, 270n, 271n

OECD, 93, 272n

oil, 96, 127, 185, 206, 274n; oil-producing/exporting countries, 88, 127, 164, 270n; oils and oil seeds, 178; *see also* OPEC

Okira, Professor Sabuto, 164

Omaboe, E. N., 277n

Oman, Sultanate of, 196

OPEC, 76, 95, 100, 121, 127, 135, 160, 161, 189, 207, 274n

open society/societies, 8, 9, 10, 15–19, 37, 38; in Britain, 26, 27, 31, 34, 35, 38, 39; income differences in, 17; and market economies, 37, 187

Orwell, George, 214
Overseas Development, Ministry of, 89, 110, 139, 141; *Overseas Development: The Changing Emphasis in British Aid Policies*, 110
Oxfam, 68; *see also* charities
Oxford University, 24, 28, 29, 31, 32, 37, 38, 195, 269n

Paish, F. W., 276n
Pakistan, 57, 88, 94, 104, 111, 123–4, 171, 274n
palm oil, 72, 178
Papanek, G. F., 273nn
Papua–New Guinea, 74, 88, 117
Paris, 2, 277
Pasteur, Louis, 10
patent laws, 81
Pearson Report, 42, 140; Annex of the, 164, 165, 277n; Pearson Commission, 92, 103, 164, 277n
Pedler, Frederick, 278n
persecution, 193, 200, 276n
Persian Gulf, 171
Peru, 71, 88
Petersen, Professor W., 57, 268n, 269n
Phelps Brown, Sir Henry, 255, 281n
Philippines, the, 127, 248
Pigou, A. C., 281n
Pincus, John A., 275n
plantations, 51, 160, 166, 167
Plumb, Professor J. H., 195–6
Point Four programme, 115, 138–9, 140, 275n
Poland, 121, 146, 233
political nation, 3–4, 24
politicization, 3, 18, 19, 23, 24, 34, 38, 83, 86, 89, 103, 104, 105, 109, 129, 133, 134, 174, 181, 188, 190, 253
Pollard, Sydney, 231, 280n
Popper, Sir Karl, 238
population, chapter 3 *passim*; decline in, 233; density, chapter 3 *passim*, 185, 274n; explosion, 68, 137, 205, 206; growth, 83, 97, 124–5, 136, 165, 185, 189, 231, 265, 268n, 270n, 274n; statistics, 120; overpopulation, 145; birth-control programmes, 124, 125; UN Fund for

Population Activities, 270n; *see also* fertility; mortality
ports, 173, 188, 194, 195, 196, 241, 244, 278n; Maputo, 209; South African Railways and Harbour Board, 209
Potekhin, Soviet Academician, 70, 271n
poverty, 11, 16, 23, 24, 33, 66, 67, 70, 72, 74, 75, 76, 79, 83, 84, 88, 92, 96, 97, 98, 99, 101, 110–15 *passim*, 117, 119, 121, 124, 125, 127, 141, 145, 149, 185, 187, 189, 192, 204, 205, 239, 247, 248, 253, 270n, 272n, 274n, 276n; causes of, 23, 24, 69; relief of, 23, 24, 87, 94, 97, 106 110, 111, 113, 114, 116, 128; Third World, chapter 4 *passim*; viscious circle of 98, 99, 100, 185
power, 3, 4, 8, 9, 10, 11, 13, 18, 19, 45, 83, 89, 92, 104, 109, 129, 132, 133, 134, 142, 147, 148, 155, 161, 174, 176, 180, 181, 183, 189, 201, 202, 208, 210, 230, 244, 245, 267n, 271n, 274n
press, *see* media
price theory, 256–7; shadow prices, 258
protectionism, 78, 155, 172, 232
public security, 121, 165, 167, 169, 170, 171, 194, 196, 202, 277n
pygmies, 70, 88, 111, 194, 205, 229; of Africa, 74, 88

Rabuska, Dr Alvin, 186, 188
railways, 29, 72, 165, 169, 209, 241, 248, 250, 277n, 278n
Ram, Rati, 269n
redistribution, 5, 11, 12, 13, 14, 15, 17, 20, 23, 24, 87, 97, 98, 101, 112, 116–21 *passim*, 124, 131, 136, 140, 148, 149; *see also* global redistribution
Reith Lectures, chapter 11 *passim*, 210–11, 278n
restrictionism, 37, 179
Rhodesia, 165, 199, 200, 202, 210; Southern, 173; Dr Ramphal, 210, 278n; *see also* Zimbabwe
Robinson, David, 28
Robertson, Field-Marshal Sir William, 29–36; Lord R. of Oakridge (son of Sir William), 36
Rolls Royce, 28, 94, 246

Romania, 276nn
Rosenstein-Rodan, Professor, 272n
Rostow, Professor, 272n
Royal Economic Society, 255
rubber industry, 67–8, 71, 159, 160, 161, 162, 276n

Sahel, the, 49, 82
Salmon (family), 28
Sanchez, N., 269n
Samuelson, Paul, 185, 272n, 274n
Saudi Arabia, 88, 95; see also OPEC
Scandinavia, 71, 75, 89
Schmidt, Helmut, 26–7
Schmitt, Dr Hans O., 273n
Schoek, Helmut, 267n, 275n
Schultz, Theodore W., 268n, 269n, 273n, 278n
Scotland, 37
SDRs (Special Drawing Rights), chapter 7 passim; see also Link Scheme
Second World War, 1, 3, 4, 29, 54, 55, 72, 78, 80, 83, 87, 88, 95, 96, 110, 115, 141, 145, 160, 163, 167, 168, 172, 173, 175, 176, 177, 182, 183, 185, 201, 214, 215, 218, 234, 239, 242, 247, 253, 257, 260, 263
Senegal, 197
Seychelles, 94, 203
Sider, Ronald J., 68
Sieff (family), 28
Sierra Leone, 173, 181, 278n
Sikkim, 67
Simon, Julian L., 42, 268n, 270n
Singapore, 43, 44, 49, 51, 57, 164, 186, 194, 229, 279n
slavery, 68, 72, 73, 122, 165, 170, 171, 195–6, 199, 227, 277n; slave markets, 165; raiding, 171, 193, 196; trading, 72, 165, 170, 192, 193, 196; Atlantic slave trade, 72–3, 195, 271n; American slavers, 122; Arab, 70
Smith, Adam, 80, 144, 225
social change/mobility, 3, 24, 26, 30, 31, 32, 33, 34, 36, 38, 83, 244
soft loans, 78, 95, 96, 102, 110, 131
Solow, Robert M., 242, 280n
Somalia, 88, 94

South, the, 87, 139, 140; see also Third World; ldcs
South America, 44, 54; Amazon jungle, 68
South Asia, 22, 44, 53, 58, 62, 117, 130
South-East Asia, 16, 44, 45, 51, 70, 71, 74, 79, 83, 88, 94, 99, 106, 108, 112, 171, 193, 200, 226, 228, 279n
Soviet Union, 15, 70, 108, 110, 121, 124, 206, 225, 226, 232, 233, 234, 249–50, 252, 253, 274n, 275n; S. bloc, 66, 89, 123, 135; Bohemia, 234; Iron Curtain, 233–4, 280n; Lenin, Stalin, 235; Prussia, 233; Siberia, 121; see also communism; Marx; Mongolia
Sowell, Thomas, 145, 148, 275n
Spain, 46; Spanish conquests, 46, 228
Spengler, Oswald, 224
Sri Lanka, 54, 106, 123, 139, 200
stabilization, see commodity
Stamp of Shortlands, Lord, 29
Stanford University, 66
state control of the economy, 80, 83, 105, 106, 109, 132, 134, 173, 174, 177, 181, 182, 183, 184, 188, 201, 202, 218, 229, 245, 251, 252, 253, 259, 275n; state-controlled economies, 89, 105, 107, 142, 144, 190
(economic) states of society, 221-3, 229, 230; city-states, 225–8 passim, 236
state subsidies, 37, 65, 181
steel, 107, 244, 250–1
sterilization, 22, 42, 61, 65, 93, 116, 125–6, 270n, 273n
sterling, 91, 183; sterling currency pool, 173, 275n
Stern, N. H., 275n
Stigler, George J., 281n
subsistence economies, 43, 49, 166, 253; subs. production, 59, 69, 81, 93, 98, 105, 112, 136, 160, 161, 175, 197, 248, 249, 254, 276n
Sudan, 197, 198
sugar, 162
Sumatra, 44
Summers, Robert, 273n
Sunday Express, 33
Sunday Times, 69, 81
Sweezy, Alan, 269n
Switzerland, 74, 75, 129, 189

Taiwan, 49, 57, 127, 186, 194

Tanzania, 49, 57, 69, 70, 88, 94, 104, 106, 111, 123, 126, 150, 169, 197, 202, 203, 272n, 273n; Tanganyika, 69, 169, 278n; Pax Tanzaniana, 203; villagization, 126

tax/taxation, 13–14, 15, 21, 23, 51, 64, 69, 77, 78, 89, 102, 105, 111, 117, 118, 122, 129, 130, 140, 149, 150, 153, 154, 158, 159, 170, 179, 180, 182, 183, 186, 187, 240, 243, 245, 246, 249–54 passim, 256, 258, 259, 276n, 278n; disincentive effects, 15, 254; negative income tax, 20; progressive, 17, 116; (proposed) tax of talented persons, 17–18; redistributive tax, 17–18, 117, 188; taxpayers, 116, 117, 122, 132, 133, 134, 146, 147, 149, 150, 183, 272n; taxpayers' money, 86, 90, 95, 108, 116, 132, 141

Tawney, R. H., 15

tea industry, 67–8, 161

Thailand, 44, 45, 93, 117, 127

Thatcher, Mrs Margaret, 29, 37

Third World, 3, 5, 16, 18–19, 20, 22–3, 24, 43, 45, 47, 56, 66–150 passim, 157–62 passim, 169, 189, 190, 192, 195, 196, 200, 205–10 passim, 217, 218, 239, 247, 248, 250–3, 260, 261, 270n, 271n, 272n, 273n, 274n, 275n, 276n

Tibet, 75

tin industry, 71, 161

Times, The, 33, 198, 270n, 272n; Times Literary Supplement, 198, 272n

Tocqueville, Alexis de, 9, 30, 189, 278n

Todaro, Michael P., 268n, 269n

totalitarianism, 19, 83, 118, 176, 183, 203

Toynbee, Arnold, 224

Townsend, Peter, 67, 270n

trade/trading, 59, 67, 72, 76, 77, 78, 79, 80, 82, 84, 105, 112, 130, 148, 173, 187, 193, 195, 208, 215, 226, 227, 228, 250, 257, 258, 271n, 274n, 279n; barriers, 130, 134, 186, 188; restrictions, 155; foreign, 52, 133, 173, 274n; free, 172, 186; trading licences, 204; traders, 98, 99, 158, 159, 173, 179, 192, 249; unions, 13, 23, 37, 38, 90, 144, 149, 188, 243, 244; unionists, 98; see also slavery; imports; exports

tribal custom, 70, 79, 171, 175, 198, 200, 202, 229; detribalization, 166; multitribal societies, 104; tr. systems of land rights, 49; tr. warfare, 121, 209, 274n; see also war

Truman, Harry, see Point Four

Turkey, 94, 97, 121, 171, 228; Turks in Cyprus, 44

Turner, Victor, 277n

Uganda, 49, 63, 68, 88, 89, 93, 104, 164, 169, 175, 177, 183, 197, 203, 272n; Idi Amin, 92, 93, 194, 203, 272n; Milton Obote, 108, 203; the Kabaka, 108, 203

underdeveloped world, 67, 87, 98, 138, 139, 141, 204, 230, 236, 247–8, 257, 258; see also ldcs

unemployment, 49, 51–2, 106, 243, 257, 265, 267

United Kingdom, see Britain

United nations, 19, 66, 87, 95, 114, 123, 132, 138, 139, 144, 185, 190, 202, 211, 268n, 275n; Charter of, 138; UN Development Programme, 123; Report on the Economic Development of Underdeveloped Countries, 139; see also New International Economic Order; Pearson Report; UNCTAD

UNCTAD (United Nations Conference on Trade and Development), 75, 132, 144, 160, 202, 271n, 275n; first UNCTAD, 139; General Principle XIV, 164

United States of America, 16, 17, 28, 30, 31, 35, 38, 45, 50, 66, 74, 75, 78, 81, 82, 88, 90–6 passim, 101, 113–14, 122, 123, 124, 150, 164, 191, 193, 194, 208, 215, 216, 227, 228, 229, 231, 242–3, 258, 273n, 274n, 275n; land rent as proportion of US factor cost of food, 50; Federal Reserve Board, 235; black vote, 168; Roosevelt, 235; Eisenhower, 139; Kennedy, 114; see also American(s); Marshall Plan; Micronesia; Point Four programme

universities, 17, 64, 66, 67, 70, 111, 129, 145, 195, 197, 235

Uruguay, 71; see also Latin America

Usher, Dan, 4, 119, 261, 274n

Vance, Cyrus, 91

Vany, A. De, 269n

Venezuela, 71

Venice, 45, 89, 194, 205, 227, 228

Vietnam, 88, 93, 94, 104, 123, 146, 271n, 272n, 276n

Wall Street Journal, 276n

Walters, A. A., 279n, 280n, 281n

war, 88, 89, 104, 121, 178, 179, 208, 215, 225, 235, 237, 248; civil, 88, 94, 104, 142, 170, 200, 201, 205; guerilla, 198, 209; local, 170, 171, 198, 202; tribal, 198, 209, 274n; *see also* First World War; Second World War

War on Want, 75, 276n; *see also* charities

Washington Post, 114, 270n, 272n, 278n

welfare, 43, 46, 64, 77, 90, 117, 137, 141, 163, 181, 183, 188, 258; services, 20; state, 13–15, 114, 188; Colonial Development and Welfare Funds, 182

West, the including Western countries, 1, 3, 8, 9, 16, 20, 24, 43, 44, 46, 49, 51, 54, 55, 56, 57, 59, 62–90 *passim*, 94, 97, 98, 99, 100, 105, 109, 111, 115–21 *passim*, 124, 125, 126, 129, 130, 131, 136, 137, chapter 6 *passim*, 155, 162, 164, 168, 176, 188, 190, chapter 11 *passim*, 237, chapter 14 *passim*, 261, 270n, 271n

Westergaard, John, 30, 268n

Weiner, Norbert, 263, 265, 281n

Wilson, Sir Harold, 37

windfall profits, 46, 100, 107, 174, 176, 177, 189.

Wolfson, Sir Isaac, 10, 28

women, 22, 100, 113, 117, 239, 270n

World Bank, 42, 51, 92–5 *passim*, 106, 121, 125, 132, 137, 140, 144, 150, 164, 219, 268n, 270n, 272n, 273n, 276n, 281n; World Employment Project, 51

Worswick, G. D. N., 255, 281n

Yamey, B. S., 276n, 277n, 278n

Yugoslavia, 94

Zaire, 49, 88, 93, 104, 123, 197, 204, 205, 208, 233, 274nn; Mobutu, 93

Zambia, 112, 123, 195, 199, 209, 210; Lusaka, 200, 210, 278n

Zanzibar, 203

Zimbabwe, 198, 199, 202